3-17-75

Economic Systems in World History

Economic Systems in World History

Stephan Viljoen

Longman

Longman
1724-1974

LONGMAN GROUP LIMITED
London
and LONGMAN INC., New York
Associated companies, branches and representatives throughout the world

First published 1974

ISBN 0582 48318 2

Library of Congress Catalog Card Number: 73-86131

*Set in IBM Journal Roman
and printed in Great Britain
by William Clowes and Sons Limited,
London, Colchester and Beccles.*

Contents

Contents

Acknowledgments

To friends and colleagues I wish to express my appreciation for numerous improvements in the form and content of this work. To the authorities of the University of South Africa I am especially indebted for the facilities extended for its completion.

Introduction
The coordination of economic activity

The central theme of economic history is the determination of the means and methods by which economic processes have been historically coordinated.

The economic process in all societies is closely related to and integrated in the total social process. There are, however, marked differences in the extent to which economies can be said to be 'imbedded' in the web of social activities and institutions that constitute each people's culture. At the one extreme are the primitive economies, which are completely enmeshed in institutions that are both economic and non-economic. But as neither the means nor the ends in such communities are primarily economic, economic processes are determined largely by factors that are non-economic in nature. At the other extreme are the modern free enterprise economies.[1] These economies tend, to a marked extent, to free themselves from the all-embracing grip of the social system. The economic process becomes that part of the total social process that consists of rational actions in the context of certain impersonal relations, rationality denoting a use of scarce resources designed to optimise the attainment of alternative ends. The economy is thus constituted into a coherent and relatively independent subsystem of society, with its own appropriate motivation and set of rules and controls.

These are matters of degree. It is, indeed, the close integration of the economic process in the total social process which accounts for the wide diversity of economies that has prevailed at all times and still exists in the world today. There are therefore other features that characterise specific economies besides the methods of coordination, and these have been dealt with where they are necessary to bring out the character or development of a specific historical system.[2] If they are nevertheless to be classified, the basis of classification must be sought in the different ways in which economic processes can and have historically been coordinated. Three distinct methods can be distinguished: first, by subsistence, reciprocity and redistribution, and collective controls; secondly, by government administration; and, finally, by the market mechanism. Three basically different types of economies can therefore be distinguished: collective, centrally administered and market-orientated economies.

Collective economies were the first to appear on the prehistoric scene and they have persisted to the present day. They can be described as traditional economies, integrated predominantly by the provision of needs directly, by the reciprocity of economic relationships and the redistribution of goods according to certain basic principles, and by collective controls. They have generally been of a primitive nature and the controls have functioned within limited areas.

Historical economies have always tended to be mixed in the sense that all three forms of coordination have played a part in the allocation of resources and the distribution of the product among the factors of production. Subsistence, recip-

---

[1] The modern free enterprise economy is today generally referred to as a 'capitalist' economy. This designation is completely misleading because it is neither meaningful nor ethically neutral. It has nevertheless become firmly entrenched.

[2] So as to avoid a mere series of semi-static and independent presentations of 'ideal types', short analyses have been made of the factors that facilitated or retarded the development of each specific economic system, as well as of the historical ties that connected the different systems.

rocity and collective controls have indeed tended to play a less important role in these societies. But to a certain extent there has always been a blending of state intervention and of laissez-faire, of development decisions made by government and by private enterprise, of the allocation of resources by public prescription and by market forces, of public and of private ownership.

The coordinative mix has varied greatly during the centuries and in different societies and has fluctuated between the two poles of almost pure central adminis- tration on the one hand, and almost complete laissez-faire on the other.

The archaic economies, the first to appear on the historic scene, retained many of the traits of the pre-existent collective economies. But in addition they had strong centrally administered features superimposed upon them. It is in the state- operated communist economies of the present day, however, that this type of organisation has found its fullest expression. A link between the archaic and the modern centrally administered economies can be found in the long and pervasive influence of Byzantine culture on Russian educational, religious and political thought and institutions.

As an 'ideal type' it may be said that centrally administered or state-operated. economies depend on overall government prescription and planning to achieve the coordination of economic activities, and that decentralised decisions by individuals can be allowed only to the extent that they conform to and can be integrated in the centrally conceived scheme of things. Economically, all activity is prescribed, directed and controlled. Administratively, the bureaucracy is centrally structured: information flows upward and decisions downward. Politically, the framework is monolithic: the state is, in principle, interested in all the activities of its subjects and can tolerate no feature that is foreign to its own nature. This scheme of things is powerfully buttressed by the appropriate ideology. Personal ambition must be directed primarily to promotion within the government hierarchy. Politically, the masses must be passive and submissive to authority. Socially, they must be fully integrated in the whole community and must accept unequivocally the standard social, moral and aesthetic norms.

In the course of history there have been two periods of comparative economic freedom: the Graeco-Roman period and the period that began gradually in certain limited areas and in limited sectors of the economies of these areas in the central Middle Ages, and has continued, sometimes rather tenuously, to the present day.

In contrast to the centrally administered economy, the free enterprise economy, as an ideal type, is decentralised and market-orientated. Every individual, to a greater or less extent, directly or indirectly participates in the decision-making process. Basically the economy is coordinated by a self-equilibrating system of price-forming markets. Economic decisions in such an economy are consequently based on prices that reflect relative scarcities, and all movements of economic significance become effective through prices.

The series of affiliated and integrated markets in which services are coordinated must therefore function effectively, and government controls must be directed to the promotion, not to the obstruction, of this end. Policies designed to promote the free enterprise economy must accordingly aim at the creation of a climate, an institutional pattern, social overheads and an infrastructure propitious to the exercise of private initiative and ensure that the economy will function efficiently. Methods of taxation must not be unduly repressive of initiative and controls must concentrate on procedures rather than on substantive issues, and must be indirect rather than direct in their scope and application.

The free enterprise economy also presents conditions that are essential to the *attainment of a large measure of political and personal freedom, though the tendency throughout history has been for only a part of the population to participate in this freedom. This is ensured by a system that relies on the exercise of private initiative and on the automatic controls of the market for the effective functioning of the economy. Not only does power tend to be widely dispersed in such economies, but opportunities of alternative sources of employment, information and leadership exist through the institution of private property and the existence of the private sector of the economy. A large measure of freedom is also ensured by the policy of leaving people to live their own lives. Hence the freedom of conviction, of speech, of the press, and of association that the system affords, and the reliance on personal initiative and responsibility that it promotes.*

Between these two broad types of economies there have been numerous intermediate categories, each characterised and differentiated from the others, not only by the forms of control and the reliance placed on the various means of coordination, but also by features that are non-economic in nature. It must again be stressed that, since historical forces are always multiple and complex, the specific character of an economy at any particular time can be explained only in terms of its own historical determinants. Each economy forms a unique entity and the grouping together of separate entities must always to some extent do violence to their individuality.

The most important of the intermediate types of economies that have appeared on the historic scene have been grouped together as 'centrally directed economies'. Dirigisme is of course a relative concept. It is used here in a specific sense to designate historical systems with certain typical features in common. Thus, in spite of the great variety of the forms, range and temper of the directives imposed and the controls exercised, these societies are all characterised by their reliance on central government decisions for the initiation, allocation and coordination of major projects and for the provision of certain basic requirements of the public economy. These services were indeed strongly supported and sustained by decentralised (though strictly controlled) market activities, supplemented by reciprocity, local and collective controls, and the basic self-sufficiency of the village communities, for the provision of most of the everyday needs of the population, as well as of its non-essential (or administratively considered as frivolous) requirements. But in principle only those spheres—outside the peasant communities—that were regarded as of no essential consequence to the central administration were left unequivocally in private hands.

The administration of these polities was characterised, in the first place, by the subordination of the bureaucracy to the central authority and its devotion to the state. A second feature was the ubiquity of the controls that were theoretically exercised: in principle all spheres of activity (outside the internal organisation of the village communities) were considered as suitable objectives for central direction. Finally, the purpose of the administration was the mobilisation of as large a share of the free-flowing resources of the economy for the service of the state as was consistent with the maintenance of stability and the requirements of the internal security of the realm and its external aggrandisement.

According to the bureaucratic scheme of values, the energies of the people had to be directed and canalised by the administration and the supporting institutional system to the service of the state, and not to be dissipated by the realisation of individual objectives through the provision of services in the private sphere of the economy. This was reflected especially in the methods of taxation and the appropriation of the surplus resources of these societies. The prime objective of policy was to enhance the power of the state, not the welfare of the people.

Politically, therefore, these societies tended to be centrally structured. Thus, in contrast to the free, decentralised, pluralistic societies of the West, they all tended basically to be centralised, controlled and directed. For this reason they have sometimes been grouped with the centrally 'administered' polities. [1]

But centrally directed economies differed from centrally administered ones in certain important respects. The most significant of these differentiating features was undoubtedly the existence of proprietary rights to the soil on the part of the members of the village communities. In the archaic economies the land was the personal possession of the monarch and the agricultural output could be mobilised and redistributed by the state because of the ready and ubiquitous availability of water transport. This made possible the centralised, if rather rudimentary, administration of the human and natural resources of these countries. In the centrally directed economies, however, proprietary rights to the land and the absence over large areas of suitable means of transport precluded the development of genuine 'hydraulic' or 'managerial' economies. But even if such an extension of the functions of the state had been within the range of vision of the governments of the time it would definitely have been beyond their sphere of competence. This must be ascribed to the fact that, since land was central to his whole existence, the proprietary rights to it held by the peasant were more vital to him than any other aspect of his life. All the state could do was to mobilise and allocate a traditionally accepted share of the human and material resources of the economy for its own purposes. To achieve this the villagers were adscripted to the land and impressed for public service. But for the rest the organisational impact of the state on the village communities, which contributed the vast bulk of the national product of these economies, was largely marginal. What is more, the state also had to protect the peasantry for the sake of conserving its own revenues and of ensuring its internal stability and prosperity and its external security.

The functioning of the centrally directed economy can be understood only if the central role played by the village communities in this type of economy is fully appreciated. Peasants have lived in nucleated villages since the dawn of history. This has had important effects from the point of view of their social relations and the coordination of resources. In the first place, because of their impotence in the face of the hazards of nature, a large measure of reciprocity has always been forced on them, inducing a system of interdependence among the members of the village community and the clan group.

But, in the second place, the village community is never entirely self-sufficient. Hence groups of villages join in the holding of periodic markets, and through interlocking market areas an exchange of specialised craft products takes place over a considerable terrain. If products produced in the villages can be traded over extended regions, these commodities, or even surpluses of staple products where the necessary transport facilities are available, are purchased by professional merchants and, with the proceeds thus obtained, the villagers buy manufactured goods and the few staples needed from outside their own economies. Though this trade may be rudimentary in form, it nevertheless forms an essential link in the life

---

[1] The best-known exponent of this thesis is Karl Wittfogel, *Oriental Despotism—a comparative study of total power*. Wittfogel's designation of China before the era of European penetration as a 'hydraulic economy' has been specially singled out for severe criticism. Joseph Needham, in a review of Wittfogel's book refers to it as 'the greatest disservice which has yet been done to the objective study of the history of China' (*Science and Society*, xxiii, no. 1, 58 ff).

and in the means of coordination of the village communities. The functioning of the market mechanism in the centrally directed economy is further strengthened by the existence of a very substantial commercial and manufacturing sector in the main urban centres, and this effectively precludes any overall 'management' of the economy.

A final characteristic of a society composed predominantly of village communities is its innate conservatism. Members of these communities tend to accept not only the phenomena of the physical world but also the basic social structure of their societies as given data that are not amenable to change. They look on the traditional hierarchical order as not merely appropriate but right, and would consider any attempt on their part to change the given order of things as improper and indeed immoral. Only when the traditional social relations are disrupted are they goaded to action. It is this voluntary acceptance of the hierarchical fabric of authority and power by the masses which explains the inherent stability of these societies. How strong the conservative decentralising force represented by the complex fabric of traditional rural society has been throughout the centuries in preventing the rise of genuine managerial economies is reflected in the difficulties that both the Russian and Chinese communist régimes experienced in their attempts to socialise agriculture.

Though the total social process in each case was highly complex and individualistic, centrally directed economies therefore tended on the whole to evolve different developmental, institutional and organisational patterns from those of both market-orientated and centrally administered economies. Each different type of economic system indeed tended over the centuries to develop and to accentuate its own specific characteristics. This must be ascribed largely to the fact that different systems represent different methods of economic, social and political integration, methods that are linked and interrelated in numerous ways and, though they may at times be at variance with one another, must be moulded into effective functioning entities. These are no doubt forces, inconspicuous in themselves but all the more potent for their lack of prominence, that have generally been of crucial importance in the shaping of social destinies.

Part 1
Collective Economies

1
The direct provision of needs, reciprocity and redistribution, and collective controls

Introduction

The history of man as a tool-user probably began nearly two million years ago. For by far the greater part of his existence he roamed the earth as a hunter and collector. The outstanding feature of human history up to the Upper Paleolithic period, as far as the technological aspect is concerned, was the uniformity and immutability of culture. The same peculiar forms were given to core tools all over the world, and for a number of glacial cycles only minor variations on a small assortment of traditional forms can be detected.

Comparatively rapid development began with the appearance of modern types of man in the Upper Paleolithic period. From perhaps as early as 12,000 B.C. men learned to cultivate plants and, somewhat later, to domesticate animals. The greater order and security brought about by an agricultural and pastoral existence were turning-points in human history. The larger and more sedentary communities developed new crafts, new ideas, greater powers of application and of planning ahead, and more elaborate systems of social organisation. In every sphere there appeared new conditions of life which demanded new methods of adaptation.

From the combined practice of agriculture and herding there evolved the first peasant economies and plough cultures. Favourable areas, such as the river valleys where continuous cultivation was possible, became forcing beds of technical development. Here more differentiated societies gradually arose. Geographically, the change was confined to the region stretching from the Aegean Sea and the Nile to Turkestan and the Indus, where the first riverine civilisations emerged from the pre-existent peasant economies in the fourth millennium B.C.

Resistance to change

No culture is completely static. Changes, however slight, are incessantly taking place either through independent discovery and invention or through culture contact, and through their interaction.

Discovery is the recognition of the advantages of something already in existence independently of the discoverer. Invention is the conception and creation of

2

something new that would not have existed but for the inventor. In practice it would usually be difficult to distinguish between the two. Many inventions, in fact, may be classed as applied discoveries. They were produced accidentally, in playful activity, or from aesthetic or religious motives, with effects quite different from those intended.

The evolution of primitive technology was a slow and laborious process. Primitive man is an inventor neither by disposition nor by training. He has little material to work on: there are few objects, situations, or processes between which his mind can perceive relationships and which he can use for educing correlates. Moreover, he is generally too occupied with the exigencies of existence to be interested in phenomena apart from their immediate usefulness.

Primitive technology on the whole, therefore, was not a self-generating process, for it was based essentially on observation, appreciation and imitation, none of which is a progressive factor. Discovery and variation were the chief processes involved in the development of the arts and crafts. Discoveries were spasmodic, and took the form mostly of the exploration of facts presented by nature. Variations were the casual byproducts of primitive man's daily activities. Deliberate experiment, though not unknown in primitive society, must have been rare; on the whole, directional research is a recent development.

The difficulties inherent in independent development are the main factors stressed in arguments between the evolutionists and the diffusionists in regard to the relative importance of the two main sources of progress in society: the development of culture by discoveries and inventions, and the influence of culture contact, which spreads the benefits of these discoveries and inventions over more or less extended areas of the world's surface.

Evolutionists ascribe the similarity of cultural traits in societies between whom intercourse is not known to have taken place to the fact that, in similar surroundings, common needs and aspirations are likely to have evolved the same basic artifacts and institutions. According to them, the psychic unity of mankind has in response to similar stimuli everywhere evolved the same fundamental means for their satisfaction. It is therefore not only possible but also probable, they maintain, that the same basic inventions were made in a number of different parts of the world.

Whereas an evolutionist like Bastian could speak of the appalling monotony of the fundamental ideas of mankind all over the globe, the diffusionists maintain that inventions were made only once in the history of mankind, usually accidentally, almost never from rational motives. From these centres of origin they then spread through the world. It is for this reason, they maintain, that progress was concentrated initially in that great thoroughfare of human intercourse—the Mesopotamian plain, the Fertile Crescent, and the Nile, where men met and mingled from the eighth millennium B.C., as they were later to do again in the narrow isthmus that connects North and South America.

But whatever the respective contributions of these two factors to any specific culture may have been, it is clear that their impact on primitive economies must have been a slow process. For the world of the primitive is small: functionally, geographically, and historically. Functionally, there is little opportunity in primitive society for economic differentiation and specialisation, and the history of civilisation has been largely the history of the extension of the principle of division of labour. Geographically, the world of primitive man ends outside the sphere of his own immediate neighbourhood. Historically, what is beyond the knowledge of his grandfathers is the realm of mythology and of imagination. The continuity of life in pre-literate communities is assured by the products of material culture and by traditions handed down orally from generation to generation. The lack of written records makes it impossible to standardise concepts and to accumulate objective knowledge beyond the mental powers of the existing members of the group. The sphere of knowledge is therefore restricted to certain limiting conditions of time, opportunity and place.

The primitive community tends, on the whole, to be strikingly homogeneous. There is little differentiation in ideas, interests, or occupation. Consequently there is little of the conflict of beliefs and interests that affords the civilised individual the opportunity to review his own ideas in the light of the ideas of others. Habits are so uniform as to be accepted automatically. Deviations tend to evoke the strongest ridicule and resistance. The control exercised by public opinion is pervasive. Action and even thought tend to be corporate affairs.

The closely integrated culture of the primitive puts no premium on progress but emphasises conformity to established rules, for the integration that he has achieved between his technique and organisation and his material and social requirements is on the whole satisfactory to him, with the result that he displays no undue interest in innovation. Hence the importance attached by historians to the presentation to such cultures of challenges, either by the physical or the social environment, which may evoke in certain communities a creative response, shaking them from the 'integration of custom' into the 'differentiation of civilisation'.[1]

Influence of the physical environment

The physical environment has exerted a pervasive and perennial influence on human development. But the physical milieu naturally affects material traits more than immaterial ones, and its influence in characterising a culture tends to be greater the lower the technical control of a people over its surroundings and the more pronounced the dominance of the environment.

The physical environment consists of a complex of factors such as soil, relief, raw materials, position and climate. These can affect a people's culture either directly by their influence on the human physique, or indirectly by presenting opportunities for or obstacles to development.

Environmental, and especially climatic, factors have a direct influence on the human physique, they create certain conditions in the human organism, and they afford facilities for the bearers of disease. These last are especially important. Thus, whereas the polar and desert regions are largely free from germs, insects or worms that cause disease, the tropics are full of the most deadly types.

Climate also has an important effect on development by its influence on the desire to work. The optimum conditions of climate for human progress would, of course, depend to a large extent on the state of a people's material development. Experiments would seem to show that, under civilised conditions of living, the optimum climatic conditions for the output of human energy vary from $38°$ to $50°$F for mental, and from $53°$ to $65°$F for physical work, with a relative humidity of from 60 to 40 per cent. The best climate to ensure human progress, according to Huntington, consists of one with a range of temperatures which, on the average for day and night, does not rise above $21°$C in summer or fall below $4.5°$C in winter. The extremes may of course be greater. These conditions would seem to hold for

[1] Cf. Toynbee, *A Study of History*, ii.

the most diverse peoples. This adaptation to a temperate climate is so universal that it might be a primitive trait belonging to the whole human race.[1]

The part of the world most penalised from the point of view of human development is undoubtedly the equatorial belt. The temperature is invariably little below that of the human body; the sluggish air is almost saturated with vapour during most of the year, and even the nights do not bring much relief. Similar conditions prevail during the rainy season in the tropical belts between the equator and the trade wind deserts. Here the cooler and drier winters, however, provide an agreeable variation.

Huntington's analysis affords an explanation of the gradual movement of the centres of economic development to the temperate zones during historical times. In the first place, the optimum conditions of climate for human progress would obviously depend to a large extent on the stage of a people's material development. The naked savage can live comfortably only in hot climates. But each improvement in the technique of providing against cold—the invention of clothes, fire, houses, glass—facilitated the movement of civilisation into colder regions. The basic features of human culture therefore had their origin in the tropical and subtropical areas. The first civilisations arose in the hot plains of Egypt and Mesopotamia because agriculture, with the techniques available at the time, could best be practised in loose sandy soils with the help of irrigation. It was only with the spread of the iron plough in the first millennium B.C. that the great grasslands of the temperate northern zone could begin to be effectively cultivated and the area successfully developed.

In the second place, it must be stressed that each environment presents opportunities for and obstacles to development, but the extent to which the opportunities will be taken and the obstacles overcome depends on the attitudes and aptitudes of the inhabitants. Given the cultural inertia described in the previous section, even the most sanguine environmentalist would therefore be perplexed by the frequent cases where the correlation between certain cultural expressions and particular environmental influences is lacking. Huntington himself notes this in a survey of culture and climate in pre-Columbian America:

> The most advanced American aborigines lived in regions which rank low in both health and climate. In the tropical plateaus where dwelt the Aztecs and Incas the climate, though cool, is so monotonous that it is unstimulating. On the other hand, in the bracing climate of the northern United States east of the Rocky Mountains, the American Indians were mere savages, living largely by hunting, while southern and central California were inhabited by almost the lowest of the aborigines.[2]

According to Nordenskiöld a surprisingly large proportion of the inventions made by American Indians came from the low-lying, unhealthy, tropical region of the Amazon basin. Those contributed by the Indians north of Mexico, on the other hand, were remarkably small.[3]

Environmental factors definitely *prevent* certain things from being done and *enable* others to be accomplished. But they are never mandatory. Had this imperative existed, mankind would have been spared an apprenticeship of thousands of years of hunting and collecting, with only the most rudimentary of stone implements.

[1] Huntington, *Civilization and Climate*, ch vii; *The Character of Races*, pp. 22, 290.
[2] Huntington, *The Character of Races*, p. 88.
[3] Nordenskiöld, *The American Indian as an Inventor*, pp. 277, 284.

The coordination of economic activities

Primitive economies are integrated primarily by the direct provision of needs, by the reciprocity of economic relationships, and by collective controls. The integration of land and labour is achieved by ties of kinship and by traditional and collective controls, and the allocation of resources is determined primarily by the self-sufficiency of the clan. Reciprocity assumes symmetrical forms of social organisation, and redistribution obtains within a group to the extent to which goods are collected in one hand and are apportioned by virtue of custom or central decision. Collective controls are based on the automatic application of cultural rules.

The acquisitive motivation characteristic of free enterprise societies is generally not found in primitive communities, which are motivated rather by psychological considerations more akin to prestige, by local and communal ties, and by social and political obligations. In these communities, in fact, attitudes that are incompatible with the competitive price system and the functioning of the self-regulating market are systematically inculcated in their members. Economic activity is directed basically not at the making of profit by means of exchange, but towards the direct provision of goods and services for use within a smaller or larger descent group. 'Nowhere', says Paul Radin, 'does there exist a surplus of goods or food accumulated either by the community or by an individual with the specific object of disposing of it at a personal profit to himself, and nowhere have the essential and fundamental types of property developed those characteristics which we, in our civilisation, regard as inseparably connected with the concept of personal and individual ownership.'[1]

As regards the basic necessities of life, the elementary requirements of all the members of the group must first be satisfied before surpluses can be disposed of. But all items of property, even the most personal ones, are enmeshed in a system of reciprocities. Goods, though formally the possession of individuals, do not have the attributes of property that would imply the right of their indiscriminate transfer to others. Transfers do indeed take place continually, usually within a prescribed circuit and, within that circuit, in a prescribed rotation. But property rights have continually to be authenticated and property must be properly used. Therefore all property rights entail corresponding obligations.

In such circumstances property can rarely become a mere commodity, an object over which an individual can have free and indiscriminate disposition. The idea of profit is alien to such a situation. Though the value of the goods is enhanced

---

[1] Radin, *The World of Primitive Man*, p. 106.

These basic differences between primitive and modern societies have significant consequences for the application of economic theory to primitive communities. Economic processes in these communities are closely integrated in the total social process. Classical economic theory, which tries to isolate the economic from the other aspects of the social process, is based on economic relations in modern market-orientated economies. Its concepts and methods of analysis may therefore not be relevant to societies in which economic processes are still strongly embedded in the institutional process as a whole. Thus the concepts of economics—capital, labour and enterprise; prices, wages, interest and profit; credit, trade, money, banking and markets—concepts that are characteristic of the institutional framework of the market-orientated economy, may have no counterparts or may have a different significance in collective economies. Economic motivation or the rational allocation of scarce resources to achieve given goals may be irrelevant to societies in which choice is socially conditioned and in which the allocative principles cannot be dissociated from their institutional framework. In analysing such societies, therefore, the tools of the economist must be used with the greatest circumspection so as not to give a completely distorted picture of the true structure and significance of these economies.

through the process of passing from one person to another, the original owner gains through the enhancement of subjective values, such as an increase in prestige, and not by an increase in its price.

It is because of these associations of property that wealth has a different quality in primitive communities to what it has in civilised societies. Since wealth consists in continuous circulation, the communal aspects of wealth—the attainment of prestige and status—are far more prominent than in a more individualist society. This gives to primitive communities a basically collective character.

The organisation of exchange relations is also basically different from that of capitalist societies in that reciprocal, ceremonial and political considerations are involved. Trade is carried on primarily between tribes. It centres in the meeting of different communities, one of its purposes being the exchange of goods. Such meetings do not produce the appropriate prices that are adjusted by supply and demand; they rather presuppose that the appropriate rates are already in existence.

Primitive collectivism

The distribution of commodities and services in primitive communities is based essentially on a system of reciprocal obligations, which ensures to each individual the basis of his existence.

> Irrespective of the type of political organisation and the method of food-production, irrespective of whether society is socially stratified or unstratified, democratic or monarchical, or whether the food-economy is that of the food-gatherer, the hunter-fisher, the agriculturist or the pastoral-nomad, all aboriginal peoples accept the theory that every human being has the inalienable right to an irreducible minimum, consisting of adequate food, shelter and clothing. This irreducible minimum is an attribute of life on a par with the biological attributes of life.[1]

The collective character of economic relations, as we have seen, is exercised especially in regard to the basic necessities of life, though it permeates all forms of movable property in the primitive community. Land, too, is held on a collective basis. Claims to the exclusive use of a given tract of land are made even by hunting and collecting peoples. The size of the land to which a group claims exclusive right varies with the size of the horde and the possibilities of making a living. Among the Andamanese it was usually about sixteen square miles; in Australia it often exceeded a hundred square miles. The intrusion of outsiders is resented, and wars among the lower primitives are often due to the violation of hunting rights.

Within the group, however, the land is held on a collective basis. Individual ownership of land among hunters is largely non-existent, though exceptions are found. Such peoples do not value individual pieces of land, but are interested rather in the animals or plants that can be obtained over an extended area. The soil itself, in fact, is usually associated with a deity with whom it is identified.

Claims to tracts of land obtain a more 'individual' character among fishermen, because good fishing spots are more restricted than hunting territories and are therefore more easily appropriated.

[1] *Ibid.*, p. 106.

Minimal formal government among lower primitives

Hunting and collecting communities have little formal government. This lack of organised control is reflected in the means of maintaining law and order. The collective character of the primitive economy and the small number of objects conferring wealth make legal relations very simple in character. Theft, for example, is largely non-existent where there is little movable property, and the few personal possessions are considered to belong directly to the personality of the owner. In such small groups, social and religious sanctions and sentiments, and the reciprocal character of economic relations, are usually effective means for bringing about the performance of obligations and of securing conformity with conventional morality. Even in the small hunting and collecting hordes, often hardly larger than the extended family, little justice is exercised by the community through the elders, and even the most grievous bodily and personal injuries are generally regarded as affecting only the individuals concerned, who have to seek self-redress either unaided or with the help of their family. Exceptions do exist. But as a rule it is crimes in regard to religion and the practice of magic that are considered as public delicts.[1]

It is only where the means of subsistence of the community are at stake that rigid control is sometimes exercised in economic affairs. This is especially the case among some of the higher hunters, who carry on hunting with an elaborate organisation and technique, requiring the cooperation of all the able-bodied men of the community. The rigidity of this control was especially marked among the Plains Indians of North America. During the period of the bison hunt the group was vested with powers to prevent individual and premature attacks on the herd, and to punish offenders with corporal punishment, with destruction of property, and in extreme cases even with death. In all other matters the members of the community enjoyed complete freedom from coercion; even homicide was not regarded as a criminal act. But with transgressions of the hunting regulations it was different. The police force which had merely advisory powers in case of murder, now assumed complete control. Such breaches of the hunting rules

> were treated as an attempt against the public, in short, as a criminal act, and they were punished with all the rigour appropriate to political offences. In other words, for the brief period of the hunt the unchallenged supremacy of the police unified the entire population and created a state 'towering immeasurably above the single individuals', but which disappeared again as rapidly as it had come into being.[2]

Economic differentiation among agriculturists and among pastoralists

The collective character of economic relations is retained among all primitive peoples, although economic differentiation becomes more important among the higher primitives. Thus communal rights to the use of land are modified among agriculturists, and lose in importance with the development of agricultural technique. Numerous intermediate forms are found, from communal tenure to the permanent family, and even individual ownership of plots of land.

With the migratory agriculture practised by the lower agriculturists, the ownership of land, as distinct from the group control of a territory, is of little import-

---

[1] Hobhouse, Wheeler and Ginsberg, *The Material Culture and Social Institutions of the Simpler Peoples*, p. 54.

[2] Lowie, *The Origin of the State*, p. 104.

ance. The population is usually sparse and abundant marginal land is available. It is the arduous task of clearing and cultivating the soil which creates economic values. The land belongs to the community, but any family is free to occupy and cultivate plots and to retain them as long as they remain in cultivation. These rights do not lapse if the ground is allowed to lie fallow in order to recover its fertility, but are forfeited if the family removes to another piece of land. Uncultivated land remains the common hunting ground of the whole community. There is therefore merely a pre-emptive possessory right to occupied land, or what may be called an 'inherited use ownership'. It is only to the products of labour, the crops, huts or trees, that more or less well-defined individual rights are attached. Even the produce of the fields is often held in common by groups, with due allowance for the status, relationship, or contribution of individuals to the enterprise.

It is by virtue of the distinction between property rights in land and rights to the products of the land, or the buildings erected on it, that trees or dwellings may belong to people other than those who hold the land. The soil as such belongs to a deity, to the community, or to the chief as its representative. Permanent alienation of land to outsiders is not allowed. Immigrants may use land only on sufferance, and their descendants only very slowly acquire permanent rights in it. So strong is the religious association of a community with the land on which it lives, that even conquerors in a new country usually hesitate to expropriate the original possessors.

Among the higher agriculturists there comes a decline in communal land tenure as a result of social stratification and the greater rights to the land claimed by the chiefs and nobles. Individual, and still more seignorial, claims to the land increase in importance. There comes a vagueness in regard to the relation of the chief to the land. It is not clear whether he is the owner or merely the administrator of the communal land. 'We seem in fact to get something of that ambiguity as between seignorial and popular ownership that we find at the beginning of our own history.'[1] The introduction of the plough, the use of manure, and the rotation of crops, especially, give agricultural land a permanent value, for with relatively short fallow periods good land can be maintained in cultivation indefinitely. 'The periodic reallotments take place less and less often, occupation grows longer and longer, and ends by becoming a life-interest. And when once this is reached, private ownership is at the door; it only needs that inheritance should be permitted or authorised.'[2]

Differences in wealth also become more important among cultivators. The personal possessions of nomadic peoples are limited by the difficulties of transport. A sedentary life increases the scope for the accumulation of property. With the development of culture, possessions also tend to lose to a certain extent the collective associations that attach to them. The number of objects made for exchange increases. The fact of exchange tends to weaken purely subjective associations and to bring wealth into freer circulation.

Social stratification is directly dependent on the production of an economic surplus. 'From all parts of the world materials are on hand to make clear that primitive societies everywhere, producing more goods than the minimum requirement for the support of life, translate their economic surpluses into the social leisure which is only afforded some members of the community—persons of privilege supported by this excess wealth.'[3] Social inequalities, however, appear not

---

[1] Hobhouse, Wheeler and Ginsberg, p. 253.
[2] Letourneau, *Property, Its Origins and Development*, p. 116.
[3] Herskovits, *The Economic Life of Primitive Peoples*, pp. 369 ff.

so much in the form of differences in the standard of living as in the amount of manual work performed and the security enjoyed by the different classes. Everywhere the highest class is represented by those who govern and those who command the technique for influencing the forces of the supernatural.

The income of the chief is derived from gifts, fines, confiscations, the labour of his subjects, and from taxes and bribes, and is further swelled by the institution of polygamy. Presents are made to him by his subjects at harvest time, to obtain favour, or as a prelude to a request. The first fruits are very generally claimed by him. Plunder in raids swells his resources. His subjects may be requested to render tribute in produce, to till his fields, herd his cattle, build his dwellings, or perform domestic service. They in turn are entertained with food and drink. Thus the essential qualities of a good chief among the Baganda have been defined as 'beer, meat and politeness'. Peasants who work for him expect to be treated. 'The chief would kill cattle when he saw that they were tired; they ate their fill, and then worked with all their might.'[1] The form of the gift is often maintained, though among the higher primitives the services tend to acquire an increasingly one-sided character. Sometimes only 'special' services are recompensed.

These resources are needed to maintain the prestige of the chief, for men of rank are frequently called on to extend hospitality to travellers, relatives, and visitors of note. Provisions are also freely distributed by the headman among his own followers, especially on the occasion of feasts, and in times of need. Contributions to the chief are, in fact, occasionally regarded as public treasuries, to which all subscribe, and from which the community is fed in times of stress, or on public occasions.[2]

Where the means of subsistence are continuously redistributed, great inequalities in the standard of living cannot arise. Since the means of satisfying human wants are relatively simple, a substantial equality in the ways of living is forced on everyone. There are few ways in which wealth can be used to acquire the comforts of life, or to gain control over human beings, or over social and economic affairs. Ways of living are much the same for everyone. Property is a source of prestige, of social and ceremonial values, rather than of material advantage.[3]

The economic inequality between chief and commoner does not consist so much in the greater accumulated possessions of the chief as in the greater amount of resources that are continually passing through his hands. The chief represents a reservoir into which wealth flows only to be poured out freely again. A system of reciprocal relations thus arises between subjects and chief. They supply him with food; he provides them with feasts and assumes the initiative in communal enterprises. The wealth of a Maori chief, Firth says, 'was utilised largely for his own aggrandisement and influence, it is true, but in so doing it contributed greatly to the material benefit of his people'.[4]

The wealth of commoners is similarly kept in a state of flux. For the primitive is 'entangled in a mesh of duties, functions, and privileges which correspond to an elaborate tribal, communal and kinship organisation'.[5] In the Trobriands about three-quarters of a man's crops are given either as contributions to the chief or as his due to his sister's or mother's husband and family.[6] Relatives have the right to

[1] Mair, *An African People in the Twentieth Century*, p. 183.
[2] Sumner and Keller, *The Science of Society*, p. 501.
[3] Goldenweiser, *Anthropology*, p. 152.
[4] Firth, *Primitive Economics of the New Zealand Maori*, p. 289.
[5] Malinowski, *Crime and Custom in Savage Society*, p. 10.
[6] *Ibid.*, p. 61.

make demands on the successful individual, friends to borrow from him. He may even be accused of practising sorcery to cause other people's property to disappear into his own house. And the evasion of obligations is difficult in these small communities. The aversion of herders to killing their cattle is no doubt a result of the practice of sharing food. In Fiji this liability to share has proved an effectual bar to the adoption of European methods of trading. 'A Fijian who sets up as a trader is liable to have his goods appropriated by anyone who comes into his store, to such an extent as to make his success impossible.'[1]

Economic control

Economic control is exercised largely by the clan or the local group, through the chief, the elders, secret societies, and the practitioner of witchcraft. The functions of the tribe are, as a rule, confined to certain formal overrights to the land within its borders. The clan, on the other hand, continues to function as an economic unit long after its political activities have been absorbed by the tribe. It ensures the maintenance of tradition and of psychological attitudes, and of effective cooperation among its members. For where labour is largely cooperative there must be central control to coordinate activities. Where the land is apportioned, this is done by the heads of the community, who settle any disputes arising from land tenure. They decide when cultivation shall begin and when cattle shall be driven to the winter grazing grounds.

The chief, through his control of ritual practices, performs an important integrating function in that he commands and initiates the correct utilisation of the community's resources. The ceremonies which he performs form the pivotal points of the seasonal economic cycle. As the centre of distribution he assumes the initiative in the construction of public works and other forms of collective enterprise, such as the organisation of trading expeditions or the building of large canoes. As the representative of the community the chief arranges its outside relations, and all external trade often has to be conducted through his agency. He declares a tabu on the gathering of crops before the appointed day of harvest, on rare trees to prevent the extermination of the species, or on fishing grounds to enable them to be replenished. The chief, therefore, plays an important part, if in an informal way, in initiating and directing the activities of his people.[2]

The group thus exercises collective control over the activities of its members and is responsible for the deeds of any individual member. In Bechuanaland, the whole village is responsible for a theft committed by one of its members. 'The head-man must assist the person robbed, and the responsibility can only be evaded by proving that the spoor extends beyond the village lands to those of another village. Thus the whole tribe becomes interested in detecting the thief.' In such circumstances the members of the group constitute themselves one another's keepers. The most profound distinction between capitalist and primitive forms of economic organisation is, no doubt, as Vinogradoff suggests, that capitalist society starts with individuals and adjusts itself primarily to the claims of the individual, whereas the primitive community starts with groups and subordinates individual interests to the claims of these groups.[3]

[1] Rivers, *Social Organisation*, p. 107.
[2] Firth, *Primitive Polynesian Economy*, ch 6.
[3] Sumner and Keller, pp. 323, 454–6.

Centralisation and decentralisation of power

With the development of culture there comes a growth of organised government within the primary groups, constituted by the clans, totemic bands, or village communities. There comes, also, a definite progress towards tribal unity, thus extending the sphere of organised society. Kinship tends to become of less importance as the basis of political attachment. The functions of government tend to become more numerous and more varied and the government itself to become more complex and specialised. With the increase in the range and complexity of organisation, the government also tends to become more powerful and more privileged, and consequently struggles for the control of the privileges and prerequisites of government tend to become more common and more vehement.[1]

It has been maintained that, from the point of view of political and economic organisation, the most highly developed primitive communities seem to represent the beginnings of a development in two different directions. Where disruptive influences predominate over centralising ones, a militant and virile nobility aided by local or ethnic ties, jealous of their rights, and recognising no superiors, may succeed in forming autocratic and virtually independent domains. An 'ideal type' of such a primitive stratified community may have an almost feudal atmosphere. The nobility is generally represented by the full-blooded conquerors of the country. But there are also internal means of differentiation, such as primogeniture or difference in wealth. The commoners are represented by the conquered community, who form a body of dependent cultivators. The relations between the two are embodied in the protection furnished by the lord, and the tribute and services rendered by the people. The clan organisation, however, generally prevents the excessive exploitation of the dependent classes and their degradation into serfs. But they perform the menial tasks, and may have to work for their overlord for certain days during the week or year. Besides the subjected classes there are often also castes of craftsmen in a more or less dependent position. Moreover the slave population assumes important proportions in certain agricultural economies. Aliens may further swell the ranks of the dependent classes. In such societies the economic area tends to outgrow that of small self-governing communities. The reciprocity of economic relations loses in importance, and the organisation comes to be built more and more on the one-sided contributions and services rendered by the dependent classes.

Favourable environmental conditions and strong personalities, on the other hand, may bring about the formation of centralised despotic states. The king claims the privileges which formerly belonged to the entire community. The whole country and everything in it are not only subject to him, but are his personal property. Hence his power over life and death, his right to tax his subjects and to exploit their labour. He makes his rights effective by a more or less centralised system of administration which, among the best organised of the primitive kingdoms, consists of a hierarchy of chiefs and officials whose ambition it is to rise in the bureaucratic order.

But though these tendencies, however vague, can be traced among the highest primitives, care must always be exercised not to transfer ideas associated with civilised societies to genuinely primitive communities. In primitive communities, untouched by contact with more advanced cultures, the heads of state, though they may theoretically be invested with very extensive power in the more centrally governed kingdoms, may lack the ability effectively to enforce their authority.

[1] Schapera, *Government and Politics in Tribal Societies*, ch 6.

Hence the necessity of allying themselves with ritualistic societies, which can act as police organisations. The system of enforcement of law and order is normally too diffused to be effectively centred in a single authority.

Part 2
Centrally Administered Riverine Economies

2
The archaic storage economies

Emergence of the first civilisations

The first civilisations that appeared on the scene of history developed out of the pre-existent peasant communities on the plains of Egypt and Mesopotamia towards the end of the fifth millennium B.C. These new civilisations, though in many respects highly individualised entities, formed a remarkable cultural unity. This is the more remarkable because, especially during the initial period, direct cultural relations seem to have been insignificant. Important factors in the shaping of similar destinies seem to have been the similarity of environment and of the tissue of existing ideas and institutions that was the common property of the world of preceding peasant peoples. Above all, the unity must be ascribed to the fact that the environment presented the early Egyptians and Sumerians with the same challenge, which evoked the same response.

It was not by accident that the first civilisations to appear on the world scene were riverine societies, developed in arid and semi-arid surroundings. Their rise can indeed be explained by the fact that initially all large and stable economies were based primarily on agriculture, and before the invention of the iron technique, agriculture could best be practised in loose sandy soils under conditions of irrigation. The great grasslands, which exist in optimum climatic surroundings and which with modern techniques offer the best conditions for social and economic development, could not be effectively cultivated before the introduction of the iron plough.

The development of a central administration

Once the river valleys became permanently settled, a strong social need would arise for certain facilities, and the environmental conditions would at the same time favour their invention. The welfare of these desert countries depended essentially on an efficient system of irrigation. The flood waters reached only the low-lying lands, and became exhausted when most needed. Under such conditions agriculture could be carried on only if there was an artificial conservation and distribution of water. But the rivers also brought down silt, which rapidly choked the irrigation system. Such conditions forced the inhabitants at an early stage to sustained collective effort and to the acceptance of a common authority that transcended their individual wills. At the same time river transport facilitated the efficient carriage and the mobilisation and centralised allocation of resources. The yearly inundations called for the accurate measurement of land, and the state required the services of a bureaucracy, of the art of writing and the keeping of careful accounts. The centralised mobilisation and use of resources must therefore have been of decisive importance in inducing the transition from Neolithic peasant to civilised societies in these countries.[1]

After an early transitional stage, archaic societies indeed became organised in centralised, bureaucratic states.[2] the king was the state by divine right. The whole machinery of state functioned for his benefit: it was to fill his treasury that taxes were levied and to honour him that public works were constructed. Land and all other fixed property and even movable property were, to a large extent, his possessions, and when he allowed anyone else to have a share in them it was merely a temporary concession that could be revoked at any time. Precarious claims to landed property arose through the grant of royal fiefs, benefices and bequests to temples and individuals. But such bequests were closely associated with and dependent on the office held by the recipients. In Mesopotamia private rights to property seem at times to have been more developed than in Egypt. But although the possession of limited rights to property might have acted as an economic incentive, it could not act as a source that conferred any corresponding political power. Politically the people remained completely passive. The privileges and powers of the king were to them not a subject for discussion but a matter of belief, and through the ages there were no popular uprisings or revolutions to secure a share in the government.

The palace was not merely the royal residence but also the centre of administration. The outstanding feature of the agro-managerial economies, in fact, was the complete dependence on and subservience of the bureaucracy to the ruler. This was reflected in the strong emphasis on service, not to the community, but to the head of the state.

Already when the riverine economies emerged in history, all economic activity was controlled, coordinated, canalised and directed by the managerial bureaucracy, and all large enterprises undertaken by the state. After the irrigation works had been completed, the most important functions of management and control were those involved in the maintenance of the works, the distribution of irrigation water, and flood control. The effective performance of these tasks became symbolic of a well-organised and efficient administration. These functions involved the development of accurate means of measurement, of recording time, and of calendar-making, all of which significantly coincided with the rise of the first riverine civilisations.

Archaic economies seem to have been particularly affected by the two typical weaknesses of all centrally administered bureaucracies. The first was the tendency for the number of officials to proliferate. As soon as the central authority weakened, 'the land became small and its leaders many'. Both in Egypt and in Mesopotamia there was a tendency for the administration to be overstaffed with

---

[1] Erman-Ranke, *Ägypten und ägyptisches Leben im Altertum*, pp. 570, 613.
[2] This does not necessarily imply that national unity was always complete. Even in Egypt the fiction of a double administration, with a granary and a treasury for each of the ancient kingdoms, was maintained long after national unity had been achieved. In Mesopotamia unity was attained much later than in Egypt and was always less complete.

minor officials and for a few of the higher officials to unite in themselves numerous functions under the pretext of centralising and coordinating the administration, and for far too great an emphasis to be laid on useless ceremony. Already Urukagina (*c.* 2781-2775 B.C.) deplored the fact that 'within the limits of the territory of Ningirsu, there are inspectors down to the sea'. In Egypt, both in the fifth and in the twentieth dynasties, the number of official drones became so large that they exhausted the resources of the state, and led to its complete collapse.[1]

This first weakness was always effectively complemented by a second: the unwillingness of officials in the centralised administration to take decisions, to exercise their own initiative, and to assume responsibility. These traits were especially noticeable in societies in which there was no appeal against the decisions of the authorities and no protection in the rule of law. This must have been especially evident in the Egyptian administration, where there was no arrangement of departments according to the functions performed and officials were continually transferred from one duty to another. Thus generals were placed in charge of commercial expeditions or the collection of revenue. The royal Meten began his career as a 'scribe of the granary', suddenly to appear as a learned doctor, to reappear as a financial official, and to end up as a superintendent of commissions. The result was that the whole administration tended to be consumed by endless friction between individuals and departments in regard to the assignment of authority and responsibility, as well as by intrigues and petty jealousies.[2]

The storage economy and the coordination of resources

The economic and financial administration of these economies was conducted very largely in non-monetary terms.

Thus as far as the state revenue was concerned, the main emphasis was laid on contributions and services in kind and on the royal domains. In Egypt contributions were collected in state depots and all payments were made from these depots in kind. Everyone literally lived from the King's Table. The central authorities were kept informed of the condition of revenue and expenditure by means of periodical reports. All this required the elaborate keeping of accounts, for nothing entered or left the treasury without the proper receipt. To the Egyptians administration and the keeping of accounts were synonymous. The fiscal arrangements were centralised as far as possible from a book-keeping point of view, though naturally the administration of all receipts in kind had to be decentralised to a very large extent.

Such an economy had little or no need of market activities. The peasants who constituted the vast bulk of the population were largely self-supporting, or obtained their rations in kind. Needs that had to be provided from outside were met by barter and reciprocity. Surpluses were effectively mobilised by the state, the temples and the nobility. The more simple manufacturing activities were imposed on the peasants by the *corvée*. Thus wool from the royal estates was deposited in central depots from which it was issued to peasants for further processing as part of their conscripted services. Specialised craftsmen formed part of the establishments of the court, the temples, and the nobility. All employees and officials were closely dependent on these bureaucratically organised economies. The more lowly paid

---

[1] Kees, *Ägypten*, ch 5; King, *History of Babylon*, p. 179; Heichelheim, *Wirtschaftsgeschichte des Altertums*, pp. 179, 195.
[2] Kees, ch 5.

ones received meagre rations in kind, but even the highest officials had to provide for their families out of their allocated fields or out of their rations, supplemented by royal presents, fees and benefices, eked out by gratuities from private persons and the occasional misappropriation of funds. Regular salaries were unknown.

Commodity and factor markets in such an economy were therefore non-existent. Land, as has already been pointed out, could normally be transferred only by bequest. A free labour force that could offer its services for payment was neither required nor available. Merchants, in so far as they existed for extra-territorial purposes, were state officials.

The Old-Sumerian and Babylonian economies also were highly centralised. In Old-Sumeria 'the population served the temple [state] and lived on it'. Trade with outside areas was carried on by merchants who were state officials. These officials, however, also participated in local trade, and especially in the sale of fish. Fish, contributed as revenue to the state by fishermen, was retailed to consumers. The fact that this purchasing power was available shows that all the free-flowing resources of the state were not appropriated by the ruler.

It was only in the New-Sumerian period that private enterprise seems to have played a more important, though still strictly subordinate, role. Merchants and moneylenders dealt on their own account as well as on behalf of the state. Contracts between private persons increased and some of the merchants owned many houses and landed estates. Some even sold their goods through subordinates and agents, financed trading enterprises, and extended credit, mainly for agricultural purposes. They carried on their activities subject to the provisions of the civil and public law. Merchants seemed to have formed a special group, who lived in a specific quarter of a town, usually close to the market quay.[1]

During the later years of Rim-Sin's reign and under Hammurabi and his successors, the royal economy again became highly centralised and trade firmly integrated in the state organisation. Merchants again acted mainly as the agents of the king, and especially as the sellers of the products collected as taxes and not needed by the state, and as the purchasers of articles required by the government. This centralisation does not seem to have been associated with the dispossession of the merchant class, but merely by the curtailment of its activities. At the same time the administration of the entire country became more strongly centred in the capital city and in the person of the ruler.[2]

Such economies had only a limited use for money. Valuable objects such as immovable property, luxury objects and slaves, where they were exchanged, were bartered, though they might have their values expressed in a common unit of account. Any representative articles could be used as currency, not only for the payment of goods but also of services, though measured food and weighed-out metals tended to predominate. The goods given in payment of services were standardised earlier than those given in payment of commodities. Specific articles, such as grain, bread, beer and cloth, were almost always used in payment of wages. The commodities paid as revenue to the royal treasury also became standardised

---

[1] Leemans, *The Old-Babylonian Merchant, his business and social position*. These views differ from those expressed in *Trade and Market in the Early Empires*, ed. Polanyi ch 2, in which it is maintained that 'Babylonia possessed neither market places nor a functioning market system of any description. . . . Contrary to traditional notions Babylonian trade and business activities were not originally market activities' (pp. 15 ff).

[2] *Ibid.*, A peculiar feature of the Late-Babylonian state, as of contemporary Egypt, was the growing importance of the temple economies, both in the economic and administrative fields. These were mere replicas of the state economy.

early. It was in the state treasury that the balance was first used. Public weigh-masters were appointed to verify weights. This system was relatively so efficient that later on the earlier and cruder forms of coined currency were considered as offering no advantage and were for a long time rejected.

State enterprise

The resources made available by the storage economy were used by the state not only for the support of the bureaucracy but also for its industrial and commercial activities. State enterprise was especially evident in the primary sectors of mining and quarrying, in the construction field, and in certain processing activities required by the army, the court, the temples and the higher echelons of the bureaucracy. The skilled craftsmen seem to have been mainly public employees, whereas the unskilled were largely conscripted by the *corvée*. The peculiar characteristic of these economies was that large-scale trading activities, and especially foreign trade, were also almost invariably undertaken either directly by the state or for the royal account, so that the merchants who engaged in these transactions occupied a semi-official position.

The shortage of timber and metals was a stimulus to trade relations that transcended the scope of the redistributive system. This foreign trade was not conducted for profit. It was not market trade, but administrative or treaty trade, and the rates at which goods were exchanged took the form of equivalences established by the authority of custom, by statute, or by proclamation. In Mesopotamia a lively trade was also carried on between the various towns within the country. The goods were waterborne, along the rivers and canals, and consisted among other things of foodstuffs, wool, wood, bricks, metals and bitumen.

Social stratification

The social structure of these agro-managerial societies tended to represent a clear differentiation between superior and privileged persons on the one hand, and subordinate and underprivileged ones on the other. At the top were the rulers, the aristocracy, the priests and the upper and middle echelons of the bureaucracy. These formed the ruling class in the most unequivocal sense of the term. Below them, the masses constituted a group of politically underprivileged persons. They had no voice in state affairs. Unlike the commoners in free economies, they lacked the means of effective organisation for securing a share in the determination of their own destinies. Socially and politically atomised, they remained politically passive, submissive and impotent.

In such societies there could be no class conflict in the Marxian sense of the word. Occasionally a group might resort to violence to voice its grievances. But this represented no organised, concerted and consistent movement. Conflict within the ruling class itself could have a more clearly defined political quality. But such conflicts were inspired, not by any desire to change the social structure, but merely to effect a reshuffle among the recipients of power.

Achievements and limitations of archaic societies

In spite of the elementary equipment available to the archaic craftsman and engineer, the material results they attained were astounding. We marvel at the ability of these people to transport colossal monuments, weighing up to a thousand tons, from the quarry to the temple; at their cleverness in raising huge obelisks to a vertical position on a narrow base, without other engineering tackle than ropes, levers and wooden rollers. The pyramids, with their polished stones of hard syenite, were built at a time when the only implements were relatively soft copper tools. But so mathematically accurate is the massive stone work that a knifeblade cannot be inserted between the blocks.

Two inventions were of capital importance for the development of archaic civilisation: the use of metals and the art of writing. It is significant that the rise of the first civilisations should have coincided with the invention of methods of working metals. The discovery of copper and later of bronze provided craftsmen with more delicate instruments for the execution of work requiring precision. Metal tools, however, at first remained extremely scarce and unspecialised. In the early Sumerian settlements tools were generally made of flint, bone or obsidian. Sickles were fashioned out of baked clay. In Egypt stone tools remained common till the second millennium. It was only after 1500 B.C., presumably as the result of developments in mining and the treatment of sulphide ores, that the use of metal became more common. The discovery of copper and bronze, therefore, did not during this period lead to the extension of control by human beings over their environment to anything like the extent that might be inferred from the revolutionary possibilities of the new materials. The aid of metal weapons in providing security to the settled peoples of the river valleys was probably of greater importance, initially, in the development of civilisation than the use of metal implements and tools.[1]

Writing enabled men to widen and deepen their ideas by facilitating the accumulation of knowledge in exact form. Illiterate and savage societies are in fact synonymous terms. The highly centralised bureaucratic states of antiquity, with their developed state economies, their well-organised methods of administration and their elaborate systems of accounts, are quite inconceivable without the craft of writing.

The great feats of antiquity were executed mainly by the abundant and systematic exploitation of time and labour. Little value was attached to either. With a few exceptions great construction works were undertaken at the command of the king. All the labour of the country was at his disposal, and he did not spare it. The natural stoppage of work in the fields during the period of the inundation facilitated the mobilisation of the peasantry. The outstanding feature of these works was that the builders invariably tried to achieve the requisite effect with the maximum use of material—a reflection of the inherent love of bureaucracy for the spectacular rather than for the aesthetic or the practically useful. Kings often boasted of the amount of material used and the number of workers employed.

The limitations of these people were no less remarkable than their achievements. It is the fate of an empirical technique that it tends to remain stationary and stagnant. Many promising developments in science and technique went no further, and even retrogressed with the lapse of time. It was a common experience that the significance of inventions originating in the Near East was realised only when they were transplanted abroad. Old processes were retained even when better methods were discovered.

Archaic science, if science it can be called, was determined by practical needs

[1] Cf. Childe, *Progress and Archaeology*, ch 3.

such as the necessity of interpreting omens, measuring the land, or healing the sick. Its character is reflected in its scope as well as in its method. All those subjects that require the clear formulation of concepts and strict logical thinking are lacking. The only attempt to systematise knowledge is by means of classification, which is determined by theological, verbal, or purely external considerations. Mental operations are confined to the concrete, and do not deal with the abstract; they are of a non-analytical character. The most diverse facts are grouped together without any attempt at synthesis, whether in law, literature or science. Mathematical texts contain no generalisations and make no attempt to prove propositions, but consist merely of sets of examples worked out. The Egyptian medical papyri, in spite of the opportunities afforded by mummification for the study of human anatomy, indicate the almost total absence of interest in the structure of the body or in the nature of disease; they merely enumerate the methods to be applied in healing specific cases. There was no desire to acquire knowledge for its own sake—people were perfectly satisfied when a given method worked.[1]

The arts and sciences were controlled by mystical and mythical notions, and these tended to increase rather than decrease with the passage of time. A technique controlled by magic, however, always implies only one correct way of doing things, the precedent having divine sanction. In Babylonia the god Ea was considered to be the inventor and transmitter of all crafts. This unbroken continuity was preserved by the Babylonian Noah, Ut-Napischti, who had the foresight to take craftsmen with him into the ark. Only things made according to the old models were considered beautiful. 'Even the sprightliness of the people was turned into formulae taught in the art schools.' In planning new public works kings always diligently set about discovering precendents, so that they might be sure to build 'as of old'. Hence there was little new in technique to mark the passage of the years, save empirical discoveries in the arts and crafts. In Egypt everything points to the fact that science attained its fullest development in the period which was responsible for nearly every good thing that the country ever produced—the period of the Old Kingdom, or roughly between 2600 and 2200 B.C. In Mesopotamia, the Sumerians believed that they came into the country with their civilisation already perfected, bringing with them the knowledge of agriculture, of the use of metals and of the art of writing. 'Since then' they said, 'no new inventions have been made', and recent excavations seem to show that there was a good deal of truth in this belief.[2]

It is this obstinate persistency that strikes one as being the most characteristic feature of archaic civilisation. The artist or craftsman lacked the spiritual self-assertion to free himself from the canons, the tradition and the ritual that limited his development in every direction. The most characteristic test of this attitude, says Eduard Meyer, is that although each of the oriental civilisations produced a large literature there is no literary work that bears the name of its author, and only in a very few of the innumerable works of art has the artist dared to introduce his name or image in some hidden way.[3]

Even at the end of the independent existence of both Egypt and Babylonia, when only a spiritual revolution could have saved them, they refused to relegate to the scrap-heap even the most burdensome of the numerous traditions that stunted

[1] Soden, 'Leistung und Grenze sumerischer und babylonischer Wissenschaft', *Die Welt als Geschichte*, 11/5, 11/6.
[2] Woolley, *Ur of the Chaldees*, p. 20; Meissner, *Babylonien und Assyrien*, i, 230, Moret, *The Nile and Egyptian Civilisation*, pp. 435 ff.
[3] Meyer, *Kleine Schriften*, p. 219.

their development. Learned antiquarianism was the characteristic feature of both the Egyptian and the Neo-Babylonian renaissance.

Nevertheless these archaic civilisations, because of their profound influence on the Hellenistic, Late Roman, and Byzantine cultures, were destined to exert an important influence on Russian social, religious and political thought and institutions, and therefore on the modern centrally administered economies.

Part 3
Centrally Directed Economies of the East

3
The Cinic economy

Natural isolation

For the greater part of her history China was very largely isolated from the rest of the world. Only in the east and south-east does she touch the sea. But in her case, the ocean was an effective means of isolation, for harbours are few and bad and the mouths of the rivers silted up with sand. Moreover the only countries within easy reach were Korea and Japan, both of which borrowed from rather than contributed to the culture of the Middle Kingdom. India was almost as inaccessible by sea as by land, for, in spite of intermittent trade relations with the West from the second century A.D. onwards, the Chinese, owing to the lack of both institutional and environmental stimuli, never became a great seafaring people, and trade with the outside world had little effect on the economic life of the country.

Communication by land was even more difficult. The rugged and wooded country of the south-west formed an effective barrier to intercourse. Elements of Indian culture entered China through north-eastern India, across the upper basin of the Irrawaddy. It was along this difficult route that rice, the domesticated fowl and, much later, American maize, reached China. The mountain ranges of Tibet close in the western approach and access on the northern side is obstructed by deserts and mountain ranges.

But in the north-west the open and fertile loess area of North China faces the Eurasian steppe zone, which imposed no hindrances on the eastward flow of western traits, however remote their original sources might have been. It was by this route that the principal elements of foreign culture, which were of importance in the shaping of Chinese civilisation, were introduced. Culture elements that originated in the Near East, such as the processing of bronze, the cultivation of wheat and other allied cereals, the keeping of domesticated animals such as horses, cattle, sheep and goats, the use of wheeled vehicles and, much later, the ox-drawn plough, spread to central Asia before the close of the third millennium B.C. Here they underwent local modification and were then passed on to northern China, where the Bronze Age civilisation made its appearance during the first half of the second millennium B.C. Nevertheless, in spite of this early indebtedness, and owing to the isolation of China during the historical period, the inhabitants of the Great Middle Kingdom came to look upon themselves as the only source of culture, the only people that contributed but never received, a relationship that made contact with the outside world both unprofitable and unnecessary.[1]

Inside China, on the other hand, there were no great obstacles to the free movement of men and the free flow of ideas. The great navigable rivers of the country, especially those of the Yangtze system, facilitated internal communication. China's wealth of fertile valleys, varied climate and diverse resources, rendered it almost entirely self-sufficing. The energies of the Chinese, therefore, were concentrated on occupying and developing their own country. In spite of original cultural and racial differences in the composition of the people, the great mass of the Chinese gradually became fairly homogeneous in appearance and in civilisation. Their culture showed an extraordinary stability and tenacity, and even when conquered they readily assimilated their rulers.

Rise of the bureaucratic state

In China the trend towards political unity and central control began at an early date. Despite repeated setbacks the movement towards the establishment of a unified empire persisted with a sense of historical inevitability.

When the Chinese emerged in the light of history they were already a highly organised people. The first dynasty was overthrown by nomadic people, the Chou, probably of Turkish stock, who introduced a type of feudal system (1054-256 B.C.). Confucian philosophy was developed during the decadence of the Chou régime, the period of the 'Warring States', and postulated moral suasion as the basis of the emperor's power. But this doctrine obviously clashed with the stern realities of Chinese life, a period of perpetual warfare in which the nobility were obliterated and Chinese society left with only two basic classes: the rulers and the peasantry. To establish order and to ensure the survival of the state amid the reigning chaos, the re-establishment of a central organisation and of discipline was required.

The natural reaction to Confucianism was the rise of the Legalist school. Its central tenet is that man's nature is intrinsically bad and that he cannot be expected to act socially if not subjected to the spur of reward and the threat of punishment. The state must therefore be governed by a clear, precise and severe set of laws, which must clearly enunciate what can and what cannot be done, and the rewards and penalties of conforming and of not conforming. To implement this policy the ruler requires a centralised, efficient and disciplined administration. The Legalist ideal is therefore 'that of a despotic, authoritarian, and even totalitarian state'.[2]

The conflict between Confucianism and Legalism was a fundamental one: a clash between idealism and realism, between feudalism and absolutism, between ethics and practice. In the state of Ch'in the Legalist theories were adopted. Every activity of the people was regulated and controlled, the economy subjected to a form of planning, and the state organised on an authoritarian military basis. A powerful unifying drive was also instituted and weights, measures, laws, and writing were made uniform throughout the empire. As head of the new Chinese empire founded in 221 B.C., the emperor became the heir of the Chou kings and of their sacred paramountcy. He held the mandate of heaven to rule the earth. Thus the position of the emperor was adequately buttressed by religious sanctions, and this traditional conception of the supreme position of the ruler became one of the strongest

[1] Bishop, 'The rise of civilisation in China with reference to its geographical aspects', *Geographical Review*, Oct. 1932; *Origin of the Far Eastern Civilisation*, pp. 14 ff.
[2] *History of Mankind: The Ancient World*, ed. Pareti, ii (2), pp. 429 ff; ii (3), pp. 770 ff.

permanent features of Chinese history. 'The Chinese heaven-willed state assumed some of the formal aspects of a theocracy.'

But the Chinese emperor, though legally vested with absolute power, was seldom a despot in the oriental sense of the term, for his power was effectively limited and circumscribed, not indeed by autonomous political units from below, but by the pressures exerted from above through a gradually perfected system of bureaucracy.

The higher echelons of the bureaucracy were recruited from a limited group of families whose members were partly officials, partly landlords, and partly scholars. The effective administration of the empire depended largely on their cooperation.[1] The intermediate ranges of the administration were recruited by a system of examinations, which was gradually opened to almost the whole population. Thus a certain social mobility was allowed in theory, though promotion in the service, as apart from recruitment, was usually reserved to certain classes. The administration was permeated with Confucian ideals and acted as a strongly conservative force, which prevented purely arbitrary rule and also tended to subordinate Legalist principles to values beyond those of mere power and efficiency. It thus contributed to the achievement of stability over long periods of Chinese history, irrespective of dynastic changes, and even under foreign rulers.

A typical feature of the Cinic state was the failure to separate the legislative, administrative and judicial functions of government. No separate and independent departments of state were formed to administer these services, with the result that the same officials were entrusted with the duties of law-makers, executive functionaries and judges. There was no recognition of the right of the subject to question the legality of the decisions or actions taken by a properly constituted authority, and there was no question of the rule of law that could act as a safeguard against the excessive or unauthorised demands of officials. The only resort that could be taken against the injustice or extortion of underlings was to appeal to the higher echelons of the bureaucracy. In theory the throne was open to the reception of any complaints or proposals that would help to improve the lot of his subjects; in practice it would have been difficult to voice grievances or to channel recommendations in such a way that these would find favourable reception.

Control over officials was, however, exercised by the institution of the censorate. This organisation observed and reported to the imperial court on the conditions of government in all parts of the empire, so as to bring to light cases of inefficiency, malpractice or corruption. The censorate was also in a position to criticise the actions of senior state servants and even of the emperor himself.

Objectives of policy

It was a typical feature of the dirigiste state that, in spite of the permeation of the officials with Confucian ideals, it was firmly believed that government was exercised not for the benefit of the people but in the interest of the state. The objective of policy was not the promotion of the public welfare but the aggrandisement and enrichment of the empire. Any advantages that might accrue to the inhabitants as the result of government action were incidental and not deliberate. The fact was also stressed that the aims of the state were best attained by deliberate, coordinated and planned effort.[2]

[1] Eberhard, *Conquerors and Rulers: Social Forces in Medieval China*, chs 2, 3.
[2] Loewe, *Imperial China*, pp. 150 ff.

Such objectives are typical of centrally directed polities. Their persistence was facilitated by the fact that, unlike European societies, the different layers of Chinese society never integrated into a 'national' entity, and the absence of nationalism further effectively prevented the conception, acceptance and implementation of broad popular policies.

Public works

As in all bureaucratic polities, the geographical and administrative unification of the state demanded the construction of public works on an extensive scale, while their creation at the same time enhanced the financial and organisational powers of the state. These comprised, in the first place, irrigation works: canals, reservoirs and protective dykes for the storage and distribution of water, and especially their use for transport and for administrative and fiscal purposes. According to legend, these were constructed as far back as the Golden Age, in the third millennium B.C. During the feudal period water conservation took place on a relatively small scale. But during the following Ch'in and Han dynasties, the ability to mobilise the peasantry in large numbers ushered in a great era of canal building and irrigation, two aspects of water control that went hand in hand and were essential to the development and expansion of the Cinic economy. Irrigation was necessary if the production of grain and other foodstuffs was to keep pace with the growing population and the ever-increasing demands of the court and the central government.

These works were complemented by the construction of public highways, chains of fortifications along the frontiers, and the establishment of new capitals, with their palaces, temples and tombs. They were supplemented by the necessary feeding services, such as mining, quarrying and the provision of the necessary means of communication. These activities were extended by the establishment of the primary and finishing industries, such as the manufacture of iron, of weapons and of durable and immediate consumer goods.

Such works required the mobilisation of human and fiscal resources on an enormous scale and the institution of elaborate means of bureaucratic organisation and control. The population had to be registered for purposes of taxation, labour service and military recruitment, and from the earliest times imperial tax systems imposed the rendering of annual service by individuals as an integral and regular part of these obligations. It is recorded that for work on the Grand Canal more than five million men were pressed into service by the Sui government 'and that there was great loss of life owing to the great hardships and also the cruelty of the administrators. The resulting unpopularity did not a little to bring about the fall of the Sui dynasty.' The emperor 'shortened the life of his dynasty by a number of years but benefited posterity to ten thousand generations. He ruled without benevolence but his rule is to be credited with enduring accomplishments'.[1]

The mobilisation of such large numbers of men required the acquisition of the necessary food and materials, which were obtained by fiscal impositions, and of the requisite services, which were provided partly by the *corvée* and partly by employment paid from the funds provided by taxation. Both the imposition of the *corvée* and the levying of taxation required the registration of the population and the

---

[1] Quoted by Tregear, *A Geography of China*, p. 79. Naturally care must be exercised in interpreting the scope of the labour resources quoted above. Ancient historians were inclined to impress their readers by speaking in millions.

elaborate mobilisation and transmission of funds. The canals and navigable rivers were especially necessary for the transport of tribute grain to the capital and to other centres where it was required.

Agrarian policy

The Ch'in government instituted the policy of favouring agriculture and repressing trade, a policy followed with greater or less consistency throughout Chinese history down to the nineteenth century. This policy, however, was of little practical value to the peasant.

During the Chou period the peasant had no right to the soil he tilled and was reduced virtually to the status of a serf. But even during the subsequent periods the peasant was never completely free. He and his land were registered for the provision of forced services and for tax purposes. Since these contributions were in relation to the land he held, he was obliged to cultivate his plot and was not allowed to leave it. To leave the land and to live unregistered in another place was a crime which was severely punished.

Attempts were made after the collapse of the feudal régime to bring about the more equitable distribution of the land. The traditional property unit among the Chinese was the family holding, and because Confucian ideology emphasised the integration of the family and the state it was easy to conceive the state as the generalised and supreme owner of the land. But despite all attempts to maintain a relatively rigid type of agricultural organisation, reforms of the property system were the recurrent theme of Chinese agrarian policy. Each new dynasty tried to tackle the problem afresh. All attempts to maintain an equitable system of distribution broke down, however, because of the weakness of the administration and the rapacity of the officials, who wanted to extend their own ownership and privileges, and consequently showed little enthusiasm in enforcing laws that limited their privileges.

The policy of the later T'ang was directed to realising the full agricultural potential of the country and to turning the peasantry into a well-organised labour force so as to obtain the maximum revenue for the state. After the collapse of this dynasty in A.D. 907, all attempts at an agrarian policy were abandoned, and under the Ming (A.D. 1368-1644) a strong tendency developed towards the building up of larger estates and the diminution of the free peasantry. The agrarian problem indeed remained one of the apparently insoluble problems of the Cinic polity and was the main cause of its final collapse in the twentieth century and its replacement by a centrally administered economy.

Commerce and industry and the coordination of resources

It is, of course, impossible to determine the relative importance of the different means of coordination in the Cinic economy. The paucity of references to economic relationships and especially to private commercial transactions is indeed a characteristic feature of Chinese historical sources.

Agriculture represented by far the most important sector. Over long periods of her history China was probably 'one of the purest examples of an agrarian state that ever existed'. The movement of agricultural produce was severely restricted in areas removed from water transport. Villages were therefore very largely self-sufficient, and this, together with reciprocity and local, clan and traditional controls, determined the methods of production and the allocation of resources. These were supplemented by the impositions of officials in regard to the appropriation of both goods and services.[1]

Chinese towns, first and foremost, were administrative centres. The inhabitants consisted primarily of officials, soldiers and landlords, and only secondarily of the shopkeepers, artisans and domestics who served them. The town was in the first place a political and administrative centre, drawing tax revenues and rents from the rural population in return for government services and proprietary rights to land, and only in the second place a centre of economic activity trading manufactured articles and mercantile services for the products of the countryside.

The size of urban centres was determined by the means of transport. The towns most characteristic of Chinese life were the numerous (perhaps as many as 3,000) small provincial centres of some 5,000 inhabitants each. The much smaller number of larger cities were those that played an important part in the political life of the country or sprang up along the lower courses of the large rivers and along the coast. In areas near rivers and canals the town markets must have exercised an important influence as a coordinative factor. Marco Polo was greatly impressed in the thirteenth century with the large number of towns located on the banks of the main Chinese rivers and their tributaries, with the volume and value of the traffic carried, and with the number of ships that plied these streams. The goods consisted mainly of articles of mass consumption such as grain, salt, wood, charcoal, hemp, and iron. He was greatly impressed especially with the quantity and variety of the victuals offered for sale in the cities. And as late as the seventeenth and eighteenth centuries, French missionaries continued to bring back glowing reports of the wealth of China, its large towns and their flourishing trade relations, and the high educational standards of its people.

How far these commodity markets reacted on and were integrated with factor markets in regard to the allocation, remuneration and price of the factors of production, however, it is impossible to determine. But in spite of the numerous administrative and cultural limitations imposed on the movement of peasants and on the transfer of land,[2] they must have exercised an irresistible, if probably delayed, effect.

So far as craft production was concerned, Marco Polo was equally impressed with the large number of workshops, each employing at least ten men, sometimes as many as forty, which supplied the local and regional requirements for a great variety of goods. As a Venetian merchant, he was especially impressed with the articles of luxury manufactured in general, and with the silken fabrics in particular.

In the social hierarchy the craftsman was indeed considered by the bureaucracy as of a lower status than even the peasant. The state imposed limitations on the transfer of his activities from one craft or place to another. But important as these

[1] It was not until the Ming period (middle of the sixteenth century) that a determined attempt was made to merge the obligations of service with those of the land tax, in the form of single payments to be made in money rather than kind. This 'single whip system' represented an important change from earlier procedures. Some reliance was however still placed on the *corvées*, and the collection of taxes in kind remained one of the duties of the provincial and local officials. Loewe, ch 7.

[2] Periods of strict control over land ownership alternated with those in which free rein was given to private enterprise. This reflected in a varied relationship between ownership and cultivation of the land, ranging from the large estate owner living on his rental income to the leasehold farmer or working tenant and the peasant living on the margin of existence on his miniature holding.

limitations no doubt were at times to the people directly concerned, they could not by themselves have had a severely restrictive effect on the allocation of services over any period of time, though they no doubt imposed limitations on the acquisition of capital and the organisation of larger private industrial establishments.

The mining and processing of certain basic commodities such as iron and salt were organised as state monopolies and were either organised as state undertakings or licensed to private businessmen. The salt monopoly, indeed, was one of the main sources of state revenue and the production, distribution and sale of salt was strictly regulated, though extensively circumvented by smuggling.

Central workshops producing silk, leather, arms and porcelain for the court and the higher echelons of the bureaucracy, also existed from very early times. The salient feature of these government-owned establishments was the use of requisitioned labour. But from the fifteenth century onwards these obligations tended to be commuted for money payments, and the craftsmen to be paid for their services.

Theoretically the position of the merchant was conceived as inferior even to that of the craftsman. He was engaged in an occupation of secondary importance to the tillage of the fields, and, unlike the craftsman, his activity was not conducive to the bringing forth of material goods to increase the output of society. His business, in fact, was merely the appropriation of profits from his fellow beings and at the expense of the state. He was regarded with suspicion by the officials, and not only were numerous taxes and requisitions imposed on him, but he was also subjected to rigid control in regard to his transactions and even his pricing policies.

Regulative policies aimed at maintaining control over the allocation of resources and were complemented by the exercise of monopolistic control over some essential commodities. According to the bureaucratic scheme of values the energies of individuals had to be concentrated on supporting the central government and on discouraging the diversion of resources to private purposes. Steps were accordingly taken at an early stage to restrict the scope of mercantile activity and to deflect it from the staple commodities to a trafficking in trivialities. The tax system provided for the collection of grain and cloth by the authorities and its movement by *corvée* labour to the centres of distribution. The essential requirements of officers and officials were paid in kind. Peasants could normally be expected to be self-sufficient. Hence the services of merchants would be reserved to non-essentials.

In practice this ideal scheme of things was circumvented because the officials would dispose of their unwanted goods and the peasants in good years would sell their surplus stocks. Besides these staples there was also a brisk marketing of manufactured goods and of luxury wares. In conjunction with the merchandising of goods there also developed a system of credit and banking. In spite of official disapproval and control, the mercantile intermediaries therefore gradually came to play an important integrative and allocative function, which helped to promote specialisation and the increased differentiation of the Cinic economy.

Corporative entities

It is a peculiar variant of the romantic illusion that the village community was an example of the existence of genuine democratic institutions in Cinic society.

> The village is as independent of the central government as any British self-governing colony is independent of the Imperial Government. . . . In China the central government plays but an infinitesimally small part in the village life. The village has perfect freedom of industry and trade, of religion, and of everything that concerns the government, regulation, and protection of the locality.

Whatever may be required for its well being is supplied, not by Imperial Edicts or any other kind of governmental interference, but by voluntary associations. Thus police, education, public health, public repairs of roads and canals, lighting, and innumerable other functions, are managed by the villagers themselves.[1]

The fact is that, through the headmen of the village communities, the bureaucracy exercised adequate authority and control over these communities for its purpose: the collection of taxes, the organisation and direction of *corvée* services and the transmission of the necessary reports to the administration. The village communities therefore by no means constituted self-governing entities. Nor were they genuinely democratic societies. The affairs they could handle were strictly local. Their fiscal contributions were determined by the government and with primary concern for the interests of the state. Finally, the personal freedom of movement of the villagers was restricted and they could be mobilised by the *corvée* to provide labour for public works.[2]

For the rest, the villagers were left largely to their own devices. Though limited in scope, the village communities nevertheless did enjoy a large measure of self-determination in regard to their own local affairs. The state, if only for its own security and well-being, also had to extend a large measure of protection to the peasantry. This provided the vast bulk of the population with a social and economic permanence and absence from government interference, which laid the basis for the stability of these communities over the centuries and supplied a genuine, if limited, scope for their initiative and self-expression.

Craftsmen and merchants, too, were allowed more scope, and their ability to accumulate possessions was less narrowly circumscribed than in the archaic economies. They were, however, denied the proprietary security that was such an outstanding feature of the rights of citizens in the medieval West. If they were not in fact living on the margin of subsistence, they often had to feign indigence to escape the attention of the tax collector, and the sweeping persecution of the merchants under the Han dynasty was provoked by the fact that prosperous merchants had the impudence too openly to display their wealth. Since official patronage and support were necessary for any big commercial undertaking, it was only by attempting to achieve a close community of interest between themselves and the bureaucracy that they could hope to rise in the social hierarchy.

Nor were genuinely autonomous and independent corporative organisations of merchants and craftsmen or independent urban entities tolerated by the state. The so-called 'gilds' were strictly controlled, and served as tax-collecting agencies for the state. The towns were primarily administrative centres. They were placed under the strict surveillance of state officials, and were even divided by walls or closed streets into quarters and wards, the passage between which was strictly forbidden at night. In the words of Max Weber, 'a city in China was a place with officials and without local autonomy'. As a result there was little evidence of municipal pride or privilege and no concept of municipal self-government. Special organs of government were rarely developed to administer the urban communities, which remained constituent members of the prefectural or provincial units. Unlike the West, the urban centres therefore never played a crucial role in determining the destinies of dynasties.

Chinese administrators and philosophers contemplated a stable, static, functional

---

[1] Leong and Tao, *Village and Town Life in China*, p. 5.
[2] In addition to the limitations on personal freedom and incentives exercised by the bureaucracy there were, of course, those imposed by the clan family organisation of society. The Chinese family formed a collective entity to which each member contributed his earnings and in which each member had a claim to the earnings of all the others.

society. In an orderly managed society people would remain in the class in which they were born, and no useful purpose could be served by their moving from one function to another. Only under such conditions could the economy function satisfactorily, for only then could the administration know exactly how many men there were in each functional category, so that it could mobilise the requisite number for each public task. Only then could it know what the revenue from farming would be and the requisitions that had to be imposed for the support of the state.[1]

The actual structure of society was indeed more complex than that contemplated by Confucian ideology. Nevertheless the framework of society was divided fairly clearly on a functional basis: the differentiation between mental and physical labour. Mental work was the duty and the privilege of the upper class, to which undisputed prestige was accorded. Physical labour was the function of the lower class. The right to social and political authority was reserved for the upper class.

Technology

Some of the most basic technological inventions of the world were made by the Chinese. Foremost among these were the invention of printing, of gunpowder and of the magnet. According to Francis Bacon 'these three have changed the whole face and state of things throughout the world, the first in literature, the second in warfare, the third in navigation; whence have followed innumerable changes; insomuch that no empire, no sect, no star, seems to have exerted greater power and influence in human affairs than these mechanical discoveries'.[2]

Of almost equal importance for economic development, though perhaps not as dramatic in their impact on the western world, were the invention of an efficient equine harness, achievements in the technology of iron and steel, the invention of the mechanical clock, and basic engineering devices such as the driving-belt, the chain-drive and the standard method of converting rotary to rectilinear motion, together with segmental arch bridges and nautical techniques such as the stern-post rudder.[3]

Nor were some of these basic inventions the product of mere empirical discoveries, but rather the outcome of deliberate experiment. Thus the invention of gunpowder arose from the investigations of Taoist alchemists, who, although they had no scientific theories to work on, systematically explored the chemical and pharmaceutical properties of a great variety of substances, inspired by the hope of attaining longevity or material immortality.[4]

The question inevitably arises why these inventions, when transferred to Europe, had such an explosive effect on the economies and institutions of the West, whereas they were assimilated without effecting major structural changes in the East. The explanation must undoubtedly be sought in the competitive nature, economically, politically and culturally, of the European countries, geographically divided into numerous separate entities, politically broken up into city and territorial states, and economically forced to seek new products in all parts of the world, as contrasted with the coherent agrarian land-mass, the unified empire, and the largely self-

[1] Eberhard, *Social Mobility in Traditional China*, pt I.
[2] Bacon, *Novum Organum*, bk i, Aphorism 129.
[3] Needham, 'Science and China's influence on the world', in *The Legacy of China*, ch 5.
[4] *Ibid.*

contained and bureaucratic economy of China. Whereas in the free enterprise economy the adoption of novelties is virtually forced on entrepreneurs by internal and external competition, there is no imperative urge to innovate in the strictly controlled scheme of things of the centrally directed economy.

Conservatism of the Chinese

Conservatism has always been a feature of Chinese civilisation. In many ways the culture of the country shows a basic unity and continuity from the Chou dynasty (1122-256 B.C.) onwards. Periods of unity alternated with periods of disruption. The centre of economic power shifted from one region to another and was gradually transferred from the central Yellow River basin to the Yangtze valley, and from the interior of the country to its periphery. Thus, whereas in the West the centres of civilisation during the historical period gradually moved ever further away from the equator, in China it was the exact reverse. But this transfer of power was not accompanied by structural changes in the economic and social system.[1]

Foremost among the conservative factors that moulded Chinese culture was the geographical and historical isolation of the country. There was an absence of independent sources of innovation within easy reach of one another that could be stimulated and fertilised by intercourse and competition, and an absence of culture contacts that could provoke dissatisfaction with existing conditions at home. China developed a civilisation of its own, rich in content, but conservative and comparatively complacent in its self-sufficiency.

The early crystallisation of Chinese culture was largely the work of the Chinese sages. Confucianism turned men's minds to philosophical speculation rather than to scientific research, to phenomena of the mind and away from the external world. Whereas European science started with matter and developed methods of precision, exactness, and the anxiety for proof, Chinese thought started with the mind and with introspection. 'Chinese philosophers had no need of scientific certainty, because it was themselves that they wished to know; so in the same way they had no need of the power of science, because it was themselves that they wished to conquer. To them the content of wisdom is not intellectual knowledge and its function is not to increase external goods.'[2] Learning therefore showed a predilection for the study of social, political and moral issues rather than of natural phenomena. The young scholar spent his most impressionable years in learning a complicated script and cramming his memory with the texts of the classics, and in later life, as an official, he often matured into a humane and disinterested scholar, but remained a member of a routinised, superior and conservative class.

---

[1] Chi, *Key Economic Areas in Chinese History*, p. 3.
[2] Yu-lan Fung, 'Why China has no science', *International Journal of Ethics*, April 1922.

4
The Indic economy

Diversity and unity

The Indian subcontinent has a great variety of races, topography and resources. The country contains representatives of all the great ethnological divisions of mankind, though broadly speaking two main types can be distinguished: a tall fair type, found mainly in the north among the upper castes and representing invaders from the north-west, and a short dark-skinned people, the descendants of the original Neolithic population. From the physical point of view every extreme of altitude and climate can be found, with a corresponding diversity of flora and fauna. Here again, however, two main regions can be distinguished: the northern plains forming the basins of the Indus and the Ganges, and the Deccan plateau with its coastal fringes. The former region forms a continuous open area but has until lately been almost completely isolated from the latter. The plains dominated the political and cultural history of the country.

This diversity is reflected in the internal strains and conflicts that characterise Indian history. From time to time great empires were formed, but these again invariably crumbled into their constituent parts. 'When no such power existed, the states, hundreds in number, might be likened to a swarm of free, mutually repellent molecules in a state of incessant movement, now flying apart, and again coalescing.'[1]

India, nevertheless, forms one of the most clearly marked geographical units in the world, cut off from the rest of Asia by mountain ranges and the sea. The only easy land entrance is from the north-west, where the destinies of the country have usually been decided. Within the subcontinent a number of strong unifying factors have always been operative. The fundamental geographical unity of the country has inspired ideals of political coherence, which, though never attained completely, have throughout the centuries remained the aspiration, not merely of ambitious monarchs but also of the people. But Indian civilisation forms a unity that is far more profound than a mere coalescence due to geographical isolation or military conquest. This unity is the work of Hinduism, with its peculiar forms of social and religious organisation. Here again the limitations imposed by diversity become apparent. Whereas elsewhere a common culture tends to level and unite, in India it

[1] Smith, *The Oxford History of India*, Introduction.

34

has divided the people into sects. The caste organisation, which has united the Hindus by throwing them into contrast with the rest of the world, has also broken society up into numerous exclusive communities and has impeded national action and effective cooperation.

The centralisation of power

In spite of the absence of enduring forms of political unity, there were nevertheless strong forces that made for the centralisation of power and the exercise of bureaucratic control within each Indian state, and at times powerful empires, such as the Gupta, Mauryan and Mughal states, succeeded in bringing a large part of the subcontinent under unified control.[1]

The ruler in Hindu India exercised supreme political and judicial power. The power was adequately buttressed with the usual religious sanctions. The divinity of Indian kings, however small their domain, says Gonda, was always accepted by the masses. The bearer of authority inspired awe, fear or admiration. Wielding power and occupying a lonely post he was credited with special qualities. The king represented the embodiment or personification of divine powers: he was the intermediary between the powers of nature and mankind, and as such he was an essential factor for the well-being of his people. It is through his mediation that the productiveness of the earth and the life and fruitfulness of all classes of beings and objects that exist on earth are set in motion.[2]

The administration was directed by a hierarchy of functionaries. The highest representatives were princes of the blood; below them were officials, whose main concern was the maintenance of the system of irrigation, the measurement of land, and the maintenance of forests, mines and roads: all typically hydraulic functions and spheres of interest. The smooth working of the bureaucratic machinery was ensured by regular circuits of inspection.

According to the *Arthasastra*, the classic of Hindu statecraft, politics is strictly a practical statecraft, exercised on a power basis, and concerned primarily with the material welfare of the monarch. But, 'just as fruits are gathered from a garden as often as they become ripe, so revenue shall be collected as often as it becomes ripe. Collection of revenue or of fruits, when unripe, shall never be carried on, lest their source may be injured, causing immense trouble.' The ruler should exploit his sources of revenue as the gardener does his trees; he should never strip the bushes to the stalk.

In Mughal India the central administration spread its tentacles throughout the state. The administration was headed by an official nobility, which was hereditary as a class but not as individuals, and was landholding but not feudal. Below these were the subordinate officials, who were mainly Hindus of the clerical castes. Their public ethic was loyalty to their superiors, whoever they might be, though they were possessed of great resources of obstruction and subtle sabotage that could be applied to an unsympathetic government.

The main function of the Mughal administration was to appropriate the bulk of the surplus resources of the country for the state. The cultivated land was recorded,

[1] During the early Vedic and up to the Gupta period, there apparently existed limited monarchies and different forms of oligarchic or republican governments. But during the later Vedic or Brahmanic period monarchies held the stage. Scharma, *Republics in Ancient India* (c. 1500-500 B.C.).

[2] Gonda, *Ancient Indian Kingship from the Religious Point of View.*

the value of the crops assessed, and the share of the government fixed. Thus the surplus agricultural product was creamed off and the cultivator left with just enough to subsist on, but without a reserve against famine. The surplus of industry, again, was collected by the administration through port, provincial and town dues, or was contributed as bribes to propitiate officials and to facilitate the evasion of fiscal obligations.

The revenue was spent on the central and provincial administrations with their large military and civil establishments. Prestige directed display in the form of personal pomp and magnificent buildings. When all these claims on the normal national surplus had been met, little remained for productive investment in the form of social overhead expenditure. 'India was the scene of much economic activity but little economic progress.'[1]

Reciprocity and redistribution in the village economy

The Indian village community formed an almost completely self-sufficient unit. Not only did it contain the vast bulk of India's agricultural population, but the artisans, too, were predominantly concentrated in the villages. All the main needs of the community were satisfied locally, and only a few necessities such as salt and metal and a few luxuries were obtained from outside.

The peculiar feature of the Indian village organisation was that most of the artisans were the servants of the community. They held their own plots of land either rent-free or at a reduced rental. In addition, each cultivator paid them a fixed share of his yearly produce. In return for these advantages the artisans had to supply the cultivators with all their general requirements without further remuneration. It was therefore only craftsmen such as the carpenter, the blacksmith, the potter or the scavenger, who performed services generally required in husbandry or in domestic life, who were the servants of the village. Those artisans, on the other hand, whose services were only occasionally required, such as the weaver, the dyer or the oilman, were free workers, whose services were paid by the job, not indeed in cash but in kind.[2]

The economic activities of the village were not based on the market activities of buying and selling and were not affected by any concern for economic efficiency. They were patterned, on the contrary, on the concepts of reciprocity and redistribution. Reciprocity implies a two-way or circular flow of commodities; redistribution means that the output of the community is brought together and then redistributed among the members. But this does not imply any equality of treatment, the allocation of fair shares, or payment for value.

The basis of the whole economy was the grain heap, to which the cultivators contributed and from which all participants received a share. The production of food was the business of the joint agricultural family; the typical unit of agricultural production the peasant family plot. The officials and servants of the community—the watchman, headman, clerk, blacksmith, carpenter, herdsman, barber, priest or potter—each performed his respective duties, and received his remuneration in the form of a share of the cultivators' grain heaps. Only during harvest time was there any exchange or payment for services rendered. Each activity was carried out in accordance with the custom and tradition of the community. At harvest time

---

[1] Spear, *A History of India*, ii, ch 3.
[2] Gadgill, *Industrial Evolution of India*, pp. 7 ff.

the means of subsistence for the rest of the year were distributed according to a complex system of distribution in which there was no bargaining and no payment for specific services rendered.

Below and above the village level the redistributive pattern continued to prevail. Below, the share that was retained by the joint family of cultivators was managed by the head of the family. Above, there was one or a multiplicity of political authorities, depending on the size of the kingdom. Whatever the economic functions performed by the authorities, the division of the grain heap at the village level was the foundation on which political authority rested. The ruler's share, again, was redistributed among the different levels of the bureaucracy in accordance with their respective acquisitive powers.

> In a large kingdom with a moderately powerful centre, such as the Mughal Empire was at times, there was a hierarchy of redistributive centres with the village grain heap at the bottom and the king's storehouses at the top. In between, the local powers and provincial governors maintained their own storehouses, retaining a share and passing on the remainder to the level above. In regard to grain, the whole political and social structure was founded on redistribution.[1]

This organisation helped to stabilise and stereotype Indian village life. It was an excellent means of ensuring the provision of essential services in times of trouble and distress, but it militated against improvements in technique and perpetuated only the most rudimentary forms of the division of labour. Thus improvements in agricultural technique have been resisted to this day because they would open the door to differing personal efforts and rewards, which would disrupt the existing social relationships. There was a complete absence of competition, for the cultivator who had paid for industrial services in advance was not likely to buy wares from outside. The result was a lack of territorial specialisation in industry. It was only the production of luxury articles centred in the towns and shipbuilding located in the ports that were localised. Indian crafts were therefore characterised by an aloofness from the outside world, concentrated as they were in innumerable self-contained and self-supplying local units, with little contact between themselves, and in almost complete ignorance of the outside world.

Industry and commerce associated with the courts

Indian towns were centres of consumption rather than of production; they owed their importance to the fact that they were the seats of courts or places of pilgrimage; hence the suddenness with which some of them disappeared as soon as the residence of the monarch was withdrawn. Sometimes they were little more than semi-permanent camps. Industry in these centres of consumption was a secondary phenomenon, dependent on pilgrims or on the needs of the court. Thus the craftsmen of Benares specialised in the production of the vessels and utensils used in worship. In the capital cities, on the other hand, were concentrated the artistic handicrafts which produced the fine textiles, embroideries, gold, silver, steel, leather and ivory work, the wares for which India has always been so justly famed, and which have called forth the admiration of all lovers of art.

It was in the urban handicrafts that Indian industry attained its greatest excel-

---

[1] Neale, 'Reciprocity and redistribution in the Indian village', in *Trade and Market in the Early Empires*, ed. Polanyi, p. 227.

lence. Craftsmen were carefully trained in all the traditions of design and process. The methods of production were crude and the division of labour rudimentary. Forms of production, organisation, and marketing were strictly regulated and unprogressive, if stable. From the earliest times to the beginning of the eighteenth century India was the centre of cotton production for the civilised world. But according to Baines, 'it cannot but seem astonishing that in a department of industry where the raw material has been so grossly neglected, where the machinery is so crude and where there is so little division of labour, the results should be fabrics of the most exquisite delicacy and beauty, unrivalled by the products of any other nation even those best skilled in the mechanical arts'.[1]

Though India before the Industrial Revolution was industrially more developed relatively to the western world than she is today, the significance of the crafts in the economic life of the country must not be exaggerated. Most of her artisans worked for a very restricted market: for an extravagant aristocracy and for the court. A middle class was virtually non-existent, the poor supplied their scanty needs almost exclusively in their own homes and the village communities met their requirements from their own resources. Even the Indian cotton industry, one of the outstanding economic phenomena of the contemporary world, was conducted on a very restricted scale when judged by modern standards. The vast bulk of the people, in so far as they were covered at all, were clothed in homemade garments of jute or sackcloth. The demand for cotton was confined to the upper classes. The result was that, though fortunate individuals might benefit from patronage, most artisans had nothing to hope for beyond the barest means of subsistence. Bernier described their plight to Colbert in the following words:

> No artist can be expected to give his mind to his calling in the midst of a people who are either wretchedly poor, or who, if rich, assume an appearance of poverty, and who regard not the beauty and excellence but the cheapness of an article: a people whose grandees pay for a work of art considerably under its value and according to their own caprice.

Large industrial establishments and also mines and quarries and the requisite means of transport were no doubt always maintained by the state to provide for its own requirements. The Mughal Empire maintained central establishments to manufacture the textile fabrics required for conventional distribution among the nobility on ceremonial occasions. Large numbers of skilled craftsmen were therefore kept at work. Bernier, who saw these central shops towards the middle of the seventeenth century, wrote of them as follows:

> Large halls are seen in many places called karkhanas or workshops for the artisans. In one hall embroiderers are busily employed, superintended by a master. In another you see the goldsmiths; in a third, painters; in a fourth, varnishers in lacquer-work; in a fifth, joiners, turners, tailors, and shoemakers; in a sixth, manufacturers of silk, brocade, and those fine muslins of which are made turbans, girdles with golden flowers, and drawers worn by females, so delicately fine as frequently to wear out in one night.

The disappearance of these native courts was therefore a severe blow to Indian industry, a misfortune further aggravated by the mercantile policy of the European powers, and finally consummated by the competition of the machine-made products of the Industrial Revolution.

---

[1] Rao, *Decay of Indian Industries*, pp. 22-9.

Commercial relations

As regards domestic commerce, the self-sufficiency of the village, the rudimentary forms of transport, and the consequent lack of territorial specialisation made the internal trade over large parts of the country of little consequence. In North India routes suitable for wheeled traffic sometimes existed, but from Golconda to Cape Comorin carts were almost unknown, and pack animals and porters were the only means of transport by land. In the rainy season traffic was brought nearly to a standstill, and in the hot weather it was circumscribed almost as effectively by the difficulty of obtaining fodder and water, so that an early English merchant complained that there were four hot and four wet months, 'in which there is no travelling and therefore unfit for commerce'. The great navigable rivers, the Indus, the Ganges and the Jumna, were the principal highways of northern India. They carried a large volume of heavy traffic, but owing to the strength of the current and the direction of the wind the traffic was largely seasonal. These rivers nevertheless facilitated the movement of bulky commodities such as grain, salt and raw cotton, and also of textiles and indigo, and made the maintenance of a centralised state and of towns economically feasible.

As regards foreign trade relations, these spread their tentacles over a considerable part of the then known world. Throughout the history of India the character of her commerce no doubt remained unchanged, and Gibbon's 'mordant aphorism', 'that the objects of oriental traffic were splendid and trifling', was in substance as applicable to the sixteenth as to the second century.[1] But these relations facilitated the rise of numerous towns along the Indian littoral, which were the centres of trade and industry as well as of administration.

As in China, the concept of a self-equilibrating market mechanism, in which economic decisions are based primarily on prices, was foreign to Indian bureaucratic circles. The activities of the merchant were strictly controlled and his prices carefully regulated. Profit had to represent 'the surplus left by the rate as regulated by the king, and not one made from rates determined by his own fancy'. The profits were also subjected to the arbitrary attentions of the tax gatherer. Merchants were therefore always careful to hide their most precious possessions and to avoid all forms of ostentation. Bernier, who spent almost ten years in Mughal India, was appalled by the frustrating conditions under which the merchants of India had to operate. Enterprise, he says, finds 'little encouragement to engage in commercial pursuits', because greedy tyrants have 'both the power and the inclination to deprive any man of the fruits of his industry'. And, 'when wealth is acquired, as must sometimes be the case, the possessor, so far from living with increased comfort and assuming an air of independence, studies the means by which he may appear indigent: his dress, lodging, and furniture continue to be mean, and he is careful, above all things, never to indulge in the pleasures of the table'. No wonder, therefore, that gradually, and especially after Buddhist times, the overseas trade of India seems to have fallen almost completely into foreign hands.

Corporative entities

As in China, no genuinely autonomous and independent corporative entities could develop in the Indian social system. We find, however, the same romantic illusion in regard to the Indian village community that we have seen in the case of the Chinese.

[1] Moreland, *India at the Death of Akbar*, ch 4.

Thus a well-known passage from Sir Charles Metcalfe's minute of 1830 states:

> The village communities are little republics having nearly everything they want within themselves; and almost independent of foreign relations. They seem to last where nothing else lasts. Dynasty after dynasty tumbles down; revolution succeeds revolution; but these societies remain the same. . . . This union of the village communities, each one forming a separate little state in itself, is in a high degree conducive to their happiness, and to the enjoyment of a great portion of freedom and independence.

As with the Chinese village, however, 'freedom and independence' are relative concepts. In the first place, the village headman was appointed as the king's representative, who 'collected taxes for him' and who also performed policing and judicial functions, all activities that linked him to the central government, although he did not form part of its bureaucracy. It is no doubt true that he could fulfil his functions successfully only by trying 'to conciliate the villagers', but the villagers would have found it extremely difficult to lodge a complaint against such an authority.

In the second place, the Hindu ruler appropriated a very substantial share of the produce of the land under the redistributive system. Although the state's share varied at different times and different places, it seems generally to have been in the region of one-fourth. But this contribution was imposed from above and inescapably tied the village community to an operational system that served the interests of the ruler rather than the villagers.

Finally, the rights of the peasant holder were enmeshed in a system of political obligations. The question of land ownership had, in fact, not yet been disentangled from that of political allegiance. The cultivation of the land was indeed a right on the part of the holder but also a duty of the subject to provide the revenues of the king. As everywhere else, these claims tended in the course of time to become hereditary, and whenever the power of the central authority weakened the rights to revenue were consolidated into claims to the land itself. A landed aristocracy would then arise and the cultivators would be depressed to the condition of tenancy.

The Muslims adopted the existing Hindu system of land tenure and taxation. Revenue was now collected by the nobility, who might therefore be regarded as the successors of the kings who had been absorbed in the empire. A certain portion of the receipts they paid into the imperial treasury: the rest they retained for themselves. From a financial point of view, therefore, the empire could be regarded as superimposed on the previous system. The state's share of the yield, however, was increased to between one-third and one-half. Such an exorbitant tax greatly strengthened the position of the revenue collectors, who appropriated the entire surplus of the cultivator.

The same dependence was reflected in the towns. Craftsmen and merchants were indeed allowed to organise in gilds, for it was characteristic of Indian society that a man standing alone had no social significance. But these organisations were always closely controlled by the state and exercised no political power or authority.

The towns were governed by state officials. As in China, there was no semblance of local authority, and no local bodies, not even the merchant gilds, were allowed to play a role in the government of these centres.

Conservatism of Indic culture

Few other countries can boast of so long and so continuous a cultural record as

India. The civilisation of the Indus may have arisen simultaneously with that of Egypt and of Mesopotamia, but this culture was effaced as completely from the tradition of subsequent Indian society as the memory of Minoan civilisation was effaced from the tradition of Greece. Whether, therefore, the 'Indus culture' was an independent growth or merely a Sumerian offshoot, it seems that Indic—like Cinic—civilisation, in so far as it was related to any antecedent culture at all, was affiliated with Mesopotamian origins rather than with the civilisation that once flourished on the plains of north-west India.

From the beginning of the second millennium B.C. northern India was gradually but thoroughly subdued and assimilated by Aryan invaders. Attacks on the Deccan, however, succeeded only in the north and the west. The assimilation of the south was the work of peaceful penetration of the Brahmin, who carried his ideas into every corner of the continent. Henceforth cultural contact between India and her neighbours led rather to the diffusion of Indian culture than to the absorption of foreign elements. Even Hellenistic influence on the country seems to have been slight and superficial. All new immigrants from the north-west, before the Muslim invasions, were in the course of time assimilated and remodelled in Hindu forms, thus reinforcing the permanent solidarity and continuity of Indian civilisation.

The conservative character of Indian culture has been ascribed largely to the overwhelming emphasis laid by Indian religion on the spiritual as opposed to the material side of life. The pursuit of transcendent ends, outside and often contrary to the natural order, could only lead to the diversion of men's minds from interest in technical and social matters. The ideal of Brahmanism is to subdue rather than to satisfy the appetite, to seek salvation in a life of contemplation and self-culture. Hence the difficulty of stimulating economic effort and concentrating it on questions of efficiency. This otherworldliness is aggravated by an enervating environment, which in many parts makes it almost fatally easy to maintain life on a bare physical minimum, with leisure as the main luxury of life.

On the other hand, even the most sublimated spiritual tenets are at least partly conditioned by material factors. Unbounded opportunities on a virgin soil awaken the creative spirit in the human being. It is only when the struggle for existence becomes excessive and enervating that the mind seeks compensation in the world of the spirit, and relief in a religion preaching quietism and fatalistic resignation. When new opportunities for creative material activity arise the old forms of religious practice may remain, but their emphasis and spirit change. Means are soon found to bridge the gulf between belief and conduct. The pursuit of material ends may be found to be not incompatible with the attainment of spiritual grace, and a religion of ascetic withdrawal to a life hereafter may gradually be transformed into one preaching purposeful endeavour in this world. Religion, therefore, merely accentuates a state of affairs gradually brought about by other factors.

One of these factors is the division of Indian society into castes, which restricts professional mobility and retards technical innovation. Another conservative influence has been the numerous communal bonds in which the individual is enmeshed, especially the village community and the joint family. Of these the effect of the latter has been even stronger than that of the former. The extended Hindu family, consisting normally of three generations and several collaterals, forms a single household, pooling its earnings and maintaining itself out of a common fund. Everyone earns according to his ability and receives according to his needs. The benefit of the system lies in the distribution of misfortune over a group instead of its concentration on the individual. Organised poor relief has therefore been unnecessary except in times of famine. The defect lies in the absence of a suitable correspondence between reward and effort. The incentive to individual initiative is removed, and the subjection of the individual to minute corporative control is not congenial to the development of individuality and the spirit of enterprise. To this institution has been attributed the small part that has always been played by natives in the foreign commerce of India.[1]

Still more deleterious has been the effect of the family system on population. Hindu belief considers the begetting of male children to be a religious necessity, whereas the joint family largely dissociates the function of procreation from the individual responsibility of maintaining the offspring. Child marriage, the intense desire for male offspring and the absence of all prudential restraint lead to the excessive stimulation of the birth rate. The physical immaturity of the mothers, insanitary conditions, overcrowding and malnutrition, on the other hand, produce an abnormally high infantile death rate. To these factors must be attributed the poor standards of Indian physique, the low efficiency, and the peculiar forms of thought that sublimate physical desires into transcendental ideals. Above all, it accounts for the continuous pressure of population on the scarce natural resources and on the capital stock of the country.

But the lack of progress in the Indian economy must be ascribed also, and above all, to the dead weight of the despotic state, with its centralised administrative machinery, which inhibited progress both by its excessive and arbitrary impositions and by the general insecurity of person and property, which is inseparably associated with it. According to Moreland these conditions effectively prevented the growth of large-scale private enterprise. 'A wealthy man would have been exceedingly unwise to invest largely in fixed capital when the administration might at any time collapse, or when a change of local officers might expose him to a campaign of ruinous extortion.'[2] Such conditions effectively maintained the Indic economy in a vicious circle of poverty.

[1] Appadorai, *Economic Conditions in Southern India (A.D. 1000-1500)*, ii, 498; Jathar and Biri, *Indian Economics*, i, 102 ff.
[2] Moreland, p. 51.

Part 4
The Free Enterprise Economies
of Antiquity

5

The rise of free enterprise economies

*c. the twelfth century B.C. to c.
the middle of the sixth century B.C.*

The rise of a new civilisation

Towards the end of the second millennium B.C. a new era dawned in the world. Large migrations of peoples, starting no doubt in Turkestan, pressed upon the settled civilisations both to the East and to the West. From Spain in the West to China in the East, the settled peoples were overthrown and partly displaced by barbarian invaders. Spain and Gaul were overrun by Celts, Germany by Teutons, Italy by Latins, Etruscans and Illyrians, the Balkans by Hellenes, South Russia, Iran and Armenia by Indo-Germanic peoples, India by Aryans, southern Arabia and Abyssinia by Arabian invaders, and north Africa by northern peoples.

Cnossos and the Hittite Empire were destroyed. The Aegean relapsed into barbarism. Syria and Palestine were overrun by Aramites, Israelites, and Philistines. Egypt and Mesopotamia were able to withstand the impact, and Assyria was even able temporarily to assume the offensive. Nevertheless, for the time bring, archaic civilisation receded into the background. For millennia races had poured into the Near East. Hitherto, however, archaic civilisation had been so superior culturally and militarily that even the most conservative alien elements had been assimilated. Everywhere, after a time, there had again arisen centralised states on oriental pattern. This time it was different. The centrally administered economies of the Orient gradually became reactionary relics in the new world. Everywhere small tribal states, with far less complicated social and economic systems, were able, with the aid of armies of free men and the new iron technique, to maintain their independence. For the first time in history the individual was able to assert his independence and become the foundation of the social system.

Syria and the Aegean were the first of the new areas to recover from the invasions. Phoenicia was freed from Egyptian and Hittite tutelage and from Minoan competition, and the Assyrian kings were occupied with Babylonia and were not yet formidable. Circumstances favoured Phoenicia and she took full advantage of this opportunity. The first half of the first millennium B.C. was the golden age of Phoenician prosperity. The same conditions facilitated the growth of a number of Aramean cities such as Harran, Hamath and Damascus. In Syria the cultural connection with the ancient Orient, however, remained close and almost unbroken. The Phoenicians were remnants of the old Canaanite inhabitants, reinforced by elements from the new invaders. For a few centuries they were almost the sole transmitters of archaic culture from Spain to southern Arabia. This strong assimilation prevented the free and spontaneous development of a new culture.

It was different with the Hellenes. They alone were able to free themselves from the influence of the Orient and to transmute their own and foreign cultural elements into a really new civilisation.

Stimuli abounded in the new era. These small, separate communities developed an arrogant self-consciousness, which, though fraught with serious political disadvantages, was not without important compensatory benefits.

> In this infinite variety of little communities all natural gifts develop with ease; in this atmosphere of absolute freedom men realize all their faculties. The Aegean, from one end to the other, tingles with an inexhaustible fruitful vigour. The spirit of independence which animates towns and individuals urges them to a constant rivalry fraught with serious drawbacks and immense advantages. Competition, the source of progress, rises here from the very womb of the earth.[1]

The physical environment of the Near East presents a continuous challenge to a vigorous, composite people. Neither Phoenicia nor Greece is naturally fertile. The Lebanon mountains hug the coast so closely that there is little land available for cultivation. The Phoenicians were virtually forced on to the sea to seek a living. Greece, in the words of Herodotus, always had poverty as a foster-sister.[2] The soil often first had to be 'made', and even then offered no more than a precarious maintenance. It was conditions such as these that forced an athletic and aristocratic people to resort to occupations that they had been inclined to regard with contempt.

Owing to the lack of land and the limited possibilities of agriculture, men had to resort either to piracy and migration or to commerce and industry. Migration is easy in the Mediterranean, for the whole area forms a homogeneous world. Everywhere, whether in Sicily, Algeria, or Spain, the colonist would find the same climate, meet the same natural conditions, and feel himself at home. Even on the coast of the Black Sea, natural conditions differ but little from those of the mother country.

The Phoenician settlements in the western Mediterranean dated from the very beginning of this period. They probably reached the Straits of Gibraltar soon after 1200 B.C. With the fall of Tyre in the sixth century the work of Phoenician expansion was taken up energetically by her former colony, Carthage, thus effectively putting a stop to further Greek expansion in the west.

The Greek colonial movement took place in the eighth and seventh centuries. In the course of these two centuries the Mediterranean was girdled with a fringe of Greek cities. The motive force of the movement was the overpopulation of the home countries, together with the social and political upheavals that were in part due to it. Emigration was the natural outlet for the surplus population of a country with limited resources during a period of quiescence. There was no desire for territorial expansion; the colonists were satisfied with the coastal settlements which they established. Nor was the colony politically and economically dependent on the mother state; only moral and religious ties bound them together. In its initial phase land hunger was the chief incentive of the movement and sites for new colonies were chosen primarily for their agricultural, fishing or piratical possibilities. In a later phase more value was attached to the commercial possibilities of the sites,

[1] Glotz, *The Aegean Civilization*, p. 6.
[2] Herodotus, vii, 102.

settlements being planted generally on the main routes of trade. The first ventures were of an unorganised, individualistic, and haphazard character. The later ones were almost always planned and directed by public authority.

Greek individualism

In the course of the eighth and seventh centuries the Greek character was formed. The varied life of the sea, the challenge presented by pioneering in new countries, and, above all, the stimulating effect of contact with the most diverse peoples, both civilised and barbarian, and the virtually unlimited opportunities offered for expansion aroused in the Greeks a spirit of adventure and developed every tendency to originality and to freedom of action. In this respect the Greek was infinitely superior to the Phoenician, too long and too intimately steeped in oriental tradition. For the Hellenic mind possessed to a remarkable degree the gift of transmuting foreign influences into its own peculiar cultural forms. Spiritually, the Greek was remarkably free from the twin obsessions of archaic thought—fear of the supernatural and concern about the hereafter. Love of freedom was the dominant characteristic of the new spirit. In art there was freedom from the slavish copying of conventional types, in science a critical and sceptical attitude towards facts, which was apt to degenerate into hair-splitting rationalism.

It was this bold and individual character, the abstract and subjective quality of its thought, that was the most characteristic feature of Greek intellectual life. Social and technical phenomena became problems that could be solved by reason, and objective methods could be applied to their unravelment. Discovery and invention, which in the Orient had been impersonal things, became closely associated with the name and individuality of the discoverer.

This new spirit was reflected in technique. Everywhere we see a groping after new forms of representation, which, after barely a century and a half of effort, were to blossom forth into the finest forms of aesthetic expression the world has ever known. The Greeks were no longer satisfied merely to classify their material and to accept a mythological explanation. They tried on the contrary to formulate general laws and to find rational explanations, and their interest ranged from the most abstract relations of things to their most concrete forms of expression. The Greeks, therefore, may be said to have been in a very real sense the fathers of modern science.

Two great inventions of the period, iron and the alphabet, slowly transformed culture and technique. Iron had probably been in daily use among the peasants of the Pontus for a considerable period before it became generally known in the Hittite empire, in the second millennium B.C. Its use then spread to Europe and India, and, in the first millennium, to eastern Asia and Africa. With the aid of iron tools, men could clear forests and drain land for the cultivation of the grasslands of Europe in a way that had hitherto been possible only in the sandy soils of the Near East. An increased density of population and the rise of city states in hitherto barbarian countries was the result.

At the same time Semites, coming in contact with both the Mesopotamian and Egyptian scripts, grasped the idea of using a sign for each of the consonantal sounds in their language.[1] The Greeks, borrowing from this vowelless alphabet, retained

---

[1] It is significant that the alphabet was invented, not by scribes who delighted in elaboration for its own sake, but by traders who sought short cuts for practical purposes.

some of the letters representing consonantal Semitic sounds not found in their own language to express their vowels. Thus the final addition was made to the alphabet. The alphabet furnished the new civilisation with an instrument of great flexibility and precision. 'No longer need the scribe spend the energy of his most impressionable years in acquiring the art of notation alone.' Writing was no longer a mystery, a knowledge of which was confined only to a few. Not that the art was immediately mastered by every member of an essentially military and athletic society, prone to despise things of the spirit. But, associated with the infinite flexibility, exactitude and logical character of Aryan speech, it was an essential preliminary condition for the appearance of the Greek miracle.

The gradual transition to a market-orientated economy

The commerce of this period was confined largely to the Mediterranean, though it filtered through to the neighbouring seas. The caravan trade through Asia Minor prospered, for these were the palmy days of the Assyrian, Neo-Babylonian and Lydian kingdoms. The Pharaohs opened their country to foreigners in the seventh century, though for purposes of easy supervision, the trade was confined to certain specified ports.

But this commerce, far as its tentacles stretched, was as yet undeveloped in form, structure and intensity. The object of Phoenician trade was still essentially the quest for metal, a typically oriental trait, which, however, declined in importance in succeeding centuries. Their exports consisted of industrial commodities, such as textiles, metal-ware and ceramics, as well as the trinkets usually sold to barbarians. The Greeks produced high quality ceramic ware, metal and woodwork, fine textiles, wine and olive oil. All these things were luxuries rather than objects of common use, for luxuries alone could bear the high costs of transport. Cheap articles of mass consumption did not begin to enter regularly into international trade until the development of coined currency in the second half of the seventh century B.C.

The royal economy still played a dominant part in Phoenician industry and trade. In Syria, Palestine and the kingdoms of Asia Minor, royal and temple economies were maintained, as in the archaic economies, working with slave, serf and wage labour. Kings lent their craftsmen to one another. Phoenician trade was still carried on primarily through the dispositional actions of status traders. Treaty prices were a matter of negotiation, the transaction having been preceded by much diplomatic haggling. But once equivalencies were arranged, they had to be observed, and all bargaining ceased. Even in private trade, however, the right to sojourn and trade in a place involved the complicated process of the bestowal of gifts and the use of a host as intermediary in all transactions. The merchant displayed his treasures and trinkets at the prince's palace or the manorial hall, and the ship often remained in harbour for a whole year. These methods changed only very gradually, but there was as yet little evidence of a market economy and of the resident professional trader.[1]

It was only in the seventh century that Greek trade showed a slight refinement over Phoenician practice. In the Homeric world there was no word for 'trader', and there existed no real market in an economic sense. With Hesiod production for the market began, but only because debt and empty stomachs drove men to it. It was

[1] *Trade and Markets in the Early Empires*, ed. Polanyi, ch 4.

the occasional trade of the small farmer and, no doubt, also of the craftsman, during the summer season. There was no mention of professional trade or of a class of Greek merchants. In the seventh century two kinds of traders arose. First, the *naukleros*, the merchant who traded in his own ship. He no doubt developed from the Hesiodic farmer who took his own produce to market. Secondly, the *emporos*, who, as passenger, shipped his wares to a distant market. This type of trade no doubt had its origin in the occasional trade of the craftsman. Retail trade also became specialised in the Hellenic world, wherever coins were in use. For the first time in history there appeared the professional and resident retailer, the *kapelos*. It is significant that, according to Herodotus, it was the Lydians, the first people to use coins, who were also the first retail traders.

But in spite of these crude beginnings, the trade of this period was different in form and structure from that of the archaic civilisations. In the centrally administered economies the initiative went out from the state and was carried out either by state officials or by merchants working on a commission basis. Such transactions involved no private initiative and no economic risk. The methods of conducting these exchanges were also the typically formal and routinised procedures invariably associated with public transactions.

In the new free economies, on the other hand, the initiative came predominantly from private individuals, whether they traded primarily for their own account or also worked on commission for the state. There was an element of enterprise and risk-bearing attached to these activities that was entirely absent from the previous transactions. Instead of displaying the stay-at-home mentality nourished by the planned economy, the Phoenician and Greek trader ventured forth into unexplored and uncharted seas to discover new fields of enterprise and adventure. Nor is an organised market, especially if viewed as a purely physical entity, essential for carrying on trade in a free economy. The market in a broad sense is merely a means by which buyer and seller are brought together. This can be done on a more or less rational basis and a trade conducted in which a gain is made on price or exchange differentials without the intermediation of organised price-making markets, or even the use of coined currency, though both these media would undoubtedly greatly facilitate the process of rational price formation and the adoption of more rational attitudes to economic affairs in general.

Class conflict

Class conflict is a characteristic feature of a free economy. Whereas the peoples of the archaic economies, like those of all managerial societies, were politically passive, those of the Hellenic world were extremely vocal.

Socially, the Hellenic world was divided into well-defined classes inherited from the pre-existing peasant peoples. These were the nobility, free commoners, serfs and slaves.

In the Homeric poems it is only the fortunes of the nobles that interest the poet. The commoners are hardly mentioned. The nobility owed a loose allegiance to a king, who, however, was merely *primus inter pares*. They represented the conquerors. The conquered population retained its private property but had to cultivate the lands and herd the flocks of the nobility. The nobles possessed the best land on the plains. They despised every form of economic activity; in Sparta such work was even forbidden by law. They monopolised the administration of justice and the priestly offices, both of which they exploited for their own ends.

From the nobility was separated by a wide gulf the demos, the 'people', the 'small', 'bad', 'unwarlike and undefended' mass of commoners, who counted neither in war nor in the council chamber. To this class belonged the small farmers and the free craftsmen, all those who were unable to live the lives of gentlemen. The commercial and industrial classes that gradually arose were recruited largely from the *Thetes* and the *Demiurges*, the free landless people who represented the lowest class of free men. Since this group consisted predominantly of foreigners, it was socially and politically unimportant.

The gulf which separated commoners and aristocracy tended gradually to widen. The increase in population led to the greater subdivision of a land poor by nature, where decreasing returns set in early and operated drastically. The nobility, finding increased scope for spending their incomes, tried to derive a greater revenue from their estates, and began to drive in the rent. In such circumstances the peasants easily fell into debt and into the power of the landowning aristocracy.

Everywhere in the seventh and sixth centuries the oppressed citizens rose against the nobility. The object of this social upheaval was the redistribution of land, the remission of debt, the removal of the political privileges of the ruling class, and the recognition of equality before the law. This shows that the society of the seventh and sixth centuries was still predominantly agricultural in character. The commoners demanded the removal of the abuses in the administration of justice and especially the publication and standardisation of the laws. They realised that the recognition of civil and political equality was the surest road to a permanent improvement in their social and economic position.

The commoners were greatly aided by changes in military technique—the displacement of the aristocratic army of nobles fighting in single combat by the middle-class hoplite phalanx, consisting of heavily armed infantry fighting in closed ranks. But, since they were usually not strong enough themselves to overthrow the nobility, they sought the support of 'tyrants'. Sometimes the aristocracy and the demos agreed to elect an arbitrator to settle their differences on an impartial basis. This was especially the case with Solon, who, in 594 B.C., was given extraordinary powers to harmonise class interests in Attica. He fought for both against both. He granted the immediate relief of debt, improved the legal relations between debtor and creditor, and fixed the amount of ground that any individual could own, but refused to redistribute the land.

The character of the reforms in different parts of the Greek world varied with the radicalism of the dictators and the strength of the commoners. The new leaders tried to stimulate local patriotism and to keep the poor employed by an elaborate building policy. But this hardly reconciled the citizen to his loss of freedom and of self-administration, and to the control, the presence of mercenary troops and the direct taxation that were everywhere an essential part of the tyrant's hegemony. No sooner, then, did the dictatorship fall into weak hands than it was overthrown. Everywhere the tyrant was merely a transitional figure, but nowhere did the nobility regain absolute power when he disappeared.[1]

These conditions facilitated the rise of a landowning middle class. Henceforth political and social privileges tended to become differentiated according to the ownership of land. The privileges of the aristocracy were now shared either by all landowners alone, or also by those citizens that did not possess land. But foreigners were not admitted to citizenship, and even the *Thetes* were excluded from import-

[1] Cf. Busolt, *Griechische Geschichte*, i, 369 ff. Hasebroek, *Griechische Wirtschaftsgeschichte*, pp. 158 ff, 189 ff.

ant official positions. Ancient democracy meant equality within the limits of an exclusive body of full citizens only. There was a slow transformation rather than a radical break with the past. Democracy itself became feudalised, not only in its privileges but also in its outlook on life. It was an association of rentiers, of politicians and of soldiers, who shared with the old aristocracy their contempt for poverty and for work, as well as their love of feasting and the agonistic spirit. Important public positions remained in the hands of the nobility, and the tyrants were drawn almost exclusively from this class. No wonder, then, that class struggles remained a characteristic feature of Greek public life till late in Hellenistic times, and again became an inherent element of the economic life of Roman times.

6
Survey

*Middle of sixth century B.C. to
c. the end of the second century A.D.*

The classical period

The middle of the sixth century B.C. saw the Hellenic world on the eve of its greatest material and cultural prosperity. Conditions were favourable for such a development.

In the political sphere, the conquest of Ionia and the Persian wars prepared the way for the greatness of Athens. Here the economic development of the Greek city state was brought to its highest perfection. Her naval supremacy in the Aegean, as well as the refined taste of her craftsmen, the high standard of her coinage, the hospitality and freedom offered to foreigners, and the consequent concentration of industry, commerce and banking within the city, assured for Athens unrivalled predominance in the Hellenic world.

But Athenian economic expansion was hampered both by the limits imposed by the city state and by the poverty of the world outside. Her markets were confined practically to the coastal regions, and even here they were restricted by the low standards of living and small purchasing power of the inhabitants, whose needs could best be supplied by local industry. Industry in Athens always had a mean and frustrated appearance. The organisation of the city state, which involved the division of the Greek economy into numerous independent units each of which tended to attain a large measure of economic self-sufficiency, led not only to a restricted home market but also to the dissipation of Greek resources in internecine conflicts.

In the fifth century, the agriculture, industry, and foreign trade, as well as the interstate commerce of Greece attained its highest development. After the Peloponnesian war, however, owing to the continuous conflicts of the fourth century and the political and social revolutions in the cities, the economic prosperity of Greece began to decline. Unemployment and poverty among the masses became acute. This decline in the prosperity of the Greek city states in general and of Athens in particular must be ascribed to the general economic development of the Mediterranean world. Whereas the market for the agricultural and industrial products of Greece had expanded rapidly in the sixth and fifth centuries B.C., it began to shrink perceptibly in the fourth. Greek colonies in Thrace, southern Russia and Italy began to provide for the needs of their hinterland, which preferred these cheap colonial substitutes to the expensive wares imported from Greece. The decline was gradual, not catastrophic, but the loss of this export trade, which paid for the imported foodstuffs and raw materials, necessitated fundamental readjustments in the economic and social structure of the country.[1]

The Hellenistic period

The opening up of the former Persian territories to Greek enterprise by the conquests of Alexander relieved the Greek city states of the acute problems of overpopulation and mass indigence, with their resultant political, social, and economic upheavals. New markets for Greek wares were opened up in the East, and excellent opportunities were offered to emigrants. The revival of the Greek mainland, however, was shortlived. Compared with the resources of the new Hellenistic countries of the Near East, those of Greece were insignificant, and the development of these countries soon reduced the demand for Greek products. Greece remained the scene of wars and class conflicts right down to the time of the Roman conquest. The most enterprising elements, which in any case consisted generally of resident aliens, or metics, migrated to the new centres, where there was far greater scope for their initiative. This spontaneous exodus was supplemented by systematic schemes of colonisation organised by the kings of Egypt and Syria. Greece, robbed of her best men, fell a prey to wars which became steadily more bitter, more destructive and more disastrous, as the resources over which they squabbled became more limited. Concurrently with these wars there raged continual class struggles which more and more had as object the redistribution of property, and after each upheaval led to the expulsion of some of the best citizens.

What was lost by Greece was gained by the Hellenistic East. Here the conquests of Alexander created a new world. The enormous influx of Greeks shook the ancient Orient out of its lethargy; private enterprise transformed the face of the Near East. The passivity of the Persian administration was replaced by the intelligent and active direction and control of the new Hellenistic monarchs. Everywhere towns arose, which became the centres of Hellenic culture and industry. The place of Athens was taken by the new emporia of the East: by Alexandria and Antioch, by Rhodes, Miletus, and Ephesus. The old towns of Asia Minor prospered once more. These centres all had access to large internal markets. The techniques of agriculture and industry were improved. Price trends show that from the third to the first quarter of the second century, the whole of the eastern Mediterranean formed a not too loosely connected economic whole.[2]

The spirit of the times was at first characterised by a buoyant optimism. 'There was confidence ... in the unlimited capabilities of man and his reason; there was an aggressiveness, a striving for life and happiness', a spirit characteristic of times of economic expansion, when people's energies tend to be deflected from introspection to outward action. Gradually, however, this creative spirit and buoyant optimism were replaced by indifference, Greek enterprise by eastern passivity. Religious and political preoccupations took the place of intellectual, economic and professional interests.

This change in spirit was symptomatic of the gradual economic decline of the Hellenistic world. The ceaseless struggles among the different states for political

---

[1] Rostovtzeff, *Social and Economic History of the Hellenistic World*, i, ch 2.
[2] Heichelheim, *Festgabe für Werner Sombart*, p. 186; *Wirtschaftliche Schwankungen*, pp. 70 ff; Kahrstedt, *Neue Wege zur Antike*, iv, 97 ff, 109 ff.

supremacy were aggravated by the struggle of the Greek cities to regain their
political independence, as well as by dissension and revolution within these cities
themselves. The continuous wars not only led to general insecurity, they also
distracted attention from home development to fruitless attempts at expansion
abroad, and the heavy financial burdens these wars imposed led to impositions that
contributed still further to making life precarious and unsettled. Nor did the new
monarchies develop into national states possessing a common language and uniform
social and economic structures and modes of thought and living. They very largely
remained military tyrannies ruling over subject peoples by means of mercenary
armies and an alien bureaucracy. The Greek language did indeed become the international means of expression and Hellenism a synonym for refinement. But Greek
culture, true to its origin, remained confined to the urban populations and never
permeated the rural masses. It remained essentially Hellenic in nature, notwith-
standing the absorption of foreign elements. Scant wonder, then, that the decline of
the central power coincided with the revival of nationalism in the Near East, which
undermined Greek prestige and the royal authority.

The Roman period

The decline of the Hellenistic world was greatly accelerated by the growing intervention of Rome. The internecine wars of the Hellenistic states, the Punic wars, the
Roman invasion of the East, and the brutal destruction of Carthage, created
anarchical conditions in the Mediterranean. The suppression of Macedonia and
Greece, the inefficient administration of the provinces and the civil wars fought
mostly in the east created conditions from which a number of Hellenistic countries
never entirely recovered.

> The Romans helped forward all the processes that were ruining the political
> stability of the Hellenistic world: separatist tendencies within the monarchies,
> dynastic troubles, civil wars, wars between the several states . . . Rome welcomed
> the gradual disintegration, nay the pulverization, of the Hellenistic states. She
> contributed to their economic ruin. By doing this, she undermined Greek
> civilization throughout the Hellenistic area, and made the advance of orientalism
> easier and more rapid.[1]

After centuries of conflict the Roman Empire did, indeed, ultimately bring
peace to the civilised world. This world was also greatly extended. The result was
that greater homogeneity, more especially in the sphere of language, of law, and of
currency, prevailed in an area that had hitherto been strongly differentiated terri-
torially. Economic conditions were stabilised, the administration of the provinces
improved, and a network of roads was built to link up all parts of the Empire.

This homogeneity was not an unmixed blessing. Economic development did not
take the form so much of a greater intensity of production as of the wider diffusion
of the centres of manufacture. But the greater uniformity stunted the development
of industrial organisation, which everywhere remained on a handicraft basis. At the
same time articles of manufacture became simplified and standardised. The sense of
beauty that permeated Hellenic and Italian wares was lost in the dull repetition of
motives that characterised western European products. Industrial technique
reflected the same sterility, unenlivened by new inventions after the first century,
save for a few minor improvements in the manufacture of glass.

[1] Rostovtzeff, p. 71.

It has been maintained by Heichelheim that the economic life of the ancient world attained its greatest differentiation and refinement during the Hellenistic period. The Augustan peace on land and sea, the protection of private property, the spread of monetary relations, and the large expenditure on public works did indeed, he says, usher in a period of prolonged prosperity. But the Empire, on the whole represented a period of restoration and of restitution rather than one of great development, and the efforts of the best emperors were persistently directed towards postponing the inevitable collapse.[1]

Rostovtzeff has, however, pointed out that there are no standards, and especially no quantitative standards, by which such an assessment can be made. He maintains that he can see no signs of a simplification of organisational forms or of a retrogression in technology during the Roman period. The Roman Empire created many institutions and devised many measures that were of great economic significance and that have survived to this day—measures and institutions that were either unknown or but little developed in the Hellenistic period. It was, in fact, only during the prolonged peace inaugurated by the Empire that many economic and social movements initiated by the Hellenistic kings could come to full fruition.[2]

[1] Heichellheim, *Festgabe*, pp. 186 ff; *Wirtschaftsgeschichte*, pp. 457 ff.
[2] Rostovtzeff, *Social and Economic History of the Hellenistic World*, p. 1311.

7

Development of the free enterprise economies of antiquity

Concept of a free enterprise economy a relative one

It must be stressed that the model of the modern free enterprise economy described in the Appendix is a limiting case. It represents an economy that has become differentiated from, and is motivationally distinct and institutionally separated from, the rest of the social complex. In the market economy the production and distribution of goods and services are carried on through the medium of a self-regulating mechanism of price-fixing markets. Economic decisions are based primarily on prices, and all events of economic significance become effective through prices. The allocation of resources between alternative uses, the distribution of incomes, even the careful weighing of the effects of social and political factors on the economy, are all basically determined within the framework of the market economy.

Naturally such an extreme dissociation of the economy from the rest of the social system did not exist in the ancient world, or for that matter even up to and during the nineteenth century. Many of the traits of a free enterprise economy were still undeveloped and undifferentiated in form and content. This applies not merely to psychological factors such as questions of motivation and of political attitudes, but also to the availability of the necessary institutions within the market economy, such as the provision of adequate markets for land, labour and capital. Above all, political considerations were too pressing and pervasive, and the interest of the dominant group in economic matters too small, for economic factors to obtain any major share in the shaping of policy. Hence, the Graeco-Roman economy was a free economy in the sense that a number of markets were more or less free to regulate themselves. The product market, however, had important constituent elements, such as, for example, the supply of grain to urban centres and the provision of amusement, relegated to the public sphere. The factor markets were still less developed. Thus the supply of slaves, an important constituent of the total labour force in the ancient world, was determined by political rather than by economic considerations, and was therefore subjected to fortuitous fluctuations. The markets for capital and land developed slowly and always remained comparatively rudimentary in scope and structure. These markets could therefore hardly be conceived as constituting an integrated and self-regulating system, in which the product markets were intimately related to the factor markets through the supply-demand-price mechanism, and in which the participants followed the principle of maximising return and minimising cost.

Economic and political freedom

The freedom of choice—the freedom to save or consume, to enter or leave any sphere of the economy, to enter into contracts with other individuals—is the primary feature, the very essence of the free enterprise economy. These freedoms imply the private ownership of the material means of production, because without these property rights severe limitations would be placed on an economy co-ordinated by the market, just as a fully planned economy cannot function where private property in these means exists on any extensive scale. The right to private property therefore does not mean merely the ability to derive an income from its ownership, but the right of control, of disposal, and of investment. It also implies the right to bequeath and to inherit, because only under such conditions can the choice between spending and saving be extended beyond the life of the individual and the free enterprise economy be placed on a permanent basis.

The assertion and maintenance of economic and political freedom were favoured by several factors in the Mediterranean world, and constituted a feature which clearly differentiated Graeco-Roman societies from both the centrally administered and the centrally directed economies and polities of the Orient.

The first factor was undoubtedly the physical characteristics of the Mediterranean seaboard, which favoured the rise of small and independent city states. The peculiar feature of these states was that they were all politically conscious and very jealous of the maintenance of their own independence, which effectively debarred the formation of larger centrally administered or directed entities during the formative period of Graeco-Roman history. The city state was, and remained, the characteristic form of political organisation in antiquity.

Of equally fundamental importance to the maintenance of the free economy was the assertion of political freedom by the individual. The Greeks and Romans, unlike their oriental contemporaries, were politically conscious. Liberty to them was an ideal that had to be striven for to be attained, and though the ensuing strife and class struggles were never satisfactorily solved, they did result in the participation of all full citizens in the formulation of the laws and the government of the state, and in the equality of rights taking, at least formally, the place of exclusive privilege. It is true that the equality of rights did not bring with it equality of opportunities, and that the failure to solve this issue ultimately led to the loss first of political and then of economic freedom. But the assertion of political liberty by the people during the period of florescence of Graeco-Roman civilisation formed the basis of the free institutions of the West, as contrasted with the centralised organisation and the political passivity of the East.

One of the first and most effective means of ensuring their political freedom was to secure the codification and promulgation of the law. To the Greeks and, especially, to the Romans law was the art of what is good and fair, and jurisprudence the knowledge of what is just and unjust. For them the business of the jurist was constantly to improve the law by bringing it into accord with ethical standards. What was particularly important to the maintenance of a free society was the fact that the social system of antiquity was based on an unequivocal recognition of private property, the right not merely to its use but also to its control and disposal by the possessor. Above all, the state effectively entrenched the rule of law, and the full power of the state was at the disposal of the individual for the enforcement of his private rights.

The law also recognised that a man could bind himself to another by engaging in effective contracts, that is, by rights and duties deriving from bilateral arrangements. Institutionally a contract is a means of self-regulation as distinguished from governmental regulation. It gives the right effectively to choose among alternatives. Thus it constitutes the institutional framework for the basic processes of exchange in a free economy, and its development in the ancient world is a reflection of the displacement of the community by the society, of the collective economy by the market economy.

The development of a market-orientated economy

The Mediterranean world presented unique opportunities for the development of trade and transport by sea, and commerce was quantitatively the most evolved and structurally the most developed branch of the economic system of antiquity.

Comparatively little improvement was indeed effected in the technique of marine transport during this period, either by the genius of the Greek or by the practical application of the Roman. Since sailing in winter was considered perilous, all ships were beached and only the most urgent business would induce sailors to take to sea. Even sailing by night was considered dangerous, for there were no adequate instruments for measuring time or distance or for taking bearings. The dangers of navigation were, however, greatly reduced by the construction of harbours. An elaborate and, considering the technical limitations of the time, ingenious system of moles, basins, and wharves was constructed to protect ships riding at anchor against the swell of the open sea and to facilitate the shipment of goods. The ports of the Empire were also provided with lighthouses.[1]

But in spite of these limitations, and because of the excellent opportunities offered to transport by sea, keen competition and low wages, freight and passenger rates remained low, provided that the freight was light and the goods easily stowed. Thus wheat was brought from Alexandria to Rome at about the modern rate, if the state covered the risks of loss. For heavy goods the transport costs were much higher, because of the difficulty of handling bulky commodities with the cranes of the time.[2]

One of the chief items of expense in sea transport was the high rate of interest on commercial loans. A favourite form of such loans was the bottomry bond, advanced on hull and cargo. In case of shipwreck the debt was cancelled; if the destination was reached, the capital was repaid with the agreed interest. Marine loans therefore had in them an element of insurance. Even in times of peace the payment for the element of risk was usually at least as high as the cost of transport.[3]

[1] Lehmann-Hartleben, *Die Antiken Hafenanlagen des Mittelmeeres.*
[2] Glotz, p. 295; Frank, pp. 315 ff.
[3] For the voyage from Athens to the Hellespont in classical times the rate of interest might be as high as 12.5 per cent, and for the voyage there and back 30 per cent. The creditor had to fear not only all the risks of the sea but also the numerous forms of fraud that Greek ingenuity could devise. The rate therefore varied according to the borrower, the place of destination, the duration of the voyage, and the political situation. Individual loans were always for very small sums, and shippers were obliged to borrow from a number of sources for the same venture. Glotz, p. 243; Hasebroek, pp. 82 ff; Heichelheim, *Wirtschaftliche Schwankungen*, pp. 91 ff.

The risks of transport were greatly increased by the prevalence of piracy. Many parts of the Mediterranean and of the surrounding seas offered ideal conditions for the pirate, and before the organisation of the Roman Empire there was no strong central government interested in suppressing the plague. It was only under the Empire that standing fleets were effectively maintained and that the Mediterranean was made safe from piracy during the first two centuries A.D.[1]

In comparison with the low cost of marine transport, the cost of carriage by land was very high. Only goods of high value could be conveyed economically; perishable commodities not at all. Traffic by land was therefore of little importance. Territorial specialisation was confined to the coastal areas of the Mediterranean; inland towns had to be largely self-sufficient in regard to the provision of cheap and bulky commodities. The ancient economy remained essentially Mediterranean in character.

Nor, in contrast to government agencies, was an efficient postal system established for private purposes. Private correspondence had to be transmitted either by messenger, who was invariably a freedman or a slave, by a friend or acquaintance who happened to be travelling in the desired direction, or by a merchant who might do it for a consideration. The absence of a more centralised and efficient system is surprising. Like so many other shortcomings of the ancient world, it can no doubt be attributed to the institution of slavery.[2]

The scope of ancient commerce

The trade of classical Greece had the seaboard of the Mediterranean and of the Black Sea as its outlets, and it spread its tentacles through foreign intermediaries as far as Germany, India, and West Africa. The use of coins now for the first time facilitated the circulation of primary products in considerable quantities. But, though trading activities were sufficiently extensive to bring into being a class of professional merchants and to provide a state such as Athens with the largest part of its revenue, the volume of trade must not be exaggerated. High profits, the persistence of the non-professional merchant, the limitation of transport to six months of the year, and the existence of numerous small states that hampered free intercourse are all sufficient evidence of the undeveloped character of the trade of the time. Wheat, slaves and wine, to which may be added fish and oil, alone were regularly traded in large quantities. Metal and ceramic ware were the only manufactured products that entered extensively into interregional trade. Attica enjoyed a virtual monopoly of the export trade in ceramic ware in the fifth century B.C. But the movement of raw material in interregional trade was small. Craftsmen, working on home materials, produced local specialities, a feature that was to remain characteristic of industry throughout antiquity. The shipbuilding industry was an exception, for it required supplies of metal, timber, pitch, tar, flax and hemp, and these had for the most part to be imported from abroad.[3]

---

[1] Ormerod, *Piracy in the Ancient World*; Ziebarth, *Beiträge zur Geschichte des Seeraubs und Seehandels im alten Griechenland.*
[2] Riepl, *Das Nachrichtenwesen des Altertums.*
[3] Heichelheim, *Festgabe*, pp. 180 ff; *Wirtschaftsgeschichte*, pp. 320 ff; Bolkenstein, *Het Economische Leven in Griekenlands Bloeityd*, pp. 165 ff; Hasebroek, *Trade and Politics in Ancient Greece*, pp. 81 ff; Ziebarth, *Beiträge zur Geschichte des Seeraubs*, pp. 59 ff; Busolt, *Griechische Geschichte*, i, 181 ff.

The sphere of Hellenistic trade was wider, its volume greater, and its structure more refined than that of classical times. It spread through foreign intermediaries from the Atlantic and the Baltic to China, India and East Africa. Commercial relations were of course not equally developed throughout this vast area. An inner circle stretched from Iran in the east to Sicily in the west, and from the Danube and the coast of the Black Sea in the north to the edge of the Sahara in the south. From this central sphere of influence commerce radiated to the peripheries with lessening intensity and increasing adaptation to more primitive methods of exchange. In this way not only Hellenistic goods but also Greek speech and culture were gradually diffused throughout the civilised world.

The staple products of agriculture began to circulate in large quantities. So important was the corn trade in Egypt that the value of immovable property came to be closely related with the price of wheat. Luxury articles entered into commerce as never before. But cheap manufactured articles of mass consumption seem to have been of no more importance than in the classical period. Nor was the trade in industrial raw materials of much more significance. The supply seems to have been too uncertain, the cost of transport too high, to facilitate territorial specialisation in the crafts. Even in the Near East each country continued largely to manufacture its own articles of mass consumption. This tendency towards self-sufficiency was strengthened by the deliberate policy of the states to meet their needs from their own resources.[1]

The economic setback that initially marked Rome's conquest of the east was reflected also in commercial relations. A decline in the trade in articles of mass consumption was accompanied by a rise in the circulation of luxury wares. For the first time since the beginning of this period, according to Heichelheim, the growing importance in interregional trade of cheap foodstuffs, as compared with luxury wares, was reversed—a structural change significant of the economic tendencies of the time. The slave trade was one of the few branches of commerce that could boast of a great expansion in volume and a considerable refinement in structure. According to Heichelheim grain, wine, and oil were the only staple articles of commerce that moved with an intensity comparable to that of the Hellenistic period. The trade in wine was so important in the barbarian hinterland that the Latin *Caupo*[2] became in the German and Irish languages the general term for a merchant.

The Roman Empire brought a much greater degree of economic homogeneity to the Mediterranean world, though this was attained partly at the expense of the more industrialised areas. Up to the first century A.D., Italy occupied a central position in a well differentiated entity, the western parts of which specialised primarily in the export of raw materials, the eastern in the sale of manufactured articles. But during the last decades of this century this balance was disturbed. Self-sufficing commercial areas tended to evolve, over the borders of which the staple articles of commerce seldom passed. Gaul formed the nucleus of such an area in the north-west, the Province of Africa in the south, Italy in the centre, and the Danubian Provinces in the north-east, while Greece and Asia Minor, Syria and Egypt represented such almost self-dependent areas in the east. The movement from territorial specialisation to local self-sufficiency was indicative of the greater

---

[1] Heichelheim, *Wirtschaftsgeschichte*, pp. 458 ff, 515 ff; *Wirtschaftliche Schwankungen*, p. 86; Rostovtzeff, *The Social and Economic History of the Hellenistic World*, ii, 1238 ff.

[2] *Caupo* = innkeeper.

cultural and economic uniformity brought about by the Roman Empire in the ancient world.[1]

But whereas the trade in staple products became localised, the interregional movement of luxury goods was greatly stimulated. Only such articles—the incense, spices, drugs, perfumes and jewels of India and Arabia and the silks of China—could bear the cost of transport. The Empire paid for these partly with the manufactures of Alexandria, but chiefly in bullion. The trade was therefore a severe drain on the monetary resources of the ancient world. Moralists inveighed against the use of silk garments that 'cover a woman while revealing her naked charms', while the emperor Tiberius fulminated against the 'vanities peculiar to women through which our money (*pecuniae*) is transferred to foreign and even hostile lands'. All the legislative measures that were passed from republican times onwards to prevent the export of coin proved ineffective. According to Pliny, in his day gold to the value of over five million dollars was exported annually to India to make up the deficit in the balance of trade.[2]

Commercial organisation

Commercial organisation in the classical period showed a definite tendency towards specialisation and differentiation. Wholesale trade was indeed still often associated with retail business, though in the larger towns it tended to become distinct. Trade and the provision of transport also tended to become distinct occupations, and there is clear evidence of the rise of a commission and forwarding business. Commerce also showed a quite remarkable differentiation according to wares. Classical Greece knew no fewer than sixty-seven different kinds of retail traders, though these were no doubt connected with one another and with agriculture and the crafts. Throughout antiquity, in fact, the amateur continued to engage in commerce as a sideline, the peasant and the craftsman to sell their own wares, and even the transport-rider, the soldier, and the traveller to derive a subsidiary income from the sale of goods. But more and more the professional, resident merchant supplemented and supplanted the itinerant hawker and the amateur.

The process of specialisation in regard to function and wares continued during the Hellenistic period. The commission and brokerage business especially showed a remarkable development. At the same time the merchant became increasingly integrated into the economic activities of the state and the landed estates of the nobility, which combined commerce with agriculture and industry. These complex *oikos* and state economies, with their elaborate systems of agents, bureaux, and transport facilities, took the lead in economic enterprise during a period that showed an extraordinary combination of differentiated and undifferentiated economic elements.[3]

The Roman Empire seems to have developed no new forms of commercial organisation. Even in the city of Rome the methods of distribution remained very rudimentary, when judged by modern standards.

> Between the petty retailers and the farmers of Campania or the shippers from Gaul there existed no machinery of distribution involving varied types of middlemen; at the arrival of a boatload of tunics from Patavium or of olives

---

[1] Heichelheim, *Wirtschaftsgeschichte*, pp. 690 ff.
[2] Cf. Speck, *Handelsgeschichte des Altertums*, iii. 2, B, 734 ff; Schmidt, *Drogen und Drogenhandel im Altertum*, pp. 93 ff.
[3] Heichelheim, *Wirtschaftsgeschichte*, pp. 493 ff.

from Picenum the small merchants themselves flocked to the open-air markets by the river to purchase their stock-in-trade and even the Tyrian and Palmyrene agents probably sold their costly stuffs directly from the warerooms.[1] It is unusual for a wholesale dealer or a jobber to be mentioned in the sources or named in an inscription.[2]

It has even been maintained that during the Roman period commerce gradually became less and less specialised until finally it was differentiated only with regard to the quantity of the turnover and the character of the wares. The merchant also tended again to become associated with transport and with the crafts.[3] As stated before, however, there is little evidence to support the general thesis that the commercial and industrial structure of the ancient world became more primitive and less differentiated after the second century B.C.

Prices and rates of interest

This period was marked also by the permeation of the economic life first of Hellas, then of the whole Mediterranean world, by the coined currency created in Asia Minor. This had an important effect on enterprise and on the development of a market economy. A common unit of account in fact forms an essential condition for the emergence of market prices, and these are essential for rational economic calculation and choice by the individual and for the transmission of economic information between individuals. The use of a common medium of exchange, again, saves time and effort by facilitating sales between individuals and places, and therefore promotes multilateral trade. Finally, the use of a store of value enables people to save. The institutional media of money and market consequently provide a set of conditions which, as Pearson has pointed out, facilitates the mobilisation and the allocation of resources and is highly conducive to the production of surpluses.

> Where money is used as a generalised means of exchange the infinite variety of substantive economic qualities are quantifiable in terms of a single measure; thus they are freely interchangeable and substitutable. Here the facilities for separating, counting, budgeting are fully provided. In addition, the institutional separation of the economic from other aspects of social existence in a market system provides a 'self conscious' economic process, as it were, directing the attention of all participants to the economic significance of all decisions. Outputs are measured against inputs. And the individuation-cum-contract feature of a market ordered economy attaches inevitable uncertainties to the roles of producer and consumer, uncertainties which can be hedged only by the creation of surpluses. Families as well as business firms save, and entrepreneurs drive for profits. It is these features of the system which necessarily direct market behaviour toward the creation of surpluses.[4]

The conquests of Alexander led to the adoption of uniform currency standards throughout the Near East. The Attic standard spread from southern Italy to the Indus, and the so-called Phoenician standard became current in the Ptolemaic Empire. At the same time large sums of money hitherto hoarded in the treasuries of the Persian king were released. By inducing profit inflation, these factors had the same leavening effect on Hellenistic society that American treasure was to have on

---

[1] Warerooms were erected in different parts of the city for the bulk storage of goods.
[2] Loane, *Industry and Commerce of the City of Rome (50 B.C.-A.D. 200)*, p. 113.
[3] Heichelheim, *Festgabe*, pp. 189 ff.
[4] Pearson, in *Trade and Market in the Early Empires*, p. 335.

sixteenth-century Europe. Great, though gradually diminishing, price fluctuations occurred, followed by a gradual fall in prices which continued till the middle of the third century B.C. This decline in prices was no doubt due to the great increase in production and exchange that resulted from the exploitation of the new resources opened up by Hellenic enterprise in the Near East. The large demand for capital in the new provinces was reflected in rates of interest much higher than those ruling in Greece at the time.

After the middle of the third century prices again began to rise. During the first 180 years of the Christian era, prices in the Roman Empire seem to have remained fairly stable, with possibly a mild downward tendency. This tendency was maintained in spite of the gradual depreciation of the currency, and can probably be attributed to the exhaustion of the silver mines of Laurium, the drain of the precious metals to the east, and the introduction of money into the new areas opened up by the Roman conquests.[1]

Banking

Banking in classical Greece gradually developed into an independent profession. It was, however, never confined to professional bankers in the ancient world, but was also carried on as a subsidiary business by shipowners, merchants, and the stewards of large estates. In the Greek city three types of banks—sacred, public, and private—functioned side by side. Temples retained their ancient function as repositories for treasure; public banks were generally adjuncts to town treasuries; and private banks, as in the Middle Ages, developed from the tables of the money-changers. In addition to transactions in foreign money, bankers received deposits in the clumsy form of the closed deposit that could be paid out only to the depositor or his representative, and lent money on collateral security, pledges, and mortgages. A favourite form of credit to commerce was in the form of the bottomry bond. Productive credit for the development of agriculture and industry, on the other hand, was rare. The state could obtain loans only at high rates of interest and on the personal security of wealthy and dependable citizens. But, whereas the rate of interest in Babylonia had usually fluctuated between 17 and 40 per cent, it now dropped to about 12 per cent for safe investments. This rate remained unchanged for decades, and even for centuries, and was obviously determined by the irrational forces of law and custom rather than by market factors. In addition to this, business bankers engaged in all sorts of speculative transactions, such as the buying and selling of real estate, the carrying on of industrial and mining enterprises, and even the lending or selling of all sorts of implements and articles. Pasion's bank must have resembled a pawnshop. This Athenian Rothschild employed a capital of only £5,000 in his banking business. The fortunes made by bankers were far smaller than those accumulated by politicians, landowners, and the owners of mines.[2]

Banking in the Hellenistic *polis* was hardly more developed than in the classical period. Negotiable paper, the precursor of the bill of exchange, came into being. But productive credit in industry, mining and retail trade was still largely lacking. These activities of production and distribution were carried on either on a small

---

[1] Heichelheim, *Wirtschaftliche Schwankungen der Zeit von Alexander bis Augustus*, pp. 2, 55 ff, 70 ff; 'Prices', *Encyclopaedia of the Social Sciences*; Burns, *Money and Monetary Policy in Early Times*.

[2] Bolkenstein, pp. 194 ff; Heichelheim, *Festgabe*, pp. 182 ff; *Wirtschaftsgeschichte*, pp. 313 ff, 349 ff.

handicraft basis or in connection with state and *oikos* economies. In both cases credit was unnecessary. In comparison with this small-scale business, the Ptolemaic banking monopoly was perhaps the most highly organised and differentiated structure in antiquity. A network of royal banks spread throughout the country was controlled by a central institution at Alexandria. But technically, as apart from their organisation, they were no doubt elementary in form. In addition to serving as a means for the collection and payment of public funds, they carried on the other functions of the banks of the time, and thus were a means of mobilising the resources of the country for state purposes.

Roman banks, though superior to those of classical Greece, were only very small establishments. They were primarily individual undertakings, though bankers sometimes formed temporary partnerships. Some of them had branches or correspondents in the more important commercial centres so that funds could be transferred without the actual shipment of coin. But the letters of Cicero show that the making of payments abroad remained a complicated matter. 'Cicero,—when he wished to establish a credit for his son in Athens—made over to Atticus his urban rentals at Rome, in return for which Atticus gave his banker in Athens orders to credit Cicero junior with the amount and to debit the account of his income from the Epirote estate.' Some bankers performed a wide variety of functions, such as the conducting of auctions, the changing of foreign money, the acceptance of deposits, the lending of money on security, the making of investments for customers, and the buying and selling of real estate for them. Bankers in Rome were generally not held in very high esteem, since their services differed but little from those that were performed for wealthy individuals by their servile stewards.[1]

Conclusion

As pointed out in the introduction to this chapter, the free enterprise economy requires certain very specific conditions for effective performance. It can function satisfactorily, in the first place, only in a progressive and expanding economy. Such a system requires, in particular, a cultural atmosphere that is sympathetic to the development of business activity, a milieu that is conditioned by an appropriate economic ethics, and that places a high valuation on enterprise, innovation and progress. A second requirement is the development of a rational technology, of rational means of accountancy, and of the rational organisation of industry generally. A third essential condition is a free market for labour and for capital, and especially the technical means and the institutional environment that favour the mobilisation of credit for private and for public purposes, as well as the commercialisation of claims and rights to business enterprise. Finally, an essential requirement is a measure of legal certainty in regard to the individual's obligations to the state, which obligations should not be arbitrarily assessed but should be subject to ordinary legal interpretation and decision by the courts of the land, and an individual who is aggrieved should have the means of redress even against the state.

These essential conditions, as will be pointed out in the next chapter, were only partly available in antiquity. The shortcomings, from the point of view of the development of a free enterprise economy, were in the prevalent psychological attitudes rather than in the existing institutional background. What was especially

[1] Frank, *Economic History of Rome*, pp. 289 ff; Heichelheim, *Wirtschaftsgeschichte*, pp. 550 ff; 722 ff.

lacking was a dynamic economy with a cultural milieu favourable to the growth of business enterprise—a general attitude among the dominent classes that valued economic activity, that encouraged the qualities of initiative, independence and self-reliance, that appraised life in terms of activity and placed a high valuation on the propensities to save and to invest, on change, innovation and progress, and that registered a corresponding disapproval of idleness, conspicuous consumption, economic dependence and waste. The free economy of the ancient world was conditioned above all, also, by the existence of slavery, which had an important effect, not only on psychological attitudes, but on the development of technology and organisation, and, finally, on the composition and character of the people of antiquity itself.

8
Psychological, technical and organisational limitations of the ancient economies

Introduction

The limiting conditions of the ancient economies were partly of a psychological, institutional and political nature, and partly of a technological and organisational character.

Economic motivation

The Aryan aristocracies of Greece and Rome were descended from a society of agricultural warriors. Their interests were centred in the land and in public life, and for the peaceful callings of trade and industry they generally professed profound contempt. Very few professions, outside the services and the law, were open to the gentlemen of Greece and Rome. Agriculture was everywhere regarded as an honourable pursuit. Foreign trade and banking were dubiously tolerated. But retail trade and the crafts were regarded as menial occupations, which warped the minds and bodies of those who exercised these professions.

The Athenian citizen indeed felt little embarrassment in acknowledging his calling, and the popular assembly was composed largely of craftsmen. Initially, no doubt, the disdain of technicians and technological problems evinced in ancient writings was confined very largely to the conservative literary class. This is shown by the importance attached to technical matters in legislative texts, and especially those from Athens, which indicates that manual dexterity and skilled labour were held in great regard. But it is the literary classes that ultimately determine the ideas and ideals of the times, and in the course of time their views and prejudices become the common property of the people. And, as Rostovtzeff has taken such great pains to point out, the relative unprogressiveness and eventual decline of the ancient world must, in the last resort, be sought in the disappearance among the élite of the will and the power to create—in the political but especially also in the economic sphere.

The duties and privileges of a citizen in the city state were also a great hindrance to the successful conduct of his business. So numerous and exacting were the demands of public affairs, that a large part of his time was taken up in attendance at the assembly, the administration of justice, and military service. For it was the principle of the city state that its administration was the privilege of all citizens. Even the Roman Empire maintained the fiction that membership of the civil service was an honour, which amply remunerated the holder for the time and effort expended, whereas, in fact, many municipal functions, such as the supervision of roads, police, water works, and the collection of taxes, were obviously nothing but a burden.

On the other hand, it was considered an essential part of state policy that citizens should be provided with the means to perform these services. The citizen, says Aristotle, must not be 'degraded' by extreme indigence. The building schemes of Pericles were intended to provide citizens with work and to make them share the advantages of a full treasury. In the fourth century B.C. a special fund was set aside to provide them with the means of subsistence. They were even amused at public expense. The result was that all full citizens were at least partly freed from the necessity of earning a livelihood. Such payments were an essential part of Greek democracy, not merely in Athens, but wherever democracy was sufficiently established to make it possible. The orators of the period assumed this to be the normal and proper state of affairs.[1]

Rome followed the same policy and carried it to its logical extreme. Not only was the proletariat fed and clothed, but it was even provided with the necessary pocket-money. Since the devil will always find work for idle hands the citizens were amused by games, which became increasingly numerous and protracted. Carcopino comes to the conclusion that the Romans finally enjoyed at least one day of holiday for every day of work.[2]

Naturally such a policy was not conducive to calling forth the necessary initiative from the citizen class. The ideal life of the citizen was that of the landowner and the rentier. Men who made their fortunes in industry and commerce tried to rehabilitate themselves socially by the purchase of country estates. 'The chief object of economic activity', says Rostovtzeff, 'was to secure for the individual or for the family a placid and inactive life on a safe, if moderate, income.'[3]

Because of the attitude of the citizen to business activity, commerce, industry and banking in the ancient world fell largely into the hands of certain penalised groups: of metics, or resident aliens in the Greek and Hellenistic economies, and of foreigners and freedmen in the Roman economy. Conditions such as these further contributed to the feeling of scorn with which these occupations were regarded, and naturally helped to keep them in the hands of the socially depressed classes. But because the idea that the competition of the foreigner might harm the interests of the citizen did not occur to the politician, the alien was never subjected to any disability in regard to his business or his trade. In fact, when the Greek states in the sixth century tried to develop home industries, they everywhere put an end to the expulsion of foreigners, and actively encouraged the settlement of foreign craftsmen. The opportunities offered to aliens, freedmen and slaves in the economic sphere in the ancient world were probably unequalled anywhere else in the history of the world.

Slavery

A peculiar feature of the free enterprise economy of antiquity was that a large

---

[1] Hasebroek, Trade and Politics in Ancient Greece, pp. 34 ff; Glotz, Ancient Greece at Work, pp. 160 ff.
[2] Carcopino, Daily Life in Ancient Rome, p. 206.
[3] Rostovtzeff, Social and Economic History of the Roman Empire, p. xi.

proportion of the workers were not free agents but servile instruments.

The growth of industry in Greece from the sixth century onwards greatly increased the demand for slaves. Constant warfare among the Greek states was supplemented, as a source of supply, by piracy and purchase from neighbouring countries, where there was little scope for the employment of slave labour. At the same time the tendency grew to employ slaves in the crafts rather than in agriculture and domestic service. But the number of slaves never seems to have exceeded that of the free population, even in business centres such as Athens.[1]

In the Hellenistic countries, too, the free population predominated. In Egypt there was little use of slaves outside Greek centres such as Alexandria and Memphis. An adequate number of simple fellaheen was available to do all the work required. Slaves might have played a more important part in Syria, and were considerably more numerous in Asia Minor, but even here the free population predominated. Alexander's policy of assimilation lessened very considerably the number of new slaves, and in Greece scope for the employment of slave labour decreased.[2]

Far greater was the number of slaves in Carthage, where they were employed on the plantations of the nobility, in naval construction, and in domestic service. The slave trade was one of the most important branches of commerce in the western Mediterranean.

Slavery became especially important in Italy from the third century B.C. The decimation of the free population in the continuous wars, the growth of latifundia, the rise of industry and the inflow of wealth from the provinces created a great increase in the demand for labour. The free Roman was unsuited, both by capacity and by inclination, to continuous monotonous labour. Moreover, he was conscripted during the best years of his life for military service, which was the real industry of the freeman. But the factors which created the demand also provided the supply. Enormous numbers of prisoners of war were reduced to slavery. It has been maintained that Aemilius Paulus sold Epirus by auction, and that Caesar reduced a million Gauls to slavery, but these statements seem to be greatly exaggerated. A swarm of human vultures continually followed the armies to prey on servile flesh. An organised slave market grew up on the island of Delos, where up to 10,000 slaves are said to have changed hands in a single day.[3] Piracy maintained the supply between wars, until finally the influx of foreign slaves seriously changed the composition of the Roman people. With the establishment of the Empire, however, there came a prolonged period of comparative peace and the suppression of piracy— factors which greatly decreased the supply of slaves available to the ancient economy.

It is not easy to evaluate the effect of slavery on the ancient economy. As the main source of supply of slaves was constituted by prisoners of war that might otherwise have been exterminated, the institution seems to have increased the supply of labour and to have enhanced its mobility. It seems also to have very considerably enhanced the supply of entrepreneurial and managerial services. For owing to the prejudices of the citizen class, one of the most effective ways for wealthy individuals to invest their money was to set their slaves up in the commerce and industry from which they were themselves excluded. Slave shopkeepers were common in the larger Greek cities. In Rome, after the second century B.C., commerce and industry fell largely into servile hands. This being the case, these

[1] Cf. Gomme, *The Population of Athens in the Fifth and Fourth Centuries B.C.*, p. 26; Kahrstedt, *Handwörterbuch der Staatswissenschaften*, ii, 658.

[2] Kahrstedt, ii, 658; Glotz, pp. 350 ff.

[3] Such numbers would have been very exceptional.

occupations came to be looked down upon more and more, and were virtually reserved for the slaves, because they were despised. Enormous numbers of cultured Greeks and orientals poured into the peninsula. These Hellenised orientals showed a capacity for business and figures which few Italians possessed. Intelligent masters therefore exploited their services by establishing them in the crafts, in retail trade, and even as bankers, business managers, tutors, and writers. A large number of slaves were also employed, throughout antiquity, in the civil service, not only in the lower, but occasionally even in the most responsible positions, especially in the administration of finance. At no other time in the history of the world were such opportunities given to the slave as in antiquity.[1]

Enlightened owners recognised that the biggest incentive they could hold out to their slaves was the promise of ultimate freedom. Freedmen played a very important part in the economic development of antiquity, and especially of Rome. The liberality of the Romans in freeing their slaves enabled large numbers of them to merge with the citizens, with the result that towards the end of the Republic freedmen already constituted the bulk of the plebeian classes. They dominated every sphere of commerce and industry. Freedmen were the builders, metal-workers, clothiers, food-merchants, slave-dealers, and bankers *par excellence*—the driving force in the economic life of Rome. They also made a name for themselves in the liberal professions. Art and science were brought to Rome by the more cultured of her captives, and remained largely in servile hands. Medicine, teaching and architecture became increasingly associated with slaves and freedmen, and the prejudice against these professions increased correspondingly.

In spite of the initiative displayed by freedmen and slaves, slavery had an extremely deleterious effect on the ancient economy and polity in several important respects. It undermined the diligence, initiative and self-reliance of the citizen and contributed very largely to the low esteem in which economic affairs was held in the ancient world, and this again was an important cause of the insufficient effort to improve the techniques and organisation of industry, commerce and banking, as well as of the means of transport and communication.

Once slavery had become the basis of the economic life of the ancient world, however, the removal of the sources of supply was also fraught with serious consequences. The slave, in the words of Polybius, was no longer a luxury but had become one of the necessities of life. The displacement of servile by free labour would therefore have required a power of adaptation and a vitality which the Roman world no longer possessed. The result was that when the cessation of the wars of expansion, which came with the stabilisation of the empire, cut off the main source of supply of slaves and created an acute labour crisis, the movement towards more primitive forms of economic organisation was an inevitable necessity.[2]

Finally, the introduction of large numbers of eastern slaves into the Italian peninsula had a profound effect on the culture of the ancient world and on the maintenance of free economic and political institutions. The old self-reliant, self-assertive, sceptical Roman stock was gradually displaced by an urban proletariat that cared for little but bread and circuses. In politics the new plebs demanded a master, in religion a saviour. In the sphere of religion, eastern, and especially

---

[1] Busolt, i, 274 ff; Zimmern, pp. 281, 392 ff; Frank, pp. 330 ff; Barrow, *Slavery in the Roman Empire*, ch 4.

[2] Weber, 'Die socialen Gründe des Untergangs der antiken Kultur', *Gesammelte Aufsätze*. The views of Max Weber have, however, been disputed on the grounds of evidence obtained from some of the peripheral areas of the Empire.

Egyptian, cults were introduced, which could satisfy the new emotional cravings—the yearning for ecstasy, for ascetic abstinence and for renunciation—emotions completely foreign to the Roman and Hellenic spirit. In the sphere of politics, the free republic was transformed first into a principate and then into a despotism.

Technological achievements and limitations

During this period the Hellenic spirit brought forth its greatest works in the arts and sciences. From the middle of the sixth century, within the relatively short space of a hundred years, the Greeks raised the arts to a standard of excellence that has rarely been equalled and never surpassed. Partly, the Greek miracle was the outcome of a freshness and a vigour that did not look back to tradition. Partly, it was a result of the rise of the lay spirit. Human reason freed itself from the shackles of religion. In the place of the mythological interpretation of the universe, the Greeks, proceeding from the assumption that nature was governed by fixed laws, fearlessly set out to discover and to formulate those laws. They were therefore in a significant sense the creators of modern science.

Initially Greek science was developed by men close to reality and experience. Both their range of ideas and the modes of thought they applied were derived from an active interest in practical affairs. This association reached its highest development with the Pythagorians.

But the achievements of the experimenters soon came under the criticism of the philosophers, who believed in seeking truth by pure reason alone, unaided by the evidence of the senses. They in fact showed a rooted objection to the practical application of scientific theories, because man, according to their views, should not tamper with nature and try to make it subservient to his end. This tendency found its culmination in Plato.

> The older view had been that there is a necessary order in the material world, and that the human mind grasps truth in so far as it grasps this necessary order. This order could only be apprehended by sense-evidence. To the interpretation of this evidence human experience in the exercise of techniques lent the necessary clue. For Plato, however, true science is teleological. It consists in interpreting phenomena in the light of the ends at which the Mind which strives to direct all things is presumed to aim. These ends are discovered, not by observation, but by reason. Not by trying to act upon nature but by argument about ends will the truth be discovered.[1]

According to Plato, the purpose of science is not to serve the vulgar ends of traders and traffickers, but to help the soul on its route from the sphere of perishable things to the contemplation of eternal truth. This became the Greek tradition. But by losing touch with experience, ancient learning was inevitably misdirected into pure formalism.

With the loss of Greek political liberty Hellenic science decayed. A mass of knowledge was indeed accumulated in Alexandria and other centres of Hellenistic civilisation, but no new conceptions of a revolutionary kind were evolved by the Greek mind. Nor did the extension of the *Pax Romana* help to revive the Greek spirit, for the Roman had no genius for science or art. In his inmost nature he always cherished for science that mixture of suspicion and contempt that is peculiar to people with a limited peasant horizon. Cicero even boasted that his countrymen,

[1] Farrington, *Greek Science*, p. 144.

thank God, were not like the Greeks, but confined their study of mathematics and that kind of thing to the practically useful. Pure science languished until the second century A.D., and by the third century it was dead beyond recovery.

The Greeks made remarkable progress in the invention of certain labour-saving devices, such as wood-turning lathes, windlasses, pulleys and cranes. Though the Romans displayed little inventive genius in mechanical matters, they perfected and disseminated some of the techniques they had inherited. The chief element in this development was the wide adoption of rotary motion, as in mill-wheels and tread-mills, which displaced human labour in the grinding of grain and ore and the crushing of olives. These inventions probably represented the most important extension of non-human motive power since the invention of the plough, the ox-cart and the sail in the fourth millennium B.C.

But in spite of these developments the technology of the ancient world was basically not progressive. Prosperity was primarily dependent, not on technological development, but on the opening up of new frontiers and on political conquest, with the result that as soon as the purely quantitative expansion ceased diminishing returns would inevitably tend to operate. And towards the end of this period both military and industrial procedures had become stationary and stagnant. Thus the equipment of the Roman armies remained unchanged from the time of Augustus to that of Diocletian; for more than three centuries no new tactics or means of warfare were applied. In spite of the importance of military matters to the Roman state, no systematic exposition on strategy or tactics was produced by any Roman writer. The methods used seem never to have been examined or criticised; in fact, they seem to have aroused no intellectual interest. Nor did new methods of any signifi-cance emerge in industry or in the administration of the state after the first century A.D. In literature and art, as in science and technology, men confined themselves to imitation, which, with the lapse of years, became spiritually ever more sterile, technically more corrupt, and aesthetically more unsightly.[1]

It is difficult to account for the prolonged stagnation after the brilliant initial achievements of Greek genius. The capacity of the philosophers to organise know-ledge logically was indeed impressive. But, after the first scientific successes of the Ionians, science failed to become a real formative influence in the life of society. It served rather as a subject of contemplation, removed from the field of technical activity in which it should have found its genuine application, and set apart from the world of practice and above it. Science, however, can develop only when it plays a positive and not merely a contemplative part in social life. Divorced from the effective life of its time it is bound to degenerate into pedantry. Technology, on the other hand, may develop gradually without the systematic determination of phenomena and the formulation of casual relations, simply through the accumula-tion of experience. But under such conditions inventions remain incidental, qualified by the experience of individuals, and difficult to improve upon. The separation of the logic from the practice of science was therefore good neither for theory nor for practice. For, as Francis Bacon put it: if you make a vestal virgin of science you must not expect her to bear fruit.

Organisational limitations

The rational organisation of the individual enterprise—the allocation of means in

---

[1] Seeck, *Geschichte des Untergangs der antiken Welt,* i, 270 ff.

such a way as to maximise returns—is one of the characteristic features of the free enterprise economy. Like so many other aspects, however, it developed only in very rudimentary form in the free enterprise economy of antiquity.

The diffusion of coinage and cheap means of marine transport did indeed initially facilitate territorial differentiation in the crafts, and the production of most articles, with the exception of basic necessities such as food and clothing, was transferred to independent establishments.

The size of the individual establishment, however, remained small. The ancient establishment was invariably a workshop, seldom a central shop, very rarely a factory. The distinction between the first two is based on a difference in size and the division of labour applied, that between the last two on the nature of the technical processes employed. The central shop is not merely larger than the workshop, but makes use of a system of labour specialisation according to the technical requirements of the work. Handwork, however, still predominates. In the factory, on the other hand, mechanical and chemical processes are employed.

The Greek term *ergasterion*, usually rendered in English by 'factory', embraced anything from a mine to a doctor's surgery. Very often it referred not to the place of work but to a body of workmen. Nor were such workmen, who were invariably slaves, always employed by the owner himself; they were often hired out. The more developed form of the division of labour, where each process is divided into a number of distinct operations, each of which is relegated to a different workman in the same establishment, was little known in antiquity. According to Xenophon, in the large Greek city, 'one man makes men's shoes, another women's, one may even live exclusively by cutting out leather, another by stitching it. One man lives by cutting cloth, another by sewing the pieces into coats.'[1] But such comparatively simple forms of the subdivision of work could be carried out even in the workshop.

Although the total volume of industrial production increased greatly in Hellenistic times, secondary industries tended to become more rather than less decentralised. The crafts certainly tended to become more diversified and more specialised, and greater technical uniformity spread throughout the Mediterranean world. But industrial production remained organised on a small handicraft basis. Even where production was centralised, as in Alexandria, there is no evidence of establishments that can be referred to as factories. The Egyptian makers of various textile specialities were artisans who operated in a small way, owned their own implements, and worked in their own homes, assisted by their families, apprentices, or a few slaves. The output of each shop was sold directly to customers, though a portion might be sold to merchants for export or sale in other centres. Many crafts in the Near East were apparently still hereditary, and concentrated in different quarters of towns.

A typical feature of Hellenistic organisation was the development of large royal, temple and aristocratic household economies. But these *oikos* economies, though large-scale undertakings, were technically less differentiated than the urban handicrafts.

A fairly elaborate organisation of industry was found only in connection with the royal monopolies and monopsonies instituted in the Hellenistic kingdoms, and above all in Egypt. But this integration was financial rather than technical. The methods of exploiting the monopolies varied greatly. Some were farmed out under control; others were administered directly by officials. Some were confined to the sale of articles; others covered every sphere of production and of distribution. The

---

[1] Xenophon, *Cyrop.*, viii, 2.5.

organisation of production itself, however, remained primitive. Even in the case of the elaborate oil monopoly in Egypt, use was made of small workshops located in the villages, and the weaving monopoly was based on home industry. From the point of view of management, considering the primitive accountancy of the time, the monopolies were indeed far more remarkable, even though the administration was often far from efficient, as may be gathered from the recorded complaints. Towards the end of the Ptolemaic regime the system of monopolies began to make way for other simpler and more direct, but equally effective, means of extracting revenue from the subject. Finally, under the Roman Empire, the whole system gradually disintegrated.[1]

In Rome the same system of small-scale production prevailed as in the east. A wealthy patron would equip a workshop for a slave or a freedman and share in the proceeds. The combined workshop and salesroom, which has been made familiar by the excavations at Pompeii, was typical of industrial activity in the Empire. Work for individual customers was very much in vogue. Even in such lines of production as the manufacture of pottery, bricks, or the construction of leaden pipes, where the development of factories might reasonably have been expected, these failed to make their appearance, though in some cases comparatively large central shops were established. Thus in the sewerage contracting industry, where there were obvious advantages in specialisation, only small contractors employing a few slaves and little equipment were to be found. They took the orders when they came, bought the metal, smelted it, and rolled it into plates, which were then cut into strips, soldered into pipes, and finally laid and connected. The contractor was therefore both constructor of pipes and plumber.

In the making of bricks there was, towards the end of this period, a concentration of yards in the hands of members of the imperial family. Building activity in the city of Rome offered the industry a steady and large market and the surrounding area deposits of good clay. Many rich landowners also had no scruples in engaging in a sphere of activity which, owing to its connection with the land, was free from the stigma attached to other industrial pursuits. Since the product was too heavy for distant transport, a few estates near the city monopolised the output, and the public building programmes created a large and concentrated demand. Conditions were therefore ideal for the large-scale mass production of bricks. But even here the individual units were small, and the development of the industry led to more, but not to larger establishments. The only sphere in which fairly large establishments were found was in the production, during the Republic, of red-glazed pottery, since the market for this product embraced nearly the whole of the commonwealth. Under the Empire, however, the Arretine ware of Italy was completely ousted by pottery from small establishments in Gaul.[2]

Forms of business organisation

The business life of the ancient world also remained wholly individualistic in character. Any form of permanent partnership with an independent legal existence was unknown. The idea of limited liability, of the separation of business capital from private wealth, was lacking, and with it any effective means of perpetuating an

---

[1] Heichelheim, 'Monopole', *Paulys Realencyclopädie*.
[2] Frank, *Economic History of Rome*, pp. 240 ff; Loane, *Industry and Commerce in the City of Rome*, pp. 101 ff.

undertaking and of making it independent of the lives and fortunes of the existing owners. Numerous temporary associations were indeed formed for specific ventures. Their object, as a rule, was to share risks, not to mobilise any considerable capital. They were the product of insecurity, not an indication of a developed economic system. The most common of these were created by bottomry loans and participation in sea ventures, where the risks and profits were shared between money-lenders and shipowners. But these associations lasted for only a single voyage. Contractors combined where even the smallest outlay had to be made. Some of these agreements did not last longer than a single day; only in the metallurgical industry, in mining, in banking and in agriculture were they of a more permanent nature.

Such associations never had a legal status; the state always dealt with the individual associates. The Roman *societas* was not in reality a partnership, but merely a business on joint account. It was automatically liquidated when the purpose for which it had been undertaken had been achieved, and more than one such agreement might be entered into between the same persons. Such associations depended mainly on the mutual good faith of the partners. They were dissolved not only by death but also by the mere verbal intimation of a member. This is the more remarkable as the corporation, the *universitas*, possessing a legal personality separate and distinct from that of the individuals comprising it, was well known in Italy. Such, for example, were the *collegia* and municipal associations. The only real corporate business entities, however, were the tax companies, encouraged by the state for the farming of public revenues. But, even here, separate undertakings seem as a rule to have been formed at each census for managing the revenue of each province and for the collection of each tax.[1]

Industry in antiquity was organised on a small scale because the large establishment was no more efficient than the small one. Little capital was required, elaborate equipment seldom being found, even in the largest establishments. There were few secret processes, for the absence of patent laws quickly made new devices available to everyone. Where such processes did exist, as in the red-glazed pottery or glass industries, there was some tendency towards concentration; this was also the case where fairly expensive equipment or highly skilled craftsmen were required, as in the production of bronze. In the iron industry, on the other hand, the absence of valved bellows, which had not yet been invented, precluded the production of molten metal in large quantities—and the production of cast-iron articles on a large scale was therefore not possible. Every iron implement had to be forged and hammered on the anvil—a process best suited to the workshop.[2]

The ancient man of means also had a conception of industrial organisation and of investment which differed from that of the modern promoter. Business undertakings are now established primarily with a view to deriving a profit from the production and sale of wares. In the ancient world enterprises seem to have been established rather as an outlet for surplus funds. Production was a secondary consideration. This difference in attitude was reflected especially in the lack of interest of the owners in adopting new devices, in maximising returns and minimising costs, and in generally improving the efficiency of their undertakings. Establishments continually changed hands because they were regarded by their owners

[1] Bolkenstein, pp. 175 ff; Glotz, pp. 301 ff; Frank, pp. 286 ff; Rostovtzeff, pp. 159 ff; Jonkers, *Economische en Sociale Toestanden in het Romeinsche Ryk*, pp. 99 ff; 'Universitas', *Dictionnaire des Antiquités Grecques et Romaines*; Endenburg, *Koinoonia en Gemeenschap van Zaken by de Grieken in den Klassieken Tyd*.

[2] Frank, *Economic History of Rome*, pp. 234 ff; 271 ff.

merely as sources of investment. The same person might own a number of dissimilar undertakings, or they might produce several different articles in the same establishment. Industrial slaves were not distinguished from domestic ones; nor were the accounts of the business separated from those of the household.

The organisation of a large industrial or commercial enterprise must have presented serious difficulties in accountancy. Business men were often illiterate. Until Hellenistic times even the granting of receipts for payments was unknown; no trader therefore delivered his goods, no banker contracted loans, except in the presence of witnesses. The absence of written documents made it very difficult to enforce commercial obligations. With the elaborate notation, before the introduction of Arabic numerals, arithmetic was also a complicated matter. Nor did means exist of drawing up adequate balance sheets, a problem accentuated by the difficulty of calculating the depreciation on slaves.[1] Small establishments were therefore easier to administer and to supervise, and wealthy individuals preferred running several small establishments to running one large one. These conditions were reflected also in the willingness of slave-owners to lease out their slaves, or to permit them to set up in business for themselves.

Because of the attitude of the ancient world to business enterprise, it is in agriculture rather than in industry that we find the most consistent attempts, under certain conditions, to effect the rational organisation of the undertaking. Already from classical times, particularly from the fourth century onwards, large properties were exploited rationally with slave labour. During the Hellenistic period, large estates replaced small farms, the technique and organisation became more refined, and the new landlords tried by rational exploitation to maximise the revenue from their estates. From the second century B.C. the large estate appeared in Italy. Aristocrats and business men, as well as enterprising farmers, acquired public and private lands, and the cheap servile labour which poured into the peninsula supplied them with an easy means of developing their properties. Under the first two centuries of the Empire, agriculture made very considerable progress. It is significant that, whereas no works emerged in the ancient world on industry, mining, or commerce, a large Greek, Punic and Roman scientific literature appeared on agriculture.

But even in Roman agriculture, the sphere of interest of the aristocracy *par excellence*, we find much the same attitude towards investment as in industry. The landowner preferred to increase his estates rather than to increase the yield of the land he already owned. Thus, according to Columella, landowners 'avoided annually recurring expenses and considered that the best and most certain form of income was to make no investments'. Similarly, according to the elder Pliny, 'nothing can be less profitable than to cultivate your land to the fullest extent'. The capitalist of antiquity hoarded his money, bought land, or distributed it among his fellow citizens as a means of acquiring political power.[2]

[1] Mickwitz, *Vierteljahrschrift für Sozial- und Wirtschaftsgeschichte*, 32, i. p. 23.
[2] Pleket, 'Technology and society in the Graeco-Roman world', *Acta Historiae Neerlandica*, i.

9
Policy

Indifference to things economic

The city state adopted an indifferent attitude towards economic affairs. The citizen of antiquity was a political, not an economic being. Industry and commerce were the spheres of interest of the metic, the freedman, and the slave, who lacked the power to give weight to their interests. Nor were there well-organised gilds that could exercise pressure on the government. Unorganised and degraded, commerce and industry had to shift for themselves, except when they were needed by the state. Carthage and the Hellenistic countries, heirs of the archaic Orient, were exceptions to the rule. In the history of Greece and Rome economic considerations seem seldom to have been the dominant factors in domestic or foreign policy. There was the same apathy in the study of economic phenomena, which is the more remarkable considering the keen interest in political theory. But, owing to the small and servile character of commerce and industry, there was apparently no inducement for the study of economics.[1]

Neither Greece nor Rome developed a consistent economic policy. There was no serious attempt to aid or interfere with commerce and industry. Only agriculture, in which the citizen had a direct interest, was to a certain extent aided and even protected. But even here the interests of the consumer were predominant. In other spheres the individual was left to his own resources. Well-nigh complete free trade existed, the duties levied on all goods imported and exported being too low to make even smuggling worth while. The merchant was exploited for revenue and was encouraged in so far as he was needed to secure the provisioning of the home market, but for the rest the state took little interest in his affairs. Protective tariffs were unknown; prohibitions of import were used for moral purposes and as a political weapon. But the problem of free trade versus protection never arose, because protection was never thought of.

[1] Bolkenstein, *Het Economische Leven in Griekenlands Bloeitijd*, pp. 227 ff, Hasebroek, *Trade and Politics*, pp. 30, 43, 100; Frank, *Economic History of Rome*, pp. 120 ff; Rostovtzeff, *Economic and Social History of the Roman Empire*, pp. 74, 89 ff. This lack of sympathy is reflected in the refusal of Aristotle to appreciate and accept the profound change that had been effected in the economic system of the ancient world from communal relations based on equivalence or reciprocity and redistribution to societal relations based on a market economy; cf. *Trade and Market in the Early Empires*, ed. Polanyi, pp. 64 ff.

In the Greek and Roman world there was nothing that resembled a 'mercantile policy' in commercial legislation, customs tariffs, the colonisation movement, or political treaties. This applied in particular to Rome, where commercial considerations were consistently subordinated to political advantages. Occasionally, social or political considerations even led to the adoption of measures that must seriously have retarded the economic development of Italy. Thus, in the later days of the Republic, legislation was passed which greatly reduced the number of men that could be employed in mining in the peninsula. The motive appears to have been the danger of concentrating large numbers of slaves near the capital. The ancient world, says Frank, has no record of any state of importance so unconcerned with its economic prosperity as was the Roman Republic.[1]

With the advent of the Empire the administration became more centralised and the aversion to state interference gradually disappeared. Throughout the first two centuries of the Christian era, however, state control was spasmodic and of little significance. Fiscal considerations were dominant, and regulation was confined to spheres where it was essential.

In this respect Carthage and Hellenistic Egypt were archaic survivals in the new economic system, though they were changed and greatly revitalised by the new economic spirit. Carthage was consistently exclusive, and her foreign policy was largely dominated by commercial interests. Ptolemaic Egypt developed an elaborate system of state control out of the centralised economy of the Pharaohs. The whole economic life of the country was systematically planned and directed with a view to fiscal and political ends. The main crops to be planted were carefully planned by a state bureau from data relating to the available stocks, the annual yield, and the needs of a rational rotation of production. Raw materials had to be delivered to state establishments at fixed prices. The whole system was completed by the centralised transport and distribution of commodities, and especially by a state banking system, which effectively mobilised the resources of the country, and supplies not accessible in this way were tapped by an elaborate system of taxes. A more refined machinery for the exploitation of the human and material resources of a country could not have been contrived.[2]

Policy of provision

It was only where the means of subsistence were at stake that the *polis* rid itself of its habitual lethargy. The doctrine that it is the duty of the state to provide for the needs of the citizen was a fundamental aspect of the Greek conception of citizenship, for the citizen had to have leisure to devote himself to public affairs. To this was added the fact that in a society based on servile labour there was an inevitable class of indigent citizens dependent on state charity. Finally, the variability of the crops was an outstanding feature of the economic life of antiquity, and the state could not rely on private enterprise to ensure adequate supplies.

To be assured of the regular supply of grain was one of the principal objectives of Athenian policy, and most of the commercial legislation had reference to the provision of wheat. During the Hellenistic period the state itself entered the market and sold grain below cost, so that all citizens, and not merely the poor, could

---

[1] Frank, pp. 112 ff; *Aspects of Social Behaviour in Ancient Rome*, pp. 101 ff; *Bolkenstein*, pp. 212 ff.

[2] Heichelheim, *Wirtschaftsgeschichte*, pp. 646 ff; Rostovtzeff, *Social and Economic History of the Hellenistic World*, pp. 541 ff.

benefit. The Roman Republic, from the time of the Gracchi, adopted an elaborate system of free alimentation for the plebs of Rome. Augustus put the administration of this service on a sound footing. A prefect of the *annona* was appointed to attend to the collection, transport and distribution of grain, and for five centuries to play the laborious and ungrateful role of minister of provisions. In the other cities this was one of the most onerous tasks of the city fathers, for not only was there no surplus of grain in the ancient world, but Rome consistently regulated and restricted the grain trade in her own favour. Nearly all the cities of the Empire, therefore, suffered from periods of scarcity, and even of real famine, with the attendant riots and demonstrations.

The civil service

A potent symptom as well as cause of the absence of control in the city state was the absence of a permanent civil service, which made effective regulation virtually impossible. The administration was largely in the hands of amateurs. It was one of the fundamental concepts of Greek democracy that the function of the citizen was not merely to make and obey the law, but also to take an active part in its administration. No special training or experience for officials was deemed necessary; a position in the civil service was an honour, not a profession. Officials were relieved annually of their duties; the only permanent posts were the lowest ones, which were occupied by slaves.

It was different in the Hellenistic kingdoms, except in so far as in the kingdoms of the Seleucids and the Attalids administrative functions devolved upon the cities. Even in Ptolemaic Egypt the Greeks in the cities lived on free and autonomous territory. But, in regard to the rest of the economy, the government took over the whole bureaucratic system of the Pharaohs. Here we find the same universality as in archaic times of the official who controls, registers, and inspects and, especially, the prevalence of financial and customs officials. The only differences were that now the higher posts were all occupied by Greeks, and that the bureaucratic system was built up in a more logical and coherent manner. Its objective remained the exploitation of the country for the benefit of the king.

The Roman Republic also adopted a policy of decentralisation, leaving the control of most matters, except political and fiscal affairs, to the individual cities. Administratively, the Republic was a federation of cities. Even when she had become the mistress of the civilised world, Rome was still able to discharge her administrative duties with a small staff of amateurs. It was only under the Empire that a civil service was slowly and reluctantly built up. One department after another was taken over by the central administration. The lower posts were relegated to slaves and freedmen, and even some of the highest and most confidential positions were initially left to the freedmen of the emperor's household. But it became the policy to reserve these for the members of the propertied classes, who alone had the general education necessary to administer them. At the head of the bureaucracy stood the emperor. Throughout this period he was not an oriental despot, but the leader of a free people. In theory it was the rule of the best man, for the ideal of the principate was that the leadership should not be hereditary but should be transmitted to the best man, whom the princeps chose from the peers of the realm. Since, however, the emperor personified the commonwealth, his person was sacred and he himself an object of veneration.

The fiscal system

The absence of an efficient civil service was reflected in the administration of the public revenue. Tax-farming played an important part in the financial system of antiquity. Greece farmed her most important source of revenue, the indirect taxes, as well as the income from the state domains. Hellenistic Egypt tried, wherever possible, to make use of the tax-farmer, even in the administration of its fiscal monopolies, not as the collector of the taxes, indeed, but as the underwriter of the royal revenue. Up to the end of the Republic certain branches of Roman revenue were also farmed out. The construction of public works, the transport and distribution of supplies, and the exploitation of the state domains were also administered by the giving out of contracts.

Nor was there a formal budget in antiquity. The various receipts were kept in different treasuries and administered by different bodies, and there was no attempt to forecast revenue and expenditure. Equally characteristic was the almost complete absence of public credit. The attitude of the state towards private property was not such as to instil sufficient confidence in the state's integrity. So-called loans were, therefore, in reality forced contributions, which were no sooner made than conveniently forgotten.

The city state was always in a precarious financial position. The characteristic feature of its public revenue was the unwillingness of the citizen to tax himself. Direct taxes, according to the notions of antiquity, were derogatory to the character of the free man. 'As the field', said Tertullian, 'has less value if it be taxed, so men are less esteemed if they pay a poll tax, inasmuch as this is a token of slavery.' In Greece only tyrants had recourse to direct taxes; in the democracies these were confined to metics, freedmen, despised professions and subjected peoples. The fiscal burden in the Hellenistic states fell not on the privileged Greek immigrants, most of whom were, in fact, employed by the kings to squeeze the native elements, but on the aboriginal population. Rome continued this policy. Frank estimates the revenue of imperial Rome under Vespasian at from 1,200 million to 1,500 million sesterces, 100 million of which were obtained from indirect taxes and the rest from contributions by the provinces.[1]

Exploitation of the provinces

The ancient state was frankly exploitive in its foreign policy. The city state was exclusive. The idea of transcending its frontiers and forming a united nation was alien to the mentality of the ancient world, and the city state remained the ideal type throughout antiquity, even in imperial entities. The Hellenistic kings accepted the city state and never tried to make any fundamental change in its constitution, for they sensed how inseverably Greek civilisation was bound up with this form of social organisation. Even the Roman commonwealth tended to disintegrate into a commonwealth of self-governing municipalities, in which there was only political and a certain measure of fiscal unity.

This attitude is evident even in Athenian policy, which initially was adopted at the expense of free allies. Aristides frankly advised the Athenians to accept the

[1] Frank, *An Economic Survey of Ancient Rome*, v, 49 ff. Gaul was rich and was made to suffer for it at an early date. Egypt had to endure fresh exactions from time to time Syria, too, was heavily exploited. Vespasian, on the other hand, gave *Latinitas* to most of Spain, an example of the arbitrary and unequal way in which taxes were levied in the Empire.

leadership of the Delian Confederation so that there could be free maintenance for all citizens. The allies were soon reduced to subjects, and their voluntary contributions converted into a forced tribute. According to Thucydides, Euboea yielded more to Athens than did Attica itself.

Hellenistic civilisation represented a superstructure of royal and urban economies imposed on the existing native populations. The kings regarded their countries as their personal property, which they had obtained by right of conquest. The natives were mere objects without political rights, whose duty it was to support the royal household. In spite of the agrarian reforms that were attempted in the Seleucid Empire, the rural masses remained impoverished and attached to the soil. There was no fusion of Greek and native civilisation; Hellenic culture remained attached to the towns.

Carthaginian policy was frankly mercenary. The subjected peoples had to pay tribute and had to acquiesce in any limitation of their foreign trade that the capital cared to impose. It even seems that Carthage alone had ships and that the other towns of the Empire were allowed to possess nothing bigger than fishing boats. On the other hand, they were allowed a large measure of independence in the management of their internal affairs. Carthage never succeeded in inspiring her subjects with affection or patriotism, and they were always prepared to profit by her misfortunes.

Republican Rome took over the Carthaginian system of imposing tribute on conquered countries. In theory this tribute was originally levied to cover the cost of administration; then the requisitions were imposed more and more openly for the benefit of the 'senate and people of Rome'. At first the expansion of the Republic was spontaneous, but gradually it became more deliberate. The cases of extreme vindictiveness, such as the wholesale plundering of Epirus, the sacking of Capua, Carthage and Corinth, and the brutal treatment meted out to Macedonia, were indeed exceptional. But Rome tended to degenerate into a powerful and irresistible bully. The loot of the provinces poured into central Italy, where it enriched, not the people as a whole, but the senatorial and equestrian classes.

Under the Republic the governors had full military, administrative and judicial powers, and the provincials were therefore largely at their mercy. Since they were unpaid and in practice responsible to no one, and since there was much jobbery attached to the acquisition of such a post, the weaker governors rarely failed to resist the temptation of abusing their powers. To obtain a province was the recognised means of setting a bankrupt on his legs again. Even the stronger ones sometimes found it difficult to protect the provincials against the abuses of the system of tax-farming, by which they were mulcted in the interests of a powerful section of the Roman public. How little interest the Republic took in the prosperity of the provinces is shown by the growth of piracy in the Aegean and the Black Sea, which severely handicapped the commercial prosperity of the Hellenistic world. It was only when the provisioning of the capital was endangered that the city roused itself from its apathy and took effective measures to stamp out the evil.

Under the Empire the provincial administration greatly improved and ultimately became the most impartial and just that the ancient world had ever known. Rome respected the culture, religion, and local institutions of her subjects. There was no attempt to Romanise these people, and this liberal policy met with remarkable success. The central control over provincial governors was strengthened and their position was assured by the payment of fixed salaries, and the financial administration was reorganised as a state department. The provincials could appeal direct to the emperor, who was informed of conditions in the provinces by his personal agents. The claim, made by the poet Claudian in the fourth century A.D., that Rome was not the mistress but the mother of her people, became more true.

But throughout this period only a small proportion of the population of the commonwealth had the privilege of citizenship. The Italians gained the franchise at the point of the sword in the first century B.C. Yet it was only in A.D. 212 that Caracalla extended the citizenship to all, and then only to increase the burdens rather than the privileges of the provincials. Rome remained a city state. The masters and rulers of the Empire were the Roman citizens. Roman opinion was strongly organised against the extension of the franchise to all the inhabitants of the commonwealth. On the other hand, it was unsafe to restrict the privilege too severely. So a middle course—the Hellenistic method—was adopted. The urbanisation of the Empire was promoted, and in this way a Romanised aristocracy of urban residents was formed. These citizens represented the wealthiest and most cultured sections of the city residents, selected because of their services to the state—an aristocracy not of birth, but of wealth and intellect. In this way the upper classes became reconciled to Roman rule. The village communities, however, continued to live under the most primitive conditions, without the schools, gymnasiums, baths, libraries and other amenities of a civilised existence. But the ancient *polis*, too, remained only in form. It was now little more than a centre of administration of an empire, whose centre of gravity was the emperor. Gradually the spirit of the city state passed away, and with it the most dynamic element in the life of the ancient world.[1]

[1] Arnold, *Roman Provincial Administration;* Fowler, *The City-State of the Greeks and Romans;* Heitland, *Last Words on Roman Municipalities.*

10

The transition from free enterprise to directed economies

*Beginning of the third century A.D. to the
third quarter of the fifth century A.D.*

Decline of ancient civilisation

The ancient economy had never been highly dynamic and progressive. Its basic weaknesses, as we have seen, were first the negative and unsympathetic attitude of the citizens to economic affairs, secondly the unprogressive nature of technology and organisation, and finally the policy of the state, which encouraged too many consumers to be a drag on the productive resources of the economy. These weaknesses were therefore inherent in the social fabric. Nevertheless the ancient economy continued to function as a viable entity because of certain promotive factors. These were, in the first place, the contributions provided by the richer economies, especially Egypt and Gaul, to the fiscal resources of the central administration; in the second place, and even more important, the excellent opportunities offered by the Mediterranean for the movement of resources from one end of the commonwealth to the other. In the third place, and above all, because of the natural frontiers provided by the Rhine and the Danube in the north, the Sahara in the south, and the Tigris and Euphrates and the Arabian desert in the east, the defence of the Empire required a comparatively small expenditure of men and material, as long as the frontiers were in a comparative condition of quiescence. Finally, because of the democratic and decentralised system of administration, the taxes could be kept on a moderate level, and the city councils performed most of the work on a voluntary and non-professional basis.

The immediate force that upset this delicate equilibrium was provided by the pressure exerted by the barbarians on the northern frontiers. This necessitated the raising of a standing professional army twice the size of that maintained under the principate. To increase its mobility, the proportion of cavalry to infantry was increased, and this added substantially to the cost of its maintenance.

To raise and administer the necessary resources, the state was obliged greatly to increase the size of the bureaucracy, which in turn proliferated with its own momentum and began to show serious signs of venality and extortion. Mistrusting the honesty and efficiency of the administration, the emperor reacted by allowing the officials less and less initative and imposed an ever greater degree of central control. But excessive centralisation involved the multiplication of clerical labour and slowed up the work of administration, without improving the efficiency or reducing the corruption.

In spite of its unwieldiness, the administration succeeded in squeezing from the taxpayers an ever-increasing revenue. So oppressive did the mobilisation of resources for the state become, and so unequal was its incidence, since it fell mainly on agriculture, the mainstay of the ancient economy, and especially on the peasantry, that it led to the progressive abandonment of marginal land. So ruthless and efficient was the collection of rents and taxes, however poor the crop, that the peasants seem, especially during lean years, to have had too little left to rear their children, and they naturally tried to evade their obligations by restricting their production to the required minimum.

To meet the difficulty of raising the necessary revenue, the government was obliged to adopt increasingly coercive measures to compel workers and property-owners to provide essential services. Certain classes were therefore tied to their professions. These were, in the first place, those whose services were essential to the functioning of the economy and the protection of the state—soldiers, peasants, craftsmen and miners—or those whose capital assets were necessary for the perform-ance of essential services, such as shippers, bakers and butchers. And whereas the work of administration had formerly been done largely on a voluntary basis and in an honorary capacity, men now had to be compelled to perform these public services.[1]

Strains and stresses on the market economy

The confusion of the third century brought about a severe monetary crisis. Coins were debased until the silver money was little more than washed copper and gold pieces circulated only by weight. Naturally after such an inflation it was difficult to restore confidence in the currency. This restoration of confidence was effected by Aurelian, who issued new plated and copper coins. Diocletian tried to establish a bimetallic coinage, supplemented by a uniform token coinage for the whole Empire, but was only partly successful. Finally, Constantine instituted a form of gold bullion standard. The silver coins represented subdivisions of the pound weight of gold, and gold coins, though issued, passed only by weight, the stamp being merely a guarantee of quality. Copper coins were also issued, but these bore no simple or stable relation to the rest of the system. Thus a measure of stability was introduced, but only at the cost of reversion to a far more primitive system of monetary arrangements.[2]

Initially the monetary sector was also greatly reduced in importance. A consider-able part of agriculture and industry, as well as of the state economy, reverted to a natural basis. Peasants and landowners provided a large part of their own needs. Transport services were undertaken more as a part of the feudal obligations of serfs than by free labourers for wage payment. Rural taxes were paid largely in kind, and officials, soldiers, and workmen were remunerated partly in goods and partly in money. The state tried to cover its needs as far as possible from taxes in kind, from the royal domains, and from state establishments. These establishments were operated to provide the needs of the army, the court and the administration, and were transformed into state concerns, managed on Egyptian and oriental patterns with staffs of workmen bound to their professions in hereditary castes. Artisans were regimented and subjected to an elaborate system of prescriptions and con-

[1] Jones, *The Later Roman Empire*, ii, ch 25.
[2] Burns, *Money and Monetary Policy in Early Times*, pp. 421 ff.

straints. These obligations were transferred from the individuals to their gilds, which were transformed from voluntary into compulsory associations. The membership of these corporations, with its duties and privileges, became a hereditary charge, which no one could attempt to escape without committing an offence against the state. In return for these public services the gilds were granted certain privileges, such as exemption from extraordinary and degrading services, military service, and municipal obligations.

In addition to central establishments for the processing of raw materials, the state also had its own mines and quarries. During the late third and the fourth centuries it obtained most of its other requirements by levies in kind assessed on the land. In this way it secured not only the necessary foodstuffs with which to feed the army, the civil service, the population of the capital, and the workers in the state establishments, but also the raw materials for these establishments and the necessary labour for the building and maintenance of public works.

But from the late fourth century onwards levies in kind were progressively commuted for payments in gold. If the government required additional provisions, it resorted to compulsory purchase direct from the landowners, and the cost was deducted from their gold tax, or, if it exceeded the amount of the tax, was paid in cash. Henceforth state servants, too, were no longer paid by issues in kind but were remunerated by the payment of salaries. These changes represented an important reversal to a market economy.

In the private sector the arts and crafts were able to maintain themselves on a fairly respectable level, especially in the East. The volume of agricultural and industrial production, however, declined and the organisation became less refined. Private establishments became smaller and specialisation less advanced, crafts again becoming integrated with retail trade.

There was a contraction of the market for medium and cheap goods because of the impoverishment of the peasantry and the lower urban classes. With the general resumption of money payments, however, the peasants were induced to sell a part of their crops in order to buy such household necessities as they did not produce themselves, and to pay their taxes and even their rents in cash.

The villagers sold their products and bought the goods not produced in their own immediate surroundings at rural fairs. As regards overseas relations, the trade in luxuries was relatively well maintained, but the circulation of staple articles showed a marked decline in comparison with what it had been during the previous period. The decrease in the volume of trade in the West was accompanied by a decline in the complexity of its structure, and this was a movement in sympathy with the gradual reversion to more primitive forms of economic organisation.[1]

The agrarian situation

Life tenancies appear to have been a normal arrangement on the imperial domains in the second century A.D., and the customary privilege whereby these tenancies were heritable gradually developed into an accepted obligation by which they became hereditary. Thus there developed in the third century a type of holding which, if it did not expressly tie the holder to the land, did produce that effect by the conditions of its tenure. In this way there evolved a system by which tenants holding land under terminable leases were transformed into colons tied to the soil.

[1] Heichelheim, *Wirtschaftsgeschichte*, pp. 796 ff; Rostovtzeff, pp. 470 ff.

A new form of feudalism thus appeared in rural areas. The owners of large estates were charged with the collection of taxes and the administration of justice. To ensure the rendering of services and the payment of their taxes, peasants were gradually adscripted to the land, and many free farmers voluntarily commended themselves to their more powerful neighbours to escape these fiscal burdens. Society became organised into two main groups: on the one hand the *honestiores*, the privileged aristocracy, and, on the other, the *humiliores*, who were often reduced to a state of serfdom. This social organisation showed remarkable powers of persistence, and survived the barbarian invasions to exercise a powerful influence on medieval society.

The landowners now generally preferred to live in their rural villas. The walled and cramped towns of the late western Roman empire were no longer the ideal places of residence, the seats of culture, outside of which a civilised existence could hardly be conceived. The main town-building factor of antiquity was therefore removed. These landed aristocrats, besides, kept numerous retainers, who readily absorbed the small agricultural surplus. The peasant, on the other hand, had to contribute to lord and state in accordance with his harvest, and he tried to evade this plight by restricting his production to the required minimum. Everywhere the state had the greatest difficulty in provisioning the smaller towns of the declining Empire.

The centralisation of the administration

The princeps of the early empire mixed freely with his fellow citizens, a *primus inter pares*. The emperor of the late Roman Empire, on the other hand, held absolute power, both in theory and in the practice of the constitution. He controlled foreign policy, could raise taxes as he willed and spend the funds as he thought fit, was the sole fount of law, and held the power of life and death over his subjects. These powers were adequately buttressed by religious sanctions. He was worshipped as a God, and from the conversion of Constantine, he became the divinely appointed vicegerent of God.

This gradual and subtle transformation of the Principate must be ascribed not merely to political exigencies, but above all also to the effect of Hellenistic ideas on the western world. This impact represented the permeation first of Greek and then of Roman culture with archaic tradition, a tradition that was to become an integral part of the Byzantine heritage.

But, though absolute, the emperor of the late Roman Empire was not an arbitrary ruler. The republican tradition in Rome was not extinct. This is well brought out in a statement made by Valentian III in 429: 'It is a pronouncement worthy of the majesty of the ruler that the emperor should declare himself bound by the laws, so much does our authority depend upon the authority of law. To submit our imperial office to the laws is in truth a greater thing than our imperial sovereignty.'[1]

Gradually the administrative services of the Empire became centralised and transformed into an all-powerful bureaucracy. In the early Empire the imperial civil service had always been regarded merely as an organ of control, subsidiary to and coordinated with the self-government of the cities. The late Roman Empire was above all a bureaucratic state, and without the bureaucracy the elaborate machine of government that held the Empire together would have collapsed.

[1] Jones, i, ch 11.

Whereas the tasks that the administration had to perform during the principate were comparatively light, very heavy duties were now imposed on it. Taxes in money supplemented by levies in kind had to be imposed on a people decimated by plague and impoverished by constant wars. The administration had to squeeze the requisite and increasing revenue from a declining national income. What was required of the service therefore was ruthless efficiency rather than impeccable honesty. The establishment also had to be greatly extended, and instead of relying on the voluntary services of amateurs, the service had to be transformed into a professional body.

It is therefore no wonder that the administration began to show all the symptoms and weaknesses of an overcentralised bureaucracy. The officials were intensely conservative, excessively devoted to form, addicted to unnecessary paper work, and unduly jealous of their own prerogatives. At the same time the service was organised on a rigid pattern and advancement was strictly by seniority. The number of posts tended to proliferate, absenteeism was rife, salaries low, and the officials apt to be rapacious and corrupt. What is more, the public servants of the late Empire seemed, on the whole, to have been an unambitious and unenterprising class.

But, despite its many failings, the service played a vital role in the preservation of the Empire. The officials alone could succeed in maintaining the machinery of state, clumsy and inefficient as it was, as a functioning entity. Above all, the officials lived among the people from whom they were never completely divorced and, if only for their own comfort, they had to show a measure of consideration to the citizens entrusted to their charge.[1]

Decline of public spirit

The most outstanding feature of the late Roman Empire is the absence of public spirit. The Roman Empire never seemed to have evoked any active patriotism from the vast majority of its citizens; it was a geographical entity without a real unifying and animating force. Men were willing to boast of the Roman name and to enjoy the privileges of citizenship, but felt no call to devote themselves to the service of the state. The Empire was to them a great and beneficent power. But though it excited their admiration and their gratitude, it was too large and impersonal to evoke the loyalty that they felt for their own cities. To them the purpose of the Empire was to promote internal peace and prosperity and to ensure external security. These paternal functions, however, were the spheres of duty of the emperor, his army, and his bureaucracy, and lay beyond the realm of responsibility of the citizen.

Gradually, and because of the transmutation of the Roman people, which was the price paid for the creation of the commonwealth, and the decline of public spirit, which was caused by the formation of the world state, there was a subtle change in the mentality of the people of antiquity. The Romans of the late Empire were no longer the same virile yeoman stock of old, who always met new situations courageously and refused to accept defeat. They would now rather hide and even mutilate themselves than do military service. They lacked the energy and the confidence in the future to recover from disasters that otherwise might have been mere temporary episodes. A wave of resignation passed over this inert mass that was too passive to react to any stimulus save religion. Men would rather seek salvation

[1] *Ibid.*, ii, ch 16.

in a life hereafter than improve their mundane existence. A new world order had arisen, completely different from that of the previous period.

It was useless to fight, better to submit and bear silently the burden of life with the hope of finding a better life—after death. The feeling was natural, for the best efforts of honest men were bound to fail and the more one produced, the more would be taken by the State.[1]

Oriental mysticism supplanted the sober, rational Hellenic spirit. The genius for invention was temporarily extinct, and men confined themselves to studying the older works, to commenting, and to coordinating. Astronomy reverted to astrology, mathematical geography to a superficial and purely descriptive art, philosophy to mystical neoplatonism, botany to a drug list, and medicine to a collection of formulae, punctuated by incantations. The creative Hellenic spirit had become impotent in the spheres in which it had achieved its greatest triumphs: in the exact sciences, in literature and in art.[2]

---

[1] Dill, *Roman Society in the Last Century of the Western Empire*, pp. 11, 236; Rostovtzeff, *Social and Economic History of the Roman Empire*, p. 470; Frank, *Economic History of Rome*, pp. 476 ff; Heichelheim, *Wirtschaftsgeschichte*, p. 834.
[2] With the exception, perhaps, of the art of portraiture.

Part 5
The Middle Ages

11

The Byzantine economy

The Byzantine state

The most direct heir of ancient civilisation was Byzantium, or the New Rome of the Near East. So much was this so that Byzantine history has generally been regarded as merely a prolongation of the death agonies of the ancient world. Yet to have successfully maintained its existence for a thousand years in the face of the most harassing dangers, Byzantium must have possessed considerable sources of internal strength. And her history was by no means one long process of decay. She knew periods of recuperation and expansion, during which she lived gloriously and formed a bulwark against the barbarism that surrounded her on all sides; she was a civilising influence on the Slav and the oriental world—without a doubt the most civilised state that Europe knew from the end of the fifth to the beginning of the eleventh century.

The sources of Byzantine strength, which enabled the eastern half of the Roman Empire to survive the barbarian invasions whereas the western half succumbed, must be sought in certain favourable economic and geographical conditions.

In the first place, the eastern Empire was economically and probably also technologically more developed and richer than its western counterpart. The Roman Empire in fact always drew the major part of its revenue from this source. Eastern peoples were also accustomed and fairly inured to being systematically fleeced. This enabled the state to mobilise sufficient resources to maintain an efficient army and an effective administration, whereas the West had to resort to continually greater exactions in its attempts to achieve the same ends, with disastrous effects on its economy.

A second favourable factor was presented by the situation of the Eastern Empire, which gave it control of all the leading ports upon which the great commercial routes of the medieval world converged.

Finally, the eastern Empire was strategically better placed than the western half. On its northern frontier it had the natural protection of the lower Danube, and the capital was strongly positioned on a peninsula, which was easily insulated by a series of protective walls. The western approaches to the Empire were protected by the sea, whereas the southern and eastern frontiers were largely flanked by deserts and mountain ranges.

The Byzantines

Nor was Byzantine culture a mere continuation of that of the ancient world. Indeed, its basic features were formed largely by the fusion of Hellenistic and Roman traditions. But whereas Hellenistic civilisation was essentially western, Byzantine culture was largely oriental in character. The people, though they spoke the Greek language, did not consider themselves Greeks by descent; they would, in fact, have regarded such a designation with disfavour. The Hellenic race occupied a subordinate position in the Empire, the dominant influence being exerted by the peoples of Asia Minor, and especially by the Armenians.[1]

This New Rome was a strange combination of strength and weakness. Perhaps its greatest weakness was the character of its people. The Empire had no national unity, because it was an artificial creation that initially united twenty different nations through a single master and a single faith. The population of the capital, which might have formed an assimilating core, lacked the spiritual self-assertion that was necessary for such a function. The plebs of the New Rome, like those of the Old, cared for nothing but bread and circuses. The Hippodrome was the 'mirror of Greek society in the Middle Ages'.[2]

Religion completely dominated the spirit of the people; it controlled every aspect of their life, their literature, their art, and even their purely mundane affairs. Each event was a manifestation of the divine will; a sermon was hidden in everything. This devout, credulous, superstitious, impressionable mass lived in a constant state of mystical exaltation.

> The Byzantine lived in a world where the supernatural was omnipresent and all-powerful. His holidays were religious festivals, his performances in his circus began with the singing of hymns, his trade contracts were marked with the sign of the cross, or contained an invocation of the Trinity. . . . His wars were crusades, his emperor the vicegerent of God, while every startling event in nature was for him a special omen sent for his warning or encouragement.[3]

The whole system of administration had a sacred character, from the sacrosanct person of the emperor to the Imperial Council, which was a 'sacred consistory', and to the ministry of finance, which was referred to as the ministry of the 'sacred largesses', and issued its decrees in the form of 'divine delegations'.

In such an atmosphere science was suspect. Byzantine scholars generally displayed more religious enthusiasm than scientific knowledge or mutual tolerance. They were passionately fond of dialectical subtleties, a trait that has been ascribed to the speculative, polemic spirit inherent in the Hellenistic mind, but that had its origin rather in the profound religious ideas of the oriental peoples—the Syrians, the Armenians, the Persians, and the Egyptians. The Byzantine was worlds removed from the sober, mundane Greek of the classical period. He was superstitiously devout, subject to incomprehensible panics, a believer in miracles, magic, and astrology. Everybody from the emperor to the least of his subjects was passionately fond of theological squabbles, and the true Byzantine would willingly have sacrificed his soul to triumph in a casuistical discussion.[4]

The spirit of enterprise, already suffering from a lack of scope, was further suppressed by ideological considerations. In the course of time, the commerce of

[1] Diehl, *Byzance*, p. 1 ff, 259 ff; Findlay, *History of the Byzantine Empire*, p. 185 ff.
[2] Diehl, pp. 76, 119, 152 ff.
[3] Baynes, *The Byzantine Empire*, pp. 22 ff.
[4] Diehl, *Les Grands problèmes de l'histoire Byzantine*, chs 9, 10.

Constantinople became increasingly concentrated in the hands of foreigners, or at best, of provincials. The Armenians supplied the best business brains of the Empire. The inhabitant of the capital was a stay-at-home, who not only would not venture abroad himself but who was too cautious to invest his money in the uncertain fortunes of sea trade. A significant contribution to this lack of initiative was the emperors' policy of granting privileges to foreigners and of feeding and amusing the people. The New Rome, like the Old, was basically a centre of consumption.

The agrarian problem

A source of considerable strength to the Eastern Empire was the effective way in which, for a long time, she controlled the agrarian problem. During the later Roman Empire the masses of the rural population had been tied to the soil and, for financial reasons, the *coloni* were deprived of their freedom of movement. To relieve himself of the financial demands of the state, the small landholder put himself under the protection of a lord and, in return, placed himself and his land in the service of his patron, thus, in fact, becoming the serf of the landowner. The early Byzantine Empire became dominated by large estates; the fifth and sixth centuries, especially, being marked by the growth in the power of the great landed proprietors. Government functions, such as the collection of taxes, the maintenance of the militia, and the administration of justice, were increasingly assumed and usurped by the large landowners.

In the seventh century, during a period of grave national danger, Heraclius solved the problem of defence by the organisation of themes and the creation of military holdings, especially on the large royal domains of Asia Minor. At the same time large numbers of barbarians were settled in the Empire. A peasant militia henceforth drew from its own soil the means of livelihood and the resources for waging war. This not only afforded great relief to the budget, but had the advantage of establishing an important body of free peasants in the Byzantine provinces, which were now increasingly characterised by small free peasant holdings. A virile peasantry enabled the country for several centuries to beat back its enemies and even to assume the offensive and to reconquer large stretches of territory in Europe and in Asia.[1]

Gradually, however, these small holdings were again absorbed. The state tried in vain to stop the process. 'The peasant holding', said Romanus I in the year 935, 'supplies two important needs of the state through the payment of taxes and the rendering of military services. Both must diminish as the peasant holding disappears.' But ultimately it did disappear, for there was no other outlet for the resources of the aristocracy than investment in land. Nobles bought up the holdings of peasants and soldiers and made their owners dependent on them. Peasants even voluntarily commended themselves to landowners to escape the ever-increasing burden of taxation. The numerous agrarian laws, passed especially during the tenth century, no doubt retarded but could not prevent the process of absorption.

In the eleventh century a succession of weak emperors lost more and more ground in their struggle against the territorial aristocracy and the Church, which was also absorbing land for its monasteries and securing for it immunity from fiscal burdens. The lands of the nobility and of the Church were more or less autonomous

[1] Ostrogorsky, 'Die wirtschaftlichen und sozialen Entwicklungsgrundlagen des byzantinischen Reiches', *Vierteljahrschrift für Sozial- und Wirtschaftsgeschichte*, 1929, pp. 132 ff; *The Cambridge Economic History of Europe*, i, ch 5.

and were, as a rule, not subject to the central administration, a fact which greatly accelerated the feudalisation of the Empire. The success of the nobility upset the system of taxation and of army recruitment, which was bound up with the system of land tenure, and was the cause of perpetual social and political unrest. A rapid fall in revenue and the weakening of the powers of defence of the Empire were the direct results. The large landholders derived their power not only from their estates but also from their control of public and, especially, of military positions. Nor did they hesitate to impose their authority on the government should an emperor have the presumption to rule without their assistance. By the middle of the eleventh century the landowners and the religious hierarchy obtained complete control of the government, amid a chaos that caused the Seljuk victories. When, in the thirteenth century the crusaders conquered Byzantium, they found a system of social and economic organisation that very closely resembled that of their own countries.

The central administration

The triumph of feudalism heralded the collapse of the Eastern Empire. But in the heyday of its existence the system of government was strongly centralised. In the late Roman Empire the kingship had tended to become orientalised, the emperor sacrosanct. The *basileus* was an autocrat. In theory his authority was absolute and universal. He controlled the civil and the financial administration, state policy, justice, and even the pastimes of his people. But while in theory there was nothing that he could not do, in practice there were ways in which he could not act. These limits were imposed by the bureaucracy, the Church, and the aristocracy. The bureaucracy imposed the necessary procedures with which the emperor had to comply. The Church, although closely integrated in the state, maintained that the patriarch stood by the side of the emperor, and during the latter half of the Empire confronted him more or less as an autonomous power. Finally, from the eighth century onward, the aristocracy began to dispute power with the bureaucracy, and attempted to make and unmake emperors.[1]

The emperor ruled through a bureaucratic system which was directly and closely responsible to him. It was only with the final disintegration of the Empire that it assumed a federal character. Under capable rulers this centralisation made for efficient government, but in an atmosphere such as that which prevailed at the court of Constantinople, the administration was prone to corruption, venality was prevalent, and advancement depended more on powers of intrigue than on ability. This bureaucracy of functionaries trained in Roman tradition, though not prone to change, nevertheless also effectively precluded purely arbitrary rule.

The administrative apparatus was expensive and cumbersome, though relatively efficient. Through the economic activity of its inhabitants and the financial exploitation of its position, the state obtained resources which, in the early Middle Ages, were beyond comparison anywhere else in Europe. Customs dues and the land tax were the two main pillars of the financial system. In order to secure the treasury against a fall in revenue, if the landowner or tenant failed to meet his commitments, communities were made collectively responsible for any deficiency in the revenue. This made it obligatory for the solvent to pay for the defaulter, and the rich land to pay for the sterile, but it also often induced small independent proprietors to sell their freeholds in bad years in order to contribute their share of the tax burden.

[1] Barker, *Social and Political Thought in Byzantium*, pt 1.

The most significant distinction between the Byzantine Empire and western Europe before the eleventh century was the existence in the former of an urban civilisation, the maintenance of fairly developed internal and external trade relations, and the functioning of a monetary economy. Its fiscal resources enabled the Byzantine state to maintain services which no other contemporary power could afford, a standing army, a fleet, and an elaborate system of administration. The only remuneration that European kings could offer their retainers was the grant of land, and this led to the gradual reduction of the royal patrimony and to the continual expansion of feudalism. The strength of the Byzantine state rested on its currency, and ultimately the state failed with it. The need of more funds, however, became a growing source of concern to the government, for without money, as one emperor said, the commonwealth could not be saved.

Resources were needed primarily for defence, diplomacy, the administration and the court. By far the heaviest item of expenditure was the first. For its defence in the tenth century the empire needed an army of 140,000 men, which was nearly half of that required by the late Roman Empire as a whole. For several centuries the Byzantine army ranked as one of the best the world had ever seen. The reforms introduced by Heraclius reduced this item of expenditure by one half and secured the safety of the state for several centuries.

In addition to the direct costs of the army there were the endless wars and the cost of subsidising the barbarians. There developed in Byzantium a veritable 'science of governing barbarians', based mainly on the maxim that each man has his price. In addition the state tried, through religious influences and a rather puerile court etiquette, to assimilate and impress its neighbours. The cost of maintaining Byzantine majesty, with its public buildings, interminable ritual and present-giving, was enormous, and the finances of the state were often in a precarious position. From the point of view of practical politics most of these items of expenditure were extremely rigid, and when the financial position of the state began to decline the government economised drastically on its military and naval establishments, with disastrous results for the Empire.

The control of industry and commerce

The Byzantine administration had to be elaborate, since every detail in the public life of the state was considered a fit object for regulation. Commerce and industry especially were strictly controlled, and an extensive gild organisation left little scope for free enterprise.

Byzantine industries were organised in two main groups: those operated by the state and by individual magnates, and those run by the gilds.

Throughout Byzantine history the state played a leading part in the conduct of business enterprise. State establishments were comprised primarily of luxury trades and the manufacture of armaments, as well as of mining and minting. Especially important was the silk industry. The raw material was produced on the imperial estates and the material was carried through the various stages of dressing and weaving within the imperial palace. The highest grades of silken wares, in fact, constituted a royal monopoly, and were kept for the use of the court or sent as presents to foreign potentates. The labour in these imperial establishments had a servile or semi-servile status.

The emperor was the only large manufacturer in Constantinople, large private establishments being disallowed in the capital for political reasons. In the provinces, however, large establishments were operated by rural magnates using servile labour. The monasteries also had their own industrial undertakings, in which they employed their lay servants.

Finally, there were the typical urban handicrafts organised in gilds. These gilds were descended from the late Roman associations and their main purpose was to enable the imperial authorities to control each industry, mainly for fiscal purposes. The control of the corporations was especially close in the 'God-protected' town of Constantinople. Conditions of production and distribution, prices, profits, wages and turnover were all strictly regulated. The corporation itself bought the raw materials needed by its members, who in turn had to sell their wares at fixed prices in public places prescribed by the prefects' bureau. As far as possible middlemen were eliminated. The gilds indeed ceased legally to be hereditary groups, and the obligation of members to perform public services was abolished, though the professions in fact tended to remain on a hereditary basis.[1]

Constantinople in the Middle Ages was a paradise of monopolies, privileges, and protection. The state inspected workshops and prohibited the import of wares competitive with local products, or the export of essential foodstuffs, weapons, and luxury articles reserved for the court. To ensure the monopolistic position of the capital, foreign merchants were induced to obtain oriental goods through Constantinople, and even through the fisc. All foreigners on arriving in the capital were obliged to report to the authorities. Their period of stay was limited to three months, unless they were exempted by special treaty, and if at the end of that time they had not sold their wares, the state undertook to make arrangements for their sale. Commerce was subjected to heavy customs duties and sales taxes, and all transactions were closely scrutinised by the administration. But to these vexatious methods of control there corresponded a system of privileges and exemptions accorded to the nationals of a few favoured states, a system which in the end was to prove ruinous to the trade and finance of the country.

The Byzantine economy thus presented the picture of a mixed but highly regulated system. The state reserved the right to interfere in the minutest details of the lives of its subjects. But in spite of the universality of control, economic planning and even a consistent economic policy was conspicuously absent. The Byzantine state, in fact, inherited the Roman tradition of deliberately sacrificing the long-term interests of the economy and of its own nationals for immediate gains in revenue and for purely political ends.

Byzantine strength and decline

The Byzantine Empire owed its economic strength largely to its position, which made it the natural highway between east and west. Initially it contained all the ports upon which the great commercial routes of the world converged.

The Arab conquest of Egypt and Syria in the seventh century was indeed a serious loss. The Empire, however, recovered; the Syrian trade routes were ruined, and the Greeks were left with the commerce of the eastern Mediterranean. Constantinople now became the clearinghouse of the world, where foreigners from all countries met and mingled. Never since has the commerce of Europe centred so completely in one city. During the ninth and tenth centuries the trade of

[1] Stöckle, *Spätrömische und byzantinische Zünfte*, ch 4; *The Cambridge Economic History of Europe*, ii, 103 ff.

Byzantium was at its height. The Arabs virtually monopolised the traffic of the Indian Ocean, but the Greeks carried on a profitable coastal trade in the Mediterranean and especially in the Black Sea. The Empire imported luxuries, such as carpets and spices from the East, timber, wheat and furs from the North, and metals, both manufactured and unmanufactured, from the West. She paid for these wares with her manufactures and especially with her textiles and metal wares, as well as with her services. Trade within the Empire, on the other hand, dealt chiefly with the necessities of life. Constantinople exploited its position on the world trade routes by charging a flat rate of 10 per cent on all imports and exports passing through the straits. This provided the imperial treasury with a constant stream of wealth, until the government embarked on the suicidal policy of exempting the Italians from these dues.

Initially the bulk of the carrying trade in the Mediterranean and Black Seas was done in Greek ships. The imperial authorities encouraged the enterprise of their citizens during the first centuries by the publication of a commercial code, and as late as the eighth century they still favoured the development of the mercantile marine. But gradually they seem to have adopted an entirely different policy. Instead of encouraging the citizens to take an active part in commerce, they were satisfied to play the purely passive role of providing an emporium for foreigners. The government seems to have believed that it would increase the power and prestige of the Empire if foreigners were encouraged to visit the capital and to marvel at its luxury and wealth. This error in judgment was to cost the country dearly when the active peoples of the West aimed, not at supplementing, but at supplanting Constantinople as the guardian of the commerce between East and West.

Towards the end of the eleventh century Byzantine trade began to undergo drastic changes from which it never recovered. The Seljuk conquest of Asia Minor robbed the capital of the source of its grain supply and the state of the bulk of the solid peasant population, which was one of the chief pillars of its strength. At the same time the emperor was induced to call in the help of the Venetian fleet and finances against the threats of a Norman invasion. Venice was compensated by the exemption of her merchants from customs dues within the Empire—a right subsequently extended to other Italian towns as well. Thus, whereas Byzantine nationals had to pay the duty of 10 per cent, the privileged Italians could export and import free of duty. The result was that the carrying trade passed almost entirely into Italian hands and that the treasury was deprived of its main source of revenue.

Despite this shortsighted policy, Constantinople was still prosperous in the middle of the twelfth century. But towards the end of the century she rapidly declined. During the last two centuries of its existence the Empire was a financial wreck. At the beginning of the fifteenth century the best quarter of Constantinople was in ruins. The population deserted the capital and the treasury contained nothing but 'dust and air'. The royal jewels were sold and the emperor fell into the hands of usurers: to such a state of humiliation had the once omnipotent emperor of the East been reduced. The Empire, in fact, was all but dead when the Turks gave it the *coup de grâce* and were welcomed by the population as deliverers. Yet, strangely enough, these last centuries witnessed a great intellectual revival, which cast a brilliant flicker on the dying Empire and heralded the transmission to western Europe of the humanism of the Renaissance.[1]

---

[1] Diehl, *Les Grands problèmes de l'histoire Byzantine*, ch 3; *Byzance*, pp. 223 ff; *Venise*, pp. 23 ff.

12
The Islamic economies

The spread of Islam

Another important link between the ancient and the modern world was that formed by Islamic civilisation. From time immemorial Arabia had served as the commercial corridor between East and West. But her cultural renaissance and political expansion began with Muhammed in the seventh century. This expansion was unique in the history of the world. For the first time the innumerable quarrelsome Arab tribes were given solidarity and leadership by a militant faith, which also instilled sufficient discipline to make them a formidable and aggressive fighting force. The vital appeal of the Muslim movement for these hungry desert nomads, however, came especially from the age-old lust for loot and power. In the East, both the Persian and the Byzantine empires reeled back before the onset. Neither the Syrians nor the Egyptians derived much benefit from the Byzantine connection. They served as intermediaries between East and West, were economically independent, and therefore resented the heavy tax burdens that they had to bear to maintain the central government at Constantinople, which contributed little in return but which involved them in continual warfare with their neighbours. In the West, religious persecution and internal dissension in Spain, and the financial exploitation of Sicily, rendered both countries easy victims to Muslim invasion. Twenty years after the death of the Prophet, the Caliphate occupied a domain half as big as the continent of Europe, and a century later it stretched from the Atlantic to the Indus.

The Muslim movement initially brought about a considerable improvement in the condition of the masses. The conquered peoples were treated with a consideration that had seldom been meted out to them by their Christian rulers. Everywhere tariffs and taxes were reduced and the land more equally distributed. Consideration for the common people was shown especially in the conquest of Sicily. The subjugation of Andalusia, says Lane Poole, was a blessing; the great estates were divided into peasant holdings, the taxes were reduced, and the slaves were emancipated on a large scale. Such measures facilitated the spread of Islam. Everywhere a new love of life and work became apparent among the people; population and production increased and the towns flourished.

The economic vitality of the Empire was greatly stimulated by this liberal policy and by the fusion of peoples and cultures it brought about. Through their conquests the Muslims entered into the heritage of both the Hellenistic and the Iranian worlds. To this new heritage the Arab contributed little besides his religion and his language. The vast majority of the men that built up the greatness of Islamic civilisation were not Arabs by birth; many were not even Muslims. The centres of civilisation shifted to the peripheries of the Islamic world: to Iraq, to Persia, and to Spain. Under the Abbasids the treatment of the client peoples showed a marked improvement; race amalgamation proceeded apace, and converted Persians, Christians, and Jews appeared in the highest positions. Commerce and industry were largely monopolised by the subjected peoples. The Arabs allowed themselves the luxury of being served by clients and non-believers, and it was only with their gradual urbanisation and impoverishment that they took to clerical and industrial pursuits as a means of making a livelihood.[1]

There are few movements more remarkable in the history of civilisation than the sudden passion for learning and travel that seized the whole Muslim world. A triumphant and militant religion might have been expected to stifle independent spiritual initiative; but the reverse was the case. The obligation of undertaking pilgrimages to Mecca and Medina, as well as the extended trade relations, brought into contact the most diverse elements. The mosques became the universities of Islam, and have remained so to this day. They were well provided with not only theological but also philosophical and scientific works, for the early Muslim Church was far more tolerant than the Christian. At a time when western Europe was steeped in barbarism, the Abbasids surrounded themselves with scholars and spent large sums on the equipment of libraries and the dissemination of learning. Under the protection of the court of Baghdad, philosophy, literature, and science flourished. In the West, Cordova, next to Constantinople, was the largest and most enlightened town of Europe. For more than four centuries the intellectual leadership of the world passed to the Islamic peoples.

The service performed by Islam to western civilisation was essentially to have preserved and developed Hellenistic culture, to have added to it important contributions from the East, and to have transmitted these to the West. Muslim thought lacked the spontaneous originality of Hellenistic science. But it perfected that science when it had ceased to be a living force, preserved it at a time when western Europeans had relapsed into barbarism, and transmitted it at a time when Europe was preparing the way for its cultural renaissance. Their original contributions were essentially in the sphere of mathematics. But even here their importance lay more in the transmission of the use of ciphers than in the development of algebra and analytical geometry. Through their transmission of the Hindu invention of the principle of position in the writing of numbers, they became the founders of the arithmetic of everyday life. Of the whole science of mathematics this is no doubt the factor that has contributed most to the general progress of culture, and it must be regarded as one of the basic inventions on which modern civilisation rests.

Commerce

The great sphere of practical activity of the Muslim lay in the field of commerce. From time immemorial Arabia had served as the intermediary between East and West. It was only in the middle of the first century A.D. that the monsoons were

[1] Mez, *The Renaissance of Islam*, pp. 39 ff, 477 ff; von Kremer, *Kulturgeschichte des Orients unter den Chalifen*, ii. 178 ff.

discovered, and that a regular trade by sea developed between Egypt and India. The Arabs naturally resented the opening up of this direct route, and the Romans had to send expeditions to prevent their interference with trading ships. But with the decay of Byzantine navigation in the Red Sea, about a century before the beginning of the Islamic movement, the Indian trade reverted to Arab mariners, and the merchants of Mecca resumed their profitable mediation in the exchange of the products of Yemen, India and Africa for those of the Near East.[1]

The position of the country and the barrenness of the soil made trade and piracy practically the only profitable occupations of the people. Strabo described every Arab as being by nature a merchant and, generally, a thief. It was in the cosmo-politan centre of Mecca, which had displaced the ancient Palmyra, that Islam was born. The leading tribe of the town, and that to which the Prophet himself belonged, was the Quraysh, so called 'from trading and getting profit'.[2] The Prophet himself engaged in commerce, which contributed to the prestige enjoyed by merchants as a class. The attitude of Muslim society was therefore more favour-able to the development of business enterprise than that of the Graeco-Roman world, with its contempt of the banausic.

The enormous expansion of the Caliphate had a stimulating effect on the distribution of goods. The wars of Rome and Persia had checked the flow of commerce between East and West. Now a united empire stretched from the Atlantic to the steppes of Central Asia. Over this whole area there was a removal of barriers—national, religious, and economic—which gave much greater scope to commercial intercourse. The internal tolls and tariffs, the numerous local taxes and exactions were initially removed to a large extent, though they soon reappeared. This trade reached its greatest amplitude with the establishment of a large centre of consumption at Baghdad. From this central sphere, and from other large centres of Muslim culture, commerce radiated in concentric circles of decreasing intensity to East Africa, Canton, North China, and Central Asia, to the Baltic by way of the Volga, and to Spain, Morocco, and the Gold Coast.

Besides the interregional trade in luxuries an important regional trade in bulky goods developed in areas where cheap river transport was available. A considerable differentiation in the functions of the different merchants also seems to have existed and a network of correspondents, brokers and transport agents seems to have grown up in the larger centres.

Commerce and the allocation of resources

With such well-developed commercial relations, the question naturally arises as to how far economic activities in the Islamic economies were coordinated by the market rather than by government prescription.

The Caliphate indeed did not have at its disposal a highly developed bureaucratic apparatus. Thus the administration of the provinces was largely decentralised, and the coordination that was effected was mainly fiscal. The Empire also soon disinte-grated into a number of independent states. But all these constituent parts were heirs to archaic, Byzantine, and late Roman traditions. Private commercial activity was therefore simply superimposed on the existing agromanagerial economies, with the result that directed economies of a loose type tended to emerge.

---

[1] O'Leary, *Arabia Before Mohammed*, pp. 79 ff.
[2] *Ibid.*, pp. 183 ff.

Thus the central administration was carefully maintained in regard to the system of irrigation, and the vast bulk of the population was engaged in irrigation farming. A very large part of the resources of all these economies, a proportion that was eventually no smaller than that which had been mobilised in Byzantine times, was also collected by the state. But where the state appropriated such a large share of the free-flowing resources of the community, and where the controls exercised were so pervasive and arbitrary, the scope of the market as an allocative mechanism must have been greatly reduced.

Commerce was largely in private hands, the typical representative being the small itinerant or bazaar merchant, who was associated with craft industry. Industry also was organised on a typical handicraft basis, with small workshops and perambulatory craftsmen.

Muslim trade, however, was confronted with formidable material, moral and institutional obstacles. Owing to the long distances and the generally intractable nature of the territory, the problems of communication were immense. On the few rivers a heavy traffic in bulky goods could indeed be economically conveyed, but over the rest of the area goods had to be carried by camel and pack-mule along desert tracks. The Roman and Sassanian highways soon fell into disrepair, and in the tenth century the last permanent bridges on the Tigris collapsed. Navigation was confined to non-communicating seas, and because of the shortage of timber and iron, the ships were extremely frail and unseaworthy. In addition to these material barriers there were constraints of a moral order. Objections against the taking of interest was a specially serious embarrassment to Muslim investors and money-lenders, though not to Jewish traders and financiers. Even more serious were the institutional factors that impeded the development of a genuine market economy.

Because of these difficulties, interregional trade was confined almost exclusively to luxuries. A proverb of the ninth century says: 'The best trade is in cambric, the best industry that in coral.' From Africa the Muslims obtained slaves, ivory, and gold; from Europe slaves, furs, arms, lumber and precious metals; from the east silks, cotton, indigo, spices and drugs. The Muslim world exported textiles—to which the words muslin, damask, and baldachin testify—carpets, paper and incense. Muslims were the leading silk-mercers of the medieval world, in spite of the fact that the Prophet had especially forbidden the wearing of silken garments.

Because of the nature of its wares, this trade must to a very considerable extent have been for the account of the royal households and their entourage, with their intense need for precious metals and exotic novelties. The needs of the royal and military establishments were also met by large state industrial undertakings, whose size contrasted strongly with the small handicrafts that provided for the requirements of the lay population. In addition, industrial products—cloth, clothing and carpets—were delivered by way of taxes, and many private traders must have fed on the luxury of the court. In Fatimid Egypt a very large share of the trade was monopolised by the government, which owned textile establishments, most of the ships, and all of the 20,000 shops and stalls that are said to have existed in Cairo in the middle of the eleventh century.

The administration

The rapid growth of their Empire confronted the Arabs with formidable problems of administration for which their past history and tribal organisation had ill prepared them. But they found in the conquered provinces a large body of trained officials. They therefore chose the line of least resistance and left the system of administration virtually unchanged. An elaborate and centrally organised bureaucratic system, such as that of the Byzantine Empire, the Caliphate did not possess. The local systems of administration in the villages, towns, and provinces were left largely to themselves, as long as they contributed their share to the revenue of the central government. Initially, in fact, governors were nothing more than tax-farmers. Nor were the finances centralised. Each province formed an independent tax area and only surpluses were remitted to the capital.

But gradually the Islamic system of administration became centralised and under the Abbasids and Fatimids the Caliphate became a despotic and bureaucratic state. The caliph, as the successor of the Prophet, became the shadow of God on earth, his power limited only by the prescriptions of the Koran. He was surrounded by a numerous court—members of his family, descendants of the Prophet, and the higher echelons of the bureaucracy.

To head the administration the Abbasids created the office of the vizier, who controlled virtually the whole machinery of state. He appointed and discharged officials, administered the finances of the Empire, directed the internal administration of the state and its relations with the provinces, and acted as controller of the royal household. Under him there was a complex of government departments, which dealt with finance, justice, defence, the central and provincial administrations, the postal service and so forth. These were administered by a numerous body of officials, who directed and controlled every sphere of the economy.

Initially the principal distinctive characteristic of the bureaucracy was its strong emphasis on service to the rulers, who, in turn, exercised close personal supervision to ensure its effective functioning. Under the later Abbasids, however, there was a clear tendency for the administration to subordinate the interests of the rulers and the state to their own self-interest. Typical symptoms of this tendency were, in the first place, the multiplication of the number of officials and, in the second place, their neglect of the interests of the community. Accordingly complaints multiplied that only the higher classes were considered by the bureaucracy as worthy of consideration. The mass of people, on the contrary, was regarded 'as mere scum, a marshy brook and lower animals, who knew of nothing save food and sleep'.[1]

At the same time the administration became corrupt. Everything had to be paid for, even the very office itself. Pious people associated officials with sinners in much the same way as the New Testament connected publicans and sinners. Chroniclers were amazed to find high officers honest. Officials who were suspected and even convicted of malpractices were often left in their posts, and when they were punished, their more successful colleagues opened subscription lists to lighten the burden of their penalty. The highest officials seem in fact to have been used by rulers as sponges. They were allowed to absorb as much wealth as they could at the expense of the public and even the treasury, only to be squeezed dry again finally by the threat of confiscation or capital punishment.

A typical concomitant of this development was the progressive inroads made on the liberty and property of individuals. Thus the functions of the postal organisation, an institution inherited from the previous régimes, were extended to include espionage on an extensive scale and on all classes of society. The development of espionage into one of the main instruments of government was typical of the orientalisation of the Caliphate. No official was trusted, and even the Caliph's own family was placed under strict surveillance. The police formed an important part of

[1] Mez, *The Renaissance of Islam*, p. 148.

the intelligence service, and their duties included interference in the minutest details of daily life. In every town a multiplicity of local officials, magistrates, tax-gatherers and stewards of public lands still further reduced the liberty of the subject.

Another typical trait was the insecurity of the individual and his property. A portion of the property of the rich was usually confiscated during his lifetime. He who escaped this fate could be sure to lose it after death. The death of a well-to-do man was therefore a veritable catastrophe to his family and friends.

> Woe to him whose father dies rich! Long does he remain incarcerated in mis-fortune's home, the unrighteous officer saying unto him: How do I know that you are the rich man's son? And when he rejoins: 'My neighbours and many other know me', they pluck his moustache one by one, assault him, knock him about, until strength ebbs away from him and he faints. And in the dungeon he languishes until he flings his purse to them.[1]

Every artifice was accordingly used by the rich to thwart the treasury in its designs on their fortunes. They deposited their properties with different persons and showed them in their books under false names; they buried their treasures in the most inaccessible places, preferably in the desert. Such an economy must of course inevitably have undermined its own foundations.

Decline of the Caliphate

The political unity of the Empire was shortlived. The rapid collapse of the Caliphate was, indeed, as remarkable as its rise to power. The Arab, like a true nomad, has always shown a fundamental incapacity for organisation and discipline. The old quarrels of the tribes in Arabia were resumed with far greater vehemence and with disastrous effects in the conquered countries. The vast and loosely-knit domain was also too unwieldy to be ruled from a single centre. The various consti-tuent parts, differing in race and social conditions, and divided by religious sects, broke up almost as easily as they had become united. Spain declared her indepen-dence in 755 when the Empire was at the height of its power. Under Haroun al-Raschid, Fez, Morocco, and Tunis seceded; later, Egypt and Syria broke away. Finally the Caliph retained only Baghdad and a part of Iraq, all that remained of the once proud Empire that had stretched from the Atlantic to the Indus.

The break-up of the Empire brought the Caliphate into serious financial diffi-culties. It had no credit, while the arbitrary confiscation of property and the numerous impositions of the customs burdened commerce and industry. In the tenth century the farming of taxes became general. In the place of the standing army and the centralised government, a system of military fiefs grew up, whose holders provided both troops and tribute. The Empire became feudalised, though the feudalism of the East was something different from that of the West, because of the fundamentally different valuation of human personality, and of the relationship of man to man, and of man to property.[2]

The political decline was accompanied by a corresponding intellectual stagna-tion. Religious tolerance of the sciences gave way in the twelfth century to persecu-tion, 'because they lead to loss of belief in the origin of the world and the creator'.

[1] Quoted, *ibid.*, p. 113.
[2] Becker, *Zeitschrift der Deutschen Morgenländischen Gesellschaft*, i, 32 ff.

The initial spiritual impetus of Islam had spent itself and the movement had become too effete to impose itself by its own inherent strength. Henceforth Islamic students merely commented, reproduced and summarised.

At this stage Islamic science was transmitted to Europe, a process that continued well into the sixteenth century. Muslim culture pervaded the medieval universities. What medieval Europeans knew of Greek philosophy and science was learned principally from Latin translations of Arabic treatises. 'From the twelfth century everyone in the West who had any taste for science, some desire for light, turned to the East or the Moorish West.' It was only with the Renaissance that the Muslim inspiration ceased. Europeans had become sophisticated enough to rely on their own resources.[1]

[1] *The legacy of Islam*, pp. 344 ff.

13

The early Middle Ages: manorial and collective controls

c. last quarter of the fifth century A.D. to
c. the tenth century A.D.

Effect of the migrations

From the time of the decline of the ancient world Eurasian humanity had been on the march once more. The ultimate source of this movement, as of all the migrations that had hitherto periodically surged against the civilisations of the East and the West, must be sought in the seething masses of Central Asia. Dyked back by the great line of frontier defences constructed by the Chinese emperors in north China and eastern Turkestan, the Huns streamed westward until the accumulated impact of the peoples that they set in motion piled up against the barriers of the Roman Empire.[1]

The Rhine-Danubian frontier had stemmed the westward flow of Germanic peoples for centuries. Gradually the adjoining territories had developed into a pressure area. This force was relieved by the safety valve of peaceful penetration into the Empire, as well as by the settlement of the eastern tribes in the regions from the Baltic to the Dnieper and the Black Sea. These tribes were the first to feel the onset. By the third century the Huns had driven the Sarmatians from the Volga region, and in the following century they invaded Europe. In A.D. 375 they overwhelmed the Ostrogoths, who were forced to seek refuge within the Empire. Soon the frontiers were forced by numerous other tribes, for the decaying Empire, no longer able effectively to defend itself, acted like an irresistible magnet on all the Barbarians precariously poised on its frontiers.

During the next few centuries Slav peoples pressed on the inhabitants of central Europe from the Baltic to the Balkans. In the seventh century the Arab drive to the West began, and early in the eighth century the Muslim invaders swept over Spain and threatened Gaul. The western Mediterranean became a Saracenic sea, and the plundered coasts were effectively closed to Christian intercourse. Finally, towards the end of the eighth century, a wave of Nordic barbarians threatened to reduce parts of Europe to a condition of even more complete confusion. After remaining quiescent for centuries in their lands around the Baltic, the Vikings were suddenly seized by a violent eruption of aggressive energy that carried them far beyond the

[1] According to Huntington a dry phase set in temporarily in the second century B.C., then persisted from the third to the eighth century A.D., reaching its greatest intensity in the seventh century. It had its most severe effects in Asia, in the latitudes 30° to 45°, from where it expanded west-south-west across Europe.

limits of their own countries. In the course of the ninth and tenth centuries their plundering expeditions and colonising and business enterprises extended from the coast of America to the Caspian, and from the Arctic to the Mediterranean.[1]

Very divergent and contradictory views have been expressed in regard to the effect of the barbarian invasions on western Europe. The Roman churchmen, to whom the Empire was a question of faith and Roman civilisation synonymous with the spiritual salvation of mankind, undoubtedly drew an exaggerated picture of the destruction brought about by the invasions. If, on the other hand, a historian like Dopsch is to be believed, the Germanic migrations involved hardly anything more than the peaceful penetration of the Empire.[2] The Belgian historian, Pirenne, has attempted a compromise between these views. The invasions indeed brought about a retrogression in every sphere of life; but the ruralisation of the Empire was a gradual process. The final transition from the ancient to the medieval world was caused by the spread of Islam, which disrupted the unity of the Mediterranean world that had been the characteristic feature of the civilisation of antiquity. The Mediterranean now ceased to serve as the thoroughfare of commerce and culture, and western Europe was forced to live on its own resources. For the first time in history the centre of European life shifted from the Mediterranean to north-western Europe. The decadent Merovingian dynasty was succeeded by a new line, the Carolingian, which was settled in the Germanic north. Up to the middle of the eighth century the medieval economy was still more or less a continuation of the economic system of the ancient world. But the Mediterranean coast of Gaul, hitherto the most progressive part of the country, now became the most desolate. The north, as a result, impressed its character on the period. The commerce of the two most progressive areas of western Europe, the towns of northern Italy and those of the Low Countries, was either greatly hampered or completely destroyed. The classical tradition was shattered because commerce was brought virtually to a standstill. Western Europe was reduced to a primitive subsistence economy.

> If we consider that in the Carolingian epoch the minting of gold had ceased, that lending money at interest was prohibited, that there was no longer a class of professional merchants, that Oriental products (papyrus, spices, silk) were no longer imported, that the circulation of money was reduced to the minimum, that laymen could no longer read or write, that the taxes were no longer organized, and that the towns were merely fortresses, we can say without hesitation that we are confronted with a civilisation which had retrogressed to the purely agricultural stage; which no longer needed commerce, credit, and regular exchange for the maintenance of the social fabric.[3]

Naturally it is extremely difficult to interpret the scanty archaeological and documentary evidence that has survived. It must not be forgotten, however, that from the fourth century western economic life had assumed an essentially domainal character, and when the Saracens appeared in the Mediterranean the western European economy was already in an advanced stage of stagnation. Thus the minting of money in the Merovingian state was no longer effectively controlled by the public authorities. This royal prerogative, like so many others such as the collection of the public revenue and the administration of justice, had been surren-

[1] Dawson, *The Making of Europe*, chs 5, 13; Moss, *The Birth of the Middle Ages*, chs 2, 15; Anderson, *Viking Enterprise*.
[2] Dopsch, *Grundlagen der Europaischen Kulturentwicklung*, i, chs 3, 4.
[3] Pirenne, *Mohammed and Charlemagne*, p. 242.

dered to various other bodies. 'Never in our history', says Robert Latouche, 'has the conception of the state known so complete an eclipse'.[1]

It would also seem that Pirenne exaggerated the violent break in economic development that occurred in the eighth and ninth centuries. No doubt the commercial links with the East and the trade in luxuries suffered as a result of the Muslim conquests. But rural settlement and production, which were of greater importance than the trade in luxuries, do not seem to have suffered. The large number of local markets and the fact that they were held weekly also suggest that there were still many people who satisfied their basic needs by the sale and purchase of goods.

But the incontrovertible fact is that the invasions did accelerate all the forces, already so strong within the decaying empire, which tended towards the clericalisation of culture, the ruralisation of economic life and the feudalisation of the state. Ancient civilisation had been essentially connected with city life. This tradition, though divested of its specific cultural, political and economic significance, was perpetuated during the early Middle Ages in the Byzantine and Islamic empires. In the West it was different. Roman institutions might have partially survived in outward form, but their content and significance changed. Thus many towns might have continued to exist as architectural facts; only the Germans, who were unaccustomed to town life, did not take up their abode in them, and they especially put an end to the system by which landowners regularly lived in towns. What had remained of municipal organisation and the autonomy of the free citizen class in the late Roman Empire ceased to exist. Political control passed to the king, the Church, and the nobility. The fact that no new town was founded in this period is incontrovertible proof of economic stagnation.

The feudal system

Historians are agreed that in Europe, outside the Byzantine Empire and Moorish Spain, there was, in the course of the early Middle Ages, a very great measure of reversion to a system of self-sufficing natural economies. Everywhere culture, to a very large extent, came to have a primitive rural and purely local character. The means of communications, towns, trade, and the independent crafts came to acquire little significance because the conditions for their proper functioning had been destroyed.

With the undermining of the economic foundations of the state, the other aspects of the classical tradition also crumbled away. Owing to the decline of commerce and the breakdown of the currency, the impost disappeared, and revenue from indirect taxes dwindled away. The kings no longer had at their disposal any regular resources apart from the revenues of their domains. The basis of the royal power became purely rural. Not only did the royal government come to depend on the exploitation of its domain, it became scarcely distinguishable from it. The reversion to a rural basis, on the other hand, greatly increased the power of the nobility. Royalty became more and more a mere form, and seignorial authority an ever greater reality. Communities became completely dependent on the owners of the soil, and the state dissolved into a disorganised mass of regional units. Power became concentrated in the hands of anyone strong enough to defend himself and his dependants.

[1] Latouche, *The Birth of Western Economy*, p. 129.

The one principle of the new society was the law of force and its correlative—the need for protection. Personal freedom was no longer a privilege, for the man without a lord became a man without a protector. Thus fealty and homage became the universal social relations, and the ownership of land became bound up with a complex of rights and obligations, both personal, military and juridical. . . . In short, the state and its public authority had become absorbed in the local territorial power. Political authority and private property were merged together in the new feudal relation, and the rights of jurisdiction and the duty of military service ceased to be universal public obligations and became annexed to the land as privileges of a particular tenure.[1]

This 'feudal disintegration of the state' was the necessary result of the ruralisation of relations and the attempt of kings to use their domains as a fund from which permanent grants were made to secure service and support—a process which continually narrowed the basis upon which their authority rested. Thus as 'parents, midwives or helpless spectators' the rulers of the early Middle Ages presided over the disintegration of their own power, a process in which economic direction became inextricably fused with the managerial powers of the great landowners.[2]

The village community

The basis of rural organisation was formed by the village community. People seem generally to have lived in nucleated villages since the dawn of agriculture, a village community consisting of a group of persons living together and cultivating a number of arable fields, dividing the meadows between them, and pasturing their cattle on the surrounding waste, to which the community claimed rights as far as the boundaries of neighbouring communities.

Initially, very extensive methods of cultivation were used, but gradually, in the course of the early Middle Ages, the three-field system spread throughout Europe. Under this system the arable land was sharply separated from the forest and the commonage. Instead of the modern rotation of crops and the use of manures, the method of alternate fallow and cultivation was used. For this purpose the arable land was divided into irregular plots or strips, usually an acre in extent, spread all over the three arable fields.[3] An individual peasant might thus own ten, twenty, or more strips, all separated from one another. Besides the cultivated fields, the village generally possessed pastures, woods and a meadow. These were common property, though as a rule the right to their use was in proportion to the members' share of the arable land.

The three-field system of husbandry represented an important improvement on methods of temporary cropping and even on the two-course system which had never been entirely displaced in antiquity, in that it involved a more intensive exploitation of land, a better distribution of the risks of bad harvests over the different seasons, and a better utilisation of labour during the course of the year. The dismemberment of property, however, which followed on closer settlement and continued inheritance, made the peasants highly dependent on one another for the improvement or regulation of agriculture, and involved the handling of the village community on a communal basis. Methods of cultivation therefore allowed

---

[1] Dawson, p. 267.
[2] *The Cambridge Economic History of Europe*, iii, 290 ff.
[3] The long strips characteristic of medieval settlement are usually ascribed to the use of the heavy plough.

little scope for innovation or improvement. The farmer was greatly restricted in the rotation of his crops and the type of tillage: the time when sowing and harvesting should begin, the crops that had to be sown, or the rotation to be followed were all distinctly prescribed.

The manor

The village community was only one element of the medieval rural economy. The other constituent was the manor. This seignorial aspect was, no doubt, as old as the communal one, though it has often been asserted, without sufficient evidence, that the lordship was of relatively recent origin, and that it was superimposed on an originally lordless community. What is true is that the storm and stress that accompanied the gradual collapse of the central authority during the early medieval period brought a far greater uniformity into the manorial system. Thus the seignorial element was present in Teutonic society, but the greater social and economic differentiation of western Europe, as well as changes in military technique, acted unfavourably on central Europe to which the king, the Church, and the nobility transferred the same institutions. The period was marked by the widespread debasement and elimination of the class of common freemen, the majority of the rural population being reduced to the state, halfway between a free and a servile status, known as serfdom. The process was slow. In the days of Charlemagne, the extent of the land in possession of smallholders and free communities still exceeded that of the great domains. After him the manor became the dominant type of rural organisation, though free village communities and free peasant holders never ceased to exist.

The powers of the lord consisted not only in the possession of land but also in rights over the labour of men and in the appropriation of political and, especially, of judicial authority. The assertion of these rights and powers was the result of the collapse of the central authority. The collection of taxes and the administration of justice were relegated to, or usurped by, local landed authorities. The duties and obligations formerly owed to the state were now converted into the private and personal services owed to the lord of the land. Property and authority became blended in the functions of government. The manor became in a very real sense the essence of the feudal system. It furnished, on the other hand, many of the services of the central government, such as the administration of justice and the maintenance of roads, and made important contributions to the defence of the country.

The inhabitants of the manor were dependent, in varying degrees, on the lord. But during the formative centuries of feudalism there was a levelling of social conditions, with the result that the majority of the rural population was gradually reduced to a state of serfdom. The average serf was a villager installed on a holding. He was bound to the land, a condition that he had inherited from the Roman colonate. He contributed regular payments in services and kind, as well as extraordinary payments at marriage, at the birth of a child, or at death, which were all signs of his personal servitude. Serfs therefore represented the main asset of the manor and, in order to increase their power and possessions, landowners tried to surround themselves with as many dependants as possible, and the exerting of pressure or the seizure of control from above to secure this end was no doubt as common as the search for protection from below.

The organisation of the manor

The new landowning class was represented by the king, the lay nobility, and the Church. Few of these landlords, except originally the monasteries, took a personal share in the cultivation of the soil. 'Not even the poorest of them—and some were very poor—would do other than "honourable" service, fighting or praying. Indeed, it may be said that leisure was the economic objective of the feudal landlord.'[1]

This attitude was reflected in the organisation of the manor. The cultivation of the lord's land was simply assimilated to that of the village community, thus assuring him of an income with a minimum of effort on his part. The lord lived on the deliveries in kind of the serfs and by means of their *corvées*. The scope and character of these services were minutely regulated by tradition. This militated against the rational exploitation of the manor and accounted for the willingness with which services were later commuted for money payments. The land of the lord lay interspersed among the plots of the peasants. This scattered ownership was accepted; with the conditions prevailing at the time there would indeed have been little advantage in rounding off the seignorial estate. The administration of even the largest estates was also completely decentralised. Different manors belonging to the same lord existed side by side, but in complete independence of one another. The owner simply moved from manor to manor, consuming the surplus of each place.

In the same way industrial production was incorporated in the village economy. The serf supplied finished fabrics as feudal dues, or merely provided the raw materials, which were then worked up in the manor house by skilled craftsmen, by the servants of the house, or by serfs. Since work on these agrarian estates was largely seasonal, there was an extra incentive to adapt the *corvée* to the crafts. But no rational division of labour was introduced. Specific functions such as baking or brewing, for example, were not relegated to particular individuals but were performed by different persons in rotation. The more basic needs of the manor were easily supplied by the local economy. With the decline of the cities, skilled craftsmen became scarce and mostly itinerant. They had to be obtained by special contract and even by diplomatic means. It was ultimately only in the monasteries and in a few lay manors that arts such as the painting of glass, enamelling, bookbinding, and the making of jewellery and musical instruments were preserved.

Basic self-sufficiency determined the organisation of the manor. There was little incentive for either the lord or the peasant to make the soil yield more than was necessary for his subsistence. The walls of the lord's stomach, in the words of Karl Marx, set the limits to his exploitation of the serf. Immediate economic needs were the only guiding incentives. What was produced was largely consumed *in loco*, and surpluses were spent mainly on the support of retainers. The attempt to secure a safe and sufficient subsistence was the leading motive of the manorial economy. Hence the disposition towards the traditional fixation of dues and the willingness later to commute services for rental charges.

Trade

The most important sources of what interregional commercial activity was left in the early Middle Ages were located on the fringes of western Europe. The earliest intermediaries in the trade of north-western Europe were the Frisians. Most of their trade seems to have flowed along the Rhine; cloth, fish and other goods were

[1] Sombart, *Der moderne Kapitalismus*, i, 61.

carried up the river to pay for the grain and wine that they brought back in return.

Even more important in the trade of the north than the Frisians were the Scandinavians. During the ninth and tenth centuries they seem to have crossed the central Russian watershed regularly on their way from the Baltic to the Black Sea, and from there to Byzantium. To the Near East they exported honey, furs and, above all, slaves; or they served as mercenaries in the Byzantine army. To northern Europe they brought back spices, wines, textiles and metal work.

Nor was all exchange between East and West severed in the Mediterranean during this period. Although it is impossible from the meagre sources that have been left to determine quantitatively the scope and significance of the commerce that remained, it would seem that oriental luxuries, and especially textiles, oil and spices, were still available to the West, and that Europe paid for these imports with commodities such as timber, iron, and slaves.

The Italian towns were the first to exploit the advantage of their central position. Gradually the Italians displaced the Greeks, Syrians, and Jews as middlemen in the trade of the Mediterranean. The Italo-Byzantine towns, and especially Venice, on the margin of and almost outside Italy, served as border markets between the Byzantine East, the Muslim South, and the Catholic West, and during the next period they were the first to take advantage of the great increase in economic activity.

Certain types of specialised merchants, such as those attached to the lay and ecclesiastical lords, the importers of oriental luxuries, dealers in foodstuffs, and slave traders remained in existence during this period, though their numbers were probably small and their functions often undifferentiated in character.

Local trade seems to have suffered less than interregional trade. The larger estates did indeed tend to become self-sufficient in regard to their basic needs. But certain manufactured goods, essential materials such as salt, and even agricultural products such as grain and wine had to be obtained from outside. Exchanges also continued to take place between estates, either through merchants or manorial officials or by the producers themselves. Some communities even in the early Middle Ages specialised as sheep-farmers, fishermen, charcoal burners, saltmakers, and miners. Some trade was also essential to agricultural areas capable of variegated cultivation and a high degree of economic self-sufficiency. Even large estates and villages had to draw certain supplies, such as salt, iron, or textiles, from outside. Specialisation within the manor must also have led to exchanges. These transactions were no doubt rudimentary in form, but from the end of the tenth century onwards trade relations—both local and distant—became the basis on which commerce, and economic life in general, could enter upon a period of rapid and cumulative expansion.[1]

[1] *The Cambridge Economic History of Europe*, ii, 174 ff; 257 ff.

14

The central Middle Ages

The expansive economy of the central Middle Ages
and the movement towards economic freedom

c. eleventh century to c. thirteenth century

A period of expansion

In the eleventh century the economic development of western Europe, which had
been disrupted and retarded by the decline of the Roman Empire and by the
migrations of the early Middle Ages, could be resumed once more, and the following three centuries constituted one of the formative periods of the world's history.
This was evident in every field of human endeavour. As far as the spiritual scene
was concerned the central Middle Ages

> was above all an age of rational and coherent advance. In every sphere of life and
> thought, an amazing variety of complicated detail was fitted into a general
> system that was at once firm, authoritative, and grounded in rational inquiry and
> widespread consent. We can observe this in law, natural science, and in the
> practical art of government no less than in theology and philosophy; and the
> great artistic achievements of the age are a reflection of the same confident
> spirit.[1]

Politically it was an era of comparative peace. This must undoubtedly be
attributed very largely to the expansive forces that operated during the period. But
an important causal factor was also the development of the idea of a universal
human society that functioned as an integral part of a divinely ordered universe
centred in the universal Empire and especially in the universal or Catholic Church.
The central Middle Ages was indeed a period in the history of western Europe when
the Church could reasonably claim to exercise an overriding political authority over
all lay governments. Further contributory factors to the maintenance of peace were
the constraints imposed on extensive warfare by the nature of the military obligations of vassals both in regard to time and place and the severe limitations imposed
by the meagre taxing authority of rulers. All these factors combined to make
prolonged offensive campaigns within western Christendom impossible and the
social impact of the wars of the period insignificant.

In the economic field the central Middle Ages was above all an age of expansion.
Agricultural production increased, commerce and industry revived, the opening up
of new mines augmented the supply of precious metals and money came to
permeate economic transactions to an ever-increasing extent. The waste lands of the

[1] Southern, *Western Society and the Church in the Middle Ages*, p. 42.

west were colonised, forests cleared, marshes drained, and new lands brought into cultivation. A large part of the Netherlands was won from the sea. In the twelfth and thirteenth centuries the process of settlement had gone so far that the surplus population broke out of the confines of what was already a comparatively thickly-populated area and spilled over into the new 'colonial' lands east of the Elbe. These developments are indicative of a rapid increase in population, an increase that more than compensated for the losses of the previous periods, and everywhere, Europe, during the central Middle Ages, became more thickly populated than it had been during the period of greatest prosperity in antiquity.

The rise of towns

This rapid development was partly initiated by and partly reflected in the expansion of commercial relations. Here and there, as in Artois, Flanders, parts of Champagne, and parts of western Germany, in the north, and in northern and central Italy, in the south, an outlet for the surplus population was found in general industrialisation. But everywhere western and central Europe became covered with a network of small towns, and this urban civilisation formed the characteristic feature of the economic life of the period.

Urbanisation in the Middle Ages naturally did not proceed on anything like a nineteenth-century scale. The townsmen probably did not exceed one-tenth of the total European population, and only in a few areas, such as the Low Countries, Lombardy, and Tuscany, was this proportion exceeded to any appreciable extent. The low yield of agriculture and the inefficiency of the means of transport imposed severe limitations on the massing of human beings. The provisioning of even a few thousand townsmen presented extraordinary difficulties, with the result that only centres with very effective means of communication and with the necessary commercial and industrial resources had any scope for expansion. The conflicting needs of the different urban communities brought them into continual conflict with one another, thus adding problems of policy to those of marketing. The population of even the largest urban centres rarely exceeded 50,000. A town of 20,000 was already considered to be very large, and most of the bigger centres had only between 5,000 and 10,000 citizens. But the significance of the medieval town cannot be adequately measured merely by the number of its inhabitants, for all the relations of the Middle Ages were on a small scale.

Towns and the development of economic freedom

When, therefore, this period is often referred to as that of the medieval town economy, the implication is merely that the townsmen formed a creative minority, a dominant economic power, into which the rural economy was incorporated as a passive partner. The towns liberated the countryside from much of its isolation and self-sufficiency by offering a market for its produce, and stimulated rural energy by the substitution of money transactions for relations in kind. They developed as centres of commerce and industry, which created new needs and built up a system of new local and interregional intercourse. Socially they formed isles of freedom in a sea of serfdom, offering to serfs the means of escape from bondage.[1] They brought into the world a new class, the third estate, and with it a transition from

[1] From the twelfth century the serf who resided in a town for a year and a day became a free man: hence the German expression 'Stadtluft macht frei'.

status to class and a new set of social relations in which position was not exclusively dependent on birth. This transformation, according to Pirenne, was in many ways no less significant than the changes brought about by the French Revolution.[1]

Charters of privilege guaranteed to the towns exemption from the feudal order. Hence the definition of Pirenne of the medieval town as 'a commune living on trade and industry and possessing rights, an administration and its own distinctive systems of law, which confers upon it a privileged corporate status'. All medieval towns were, in a legal sense, communes. They formed corporate bodies endowed with their own rights and were recognised as such by the public powers. This was a fact that was of fundamental significance to the gradual emergence of economic freedom in the western world.

'Liberty', says Pirenne, 'is a necessary and universal attribute of the townsman', even though the liberty was a *de facto* rather than a *de jure* condition. The liberty of persons together with the freedom of urban land, reflected in the emergence of free tenure, brought about a mobility of men and goods. Tenants of urban land could let, pledge or transfer their properties without the intervention, or even without the agreement of the proprietor, and were thus able to acquire the means of raising capital for commercial and industrial ventures. Urban property, on the other hand, also became in the course of time a favourite source of investment for wealthy merchants. But perhaps the greatest gift of the period was the continuous creation of new opportunities offered to everyone by the commercial expansion and the chances that were provided to people to improve their position in the social hierarchy.

This period was characterised by the dominance of the merchant classes and by the primacy of their interests in all the major towns. Power was concentrated in the hands of the propertied classes: the landowners, rentiers, and merchants. Hence the absence of restrictions on commercial transactions, from which the propertied classes derived a benefit. The craftsmen, a naturally protectionist class, had neither the economic nor the political power to support policies of restriction; hence the freedom of entry of both men and goods into the towns during this period. Not only were the central Middle Ages a period of rapid development, but western Europe was still clearly differentiated into developed and underdeveloped areas, into centres that specialised in manufacturing and those that produced agricultural products and raw materials, and the development of commercial relations between them was favourable to all the interests involved. Not until the Industrial Revolution would conditions become so favourable again for the development of economic freedom and the rise of a market economy.

Most communes also succeeded in obtaining the right to control their own civic and economic affairs, though conditions varied greatly from country to country and from town to town. Where there was a sufficiently exact equilibrium or prolonged stalemate between the territorial powers, as in Italy, Germany and the Netherlands, city states arose with more or less complete political and economic independence. But in all cases the medieval city was left largely to its own resources. It had to care for its own defence and means of existence, levy its own taxes and control the industrial and commercial life within its boundaries. The medieval commune therefore developed an assertive consciousness of its own rights and responsibilities, with a consequent emotional tension and a constant devotion to the public cause that contrasted strongly with the peaceful existence of the presentday town.

[1] Pirenne, *Les Anciennes démocraties des Pays-Bas*, pp. 20 ff.

The expansion of commerce

The commerce of this period expanded both in volume and in the area of its operation. The routes of communication became safer, the means of transport better organised, and the various centres more closely knit together, so that by the end of this period western and central Europe and much of eastern Europe had become a single trading area.

The growth of trade was a reflection of closer settlement, of increasing population, and of increased differentiation and specialisation between the various areas. During the early Middle Ages trade had suffered more from the general upheaval than any other economic activity; now it registered the greatest recovery. Internal colonisation tended to remove many of the physical barriers between communities and external colonisation to bring outlying areas within the western economic orbit. The numerous country towns that arose all over Europe served as centres of exchange of low-grade industrial wares for agricultural staples. These were exchanged at fairs and markets or were bought in the workshops of craftsmen. Gradually these channels of distribution were supplemented, first in the larger and then in the smaller centres, by permanent stores. The fact that peasants could to an increasing extent pay their rents in cash is significant proof of the gradual penetration of commercial and money relations to all spheres of the medieval economy.

Whereas the production of the coarser types of cloth, leatherware, cutlery and other utensils and implements was widely distributed throughout Europe, certain centres from the beginning specialised in the manufacture of high-grade wares. Such trades were the cloth industry of Flanders and Artois, the manufacture of the metal wares of Cologne, Liège and Dinant, and the production of metals in parts of England, Hainault, eastern France and southern Germany. Certain agricultural areas also tended to specialise in the production of wine, others in the growing of wool; and even areas that were predominantly arable, such as parts of western and northern France and southern England, contained large units that produced mainly for the market.

But, above all, certain towns from the beginning of this period became the centres of long-distance interregional and international trade. These centres were especially the Italian and north German towns, Bruges, and the towns of Champagne. According to Pirenne it was the merchants engaged in distant trade who acted as the driving force in the economic life of the central Middle Ages, and stimulated economic specialisation and interterritorial differentiation up to the limits permitted by the technical conditions of the time.

Commercial routes

Comparatively effective means of water transport accounted for the two main streams of medieval commerce. The first was the Mediterranean. The trade of this area was largely a matter of shipping oriental and Levantine luxuries to the West and of moving European cloth and raw materials to the East; but partly it was also an interregional trade between the various Mediterranean countries. The rise of the Italian towns to commercial primacy was due initially to the policy which stopped the barbarians on the fringes of the Byzantine Empire and the infidels on the borders of the Muslim world, thus enabling the Italo-Byzantine ports to develop into intermediaries between East and West. The Crusaders gave the Italian towns, and to a lesser extent Marseilles and Barcelona, the undisputed mastery of the

Mediterranean. By the twelfth century these towns had surpassed the greatest business centres of the ancient world in wealth and in the value of their commerce. By the end of this period, when they attained their greatest prosperity, their commercial activities reached from England in the west to China in the east and from Flanders in the north to the Sahara in the south.

During the twelfth and thirteenth centuries Venice, Genoa and Pisa built up extensive networks of trading posts all along the Mediterranean and virtually monopolised the trade of this inland sea. They took from the Muslims and the Byzantines not only the trans-Mediterranean trade but also an ever-increasing share of the coastal trade within these empires.

From the east the Italians imported not only luxuries such as silks, velvets, and damasks, Russian furs and eastern spices, but also raw materials, especially dyestuffs, for the cloth industry. These they distributed all over western and central Europe. In return they shipped timber, arms and slaves, and especially woollen goods, which soon became their chief export. The cloths of Flanders and northeastern France were unrivalled for their flexibility, softness and beauty of colour, and the high prices they fetched and the ease with which they could be transported made them an effective return for the spices—the seasonings, dyestuffs and medicinals—imported from the East.

What gave the trade of the Mediterranean its peculiar character was the shipment of luxury articles, even though foodstuffs and raw materials also entered into this traffic and might in fact, as far as volume was concerned, even have exceeded the movement of the high-grade wares. By contrast, the commerce of northern Europe was confined almost entirely to necessities.

First and foremost among these essentials was grain. Initially this was supplied by the valleys of the Somme and the Seine, but, towards the end of this period, and as a result of the German colonisation of the lands to the east of the Elbe, Prussia and Poland became the granaries of Europe.

Another staple article, also obtained from the Baltic, was fish. It was obtained during this period from the fisheries of Skania, off the south coast of Sweden, and shipped to western Europe and along the rivers into the heart of Germany.

Besides these two commodities, no other product played a more important part in the medieval diet, or was carried in larger quantities, than wine. The wine trade of Bordeaux was so important that the methods used by the wine fleets gave rise to the maritime law of northern Europe.

Associated with these articles and rivalling them in value and bulk were the basic raw materials. Timber was carried especially from the well-wooded countries around the Baltic to the treeless plains of Flanders and the Netherlands. Wool was another important raw material needed by the industries of Flanders, together with flax and the more common dyestuffs. Of the mineral products by far the most important was salt, which was obtained especially from the Bay of Bourgneuf.

The intermediaries in this trade were the north German towns. They occupied favourable positions at the mouths of the great German rivers, from where they had easy access to the interior. To the peoples of the west, and especially to those of Flanders and Brabant, they offered markets in the east and, in return, supplied these areas with an abundance of food and raw materials. These services made them indispensable, and this accounts for the privileges that they obtained in the countries of the west.

The connection between these two major commercial areas was formed during this period by the fairs of Champagne. Here, on neutral ground, in an independent province lying between Germany, France, and Italy, merchants from all parts of

Europe met and mingled, exchanging their wares as well as their ideas. The routes from Italy and the Rhone Valley to Flanders and England led naturally through this province. In the course of each year six fairs were held in successive places, thus constituting one continuous market. Here the merchants of Italy and Provence exchanged the products of the East for the cloth of Flanders, the wool of England, and the wares of northern Europe. The fairs were also centres for the settlement of commercial debts contracted over a large part of Europe.

The volume of interregional trade

The volume of interregional trade of this period was indeed not large when compared with that of the present day. There still remained a subsistence core to much of the life of the Middle Ages. The bulk of European society was comprised of relatively small groups, which were largely self-supplying in character or at least provided their needs from the surrounding areas. Thus, out of some 3,000 urban communities in Germany at the end of this period, only a very small minority of some twenty to twenty-five lost their original agrarian character and developed a really urban economy.

The purchasing power of the lower classes was still too low to create an effective demand for foreign goods. Outside Italy, Flanders and the north German towns, the demand for these goods was confined to the upper classes. In these centres the demand of the growing middle class probably already exceeded that of the nobility and the clergy. The bourgeoisie not only formed a small minority of the total population, but was also interested more in the quality and durability than in the quantity and cheapness of the wares they bought. The bulk of the people of Europe were still clothed in homespun cloth, except perhaps on Sundays, and were dependent on local products for their food, furniture, accommodation and other requirements.

The mass movement of goods was indeed confronted with numerous obstacles such as tolls, monetary chaos, and, above all, the inadequacy of the means of transport. It was only where sea and river transport was available, and where time was not material, that the carriage in bulk of goods was economically feasible. In the Mediterranean the *naves*, the slow sailing ships that cost only a third as much as the galleys but carried four times as much freight, in the North Sea the 'cogs' developed by the Hansa towns, and on the rivers the canal barges towed by men or horses, were by far the most effective means of carriage.

Examples of the mass movement of goods in the Middle Ages were therefore all dependent on cheap water transport. Thus the wool exported from England in 1273 amounted to 35,000 sacks. From the southern extremity of Sweden, then under Danish rule, 100,000 tons of herrings were exported annually to the Hanse towns, which again distributed the fish throughout the Empire and as far south as Vienna. In return some 24,000 tons of salt were imported during the curing season. Sweden exported butter to the value of more than one million marks to Lübeck, which again transported it as far south as Nuremberg. At the beginning of the fourteenth century wine exports from Bordeaux reached 100,000 tons annually.[1] Imports into Venice, the greatest port of the Middle Ages, are said to have amounted to 250,000 tons annually at the end of the fifteenth century. Of these 10,000 tons were exotic products, 50-60,000 tons were salt, 20-30,000 tons cereals, and the rest foodstuffs and raw materials.

[1] *Annales*, Jan.–Mars, 1955, p. 68.

These examples show the importance of foodstuffs and raw materials in the interregional trade of the time. The large towns of Flanders and Italy were fed almost exclusively on imported grain, and depended largely on imported raw materials for their industry. The cost of transport even for carriage by sea was nevertheless comparatively high. Thus the cost of shipping English wool to Florence by galley was about three times the home price. The freight charge for grain from Prussia to Flanders amounted from one-half to two-thirds the price at the place of shipment, and often to considerably more; the cost of transporting wood was often three times the article's original value. For valuable wares, on the other hand, the incidence of the cost of transport was of course much lower.[1]

Currency

Money came to permeate economic transactions increasingly during the central Middle Ages, although its value as a unit of account and a means of payment was greatly reduced by the multiplicity of minting centres and the continual depreciation of the coinage. The position differed in various countries. Germany occupied the worst position. Here every prince and duke, archbishop and bishop issued his own coins, and even abbots, margraves, and towns assumed the right, until the emperor's prerogative was finally confined to his own hereditary lands. Even agreements to unify standards could not bring order into such a currency chaos. Italy and the Netherlands were in much the same position. In France, too, there were no fewer than 300 issuing centres, though their number was greatly reduced in the thirteenth century. Conditions were much better in England, for not only were there fewer minting centres but a uniform standard was maintained. Moreover, the number of these centres was reduced from forty to twelve at the end of the thirteenth century.

Depreciation was another evil. It was a result partly of the imperfect technique of minting, testing and weighing, which made the maintenance of uniform standards impossible. New pennies might, for example, differ in weight by as much as 40 per cent; also, such coins could be easily clipped and counterfeited. If good coins were issued they were immediately bought up by forgers and melted, so that only the bad ones remained in circulation. The prudent minter therefore accepted the depreciation of the coinage when making new issues, appropriating for himself the profits that would otherwise have accrued to criminals. But the authorities were by no means motivated exclusively by the exigencies of existing facts. The policy of securing a revenue from coinage led naturally to a reduction in the weight and a deterioration in the standard of coins; new issues were deliberately debased by feudal lords and kings, who forcibly exchanged these against the old, which were withdrawn from circulation.

The result of these conditions was that a distinction always had to be drawn in the Middle Ages between the unit of account and the medium of exchange. The money used in actual payment was first converted into the standard of value, and such revaluations appeared regularly in account books. Larger transactions were always paid by weight, which greatly reduced the value of a system of coinage, for people in accepting coins evaluated them not at their face value but according to their metal content. Under such conditions coins were more a convenience than a true monetary standard. The limited scope of coinage indeed makes it hazardous to

---

[1] Sombart, i, 290 ff; Kulischer, i, 301 ff; Bechtel, *Wirtschaftsstil des deutschen Spätmittelalters*, pp. 107, 145.

assume, says Usher, that coined money constituted an exclusive and comprehensive means of payment in the central Middle Ages.[1]

Credit

These conditions led to the rise of the money-changer or banker whose profession was as difficult as it was profitable. Since the money-changer was usually provided with a strong vault for storing money, the merchants with whom he was in constant contact began gradually to deposit their surplus cash with him, as a rule paying a small fee for its safe keeping. These deposits became the basis for a book transfer or clearing system of settling local debts. They could even be used, without the knowledge of their owners, as a means for the extension of credit.

Because of the connections of the money-changers with associates in other centres these deposits also gave rise to a system of settling debts between different places. The close of the twelfth century provides the first evidence of the bill of exchange. The actual transfer of coin was replaced by the written promise of the money-changer to pay abroad in foreign money the equivalent of the sum received in domestic coin. In this way the currency of one region was converted into that of another, without incurring the risk of transporting specie or evading restrictions on the export of bullion. The merchant thus suffered less from the defects of the existing monetary systems than might have been expected. The granting of credit to the recipient of the bill of exchange would, under such circumstances, appear as natural as the establishment of credit relations among the money-changers operating in different places. The bill of exchange was in this way transformed from a currency instrument into a credit medium. Owing to the outstanding importance of fairs in the interregional trade of the central Middle Ages, bills of exchange were made payable mostly at these gatherings. The development of an ideal unit of account further favoured the growth of clearing arrangements at fairs and the granting of credit from one fair to the next. Naturally the largest part of this European credit business based on the bill of exchange concentrated at the fairs of Champagne. Gradually the fairs evolved from institutions dealing in commodities into predominantly financial centres. A semipermanent money market developed, where large sums could be borrowed, not only by merchants but also by public authorities. The regulation of the capital market in fact became the main function of these institutions.[2]

By the end of the twelfth century, therefore, the money-changers had invaded the field of banking proper. Not only did they accept time and demand deposits and extend credit to customers, but they even participated in business overseas. They formed partnerships and, by arrangements between themselves, made it possible to transfer funds even when debtors and creditors had accounts with different establishments. Cheques were not used for this purpose. Though the merchants had long since ceased to be illiterate, written contracts were distrusted and used only in very exceptional cases. Transfer orders therefore had to be given by word of mouth and written down by the banks. This practice militated against

---

[1] Usher, *The Early History of Deposit Banking in Mediterranean Europe*, ch 7; Kulisher, i, 315 ff.

[2] Cf. Judges, in *European Civilization*, p. 454. 'It is interesting to observe that even as late as the eighteenth century it was customary both in France and Germany to make bills drawn for purposes of inland trade payable at fairs' (*ibid.*, p. 455).

the establishment of resident banking establishments and the development of more advanced banking practice until the use of non-negotiable bills and notes became common in the second half of the fourteenth century.[1]

The handicraft basis of industrial organisation

Industrial production in the Middle Ages had a predominantly handicraft basis. This was a form of organisation in which production was carried on by economically independent artisans. The master of the craft combined all the qualifications of property and ability required for the production of his wares. He worked in his own shop with his own tools, on raw materials purchased by himself or supplied by a customer or a merchant, and marketed his own wares, either directly or through the merchant as intermediary.

The various crafts were differentiated according to technical aspects: the object of production was the attainment of quality not quantity. The ideal of the medieval craft system was that each artisan should be responsible for the complete production of a specific article, an ideal which was never completely realised in practice. Thus differentiation appeared, for example, between the spinners, weavers, fullers and dyers. Trades were differentiated according to their finished products. For the production of each article there was a corresponding craft; each task formed the basis of an independent existence, the means of subsistence of a citizen. Thus, besides the blacksmith, the nailsmith and the tinsmith, there were the cutler, the sword-cutler, the maker of spurs and the manufacturer of helmets, as well as specialists in the production of different kinds of armour. The extent of this subdivision, of course, depended on the scope of the market. In a large medieval town there might have been as many as 200 independent trades.

The central Middle Ages to a large extent fulfilled the conditions necessary for the successful operation of the handicrafts. These consisted, first, in the easy coordination of all the processes of production, even for the limited means and experience of the craftsman. This condition was assured by the small capital required in the productive process and by the absence of changes in fashion. The crafts also required a sellers' market. There had to be no cut-throat competition. This condition was assured by the rapid expansion of the market in relation to industrial output. The craft system, finally, required technical stability, and the medieval world favoured leaving things as they were.

Technical stability was assured above all by the empirical and traditional character of industrial technique. The craftsman worked as he had been taught to do, using methods sanctioned by experience and by communal usage. Technical knowledge was the subjective property of the master of the craft, who passed it on orally and visually to his successors. Its perpetuation was assured by the institution of apprenticeship and by family relationships, which transmitted it from generation to generation. Work was the concrete embodiment of the creative personality of the artisan, not of an impersonal establishment. Within the confines of the handicraft system minor variations were indeed possible in the use of materials or in the techniques of production. But the objective of all craft associations was always the creation of conditions of complete equality for all, and the crafts were receptive to new techniques only if they did not threaten to undermine the equality of their members. The social relationships fostered by the crafts were intended to strengthen the maintenance of artisan independence rather than to foster economic

[1] Usher, p. 12; *Cambridge Economic History of Europe*, iii, 66 ff, 448.

growth or the pursuit of profit. The rational organisation of the work—the use of means in such a way as to minimise costs and to maximise returns—was not a feature of the crafts.

The handicrafts were ideally suited to production for the local market. In France and England and in western Germany it was customary for artisans to visit the country fairs to sell their wares. Some artisans might even specialise as merchants. Even in cases where the output of artisans exceeded local requirements and the surplus had to be exported, and this could be arranged by merchants who contracted to take the output of groups of producers, the craftsmen could still maintain their independence. Such conditions were found in the Middle Ages in certain metal trades and in the manufacture of the coarser textiles. It was only when the different processes of production themselves had to be coordinated by the merchant-entrepreneur that the artisan tended to lose his independent status and to become fully integrated in the capitalist process of production.

The craft structure was characteristic even of an industry such as mining. Coal and base ore were obtained in very shallow pits. It was only in the mining of silver in central Europe that shaft mining had become at all general by the end of this period. But even in these mines the shafts seldom went far below the surface, for a sloping field would be covered with numerous shallow pits, and as soon as they became waterlogged, they were abandoned. In many parts of Europe manorial undertakings employing fewer than a dozen villagers remained the normal type of mining throughout the Middle Ages.

It was common for miners to combine in associations. They then worked their concession on a collective basis in much the same way as the peasants cultivated their fields in common. Participation in these associations could be handed from father to son or could be disposed of to outsiders.

The preparation and the smelting of the ores and the refining of the metals were no more elaborate than the mining. The washing, breaking and crushing of the ore were usually performed by hand labour; the forges were small and required no more capital than that invested in the workshop of the smith.[1]

Capitalist coordination

The craftsman who produced for the local market could himself buy the materials that he required and sell his wares direct to the ultimate consumer; alternatively he could work on commission for his client. Such direct relations between the supplier of raw materials, the producer and the ultimate consumer would dispense with the services of the middleman. It would therefore involve no dependence of the crafts-man on a merchant who supplied the raw materials, financed the productive process and distributed the finished wares. Local and direct relations of this nature were characteristic of a large part of medieval Europe.

These direct and partly local relationships were, however, not suited to the large specialised markets that developed in parts of Europe and specifically lent their imprint to the economic development of the central Middle Ages. The industries peculiar to these markets were characterised by the facts that they drew their raw materials from abroad and produced for export, and that it was the merchant who served as the activator of economic activity and the coordinator of the economic process.

[1] *Cambridge Economic History of Europe*, ii, 459.

A typical example of this *grand commerce* was the cloth trade, the great industry of the Middle Ages *par excellence*, and especially the cloth industries of Flanders, Artois and Brabant, and, later, of Florence. Here from the twelfth century onward, the crafts were supplemented and coordinated by the putting-out system, a typically capitalist form of organisation.

The raw materials of this industry were drawn from many countries. Dyestuffs were obtained from different parts of Europe, from the Near East, and even from the Indies. Potash, used as a mordant, was imported from the forests of the Baltic, and wool was obtained from the pastures of western Europe, especially from England. The finished products, on the other hand, were sold in all the countries of Europe and were exported to the Near and the Far East.

The processing and marketing of cloth, therefore, required numerous specialised skills and a considerable subdivision of labour. The coordination of all these activities was performed by the merchant. In each sphere—the import of the raw material, the processing of the product and the export of the finished article— entrepreneurial activity was required. The dominant figure in the new process of production was the draper. Certain preparatory functions, such as the sorting and cleaning of the wool, were performed in his own establishment, but the further processing of the materials was performed by craftsmen working at home. All the people, whether spinners, weavers, fullers or dyers, were in complete dependence on the cloth merchant. The position of the cloth merchants was all the stronger in that they wielded not only economic but also political power, for through the merchant gilds they controlled both the economic life and the civil affairs of the commercial and industrial centres. Thus prices, wages and hours of work were prescribed by the municipal authorities, and the craftsmen were effectively kept in their place. This identity of political and economic power, which placed the commercial towns under the political leadership of the most enterprising citizens, helps to explain the vitality of the Flemish, Italian and the Hanse towns during this period, for as a result of the hegemony of the successful merchants, the town councils concentrated all their energies on the promotion of trade.

Capitalist organisation became characteristic of all the great regional industries of the time, not only of the cloth trade of Artois and Flanders, but also of the metal goods of Cologne, Liege and Dinant, and the metals of England, Hainault, eastern France and south Germany.

Interregional trade in particular assumed a capitalist basis. From the beginning the profits made by the Italians and Hanses in foreign trade must have been considerable, for neither the high costs of transport nor the numerous tolls prevented the sale of goods at a satisfactory profit. In the larger trading centres functions became more specialised, business methods more competitive and less corporative, the operations organised on a larger scale and more carefully planned, and business activities directed more deliberately towards the attainment of profit as the leading motive of commercial activity.

Merchants were still largely peregrinatory and they and their servants accompanied their goods either by land or by sea. To protect themselves, they formed fraternities, which in northern Europe were called merchant gilds. As a means of raising the necessary capital they formed partnership agreements. The Italian *commenda* and the *societas maris* were concluded, not for a period of years, but for a single venture or voyage, usually a round trip to the Levant or to Africa. They involved the cooperation between a travelling and an investing partner. The ensuing profit on the venture was divided on an agreed basis, and generally to the advantage of the sleeping partner, for life in the Middle Ages was cheap and capital dear.

Terminal partnerships, which extended over several years, were rare in overseas trade, but more frequent in local retailing and in manufacturing.

To the investor these agreements provided the advantage that he assumed only a limited liability; he could lose no more than his initial investment. He could also spread his risk by dividing his capital between different ventures. This flexibility made the agreements admirably suited to the conditions of the Middle Ages. The sea loan, already used in antiquity, was another means of financing overseas ventures. In this case repayment was contingent on the successful completion of the venture. These agreements made it possible to experiment with joint business ventures, at first on a small, and later on a large scale. They were to exert an important effect on future economic development.

Traders who proceeded overland, on the other hand, made use chiefly of the *compagnia* partnership, which could associate a large number of partners for many years. It could combine men who supplied both capital and management and who alternately travelled and remained resident. The disadvantage of this form of association was that each partner was liable towards third parties for the debts of the entire company, without limit.

Association between merchants thus played a prominent part in the provision of early mercantile capital, and the reinvestment of the profit the means for its rapid expansion. Nor were the profits realised by merchants all reinvested in trade. Many merchants combined business with banking and advanced considerable funds to kings and municipalities. In addition, they invested their surplus funds in land; and in the course of the twelfth and thirteenth centuries they acquired most of the ground in urban centres. The rapid expansion of land values tended to transform the mercantile class into an urban patriciate.[1]

Commercial policy

The extreme dispersal of authority was a characteristic feature of the central Middle Ages. Consequently the effective political authority tended to be localised and small and, as regards economic policy and control, the towns were left largely to their own devices.

Commercial policy during the central Middle Ages can best be explained by the fact that this was an era of rapid expansion in which a few developed and specialised commercial and industrial centres coexisted with large unspecialised but rapidly developing areas. These were ideal conditions for the maintenance of a large measure of freedom in the international sphere. In a rapidly expanding economy, in which the main limitations were those imposed by inadequate techniques of production and inadequate means of transport and in which there was a natural territorial division of labour between the specialised and unspecialised areas, there was no need for restrictive policies.

In the developed centres the interests of the mercantile class tended to predominate. This can be ascribed, first, to the fact that, numerically, the merchants constituted an important section of the population. In the second place, it was due to the fact that the artisan population was largely dependent on the merchants for their employment and their livelihood. In the third place, many other citizens drew an income from trade in a less direct way, either as sleeping partners who financed those directly engaged in commerce or as property owners

[1] *Ibid.*, ii, 323 ff.

who let their properties to those engaged in production and distribution. Finally, the towns were dependent largely on tolls and other commercial levies for their income.

The dominance of mercantile interests was clearly reflected in the two main lines of commercial policy. The first was to improve the conditions of interregional and international trade, the second to improve the conditions of supply of manufactured goods by keeping down the costs of production.

In an expansive market the only requirement of commercial policy, as far as the first objective was concerned, was to organise production and distribution on an efficient basis and to remove political and physical obstacles to the exploitation of the market. Until the last half of the thirteenth century there was little evidence of the existence of exclusiveness or of the appropriation of monopoly powers. Thus one of the characteristic features of this period was the tolerance shown towards, and even the active encouragement given to, foreigners, who were allowed to do business under conditions of remarkable freedom both in the developed and in the underdeveloped areas.

The formation of free confederations of trading towns was another characteristic feature of this period. The purpose of these federations was, on the one hand, to overcome physical insecurity, to offer joint protection against feudal disruption, and to put collective pressure on political authorities. Individual towns, on the other hand, were often hampered by lack of capital or by an inadequate economic organisation. Town leagues consequently represented an attempt to combine the strength of a number of commercial centres and thus made it possible or easier for them to penetrate new markets and to organise their activities in an effective way. A typical example was the 'hanse' of seventeen north European towns, which was formed to penetrate new markets and not, as later, to retain their grip on existing ones. One of its main objectives was also to safeguard the northern route that led from Novgorod in the east to Bruges in the west.

The same spirit was reflected in the establishment of the gild merchants of this period. The privilege, originally, to establish a gild merchant was a right granted to a whole town community and not to any specific group of citizens. Moreover it was a right not to a specific kind of association but to a particular method and purpose of associating. The object of its formation was basically that all the individuals and interests in the trade of the town should 'geld' together—i.e. should submit to joint taxation. Not only, therefore, did it include all the local trading interests, but it could also include outsiders. The fund thus raised served to replace the former tolls levied on trading activities.

Any monopoly which the gild merchant held could therefore be explained as the insistence that only those who paid for a privilege could enjoy its benefits. Nor was the gild merchant initially a gild of merchants only; it included all those with trading interests. Up to the middle of the thirteenth century artisans were freely admitted and often constituted the bulk of the members.[1]

Organisation among craftsmen during this period seems to have been a weak and ineffective means of raising wages or of applying pressure as a means of bargaining. Immigration into the towns was encouraged, and this enhanced the supply of labour. During a period of expansion employment was readily available and this further discouraged craft organisation. Separate craft gilds were therefore comparatively late in making their appearance and were of little account before the thirteenth century. During the great centuries of expansion these gilds were too few

---

[1] *Ibid.*, iii, 181 ff.

and too scattered to exert any effective influence either as a help or as a hindrance to·economic development.

It was not until the latter part of the thirteenth century, when the expansion of the main industrial centres was slowing down, that the craft gilds became at all widespread. When their organisation improved towards the end of this period, at a time when competition was becoming more intense, the dominant mercantile interests in the towns were not slow in imposing drastic controls and even in barring any sort of association or collective agreement among the workers. Recourse to such policy was especially vigorous in the textile trade. In most of the Italian towns the artisans who worked in this industry were prohibited from associating in gilds. The object of these bans was to prevent collective action on the part of the workers to control the supply of labour and to impose collective bargaining on wages. Similar bans were not imposed on the employers. These were, on the contrary, prohibited by the town statutes from enticing away the workers of their colleagues, and gild statutes imposed the maximum wages agreed to by the employers among themselves.

In the important textile towns of western Europe towards the end of this period attacks on craft gilds became a common phenomenon. They were prohibited in Dinant in 1255, in Tournai in 1280, and in Brussels in 1291. Ghent had virtually no craft gild organisation before 1302. In the towns of Brabant craft fraternities were not officially recognised until after the middle of the fourteenth century. Power rested in the hands of the urban patriciate, and where associations of craftsmen were allowed, they were rigidly controlled.[1]

The policy of provision

The overwhelming preponderance of mercantile interests during this period had one important limitation. Where these interests conflicted with the policy of provision, it was this objective that always prevailed. The policy of provision was the procedure of retaining goods in, and to a lesser extent of attracting them to, a country or a town. The object was secured by the setting up of obstacles to exports and the facilitating of imports. Export prohibitions were prevalent throughout the Middle Ages, and import prohibitions conspicuous by their absence. Commercial treaties aimed at securing imports, exports being granted only by way of compensation. Foodstuffs everywhere occupied a central position in this policy; next came armaments, raw materials, semi-manufactured goods and the instruments of production.

The important role of foodstuffs can be explained by the tremendous and perennial fear of famine in the Middle Ages. In this respect the policy was a continuation of that of antiquity. Inadequate means of transport made it difficult to ensure the provisioning of the larger towns, especially of those located in the interior of the country. Crop failures in any particular area therefore entailed famine in that area, and famine led to unrest, economic depression, and finally epidemics.

Consequently town administrations exercised a continuous control over the supply and distribution of foodstuffs. Concern for the supply of grain was combined with concern for the supply of the other necessities of life: of foodstuffs

---

[1] 'Guilds', in *Encyclopaedia of the Social Sciences; Cambridge Economic History of Europe*, iii, **204** ff; 425 ff.

such as wine, oil, meat, fish and vegetables; of raw materials such as straw, wax, timber and building materials; and of finished products such as candles. On the one hand, policy measures were designed to ensure the continuity of supply by means of the direct purchase of grain from abroad, the granting of facilities to importers, threats to speculators, and measures to increase local production and local self-sufficiency or the maintenance of adequate stocks. On the other hand, various trade restrictions were imposed on exports. Finally, there were controls aimed at the maintenance of price stability. Nor was the fixation of prices confined to necessities; it extended to the wages of those workers whose services most directly affected the cost of living of the masses, such as the millers of grain, the bakers of bread, the transporters of wine and the slaughterers of animals. This was therefore no part of a protectionist policy to build up productive powers, for often the export of the finished commodities was prohibited, even when these constituted the principal products of the producing centre. This policy of plenty was due not merely to the 'hunger for goods', that is, the excessive growth of demand in relation to supply during a period characterised by rapid expansion and poor means of transport, but also to the fiscal needs of the chronically embarrassed authorities—imports increasing the supply of goods available for taxation—and to military motives. It arose in various centres in the course of the twelfth century and culminated in the fourteenth century.

But in spite of these restrictive policies there was a very large measure of freedom in the central Middle Ages. Thus there was nothing like the detailed and comprehensive regulation of the town economy that was to become so characteristic a feature of the late Middle Ages. This was true of both internal and external aspects of policy. There was as yet a large measure of freedom from the numerous restrictions, both aggressive and defensive, that were to become characteristic of the following period, when merchants and craftsmen alike found themselves in a more highly competitive situation because of the more even spread of industrial activity throughout western and central Europe. Restrictions on foreigners, so common in the late Middle Ages, were still very little in evidence. Nor were the weaker groups of the town society as yet subjected to such rigid control by the urban patriciate and the mercantile interests. What exploitation there was, was more of a general fiscal nature. As long as the entrepreneurial and propertied groups formed the governing class, the economic and social policy of the commune was one of expansion, free immigration, and relatively free trade. Growth and expansion were the hallmarks of the age.[1]

---

[1] *Cambridge Economic History of Europe*, iii, pt 2; Heckscher, *Mercantilism*, ii, 80 ff.

15

The late Middle Ages

A period of arrested development and of increasing urban, corporative and central control

c. Beginning of the fourteenth to c. the end of the fifteenth century

A period of arrested development

The late Middle Ages had all the symptoms of a period of arrested development. It was a time of fermenting diversities, of schism, struggle and strife, a period characterised by wars more protracted and destructive than any that had taken place since the barbarian invasions, an age represented by the transition from rapid expansion, internal order and social solidarity to constriction, class friction and civil strife.

> Nothing more involved and bewildering and more full of contrasts can be imagined than the period extending from the beginning of the fourteenth to about the middle of the fifteenth century. The whole of European society, from the depths to the surface, was as though in a state of fermentation. . . . The peoples were perturbed by social insurrections, excited by the hasty quarrels of the parties, or the prey of a general unrest which sometimes found expression in tentative reforms, and sometimes by the oppression of the weaker classes by the more powerful. A spirit of restlessness was abroad, affecting men's minds as well as their policies; even religion was not immune; it was a restlessness that almost amounted to mental confusion. The world was suffering and struggling, but it was hardly advancing. For the only thing of which it was clearly conscious was the fact that all was not well with it. It longed to escape from its ills, but it did not know how it would do so. No one had anything to offer in the place of the tradition that weighed upon it and from which it could not liberate itself. . . . Everywhere the world was in labour, but it produced only abortive births. There was a definite feeling abroad that it was waiting for a spiritual renewal.[1]

The social unrest was due, at least in part, to the fact that the process of secular expansion in population and in territory had ceased. All the free land so abundantly available in the West at the beginning of the Middle Ages had been occupied by the end of the thirteenth century, and marginal land was no doubt beginning to show signs of exhaustion under excessive cropping and a static technique. The Black Death that ravaged Europe in the middle of the fourteenth century is generally considered to have marked a turning point in the growth of population in the Middle Ages. In reality the population of western Europe had already become

[1] Pirenne, *A History of Europe, from the Invasions to the XVI Century*, pp. 379—80.

stabilised before the plague, though it continued to grow rapidly in the Slav countries of the east. The extensive colonisation of the period of florescence, the clearing of forests, the draining of swamps, the founding of new towns, ceased. It was not that the fecundity of Europeans had fallen off, but that their *Lebensraum*—the opportunities offered by the opening up of new lands and the advantages that could be derived from further territorial differentiation through the extension of commercial relations—had ceased to expand. Pestilence became a regularly recurring evil. Between 1326 and 1500 no fewer than seventy-two years of plague were recorded in Germany. The Black Death alone carried off from a third to a half of the people of Europe. At the end of this period the population of western and central Europe seems to have been no more than at the beginning. The fact that a very high birth rate could no more than restore the ravages of the plague shows that, from the point of view of population, western and central Europe had reached saturation point.

Everything, in fact, indicates that at the end of the thirteenth and beginning of the fourteenth century the western and central European economy had reached the culmination of its process of expansion. All the indications are that, in relation to the cooperant factors of production, and especially the supply of land, that were available, western Europe in the later thirteenth century had become heavily over-populated. All the most fertile land had been taken up, the best and most accessible stands of timber felled, and the more easily reached ores exhausted. The excessive parcellation of land and the growth of uneconomic holdings had become a charac-teristic feature of the late thirteenth century. With no new discoveries or improve-ments in technique to offset these effects, increasing costs were the inevitable result.[1]

'With a population pressing against the means of subsistence', says Ricardo, 'the only remedies are either a reduction of people or a more rapid accumulation of capital.'[2] This is correct, of course, provided there are sufficient investment oppor-tunities. In the western Europe of the late Middle Ages it led to famines and pestilences of unprecedented proportions, which temporarily more than restored the balance. The reduction in numbers did indeed lead, at least temporarily, to a remarkable improvement in the standards of living of those that survived. For a time the moving frontier that had existed in the earlier Middle Ages seemed to have returned. Shortages of labour led not only to improved standards of living and greater freedom from restraint in the countryside, but also to improved wages in the towns. But these were temporary and local phenomena.

Associated with the demographic stagnation, partly as cause and partly as effect, there came a cessation in the expansion of the total volume of commercial activity, the great extension of which had been the main feature of the central Middle Ages. This secular stagnation was also associated with a redistribution of business and wealth from certain areas to others and with the replacement of certain types of activity by others, so that the process of slowing-up of the economy was not equally distributed between the different centres and the different industries. At the same time the rural economy underwent a process of adjustment which reduced the total level of agricultural production and, because of the greater home con-sumption of the peasants themselves, also of the surpluses sold on the market; hence the preoccupation of towns with the food supplies of their population. The mines of central Europe were also producing under conditions of rapidly

[1] Slicher van Bath, *De agrarische geschiedenis van West-Europa (500-1850)*, pp. 147 ff.
[2] *On the Principles of Political Economy and Taxation*, ed. Straffa, i, 99.

diminishing returns, because the superficial seams had become exhausted and the deeper seams had to be worked under conditions that were raising technical problems which medieval technology as yet could not solve. The result was that, whereas the previous period had been characterised by a steep rise in prices, the fourteenth and fifteenth centuries were in general associated with prices, and especially grain prices, that were either falling or stagnating, and this must have been an important contributory factor to the secular stagnation of the time.[1]

Commercial routes

The main currents of commerce continued to flow from east to west along the Mediterranean and along the North and Baltic Seas. Up to now the exchange of goods between these two regions had taken place at the fairs of Champagne, and a secondary stream of goods had followed the northern route from Venice through the south German towns of Augsburg, Nuremberg, and Ulm.

The French fairs now fell into complete decay. This was due to the establishment of more permanent means of distribution; the substitution of 'continuous' and resident for peregrine practices. Thus there was no longer any need for the Italian merchants to visit the fairs after their companies had set up permanent branches in the main commercial centres of the West. The process was greatly facilitated by the establishment of direct commercial relations between northern and southern Europe. From the beginning of the fourteenth century a direct service by sea was instituted between the ports of Italy and those of western Europe. Henceforth the two main commercial routes of Europe were bound together directly by way of the Atlantic.

The increased importance of sea routes reflected considerable improvements in the technique of navigation. By 1300 the compass, indispensable to regular sailing, was in general use. The great extension of seafaring in the late Middle Ages would, in fact, have been inconceivable without it. It was followed by the introduction of the astrolabe and the cross-staff. Most important of all was the rapid transformation in the art of sailing because of the progressive adaptation of ships to new means of steering, rigging, and long voyages. Up to the fourteenth century most European ships were single-masted and fitted with one square sail, and were therefore wholly dependent on a favouring wind. By the end of this period the three-masted ship,

---

[1] *Cambridge Economic History of Europe*, ii, 191 ff, 338 ff; Slicher van Bath, pp. 147 ff. It is difficult to reconcile a condition of overpopulation with the reduction in the total level of agricultural production and with the fall in agricultural prices during this period. It is not easy to unravel the strains of cause and effect in the historical process, but it seems likely that the technological and organisational factors analysed in chapter 19, strongly buttressed by external factors, may have been the main causative factors of the secular stagnation in general, of which the stagnancy of population and of agriculture were largely concomitant features. Thus, according to Slicher van Bath ('The Yields of different Crops (mainly cereals) in relation to the Seed, c. 810-1820', *Acta Historiae Neerlandica*, ii, 26 ff), there was both a fall in the yield ratios of virtually all cereals and a decline in the acreage of cultivated land, and as cereal prices fell in comparison with those of industrial products and wages, it became unprofitable to devote much time and money to their cultivation.

According to Prof. Helleiner (*Cambridge Economic History of Europe*, iv, 68 ff), there was an upward revision of the standard of living during the late Middle Ages, which involved a partial shift from a cereal to a meat diet. The result was that animal husbandry expanded at the expense of cereal production. This 'decerealisation' helps to explain why the last century of the Middle Ages suffered scarcely less than the previous century from death and famine. The shrinkage of economic opportunity seems also to have encouraged a measure of demographic control.

able to sail reasonably close to the wind and consequently able to go anywhere, was in common use. The era of geographical discoveries had been made possible.

In the towns of Flanders, first in Bruges and then in Antwerp, the commercial current from the south met that of the north. The Flemish themselves grew rich 'by exploiting commerce rather than by practising it'. Their own share in the business became less and less important as the trade of their ports became more and more international. From the fourteenth century Flemish merchants no longer had establishments abroad; they had no commercial fleet; and all their foreign trade was in the hands of aliens. Whereas the trade of the Hansards and the Italians was reserved for citizens, the burghers of Bruges were content to serve as hosts or brokers for their guests. Bruges in the north, like Geneva in the south, took up the heritage of the fairs of Champagne.

At the same time the supremacy of Flanders as the leading textile centre of Europe was increasingly challenged. First the Italians, who had built up a finishing industry by importing cloth in the grey and dressing and dyeing it at home, developed the preliminary manufacturing processes as well, and organised an elaborate cloth industry, using African, Spanish, French, and English wools, Mediterranean and oriental dyestuffs, and local capital and enterprise to produce high-quality textiles of European repute. Secondly the English, assisted by the increasing use of fulling mills driven by water power, strengthened their hold on the cloth market, and by the time of the Tudors England had superseded Flanders as the leading centre of cloth manufacture in Europe. While the Italian and English cloth industries were developing, the Flemish industry was increasingly subjected to internal and external pressure, to economic fluctuations, and to labour unrest, and two centuries of expansion were succeeded by a period of recurrent crisis, readjustment, and gradual decline.

During this period the Flemish merchants also became increasingly dependent on the Italians. The Flemish draper now bought his wool from foreign importers, generally Italians, and sold his cloth, usually through the agency of brokers, to exporters, most of whom were also Italians. During this period the Italians, whose profits were being squeezed by the countries which controlled the eastern terminals of their trade and by the impoverishment of important markets in the West, and especially of France, as well as by the increase in the number of intermediaries in the Mediterranean trade, began increasingly to supplement commercial with financial transactions. The Italian merchant-bankers, because of their connection with the collection and transmission to Italy of the economic tithes collected by the papacy throughout Europe, had indeed been drawn gradually but irresistibly into trade and private and public finance during the central Middle Ages.[1] They now came to play a dominant part in the financial and commercial transactions of western Europe. In return for loans they obtained all kinds of commercial concessions from necessitous kings. So indispensable were they in the fiscal arrangements of western European countries that the mere threat of the Genoese in 1434 to leave England induced the king to take their part in their quarrel with the customs officials. Although favoured and protected by the governments, the Italian merchants were the object of a good deal of opposition from the local business communities, mainly because of the one-sided character of their privileges. Thus,

---

[1] The needs of its financial administration brought the Church into continual contact with commerce and banking. It was the irony of fate, says Strieder, that nothing furthered the development of credit and of capitalism more than did the papacy, that is, the head of an institution that was theoretically most opposed to the capitalistic spirit (*Studien zur Geschichte kapitalistischer Organisationsformen*, p. 64).

whereas the Italians enjoyed important advantages in England, they prevented English ships from appearing in the Mediterranean.

The commercial domain of the Hanse merchants, on the other hand, stretched in a great semicircle from Novgorod in the east to Scandinavia and Iceland in the north, England in the west, and Lisbon in the south. These were the colonial countries of the time, commercially passive, which were 'traded with', and whose commercial policies were influenced largely by the aliens who served them. The Hanse merchants had, during the previous period, become the first, and soon the indispensable, link between the Baltic states and the countries of western Europe, and they had gradually succeeded in wringing concessions from the countries they served. Thus in England the Hansards had acquired liberties and privileges which sometimes favoured them even above the English merchants themselves. In Flanders they formed a privileged community. They monopolised the Russian trade and obtained control over the mineral wealth of Sweden, the fisheries of Skania and the fish and fur trade of Norway. The Hanseatic League was formed at the beginning of this period to defend the foundations of German trade and to organise military and political action against any possible change. Unity became more than ever necessary in the late Middle Ages in view of the changing economic and political constellation of Europe. From the third quarter of the fourteenth century the League was threatened with both internal and external disintegration, for with the cessation of the Germanic *Drang nach Osten*, the Hanse commerce ceased to expand. Danzig was the last of the German towns to be founded in the Slavonic east, and the later German settlements remained outposts in the midst of a foreign culture which they could not assimilate and whose economies they could not integrate with their own. The League, therefore, was a manifestation of the tendency towards collective protection rather than a symbol of virility and expansion. From the fourteenth century onward the German towns, in fact, were interested more in consolidating the position they had won than in furthering expansion.

This was the purpose of the Hanseatic League. It tried by political action to retain in the late Middle Ages the place in the commerce of Europe that its merchants had won during the central Middle Ages. The Hansards adopted the same methods as the Italians. They financed kings in return for financial and commercial privileges. But to an increasing extent they followed the policy of excluding the nationals of northern and western Europe from their own commercial preserves.

This trend towards the local protectionism and growing urban exclusiveness in the fourteenth and fifteenth centuries was a symptom of the contraction of the foreign market and of the secular stagnation of the time. In the centuries of growth and expansion there had been little evidence of exclusiveness in town policy. Now the interests and policies of the individual towns concentrated more and more on the local market. In town policy considerations of local trade began to predominate over those of foreign commerce. The exclusion of outsiders from the local markets became the settled object of municipal policy. Thus merchants not belonging to the League could neither visit Hanse towns nor obtain ships from them, and Hansards would not even take their goods on commission. The direction of economic affairs tended to pass from the hands of the enterprising merchant class to those of the wealthy rentiers, who were concerned only with assuring their own privileges and possessions. The creative spirit of the Hanse merchants was sapped at a time when their prerogatives were being increasingly threatened from outside.

No wonder the League failed to arrest the development of the economic forces that were coming, to an increasing extent, to determine the course of European commercial and political development. Since sailors had been afraid during the previous period to navigate the waters around Denmark, goods had to be carried across the isthmus from Lübeck to Hamburg. This had contributed greatly to the leading position of these towns in the League. In the second half of the thirteenth century, however, the means of communication had improved so much that Lübeck established direct communications with Norway and England. In the following century the Dutch and the English followed this example. In the West—in England, in the Burgundian countries, and in Scandinavia—states were arising which were growing continually stronger, better organised, more centralised, and more self-conscious, and these were factors that heralded the approaching end of Hanseatic tutelage. In the East the League was unable to maintain its position in Novgorod in the face of the rising power of the Tsars. Owing to differences in the interests of the various towns, there was also a progressive disruption of the internal unity of the League. Confronted by such dangers the German towns, unsupported by the Empire and even threatened by the territorial powers, could only try by astute diplomacy to hide from their adversaries the weakness of their political and economic position.[1]

Defensive restrictionism

Business men can face the problem of contracting markets in two typically different ways. On the one hand they can withdraw from the competitive struggle and invest their money in comparatively safe fields such as urban property or municipal loans. On the other, they can attempt to weather the competitive storm by the rationalisation of their activities. Resort was taken to both these methods in the late Middle Ages.

The tendency for men of means to participate as sleeping partners in the activities of others—to buy urban tenements, to invest in public bonds, and to advance loans—was a noticeable feature of the times, both among the Italians of the south and the Flemish and Hansards of the north. The fifteenth century, which was the period of the intellectual and artistic renaissance of Europe, witnessed a tendency in the reverse direction in the economic field: the disposition of business men to fatten and degenerate, and to cultivate a mentality which no longer found satisfaction in the field of business enterprise and civil duty, but in the enjoyment of their incomes, in the purchase of country estates, or in scientific and artistic pursuits. Such a transmutation of the commercial class into an urban patriciate is indeed typical of all times when economic frontiers recede and the rewards of the assumption of risk are reduced. In all the leading commercial centres there was a tendency for accumulated profits to be spent on the purchase of durable consumer goods or to be invested in fixed property as the best means of securing the family patrimony.

Men looking for safety rather than for expansion could also find this safety in cooperation and in combination. The growth of commercial associations was therefore a typical sign of the defensive restrictionism of the late Middle Ages. Corporate trade was the reaction to the restricted opportunities of a contracting economy, the tendency to trade in a smaller way in well-organised and protected markets. These corporations both protected and circumscribed the trade they controlled, and if they conferred collective privileges on their members, on the one hand, they also

---

[1] Rörig, *Annales d'Histoire Economique et Sociale*, 1930, pp. 481 ff; *Studies in English Trade in the 15th Century*, ed. Power and Postan, pp. 91 ff.

assumed collective authority over them, on the other. Thus they regulated the scale and the methods of operation of the participants, the prices they had to charge, and the credit they could extend, as well as the places in which and the channels through which they had to conduct their business.

The other method of rationalisation was the reduction of costs, either by the use of improved techniques or by the exercise of collective pressure on the part of entrepreneurs on the cooperant factors of production.

Both the secular decline which set in during this period and the intensified competition which was the result acted as a spur to merchants to improve their methods, to increase their efficiency, and to reduce their costs. This was especially necessary in the case of the Italians, whose profit margins were being squeezed at both the eastern and western terminals of the distributive chain. The result was that they developed some of the most basic techniques of the modern western economy.

The development of business and banking techniques

The development in Italy of mercantile and banking concerns with branches in other parts of the world involved the use of new methods of doing business by correspondence rather than by personal contact. This presupposes a fairly high standard of education. The Italians also diversified their activities, and all the leading companies combined banking with foreign trade. For commercial privileges were often accorded only in return for loans; and bankers, again, were obliged to exploit trade concessions. Not only were their techniques more advanced than those of their competitors, but the various firms of merchant bankers attempted to coordinate their services. Thus they divided their risks and shared them between themselves. They made extensive use of credit and frequently drew on one another's resources, resources that were further supplemented by deposits from the public.

The banking services were greatly improved during this period. In many of the larger commercial centres the offices of the money-changers became local transfer and deposit banks, which operated on a fractional reserve ratio and extended credit to their customers by means of overdrafts. The exchanger had performed an invaluable service to international trade in the central Middle Ages by the introduction of the bill of exchange. Such bills were at first made payable only to the persons who actually deposited the money, but from the fourteenth century onward they were made transferable to third persons. Thus the bill of exchange made it possible for the first time to develop business systematically between parties not present at the same place, in this way obviating the need for travel on the part of merchants, and creating types of business hitherto unknown. By the end of this period international trade was financed almost entirely by bills of exchange, and only small amounts of specie passed along trade routes for the settlement of interregional balances.

Local payments were facilitated by means of book transfers, which were still very clumsy and circumstantial, since both parties had to be present at the transfer. But by the end of this period the bill of exchange, the promissory note and the rudimentary cheque was already available to meet the needs of the commerce of the time. None of this paper was transferable by endorsement. Discounting operations could therefore not be carried out.

Banks could not buy and sell short time paper in the open market. They could accumulate credits and sell exchange. They could lend deposit credit against a bill or a note. But they could not convert particular bills or notes into cash before maturity. The paper work of a bank could not assume its modern form before the jurists had developed the concept of negotiability.

Rudimentary as these developments of organised dealings in foreign exchange and improvements in the technique of banking were, they represented an important contribution of the late Middle Ages to the rise of modern financial institutions.[1]

It was probably the difficulty experienced in transferring claims, and the lack of negotiability of commercial paper, that gave rise to the development of the giro system. This system was introduced by deposit banks that were established by municipal authorities from the beginning of the fifteenth century onwards. It allowed depositors to order their banks by letter to transfer specified amounts from their accounts to those of other depositors. The giro system developed in the Mediterranean commercial centres in the fifteenth century, spread to Germany in the sixteenth century, and was transferred to the Netherlands at the beginning of the seventeenth century.

The development of accountancy

An aid in making the business an objective, impersonal, 'capitalistic' entity was the development from the middle of the thirteenth century of the art of keeping accounts. The extension of credit transactions that were only gradually liquidated, the administration of property by factors and other third persons, and especially the formation of commercial associations made the elaboration of means of cost-profit calculation essential and almost inevitable.

During the central Middle Ages the keeping of accounts had consisted of little more than the collection of memoranda of credit transactions interspersed with domestic details. The Venetians were the first to write debits and credits in collateral lines, and the idea of balancing the two sides soon suggested itself. With the introduction of the principle of double-entry in the first half of the fourteenth century, a decisive advance was made in the history of accountancy.

The Italian merchant of the late Middle Ages was by no means an untutored person. He kept his books with order and precision, and these were perfectly intelligible to third persons who were able to read and interpret them. Nor do faults in reckoning seem to have been much more common then than they are today. This was true not merely of simple arithmetical calculations such as addition and subtraction, but even of more complicated computations such as the conversion of one sum of money into another.

Side by side with the rise of commercial accountancy there also developed means of controlling the course of industrial production and the use of raw materials. Since it was the merchant who directed industry, this was to be expected. With the development of the putting-out system, in which the process of production was subdivided and dispersed, such control became essential. The object of industrial accountancy was at first to supervise the employment and the transformation of raw materials in order to eliminate waste, to trace cases of embezzlement, and finally also to estimate the cost of production, by allocating, for example, to each piece of cloth its share of overhead and indirect costs. This was a major contribution towards the rationalisation of the business enterprise.

[1] Usher, *The Early History of Deposit Banking in Medieval Europe.*

Double-entry book-keeping developed under the favourable conditions that existed in Italy during the fourteenth and fifteenth centuries. In the course of these centuries it spread all over the peninsula and was probably diffused also to Flanders, where there was a large Italian colony. But, in the other countries beyond the Alps, the merchants throughout the Middle Ages continued to keep their books according to more or less empirical rules. Thus, even the Fuggers at the commencement of the sixteenth century still kept their accounts on the principle of single-entry. Here it was only in the following centuries that rational methods of accountancy began to make headway through the increased trade brought by the geographical discoveries and the greater enlightenment spread by the printing press.[1]

Extension of the putting-out system

The domestic system became characteristic not only of the textile trade but also of the metallurgical and mining industries in some areas. The exhaustion of the superficial deposits necessitated the sinking of shafts and the installation of horse-powered and water-powered equipment to pump the water out of the mines. This equipment became a common feature of the argentiferous copper mines of central Europe towards the close of the Middle Ages. But remarkable as were some of the appliances of this period, they cannot be said to have revolutionised the mining industry which, outside the few specialised mining areas, changed little from what it had been in the central Middle Ages. More success was achieved with the application of water-driven hammers for crushing the ore and of bellows in blast furnaces for smelting it. These furnaces began to replace the older blowing forges in the fourteenth century. The new equipment added greatly to the capital cost of the mining and metal industries. Merchants advanced to miners and smelters the funds necessary for their maintenance and equipment in return for the right to be supplied with the mineral output for a specified number of years at a predetermined price, and when the workers defaulted in their payments, the works were taken over by their creditors, and the once independent undertakers were reduced to the status of wage-earning employees.[2]

Rise of the craft gilds

The competitive and shrinking markets of this period gave rise, particularly in the textile industries of the more specialised centres, to unemployment among artisans and to attempts by the merchant manufacturers to improve their competitive position by squeezing wages. The reaction among the workers was to present a united front by the improvement of their own organisation. Thus, whereas craft

---

[1] De Roover, *Annales d'histoire economique et sociale*, nos 44 and 45. 'In the opinion of experts, the greatest progress in bookkeeping was accomplished during the period from 1250 to 1500. From then on, accounting made little headway until the growth of large-scale enterprise in the nineteenth century brought to the fore new problems and new solutions' *Cambridge Economic History of Europe*, iii, 93—4. 'Premium insurance also started during this period. But despite the high premiums charged by the underwriters, the insurance business does not seem to have been a very profitable one. Not only was the business apparently highly competitive, but it lent itself to fraud. Thus ships were sometimes deliberately shipwrecked in order to claim insurance for goods that were not even on board' *Ibid.*, iii, 99 ff.

[2] *Cambridge Economic History of Europe*, ii, 119 ff, 257 ff.

gilds had been of little importance during the previous period, they now began to multiply rapidly.

In the course of the fourteenth century the gilds succeeded in most centres in asserting their authority and in obtaining a share in the control of the municipal government. The effective countervailing power that they could exercise in the centres that depended on export was, however, narrowly circumscribed by the limitations imposed by a stagnant market. The history of the Flemish artisan gilds was a tragic record of the futility of attempting to resist the efforts of the entrepreneurs to lower their labour costs under highly competitive conditions, with the inevitable result that the trade was diverted to other centres.

The craft gilds had more success in the non-specialised areas, where they could exert pressure to secure the local market for the wares of their own members. They therefore came to play a leading part in the application of the restrictive commercial policies of the late Middle Ages. Their principal aim was to protect their members against the competition not only of other cities but also of their fellow-workers. Thus access to the city markets was reserved exclusively for gild members and attempts were made to prevent any member of the profession from enriching himself at the expense of others. It was to achieve this end that gild regulations imposed, with ever-increasing minuteness, the techniques that had to be observed by all; that working hours, wages and prices were rigidly prescribed; that advertising was prohibited; and that the tools used and the number of apprentices allowed to be employed were carefully decreed. All these measures reflected the spontaneous efforts of the gilds to create conditions of complete equality, and were rooted in the belief that only the granting of equal shares would guarantee sufficient work for all. These regulations became an integral part of town policy and show the extent to which the craft gilds had been incorporated in the town authority and the craft mentality in urban policy.

Break-up of the manorial economy

Because of the drastic fluctuations in the ratio of population to land resources and the decline in grain prices, this period witnessed a considerable contraction of large-scale demesne farming. Labour charges, at times, were increasing, whereas grain prices were falling, with a consequent decline in the profitability of farming. Manorial lords were therefore forced to break up their estates into portions small enough for independent cultivation by peasants.

The result was the increased commutation of feudal dues and services for money payments, a process greatly furthered by the financial needs of the landowners, by the requirements not only of the impecunious nobility, but even of the Church, and especially of the kings. The peasants welcomed this release from burdensome control and degrading obligations. Villeinage was gradually dissolved, and the manorial economy was transformed over the largest part of Europe into a system of tenancy. The seigneur became a rentier—often an absentee landlord—and the peasant gained a greater measure of freedom in the exercise of his calling.

The disappearance of the old centralised administration of the manor gradually led to the dissolution of the personal relations between lord and peasant. The tenant therefore came to look on himself as the owner of his holding and to resent any obligations that he had to render to his landlord. The seigneur, on the other hand, tried to protect himself by transforming the dues owed to him by individual peasants into perpetual servitudes attached to the holdings. What now came to determine the obligations of the peasant was not his original status but the legal duties attached to the holding that he happened to occupy. The lord's right to property was therefore transformed into the peasant's rights, to which perpetual servitudes were attached. The result of this process of dissolution was the blurring and gradual effacement of distinctions of status based on birth.

It was, however, a serious disadvantage to the peasant that this transformation of seignorial institutions and his consequent emancipation was only half completed, and not finally consummated until the French Revolution. With the disappearance of the old centralised administration of the manor and the weakening of personal relations between lord and peasant, the seignorial dues and obligations were felt to be increasingly unjustified and therefore oppressive. The late Middle Ages also witnessed a general decline in grain prices, which increased the burden of money rents and led to a further deterioration of relations. The close of the Middle Ages was marked by a prolonged struggle in western Europe between the peasants striving for complete independence and the landlords clinging tenaciously to rights that were the basis of their existence—a struggle which in England, France, and Germany flared up into open civil war.[1]

The movement towards control

The previous period had been characterised by the prevalence of undeveloped resources. The towns that were initially in a favourable position to exploit these resources developed into highly specialised centres, with the result that striking differences in the levels of technical skill became apparent in many parts of western and central Europe. These factors favoured freedom of enterprise and of inter-regional trade and created a new mobility of both men and merchandise.

This situation began to change fundamentally towards the end of the thirteenth century. Many areas, which in the previous period had remained relatively under-developed, now entered a phase of rapid expansion. The result was that during the course of the fourteenth century industrial activity came to be far more evenly spread over the whole of central and western Europe. Regions that had previously served as sources of supply of raw materials and as markets for the finished wares of the developed centres, now became competitive sources of supply of finished goods. With static techniques, profit margins began to decline, and this had a deleterious effect on the inducement to invest. The secular stagnation that followed had important effects on the temper of townsmen and on the policies adopted by the urban authorities.

Such a situation was likely to call forth two types of policy. Those economically advanced centres that wielded sufficient economic and political power, or that could improve their techniques, could apply monopolistic pressure in an attempt to maintain their position. The economically less developed centres, on the other hand, could resort to protectionism and control to achieve this end. Both these policies were adopted.

[1] Nabholz, in *Cambridge Economic History of Europe*, i, ch 8. 'The general impression is that in the second half of the fourteenth and the first half of the fifteenth centuries tenements burdened with heavy dues could not as a rule be re-let except by altering, i.e. by improving, the terms of the contract other than the money rent itself. Agreement to commute was one such improvement; more liberal re-definition of services was another' (Postan, *Economic History Review*, second series, ii, no. 3.

There was a definite and significant trend in the late Middle Ages for a small number of towns to achieve superiority over a large number of their less successful competitors. Thus in England, London, Southampton and Bristol rose to a leading position; in Flanders the 'big three'—Ghent, Ypres and Bruges—crushed their smaller neighbours as well as the rural industries in their neighbourhood; in northern Germany the small group that dominated the Hanseatic League obtained a monopolistic position; and in Italy a few cities obtained control over extensive territories and completely subordinated their lesser rivals. The means employed were always the same: the use of a combination of political and economic power to crush their rivals. The objective was to secure or to retain a privileged position, and especially to keep control of the carrying trade.

The smaller centres tried to attract to themselves what economic activity could be obtained by a policy of exclusiveness and protection. This was reflected in attempts to preserve the environs of the town as a strictly private source of raw materials and as a sales outlet for finished wares. Where the towns formed small autonomous states, which ensured the effective political domination of the sur-rounding country, competitive rural industries were completely prohibited. Towns also tried to attract productive resources to themselves and to prohibit their export to other centres—whether these resources were skill, capital, or raw materials.

This policy of exclusiveness was reflected in the antagonism shown to foreign merchants who tried to encroach on the local commercial preserves. Not only were duties imposed on foreign merchants from which local merchants were exempted, but a complete prohibition was often imposed on the importation or sale of outside goods. Since medieval states were far less integrated than modern ones, this protec-tion had a local rather than an international aspect. Thus everywhere attempts were made to keep local trade for the merchants of the town; strangers were forbidden to engage in retail trade or to trade directly between themselves; and, finally, attempts were made to establish an absolute monopoly for the town in specific commodities or along a specific route.

These defensive restrictions reflected the growing strength of craftsmen and of the affiliated retailers in urban policy, men whose economic horizon was bounded by the town walls, and who were imbued with the idea that local prosperity during a period of contraction could best be secured by the twin principles of external exclusiveness and the internal regulation of economic activities. It shows the change from the previous period, when power was normally in the hands of the urban patriciate—the landowners and the leading merchants—and when the only associations were the merchant gilds. It was at once a change in outlook, in interest, and in policy.[1]

The dominance of the large commercial centres

The economic life of the late Middle Ages can be understood only when viewed in the light of the predominance of the great commercial centres over the undeveloped

[1] The canonical concept of the just price and the prohibition of usury reflect the same craft mentality. The idea of a mechanism such as a market functioning automatically and indepen-dently of the needs of the community was abhorrent to the clerical thoughts of the later Middle Ages. The prices of commodities should, on the contrary, be determined by their proper function in the communal order. Prices should conform to the cost of production, and the craftsman should be rewarded in a way which would enable him to maintain his proper station in life. The concept of the just price thus reflects the basic conflict between distributive shares based on value and those required by status.

territorial states of the time. The revenue of a city state such as Florence or Milan exceeded that of large medieval kingdoms, and as intermediaries in the circulation of goods and as financial centres they were indispensable. Even in smaller towns, situated in territories in which the central authorities had gone further in the work of 'state-building', the functions of economic control were still in the hands of the largely autonomous local authorities. This was, in fact, one of the main obstacles to the attainment of 'national' entities and the formulation of 'national' economic policies, even in those western countries where political integration had made the greatest progress.

But important changes were now taking place within the communes themselves. The previous period had been one of social and political solidarity; class interests had been complementary rather than competitive, and political power had been firmly vested in the hands of the patriciate. Now strongly divergent interests emerged, politically, socially and economically. Politically, the most important factor was the emergence of the craft gilds and their growing participation in town government and in the formulation of urban policy. The control of the commune was henceforth shared, and rested on a precarious balance between an oligarchical minority and a majority composed of a variety of craft gilds. Socially, this period was characterised by intense conflict between the various groups within the town walls. Economically, the scene was dominated by struggle between the entrepreneurial and propertied classes on the one hand, and the craftsmen on the other hand, between the conflicting interests of different centres, and between the communes and the emergent national states.

During the course of the fourteenth and fifteenth centuries there came for many towns a period of genuine crisis. They suffered heavily from a periodic or permanent decline in population; they had to fight bitterly for a share in a stable or diminishing volume of international trade; they were faced with serious financial problems, and they had to struggle to preserve control over their own destinies from the encroachment of the territorial powers.

The towns therefore had to make heroic efforts to maintain themselves. In Germany the larger Hanse centres spent from 75 to 90 per cent of their revenue on defence and diplomatic services. In the Flemish, north French and west German towns a large proportion of urban revenue had to be spent on the servicing of the communal debts; and in Flanders and in France the towns were ultimately subjected to control so that the available financial resources could be more effectively mobilised by the territorial authorities.

The communes tried to maintain themselves by resorting to a policy of exclusiveness. The late Middle Ages were characterised by a general diminution of economic freedom, by a decline in the tolerance shown to outsiders, and by a fundamental change in the liberal policies of the previous period. The result was that the commune, which had been the standard-bearer of emancipation and progress during the previous period, now became a reactionary force retarding the growth of larger and more virile societies. It was clear that the western world was not to be reconstituted into a society of city states. But what a different world might have emerged if this could have been achieved.

The rise of national states

During the central Middle Ages the extreme disintegration of the previous period had gradually given way to greater internal unification. The movement had proceeded slowly, for there were very formidable obstacles to the attainment of unity in the form of inadequate means of communication and inadequate resources of the central powers. But above all the movement was impeded by the lien that had been established on government power by the beneficiaries of the previous period of disintegration, and in particular by the feudal nobility and the urban authorities. By the end of the Middle Ages, however, much progress had been made in this direction in western countries such as England, France, and Spain. In central and northern Italy the territorial principalities came gradually to replace the city communes as the prevailing form of political organisation, and even in a deeply fragmented country such as Germany there were signs that the further process of disintegration had been stopped.

The tension created during the late Middle Ages between the different classes in the towns, between the conflicting interests of different centres, and between the towns and the countryside, called for increasing intervention on the part of the central authorities. Endeavours to safeguard established interests, whether in the face of contracting markets or new competition, created a demand for the intervention of these authorities. Thus the old industrial centres of Italy asked for protection against the new developing areas, the Flemish cloth towns demanded protection against English competition, the English merchants cried for help against the privileged Hansards and Italians. Restrictive policies, again, required government sanction and enforcement.

The central governments strengthened their financial resources to cope with these new responsibilities. The traditional revenues they obtained from their own domains were increasingly overshadowed by the 'extraordinary' levies, from direct and indirect taxes, and from loans. Kings were indeed continually exhorted to 'live on their own'. But it became increasingly accepted that the earlier type of state, which lacked an elaborate administration and which depended on the political support and the unpaid military service of feudal vassals, was disappearing, and that it was being superseded by better organised and more centralised administrations, supported by mercenary armies and by a salaried bureaucracy. The difficulties faced by central governments to obtain the consent of their subjects to the imposition of regular taxation, however, remained one of the greatest sources of weakness of medieval kingdoms. Hence the necessity of relying on the loans of foreign merchant-bankers to tide them over the difficult period of fiscal reform, during which western society could adjust itself to the painful necessity of regular taxation.

National policy was still timid, compromising, and vacillating, but it was gradually proceeding in the direction of mercantilism; towards a system of national self-sufficiency and power as opposed to both urban exclusiveness and internationalism; towards a policy of freeing the countryside from the domination of the towns; and towards the subordination of particularistic to state interests. The economic penetration of the West by the great commercial centres had come to an end. A new political and economic era had emerged.[1]

---

[1] *Cambridge Economic History of Europe*, iii, pt 2.

Part 6
The Early Modern Period

The imposition of central controls and the
movement towards economic freedom in the West

*End of the fifteenth century to the last quarter
of the eighteenth century*

16

The discoveries, the price revolution, and the rise of national states

The discoveries

The turning point between the fifteenth and sixteenth centuries was a time of great changes, a time pregnant with possibilities for the creation of a new economic order. The Renaissance released the pent-up energies of western Europe, energies that found expression in a new joy of life—in aesthetic presentation, intellectual inquiry, and the faith of men in their ability to control the environment by observation and reason. A secular, materially orientated, and intellectually curious society was emerging in western Europe. The secular individualism of the Renaissance no doubt contributed to the religious individualism of the Reformation, which was soon challenging the authority of the papacy. The printing press was facilitating the diffusion of knowledge. National states were consolidating themselves. Finally, there commenced an era of geographical discoveries, which within a relatively short time opened up three-quarters of the globe. These forces created favourable conditions for the development of the market economy.

The discovery of America and of the sea route to India was probably the main contributory factor to the development of this period. Many mixed motives, 'gospel, glory and gold', stimulated the process of discovery, and a number of improvements in maritime knowledge and equipment made it possible.

Although moral considerations no doubt contributed to the issue, the main motive for the voyages of discovery was without a doubt to establish a direct sea route to the source of the spice trade, and thus to break down the monopolies of the Arabs and the Italians. At that time spices played a role in drug lists and in the culinary art, and consequently in international trade, that is difficult for us to conceive today. Spices were rare and precious wares worth their weight in gold. Only the search for spices and precious metals could induce navigators to equip fleets and to venture forth in their small ships into unknown and uncharted seas. Columbus was never forgiven for having discovered the wrong route, whereas the Portuguese held the right road to the spice country. Nor was he pardoned for having discovered so little gold. It was the thirst for precious metals that drove his successors on to the mainland, and it was only when gold and silver were discovered that America ceased to be regarded as a barrier and became an asset valued in itself.

Whereas the discovery of America was the result of a lucky accident, that of the Cape route was the fruit of long and rational effort.[1]

The discoveries in their turn contributed to the development of the market economy. The expansion of the European market into a world market gave increased scope for commercial enterprise and encouraged new forms of organisation and control. The new countries called for increased quantities of European manufactured goods, and the introduction of eastern wares soon led to their imitation and production at home. The enormous profits made in the East Indian trade were for the most part reinvested in commercial, industrial and financial undertakings.[2] Long-distance voyages improved the technique of navigation. Above all, the discovery of new lands and strange peoples widened men's mental horizons. The discovery of the New World and of the sea route to India was therefore of primary importance for the development of capitalist enterprise through the enlarged economic horizon that it created, the larger fields of competitive activity that it originated, the profit inflation that it induced, and the more favourable forms of economic organisation that it brought about.

The price revolution

An important and immediate effect of the discoveries was to augment the supply of precious metals. Not only were new mines opened up in central Europe during the second half of the fifteenth century, but the Portuguese soon began to ship large quantities of gold from Africa, and the Spaniards imported increasing amounts from the New World. Improved methods of extraction, smelting, and refining further helped to increase the supply. This output, though small if compared with the production of today, meant an important addition to Europe's accumulated stocks. The new sources of supply were especially necessary as large quantities of gold and silver were exported to the East in payment for oriental imports. A severe decline in prices, with deleterious effects on enterprise, would therefore have followed the opening-up of the sea route to India if the American supply had not been forthcoming. 'The voyage of Columbus was an imperative supplement to that of da Gama.'[3]

During the last quarter of the fourteenth century a decline in prices set in, which reached its lowest point about 1475. From that date there began the tremendous upward swing known as the price revolution. For the first fifty years the increase was moderate, then it gathered speed, until, towards the middle of the seventeenth century, a peak was reached. Commodity price indices in France and England during this period seem to have increased by about 200 per cent. In Spain the price level soared rapidly during the sixteenth century—the increase amounting to nearly 500 per cent—to reach its highest point near the end of the century. The advance in the Spanish price level during the sixteenth century was about twice as great as that of France and England over the longer period from 1475 to 1663, and the upward trend was exhausted about fifty years earlier than in the northern countries. During

[1] Hauser and Renaudet, *Peuples et civilisations, les debuts de l'age moderne*, pp. 55 ff.
[2] Profits made in the East Indian trade were very high. Vasco da Gama returned to Lisbon in 1499 with a cargo that repaid sixty times the cost of the expedition. During the 198 years of its existence the Dutch East India Company paid an average yearly dividend of 18 per cent. During the seventeenth century the dividends of the English East India Company averaged about 100 per cent.
[3] Hamilton, *Economica*, ix, 338 ff.

the seventeenth century the European mines gradually ceased production, the world output of silver declined, and gold production increased only slightly. Since both production and commerce continued to advance, the result was that the upward surge of prices had spent itself by about 1660. From that year until about 1745 there was a mildly downward trend in the price levels of western Europe, followed by a renewed advance after 1746, an increase that continued till the close of the Napoleonic wars.[1]

It is of course not the mere increase in prices as such, except in so far as it acts as a transfer of resources from the more passive rentier to the more active entrepreneurial class, but an increase in prices more rapid than the increase in costs, with a consequent inflation of profits, that acts as a stimulus to enterprise. American treasure acted as a spur to enterprise by influencing the two factors which condition that iniative, namely, the expectation of profit and the command of resources. In Spain during the first sixty years of the sixteenth century prices always kept comfortably ahead of wages, and conditions were propitious for a rapid accumulation of wealth. 'The resultant material prosperity, together with the effect of the specie on national psychology, played a part in the passage of Spain through her golden age of literature and art.' But after 1588, and especially after 1600, wages began to rule permanently above prices, so that a severe profit deflation set in. Spain had lost the most enterprising elements of her population through immigration or expulsion. Too much wealth sapped the vitality of the people. Instead of being used for investment at home, most of the American treasure was wasted by imperial policy abroad. Senseless ambitions drained away not only the wealth but also the lifeblood of the people, while the illusion of wealth encouraged extravagance and vagrancy at home.[2]

Things were different in other parts of Europe. Here the new purchasing power filtered in through the channels of commerce and was largely reinvested in that source. Wages and rent were slow to react, with the result that profit inflation continued in England until the mid-seventeenth century and in France until the end of the century. The 'common labourers' and the nobility, whose lands had been leased by their ancestors at a fixed rental charge, were the principal losers; peasants, and to a greater extent wealthy merchants, bankers and usurers were the greatest gainers. The price movement was at times so rapid that it caused grave discontent among the classes that were being dispossessed. Almost every European government in turn tried ineffectively to cope with the price problem.

The price revolution offered unparalleled opportunities to the middle-class capitalist. In the course of this period a large part of the property of the French nobility passed into the hands of the urban bourgeoisie, who in turn were ennobled, so that the nobility of France came to consist for the main part of an enriched third estate.[3] 'Never in the annals of the modern world', says Keynes, 'has there existed so prolonged and rich an opportunity for the business man, the speculator and the profiteer.'[4]

The tendency towards a contraction of the European economy, which followed the slightly downward move of the price level after the middle of the seventeenth century, then led to an increased competition among the powers for precious

---

[1] 'Prices', in *Encyclopaedia of the Social Sciences.*
[2] Hamilton, *American Treasure and the Price Revolution in Spain.*
[3] Hauser and Renaudet, *Peuples et civilisations—La Preponderance espagnole*, pp. 202 ff; See, *Französische Wirtschaftsgeschichte*, i, 118 ff.
[4] Keynes, *A Treatise on Money*, ii, 152 ff.

metals. Mercantilist policy entered a pronounced protectionist phase bringing with it navigation laws, protective tariffs, and wars to disturb European relations.

Professor Nef has cautioned against unduly exaggerating the part played by the price revolution in the development of early capitalist enterprise. For not only have new discoveries of price records, according to him, shown the profit inflation to have been less than was formerly thought, but industry also responded in different ways in different countries to the strains and stimuli provided by the inflow of American treasure and the debasement of the coinage. Thus, whereas in England industrial advance was more rapid between 1540 and 1640 than in any other period before the Industrial Revolution, progress seems to have been slower in France between the death of Francis I and the accession of Louis XIV than during the previous hundred years, when the inflow of treasure from America had hardly begun. The period of profit inflation therefore coincided with conditions of stagnation as well as of economic expansion.[1]

It must however be pointed out that, while the century mentioned was one of peace in England, where strong rulers governed the country, it was a period of almost continuous warfare in France—which merely goes to show that historical causation is always complex. The mistake of overestimating the effect of American treasure on European growth is that the supply of capital merely provides the condition for economic development, whereas it is the demand for resources that calls forth the productive investment. It is therefore rather in the factors on the side of demand that the main causes of development—or the lack of it—during this period must be sought. This is reflected by the fact that the period of rapid development during the nineteenth century was one of almost continuous deflation; but the technological improvements and cost economies more than offset the effects of falling prices. The influence of American treasure on European development during this period must therefore no doubt be sought in the conditions that it created for the provision of capital, necessitated by the fact that increased trade required additional money to finance business, rather than in its effect on the price of capital.[2]

The rise of national states

An important factor in the rise of modern capitalism was the formation of strong centralised states. Large and well-ordered kingdoms arose from the ruins of feudal chaos. Instead of each tiny community's maintaining an exclusive policy towards the outside world, larger areas appeared, within which law and order were established, greater uniformity brought about in commercial legislation, currencies and weights and measures, and from which some of the internal impediments to the free circulation of goods were removed. What was of even greater importance was the formulation of deliberate national policies to further the general interest against the sectional aims of town, gild, and manor.

[1] Nef, *Economic History Review*, vii, no. 2.
[2] The following dates show a marked correlation, both as cause and as effect, between secular swings in agricultural prices and secular changes in economic development during a period of relative technical stability. Periods of rising agricultural prices were 1150-1300 and 1460-1650. These were characteristically the periods of land reclamation, expansion of arable *vis-à-vis* livestock farming, and a trend towards larger holdings. Periods of stationary or falling agricultural prices were 1300-1450 and 1650-1750. A variety of other developments, such as the course of real wages and the incidence of agrarian disorder, were related to these swings.

The present economic system would be a pure impossibility at a time when goods and travellers were held up by customs barriers at about every six miles on the best of routes; when the currency changed with every day's journey; when industrial activity was confined to the handicraftsmen of the locality, and agricultural production was subordinated to the interest of the neighbouring little municipality, and every little community governed as it thought best. The expansion of production was hampered, even more, by the particular attitude of mind insolubly bound up with particularism, whose ideal was a static one, firmly anchored in a religious system and believing in 'subsistence' according to rank; with a technique which was certainly often artistically high but unalterable in principle; and in which economic activity was considered to a very great extent as an end in itself. . . . There is little doubt that the destruction of medieval particularism was one of the indispensable, fundamental conditions for making life physically possible for the mass of people of the present time.[1]

The term 'mercantilism' was given by the physiocrats and was popularised by Adam Smith to designate the economic policy that the early modern state applied to stabilise and to extend its power. Mercantilism aimed at the mobilisation of all economic resources to strengthen the power of the state, a policy which reached its clearest expression and its most forceful application in the France of Louis XIV.

In the autocracies the officials tried to encourage private enterprise as a means of promoting the interests of the state. In the 'democracies', on the other hand, the commercial interests succeeded to a very large extent in the seventeenth and eighteenth centuries in making the state serve their own specific interests. For if the state was eager to promote the wealth of its citizens to further its own ends, the rising capitalist class was as anxious to use state action to serve its own purpose, under the pretext of contributing to national power and the public purse. According to Professor Unwin nine-tenths of the inventive ingenuity of the seventeenth century was employed, not in exploiting the powers of nature, but 'in the endeavour to manipulate the power of the state and the wealth of the community for the benefit of individuals'.[2] Adam Smith, commenting on some aspects of British commercial policy, remarked that 'the sneaking acts of underling tradesmen are thus erected into political maxims for a great empire'.[3] In the restrictive aspects of colonial policy he saw nothing but a 'project fit only for a nation of shopkeepers'.[4] No wonder that there were persistent demands in the democracies for a 'business government'.[5]

But then both these writers were strongly prejudiced against mercantilist theories and their exponents. The dynamic force behind the achievements of this period was undoubtedly the energy and quest for material gain of the entrepreneur and the organised pursuit of power by the state. And if the merchant was dependent on the resources of the state, the state was in as much need of the drive and resources of the private entrepreneur. By the end of this period the symbiosis of public and private interest, of power and plenty, and between the state and the capitalist class had been largely attained in the maritime powers of the West.

[1] Heckscher, *Mercantilism*, i, 43.
[2] Unwin, *Studies in Economic History*, pt 2, ch 9.
[3] Smith, *The Wealth of Nations*, bk iv, ch 3, pt 2.
[4] *Ibid.*, bk iv, ch 7, pt 3.
[5] Robertson, *Aspects of the Rise of Economic Individualism*, p. 69.

17

Commerce and the development of private enterprise

The rise of a world market

Commerce offered the most extensive scope for capitalist enterprise during this period. It was a typical sphere of concentrated large-scale operations, and the joint stock companies of the time consisted very largely of commercial concerns. Production was controlled mainly by the merchant, who, in the worlds of Mantoux, was 'the exciter of industry'. The English word *trade* and the French *commerce* referred to industry as well as to trade. Industrial economics went under the name of 'commercial science'. The importance of the merchant was reflected in the almost fanatical admiration expressed for him in the economic literature of the time. 'The Merchant', said Davenant, 'deserves all Favour as being the best and most profitable member of the Commonwealth', and in the opinion of Petty, 'a Seaman is in effect equivalent to three Husbandmen'.[1]

The discovery of the New World and the opening up of direct relations with the East introduced a new era of commercial enterprise. International trade was no longer confined to a few inland seas but became a worldwide traffic. Commercial supremacy passed from Italy and Germany to the countries on the Atlantic: to Spain and Portugal in the sixteenth century, to Holland in the seventeenth, and to Britain in the eighteenth. Even in Germany the lead passed from Lübeck to Hamburg. Everywhere in the West the ports grew more rapidly than the towns of the interior. At the same time many medieval restrictions on intercourse were removed. Other restraints, however, remained, and new ones were imposed. With the rise of national states and the ruralisation of industry, territorial specialisation seems on the whole to have decreased over large parts of Europe.

The volume of transactions increased fairly steadily throughout the early modern period, although naturally it remained on a very modest scale when compared with the commerce of the present day. Hitherto the trade of Europe with the outside world had been limited largely to oriental luxuries, consisting mainly of spices, silks, tapestries, precious stones and the like, which were articles consumed only by the rich. Not only was the supply of these wares now greatly increased, but

---

[1] Hull, *Economic Writings of Sir William Petty*, i, p. 259. This high estimation was also probably not unassociated with the fact that from the fifteenth to the eighteenth century economic theory in England was provided mainly by the merchant class.

a whole new range of commodities was added. Overseas commerce no longer adapted itself exclusively to the needs of the rich but also to the requirements of the middle classes. A large number of colonial wares came into fairly common use. Towards the end of this period commerce began to cater increasingly also for the labouring classes, thus preparing the way for the mass production of commodities that was to characterise the Industrial Revolution.

Inter-European trade was characterised by the absence of any pronounced territorial specialisation. In spite of high protective tariffs the greatest variety of manufactured goods passed from one country to another, similar articles often being imported and exported by the same country. The export of manufactured wares between the different countries of Europe was however not balanced by a corresponding import of raw materials. In the Middle Ages the textile industries of Flanders and Florence had been dependent on imported wool. But in the early modern period this specialisation tended, to a certain extent, to disappear. It was one of the fundamental tenets of mercantile policy that raw materials should not be exported—except, of course, by the colonies—but should be worked up at home. Early modern industry was largely rooted in the native soil. The linens of the Continent, the woollens of Britain, and the silks of France were manufactured from raw materials supplied by the home market. This mercantilist ideal, however, was sometimes more honoured in the breach than the observance. Thus important industries, such as shipbuilding and the metal trades, were largely dependent on foreign raw materials.[1]

Staple markets, commodity exchanges and shops

Not only the wares but also the character of commerce underwent important modifications. In the Middle Ages trade relations had to a certain extent retained a periodical, perambulatory and highly personal character. The personal element was to a certain extent maintained. But there was a tendency for the determination of prices to become more rational and impersonal, and with the commodity exchanges, almost mechanical. The face-to-face bartering and haggling of the medieval market was superseded in the case of larger transactions by contracts for delivery at a given price at some specified future date. The increasing need of armies and cities for commodities in bulk and the growth of overseas trade made such methods imperative. The goods, however, or at least their samples, still had to be physically present, inspected, and handled on what were known as the 'exchanges' or 'bourses' of the time. 'After the bargain is struck, the merchants or the brokers go to the warehouse with their samples in order to show the buyers that the goods conform to the samples, whereupon delivery is completed.' Wares were not yet sufficiently standardised to be sold by grades. Even the 'selling by samples only' was deprecated by the more conservative commercial elements. Defoe referred to it as 'utterly unlawful'.

The growth of international traffic made the concentration of commerce in central staple markets necessary for the determination of freights and prices. In these 'continuous fairs' the goods were sold at the bourse or exchange. The existence of these institutions was conditioned by a volume of trade large enough

[1] Kulischer, *Allgemeine Wirtschaftsgeschichte*, ii, 227 ff; Sombart, *Der Moderne Kapitalismus*, ii, ch 47, 62; Rörig, *Mittelalterliche Weltwirtschaft*, p. 36; See, *Französische Wirtschaftsgeschichte*, pp. 310 ff.

to cause a steady and continuous flow of wares. The objects also had to be sufficiently valuable to bear the extra costs of transport and reshipment. The big oversea companies sold their wares by auction on these exchanges. 'At the "candle-auctions" on the Royal Exchange of London in the seventeenth century, goods were offered with an inch of lighted candle on the desk, and were knocked down before the candle went out. A single parcel of silk, indigo, or spice sold in this way was sometimes worth half a million dollars.'[1]

It was however not before the nineteenth century that the commodity exchange reached its full development. In the second half of the eighteenth century, on the other hand, staple markets declined. With the increased movement of articles of mass consumption, the circuitous transport, transhipment, and assessment of goods no longer proved profitable. As the means of transport became cheaper, safer, and more regular, the central market was no longer indispensable. Consequently international trade became more decentralised.

At the same time there was a tendency for commerce to become less migratory and more settled. Resident retailers increased rapidly in the seventeenth and eighteenth centuries until, at the end of this period, every town and even most villages in central and western Europe possessed their own retail establishments. In the larger towns the shops became specialised: there arose fruiterers, greengrocers, drapers, mercers, jewellers, and so forth. By 1725 there are said to have been more than 6,000 retail shops in London alone. Price maintenance and even the fixed or one-price system were already employed by English retailers at the beginning of the eighteenth century. Distinctive retail shop architecture, with attractive store fronts, effective window displays, artistic signs, and the clever use of lighting effects, was also coming into evidence.

Commercial organisation

The functions of distribution became differentiated and specialised. Under the domestic system the wholesaler assumed the function of coordinating production and of finding a market for the finished wares. Besides the itinerant merchant there appeared many general merchants (wholesalers), jobbers, brokers, and factors. But the separation between wholesale and retail trade was seldom complete, especially in the provinces, and, even when separate, the two functions might still be performed by the same person. Merchant manufacturers sold not only to shopkeepers but also direct to consumers. In central Europe, wholesalers still dealt in the greatest variety of goods. In the West, however, specialisation according to functions, wares, and markets proceeded apace, and by the end of the sixteenth and the beginning of the seventeenth centuries the separation of retail from wholesale trade and of local from foreign trade was recognised in the main in England, though the principle was never really applied in the provinces, and exceptions were occasionally found even in London. The export trade was organised mainly on a commission basis, whereas selling on consignment became increasingly common towards the end of this period, both in domestic and in foreign trade.

Currency and credit

The means and methods of payment also underwent considerable modification

[1] Day, *A History of Commerce*, p. 155.

during this period. The growth of large territorial states in the west led to a reduction in the number of minting centres. In central Europe each territorial state and many towns still issued their own currency, and many centres, and especially the smallest, systematically depreciated their coinage. In addition, from the thirteenth century onward, gold was generally adopted in conjunction with silver as standard money, and this introduced a further source of confusion, since the ratio between the metals prescribed by the European mints varied constantly, and German contracts not only specified whether payment had to be effected in gold or silver but also stipulated the specific coins that had to be used. Even in the west there was a marked absence of determination on the part of the state to create a good and uniform currency system. Fiscal motives predominated, and in times of financial stress currencies were frequently debased. Almost up to the end of the seventeenth century the technique of minting was so inefficient that coins could easily be counterfeited and debased. Towards the end of this period, however, methods of minting improved so much that better and more standardised coins could be produced at a lower cost. In spite of the influx of American treasure there was often a great scarcity of small change, and local merchants tried to make good the deficiency by circulating their own currency.

Owing to the condition of the currency, various substitutes for coins came into general use. Bills of exchange had been regularly employed in the Middle Ages, both as commercial and as credit instruments. The practice of endorsing these bills appeared early in the sixteenth century, making them negotiable and greatly encouraging their use. Exports to the Orient and to the colonies were paid for largely by bills drawn on the large commercial centres, and especially on London and Amsterdam.

The discounting of bills was introduced in the seventeenth century, though it was still regarded with distrust. 'Borrowing money upon interest', says Defoe, 'is very dangerous; but this discounting of bills is certain death to the tradesman.' The discounting of bills and the granting of other forms of commercial credit by private individuals often developed out of wholesale trade, shipping and commission business. It was largely through the liberal grant of acceptance credit that Dutch merchants were able to maintain their position in international trade during the eighteenth century.[1]

The bad condition of the coinage also facilitated the settling of accounts by means of clearing arrangements. This system created an ideal unit of account called bank money, in which wares and currencies could be valued. The desire to perpetuate this unit of account led to the establishment by municipal authorities in the seventeenth century of numerous public transfer banks, of which the banks of Amsterdam and Hamburg were the best known. Balances in bank money were established with these institutions by the deposit of coin or bullion. These deposits were to be used not for the extension of loans but as the foundation of a book transfer system. Few of these banks, however, could resist the pressure of public authorities for unauthorised and often secret loans. This impaired the ability to convert their money into precious metal on demand, and most of them had been dissolved by the end of the eighteenth century.

While the market for the discount of commercial paper was developed by private finance, and the deposit and clearance mechanism was forged by money-changers and transfer (giro) banks, the other component of modern commercial banking, the banknote, was supplied by banks of issue. These banks of issue were established at

[1] Romein, *De Lage Landen bij de Zee*, p. 328.

the end of the seventeenth and the beginning of the eighteenth century to provide funds for the state as well as for commerce and industry.

In the seventeenth century, goldsmiths in England received deposits from the public which they lent out at interest to the government and to business men. Demand deposits could be transferred by book transfers, by means of drafts, which led to the development of the cheque system, or by the circulation of the deposit vouchers, which thus came to represent the oldest form of English banknotes. The goldsmiths soon discovered that the amount of vouchers outstanding could be kept considerably larger than the available cash balances. When, however, loans were no longer made exclusively to merchants through the discount of bills of exchange, but to the Treasury as well, this lending beyond their resources proved fatal. With the suspension of payments by the government in 1672 many of the goldsmiths went to the wall.

This disaster led to the establishment of the Bank of England in 1694, an institution which was to be independent of the state and was to engage in banking operations such as the purchase of bullion, the discounting of bills, and the granting of secured loans. It was the first modern bank of issue that combined the functions of a transfer bank with those of a commercial bank. The success of the institution led to the foundation of a number of similar banks on the Continent. But the pressure of their governments for loans soon forced these banks to suspend payment. By the end of this period, however, Europe was well on the way to developing all the essential elements of the modern commercial banking system.

Partnerships, regulated companies, and joint stock companies

One of the outstanding features of capitalist organisation has been the rise of the impersonal business entity, the firm or the enterprise, in contrast to the other collective forms of association, such as the family and the gild. But business enterprise during this period in the main retained its personal and individual character. The one-man business and the partnership met most of the requirements of the time.

The partnership had been a common form of organisation in medieval commerce and banking. With the growth of businesses that required any appreciable investment of capital, it was applied also to other forms of enterprise. French trade and industry, with the exception of the few state undertakings, were organised on this basis. Dutch commercial and shipping ventures, outside the few large oversea companies, made use almost exclusively of ordinary partnership relations. Coal-mining, a great source of speculative investment in England, was financed mainly by partnerships. When the English goldsmiths turned their attention to banking, many of them organised their businesses in this way. Many of the large manufacturing establishments were similarly organised.[1]

---

[1] A major difficulty in the efficient organisation of the large industrial enterprise was the inadequacy of the financial procedures used. Mercantile accounting made little progress during this period and was still largely of the single-entry type. This method of accounting was also adopted for industrial purposes, but was not adapted to the needs of establishments which required a considerable outlay of capital. Such were, for example, the new enterprises that developed during this period for the manufacture of paper, glass, printing and powder making. The financial results of such undertakings could obviously be controlled only if provision was made for depreciation. But for this to be done, fixed capital had to be transformed in the minds of industrialists from concrete entities such as buildings, equipment or machines into abstract money values, and this was a difficult mental achievement for the businessmen of the day. Freudenberger and Redlich, in *Kyklos*, xvii, 1964, no. 3.

The partnership facilitated the accumulation of capital and its investment in business. Grave defects, however, were the unlimited liability of the partners and the lack of permanence of the enterprise. The division of the capital into transferable shares was already a common practice in German mining partnerships of the early sixteenth century. The same procedure was followed at an early stage in the history of British coal-mining and shipping, and it was the normal usage of syndicates contracting with the English government in the early seventeenth century.

On the basis of the private partnership and the merchant gild there arose the regulated company. This form of association obtained its highest development in England, the best examples being the Merchant Staples and the Merchant Adventurers. In these regulated companies there was no common capital. Each member traded on his own account, but subject to the rules and with the aid of the company's organisation. These companies were really associations organised for limited tasks, and not enterprises in which the members formed part of a superior entity. The associational form, however, secured for them special powers and privileges. They held exclusive trading rights and possessed a common purse out of which was defrayed expenditure for defence, the maintenance of ambassadors, and charitable assistance to members.

Within the framework of the regulated company, though foreign to it in spirit, there arose the joint stock company. Instead of each member trading on his own account, the participants united their resources in a common purse for the purpose first of a single voyage and then of a number of voyages, the stock finally becoming the permanent capital of the firm. This stock was made up of transferable shares, the management falling into the hands of a body constituted by the largest shareholders.

The impersonal unity of the corporation developed slowly. Each of the first voyages of the English and the Dutch East India Company was financed by a separate contribution of capital. At the termination of each expedition the capital with the profit was paid back to the shareholders, and then the same individuals, or others, among themselves subscribed the stock for the next venture. But independent merchants or associations were no longer allowed to operate within the corporation. The idea of a fixed capital bound up indissolubly with the enterprise developed gradually, largely because the share market met the needs of individuals who wished to liquidate their holdings.

This impermanence of the capital did not seem initially to have conflicted to any important extent with the economic needs of the times. During the early modern period joint stock enterprise played a small part in those branches of activity that today demand a large investment of fixed capital. The only important sphere was overseas trade, and even here the possibilities afforded by joint stock organisation for the distribution of risk seem to have outweighed the opportunities for the concentration of capital. Nor was the value of the shares standardised. Relations within these companies were still largely personal in spite of the impersonal character of the corporation. Shareholders were referred to as 'brothers', and the transfer of stock was limited. Stockholders were drawn from a limited social and geographical circle: the family, friends, the town, or the county. Preferably they were limited to important personages. According to Hume, the foreign commerce of Britain in his time was controlled by 200 wealthy merchants.

These overseas companies were not exclusively commercial undertakings. In countries where European methods of government were not in force, certain state functions had to be delegated to business corporations. Commerce assumed a 'political' complexion. A large investment of fixed capital was required not so much for the business establishment itself as for the exercise of military and political functions: for the maintenance of defence works, military forces, and diplomatic representation. Duties such as these could be effectively carried out only by the state or by chartered companies that were given a privileged position in the areas they opened up to European penetration.

In Portugal the problem was solved by the state's assumption of control and by the organisation of colonial trade as a state monopoly. Spain adopted the same method, but in a modified form. In France the great oversea companies were merely thinly disguised public undertakings. The state took up a large part of their shares and exercised a rigid control over their management. In Holland and England, on the other hand, the difficulty was solved by the delegation of state functions to private corporations. The grant of the exclusive right to trade in the areas they opened up was held to be indispensable to the successful operation of these companies.

State enterprise was faced with the insuperable difficulty of the absence of an efficient and honest administration. Chartered companies, in spite of numerous failures, were on the whole more successful, though their management and direction, too, were by no means models of efficiency. From a survey of the history of joint stock companies up to his time (1776), Adam Smith came to the conclusion that corporations could not profitably carry on any branch of foreign trade of which they did not hold the monopoly. The skill and judgment needed to adapt the supply of goods to the vagaries of the market under competitive conditions resembled 'a species of warfare which can scarce ever be conducted successfully without such an unremitting exertion of vigilance and attention as cannot long be expected from the directors of a joint stock company'. The only functions that, in his opinion, could be efficiently carried out by a corporation were those that could be reduced to routine, such as banking, insurance, the making and maintenance of canals, and water supply.[1]

The corporate form of organisation was characteristic only of the great oversea commercial companies, in which the capital and the risk required were too great to be undertaken by anything but 'by a joint and united stock'. Outside this sphere it was represented spasmodically in public utilities, insurance, banking, and industry. Towards the end of the seventeenth century, the speculative possibilities of freely transferable stock and the craze for company promotion greatly stimulated the formation of unincorporated associations called companies, but regarded by the law as partnerships. Their inability to sue or to be sued except in the names of all their members as well as the unlimited liability of the shareholders gave rise to great confusion.

The frenzied speculation in the shares of companies during the early years of the eighteenth century culminated in 1720 in the South Sea Bubble in England and the failure of Law's Mississippi Scheme in France. The Bubble Act of that year prohibited the formation of joint stock companies in Britain except by royal charter or by private act of parliament. The unincorporated company, however, continued to serve as a more or less efficient substitute. For the rest, individual firms and partnerships satisfied the needs of an age which, in spite of exceptions, seldom required a very large investment of fixed capital.

Conclusion

On the whole the development of foreign trade during the early modern period

[1] Smith, *The Wealth of Nations*, bk v, i, pt 3, ar 1.

fulfilled the functions demanded of it by the state and by society. It supplied the commercial world with the precious metals necessary for its development; it provided Europe with colonial produce; and it made substantial national surpluses available for export. But above all it stimulated manufacturing industry to a steadily greater output, made imperative its reorganisation and its re-equipment, and supplied the means for the realisation of these ends.

In north-western Europe, and especially in England and the Netherlands, commercial forces had by the end of this period gone a considerable way towards the development of a genuine market economy in which the production and distribution of goods and services were carried on predominantly through the medium of a self-regulating mechanism of price-fixing markets, in which prices and price movements were the primary factor in the allocation of resources, and in which economic considerations played an important role in the determination of national policy. Many forms of interference with the free functioning of the market mechanism nevertheless remained. Tariffs and tolls, subsidies and prohibitions interfered with the free movement of goods and productive resources in accordance with economic considerations. Gild and state regulations interfered with attempts to minimise production costs by the imposition of regulations in regard to the techniques of production, while the putting-out system prevented the mobility of labour and the rational organisation of production. A number of important factors—psychological, technical, organisational, and political—still militated against economic development in general and the smooth functioning of the market mechanism in particular. These forces will be discussed in the next chapter.

18

The low rate of economic growth

Slow economic growth before the Industrial Revolution

Werner Sombart concluded his monumental work on modern capitalism with the statement that what the capitalist system had achieved at the end of the early modern period in transforming the economic life and culture of Europe, and especially what it had attained in creative performance, must be judged by modern standards as surprisingly small. This he considered the more surprising because the basic conditions of economic progress had been firmly laid during the period.[1] As a general survey, and viewed in its historical perspective, his conclusion undoubtedly contains a large measure of truth.

The economic growth that took place before the Industrial Revolution differed not merely quantitatively but also qualitatively from that which has taken place since that time. The growth that came with the Industrial Revolution was of a self-sustaining and irreversible nature. On the other hand growth in the early modern period, as indeed the growth that had taken place throughout history was due primarily to the opening up of new physical resources and the spread of existing methods, and only secondarily to new technical developments. But the discovery of new resources is of course not a progressive phenomenon. The result was that an amelioration of the conditions of existence and an enlargement of the economic horizon were always followed by a rise in population that tended eventually to consume the gains achieved. For no sooner did the population catch up with the new resources than decreasing returns would tend to set in. After that stage was reached, the increasing pressure of population on resources would cause the product per head to fall, and it would rise again only if, through some vicissitude, the population temporarily declined.

Factors that generate economic growth

Economic growth is dependent primarily on factors such as capital accumulation, total expenditure, technological change, exports, import replacement, and advances in the educational level of society in general and in entrepreneurial, managerial,

[1] Sombart, *Der Moderne Kapitalismus*, ii, pt 2, 1111.

technical and labour skills in particular. These are interrelated and interactive factors in the sense that the efficient functioning of any one of them requires the efficient functioning of all the others. They also constitute an integrated system in the sense that any significant variation in the activity of one component will be associated with significant variation in the activity of all the others. Besides these constituents there are also a number of other factors that influence the rate of economic development, such as the nature of the public administration, the measure of freedom and security enjoyed by citizens, and the size of the market.

Capital formation and economic growth

Self-sustained growth consists largely in the generation of sufficient savings and their conversion into productive investment projects. This requires, in the first place, the provision of sufficient voluntary or forced savings. It needs, in the second place, the availability of profitable investment opportunities into which the savings can be channelled. Finally, it calls for the ability to transmute the available savings into specific investment projects. The reason for the relatively slow growth of the early modern economy, as compared with the more rapid development that commenced with the Industrial Revolution, must therefore be sought partly on the supply side, in the small flow of resources available for investment, and partly on the demand side, in the weakness of the inducement to invest.

It has been pointed out that *ex post facto* data can never provide adequate proof of the correctness of two alternative hypotheses, each of which refers to *ex ante* assumptions, namely that wouldbe savings were smaller than wouldbe capital investment opportunities, and that therefore, the former served as the brake; or that, alternatively, wouldbe savings were greater than wouldbe capital investment opportunities, and that therefore the latter served as the curb on economic development.[1] Very general historical considerations would seem to indicate, however, that the limiting factor must be sought more on the demand-for-capital than on the supply-of-savings side.

Inadequacy of the flow of resources seeking investment

Sustained economic growth, as has been said, requires and depends on capital formation. The rate of capital formation that is required for a given rate of growth is a function of the incremental capital-output ratio and the rate of population increase. It has been maintained that for stationary economies to achieve self-sustained growth, the rate of capital formation has to increase from approximately 4 to 5 per cent to about 10 per cent of the net national product. A considerable proportion of this investment must also be financed from local sources. The requirement of such a substantial increase in capital formation as a condition of sustained growth is however almost certainly exaggerated.[2] What is required is rather a material improvement in the efficiency of investment—that is, in the increment in output per unit of investment.

[1] Cf. Kuznets, *Capital in the American Economy*, p. 399.
[2] See Kuznets, 'Notes on the take-off', in *The Economics of Take-off into Sustained Growth*, ed. Rostow, which deals with many of the same countries during the same periods as Rostow. He finds that in none of the cases dealt with did the percentage of capital formation during the critical period of the so-called 'take-off' approach a doubling of its value.

Gregory King's estimate of English experience during the seventeenth century indicates an annual rate of productive capital formation of about 3 to 4 per cent of national income. This growth was represented largely by an increase in the number of farm animals, buildings and ships, and an enhancement of traders' inventories and of the stock of gold bullion. Its earning power was therefore both low and erratic. If this rate of capital formation can be assumed to be more or less correct for England, it is very unlikely to have been exceeded by any other European country, except perhaps the Netherlands during the first half of the seventeenth century.

The experience of the seventeenth and eighteenth centuries would seem to indicate that when the occasion arose European peoples were able to save considerably more than they normally did, and that consequently the cause of the low capital formation must be sought not in the inability to save but rather in the shortage of sound opportunities for profitable investment. As regards the early modern period, Keynes was probably correct when he maintained that the basic weakness of the free enterprise economy has always been that the propensity to save has generally been stronger than the inducement to invest.

It has, indeed, been maintained by Professor Ashton that the significance of the lowering of the rate of interest in the half-century that preceded the Industrial Revolution as a causative factor of this movement has not been sufficiently appreciated by historians.

> If we seek—it would be wrong to do so—for a single reason why the pace of economic development quickened about the middle of the eighteenth century, it is to this we must look. The deep mines, solidly built factories, well-constructed canals, and substantial houses of the industrial revolution were the products of relatively cheap capital.[1]

In a later book the author seems to have modified this view, stressing the importance not so much of the cost of capital as of its availability.[2] The cost of capital was no doubt an important factor in timing the construction of expensive projects of slow gestation such as turnpike roads and canals. But in the case of projects that required a comparatively modest outlay, such as textile ventures, the major consideration was not whether the prospective yield would cover the cost of a slightly higher or lower rate of interest, but whether the required capital would be raised at all. It would seem, however, that the primary cause of the lack of progress in the early modern period must be sought not on the side of the supply of capital, nor so much in the lack of sensitivity and the unresponsiveness of the business community to the opportunities offered for economic advancement, but primarily in the fact that the slow development of technology during this period failed to create adequate opportunities for profitable investment and thus to serve as an 'engine of growth'.

Factors inhibiting the inducement to invest

The inducement to invest is determined by the marginal efficiency of capital in relation to the market rate of interest, the marginal efficiency of capital designating the rate of return over cost. The low rate and low productivity of investment during

[1] Ashton, *The Industrial Revolution 1760-1830*, p. 11.
[2] Ashton, *An Economic History of England: the Eighteenth Century*, pp. 76 ff.

this period can be ascribed to a great variety of political, social, economic, and technical factors, factors which assumed different forms in different countries and which are consequently difficult to isolate from their peculiar settings. The achievement of self-sustained growth, as Professor Rostow has pointed out, 'requires a massive set of pre-conditions going to the heart of a society's economic organisation and its effective scale of values'.[1] It must of course be stressed that historical growth is a continuous process, and that the conception of a 'take-off' is completely misleading if it invokes the idea that the conditions necessary for the more rapid expansion that came with the Industrial Revolution had not been carefully laid during the previous period, and that this preparation was not an essential condition for the accelerated rate of development during the following period.

Technological factors

The very gradual growth of the early modern period must be ascribed primarily to the slow development of technology in all sectors of the economy, which exerted a depressing effect on the rate of return entrepreneurs could expect from capital investment in new ventures. But the basic causes of the slow rate of technical innovation during this period and its great acceleration during the next phase are not easy to conceive and to formulate.

It has been maintained that the early modern economy suffered from the disadvantage, as far as technological development was concerned, that the men who controlled industry under the domestic system were merchants, men who were not technically minded and not in the position either to analyse industrial opportunities or to organise and operate undertakings for the exploitation of resources outside their own confined and specific fields. That this was not a serious drawback, however, is shown by the eagerness with which the investment opportunities opened up by the Industrial Revolution were seized by the commercial class. Though there is undoubtedly a measure of truth in this contention, it would be equally correct to say that the low rate of investment acted as a drag on technological change and on the acquisition of the entrepreneurial, managerial and technical skills necessary to generate further economic growth.

So far as the development of technology is concerned, it would seem that invention and innovation are nearly always the result of the conscious or unintentional cooperation of many minds working on the same project, when the time is ripe for its application. From the point of view of industry, however, production was not sufficiently concentrated and rationalised to fix the attention on technological improvement. The world of business was divided into numerous self-contained units, their trade secrets jealously guarded from one another, and therefore from scientists as well. Moreover, the means of communication and transport were still too ineffective, and gild, urban and territorial restrictions too universal, to make market forces the compelling factor required to induce the adoption of improved methods of production.

No more effective was the collaboration from the point of view of science. Technology still lacked a scientific basis. Science was not yet ready for the task: the technological problems were too complex and the scientific data and theories too disjointed and incomplete to be of much practical use. Nor were adequate sources of power available. The sources of motive power remained fundamentally the same

[1] Rostow, 'The take-off into self-sustained growth', *Economic Journal*, March 1956, p. 47.

as in all previous ages—man and animal, wind and water—though human and animal labour was increasingly supplemented by the elementary forces of nature through the creation of mechanisms to facilitate the transmission and utilisation of energy. But the weakness of early modern technology lay in the irregularity and the localisation of its resources of power even more than in its ineffectiveness.

As in every social process, the first steps are the most difficult to take. Change involves not only the displacement of existing methods but also damage to vested interests and serious human dislocation. Before an innovation will be adopted there must first be an acute appreciation of the inadequacies of the existing techniques, and the adoption of the new methods must be encouraged or induced by their obvious competitive advantages. Once it is initiated, technological discovery tends to become a cumulative process. Any given discovery or development facilitates further discoveries and development, and investment in itself tends to create new investment opportunities. Accordingly the development of investment opportunities tends to advance along a broad front.

During the early modern period improvements in production techniques were especially necessary in three fundamental sections of the economy: in the textile industry, which absorbed more labour than all the other industries combined; in the iron industry, the development of which was being seriously hampered by its organic basis; and, finally, in the methods of land transport, which constituted probably the main limiting factor in economic development before the Industrial Revolution.

The concomitant effects of such a development would have been the transfer of income to those classes and individuals that could plough it back into highly productive investment, thus setting up a cumulative chain of repercussions in the demand for the products of the other sectors of the economy: for primary and intermediate products, for improved means of transport, for more effective banking and distributive systems, and for enlarged urban areas. Such a development would also have made available a whole range of external economies, which would have ensured that new leading sectors would have emerged once the stimulus given by the initial sector had begun to wane.

Education and vocational training

The third determinant of economic growth is of a more intangible and intractable nature. A prime factor in bringing about economic change is the general level and advances in the level of education. It is a question not merely of the amount of education but above all also of the kind of education received. Its influence on economic growth is primarily to lift people's mental horizons: to provide the general incentive and inclination to change.

The Renaissance formed a landmark in the history of western education. One of its main features was the revival of classical learning and a strong yearning for a new world with a fuller and more interesting way of life. The language and literature of Rome and Greece were the central features of the curriculum. Primary instruction consisted largely of the inculcation of the three R's, and was liberally spiced with religion. Such studies unfortunately encouraged the receptive and the reproductive faculties of the pupils at the expense of the rest of their mental equipment.

The Reformation, although it might ultimately have laid the foundation for the organisation of universal elementary instruction in the vernacular, initially had a disruptive and disintegrating effect on education. First, the secular authorities appropriated the endowments of the schools; secondly, the contestants used the schools to propagate their specific ecclesiastical cause. The result was that during the course of this period teaching tended to become even more remote from the real needs of life, whether cultural or professional. In vain a man like Bacon deplored the obsession with 'words, not matter', and, with an appreciation of the need for scientific research, urged that 'other helps are required besides books'. The universities, like the schools, were too deeply involved in the religious conflicts of the time, and declined for the most part to contemplate any enlargement of the frontiers of knowledge.

No wonder therefore that the main current of intellectual life tended to drift away from the orthodox centres of learning and to centre in the learned societies which became a characteristic feature of western Europe during the latter part of this period. The sterility of the universities stood in strong contrast to the brilliant contribution made to human knowledge by the mathematicians and physicists of the time. During the seventeenth century modern science may indeed be said to have been born. For with the enunciation of what has been called 'the first physical synthesis', the whole universe was brought into the range of man's inquiry and was shown to work in one gigantic mechanism, in accordance with the dynamic principle established by the experiments and inductions of Galileo and Newton. Towards the end of the next century, the principles established in mechanics were carried over into chemistry, and the road opened for the tremendous developments of the next hundred years.[1]

Vocational training—the type of education which prepares the individual specifically for the pursuit of his profession—continued during this period to be confined to apprenticeship. Apprenticeship not only trained youths in the acquisition of technical skills; it familiarised them with the rudiments of marketing, the purchase of materials, stock-keeping, and capital requirements. Moreover the numerous town ordinances that dealt with the conditions of employment, quality of wares and other matters had to be understood and applied. It therefore remained the most significant form of education for business until the Industrial Revolution.

The craft organisation of industry, however, as has already been pointed out, was not conducive to technological development. Within the limits of the handicraft system minor variations were indeed possible in the use of materials and the techniques of production. But the promotion of innovation was not a significant feature of the craft and gild organisation. Its main objective was to preserve artisan independence and economic stability—not to foster economic growth.

The putting-out system did indeed encourage the development of more rational methods of organisation, and especially of accounting practices, and a broader economic vision. The remarkable fact, however, is that these developments, which showed such great promise during the late Middle Ages, made little or no headway during the early modern period. This can be ascribed only to the close interrelationship that exists between inputs of physical capital, technological advance, and human skills. For if the accumulation of skill is the essential means of transmitting knowhow to industrial equipment, it is equally true that industrial and managerial skills can unfold only if presented with the challenge of being applied to new technological advances and to a growing capital stock. If therefore it can be said

---

[1] Neither a purely literary (or humanistic) education nor the study of the pure sciences would seem to be directly conducive to rapid economic growth, but rather concentration on the social and the applied sciences; cf. Bieda, *The Structure and Operation of the Japanese Economy*, pp. 24 ff.

that new technological processes, representing a deepening of capital application, can be made possible only by the generation of new labour skills, the reverse equally holds that it is only by the development of new technologies and investment in capital-intensifying processes that the enhancement of entrepreneurial, managerial and technical skills can be achieved.

Psychological factors

An important influence affecting the discovery and exploitation of investment opportunities is the system of values that prevails in a community, and especially the energy, diligence, and assiduity of its business men and their sensitivity and responsiveness to economic opportunities, as well as the vision and perseverance of its government.

The entrepreneurial class had fitted rather uneasily into the medieval scheme of things. The spiritual foundations of the Middle Ages were built on religion. 'All medieval thought', says Coulton, 'is characterised by the conviction that each man has a soul to save, and that, therefore, salvation is the main end of every human being, not a distant ideal, but the most practical duty that is set before us all'.[1] The Christian religion, however, is one of renunciation. The relations between Christian doctrine and economic activity directed at gain are therefore naturally strained. *Homo mercator vix aut nunquam potest Deo placere* (The merchant can hardly ever or never please God). Such doctrines weighed heavily on the conscience of the medieval merchant.

> It prevented the merchants from growing rich with a free conscience and from reconciling the practice of business with the prescripts of religion. For proof of this we need only read the many wills of bankers and speculators, directing that the poor whom they had defrauded should be repaid and bequeathing to the clergy a part of the property which at the bottom of their hearts they felt to be ill-gotten.[2]

Large sums flowed into the church coffers as 'conscience money'. Good giving apparently expiated bad getting.

The attitude of the early modern period was, on the whole, more positive and promotive. The psychology of the ruling and business classes nevertheless still exercised a deleterious effect on the volume of new investment, especially in France, the leading industrial country of the time, and to the despair of an official like Colbert. This was reflected in the low valuation of economic activity: the often ill-advised interference with these activities on the part of the ruling classes and the high premium attached to leisure, as compared with active participation in business ventures, on the part of the entrepreneurial classes, and the tendency for successful merchants to transform themselves into landed gentry, to retire early, and to purchase estates and titles of nobility for themselves and public posts and commissions for their descendants. In this way both enterprise and capital were withdrawn from the sectors that could have supplied the necessary momentum to a more rapid rate of economic development.

The general climate in Britain and the Netherlands was indeed more favourable

[1] Coulton, 'The mind of medievalism', in *Universal History of the World*, v, 3012.
[2] Pirenne, *Economic and Social History of Medieval Europe*, p. 29.

to investment. In Britain, especially, the comparatively close relationship between the English aristocracy and the higher echelons of the business community, the comparatively free intercourse between all levels of society, and the consequent tone of respectability that was lent to business enterprise were no doubt prime causes of the assumption of economic leadership by Great Britain towards the end of this period.

Nor was collaboration very effective on the part of the rather rudimentary public administration of the time. As a precondition of rapid and sustained economic development it is necessary that the surplus funds above the mass consumption level must not flow into the hands of those that will sterilise it by hoarding, luxury consumption, or low productivity investment outlays, but that they be directed to economically useful projects instead. For this to be attained, in so far as the funds that can be mobilised by the central administration are concerned, it is necessary that governments or politically and economically important groups in the community must come to perceive that it is both possible and necessary to undertake acts of capital investment, and for their efforts to be successful they must act with a certain measure of rationality in selecting the directions towards which their enterprise is directed and in the effectiveness with which the resources are applied. These conditions were present in a very small measure only in a period that was generally characterised by the prevalence of conspicuous consumption, royal improvidence, the maladministration of public finances, the arbitrary incidence of taxation on certain classes, and the subservience of economic to political considerations. The absence of genuine nationalist movements that could induce investment in productive enterprise as a means of enhancing national power and prestige was undoubtedly an important factor in retarding the growth of European economies during this period.

The lack of security

The inducement to invest is of course determined primarily by expectations in respect of the *future* yield of investment. Since the outstanding feature of prospective yields is the precariousness of the data on which the estimates have to be based, the state of confidence with which forecasts can be made, or the general climate of business expectations, is of the greatest importance in determining the volume of new investment.

In a free enterprise economy a state of uncertainty affects both the borrower and the lender. The borrower will, in such circumstances, require a wider margin between the prospective yield and the rate of interest to make the loan worth while, and, for the same reason, the lender will demand a wider margin between his price and the pure rate of interest as an inducement to lend.

The insecurity of this period was brought about in the first instance by the endless wars, which not merely disrupted communications and disorganised established business connections, but also destroyed valuable assets and undermined the will to work, to save, and to invest in new undertakings. A second cause of insecurity was that engendered by the power and intolerance of the established Churches, which meant that for economically important sections of the population there was security for neither their persons nor their possessions. This was an important cause of the economic stagnation of Spain and France during much of this period, and especially for the disinclination to invest in manufacturing industries, and more particularly in those industries the capital requirements of which were high, as contrasted with investments in commercial and financial ventures. In the third place, a lack of security was brought about by the dangers to which the means of communication were subjected, both on land and sea, and which were reflected, for example, in the high rates of marine insurance throughout this period. A final cause of insecurity was represented by the mismanagement of the public finances and by the arbitrary and inefficient methods of their administration.

Market limitations

A further restrictive influence on economic growth was the limitations imposed by the market. This period was inaugurated by the discovery of large new territories and of important new natural resources. The use of these resources, however, had to wait upon the development of new industrial processes, since the few and simple industrial processes of the time could make use of only a very limited range of raw materials. But severe restrictions were imposed even on the resources that could be used.

These limitations were represented by the numerous tolls on roads and rivers, by the inadequacies of the means of transport, by the restrictions placed on international and especially on colonial trade, and, partly as cause but mainly as effect, by the small proportion of the population that was urbanised and that created an effective demand for the goods and services of commerce and industry. The gradual growth and expansion of markets and market transactions, and the stimulating effect this had on industrial technique and on capitalist methods of organisation, must be regarded as one of the main factors which encouraged the economic development of the maritime nations of the West during this period, a development which laid the basis of the Industrial Revolution.

A factor which also exercised an important restrictive effect on economic development were the numerous restrictions imposed on business enterprise during a period which considered all economic activity to be essentially privileged. Of these restrictions the regulation of industry by state and gild, the limitations imposed on international trade and on colonial development, and the grants of monopoly were undoubtedly the most important. Grants of monopoly could indeed, if judiciously applied, promote the economic development of a country. On the whole, however, they exercised a deleterious effect on the economic development of this period, not only by reason of the exclusiveness of the rights granted, but also because of the narrowness of the circle and the nature of the participants on whom the rights were often ill-advisedly bestowed.[1]

The prevalence of underemployed resources

The combined effect of all these factors was that the economies of the early

---

[1] They were restrictive also in another way. Privileged companies played an important role in the financing of government expenditure. A large part of the capital of English companies was invested in 'governments', which were usually at considerable discount and fluctuated violently in response to changes in the political situation. Owing to their dependence on the state for privileges, and in other ways, the demands of the government could not be refused. 'Thus, company promotion provided a channel through which funds flowed away from, rather than toward, productive purposes, which is an important fact to remember in the interpretation of the economic history of that epoch' (Schumpeter, *Business Cycles*, i, 249).

modern world were doomed to a low rate of effectiveness of their capital invest-ment—that is, to a low increment in output per unit of investment. They conse-quently also lacked the incentives to induce a rate of investment sufficient to effect rapid and sustained growth and to assure a regular increase in the standard of living of the masses of the population. Outside a few favoured areas the growth of population outstripped the growth of industry, and this gave rise to the develop-ment of a pauperised rural proletariat whose marginal productivity was negligible. Hence the spontaneous opposition on the part of workers to the adoption of inventions in the textile industry, which they feared would still further accentuate the existing unemployment and underemployment, while the low cost of marginal labour in turn helped to slow down the demand for technological improvements. What the workmen did spontaneously, kings and statesmen did deliberately, and the introduction of labour-saving equipment in the textile industry was discouraged from Prussia in the East to Britain in the West. Since the central Middle Ages large sectors of the European economy had indeed become bogged down in a vicious circle from which it could be jerked only by a technological and psychological revolution.

19

The centralisation of authority and the gradual development of economic freedom

The centralisation of authority

During the early modern period the work of state-building, which had started in the Middle Ages, was carried on deliberately and with a very large measure of success, and by the end of this period the geographical consolidation and political integration of the modern national state had been largely completed.

The first step in the formation of the new national state was the liquidation of the peculiar medieval heritage of universalism and particularism. The former presented few difficulties. For a thousand years after the fall of Rome, European policy had still been dominated by its twofold legacy: the idea of the universal Empire and of the universal or Catholic Church. The spirit of medieval Europe was not nationalistic but oecumenical. The paramount theme in the rebuilding of society in the early and central Middle Ages had been that the unitary authority of the Empire should be replaced by the unitary authority of the Papacy. It was this attempt at imperial reconstruction under papal auspices that had given such a large measure of unity to the central Middle Ages—the ideal of a universal human society as an integral part of a divinely ordered scheme of things.

The secular and religious movements of the late Middle Ages destroyed forever the possibility of recreating the Roman Empire on a religious basis, and during the early modern period kings and their ministers, with the aid of the Reformation and the rising tide of nationalism, succeeded in completely disrupting this heritage.

Far more formidable were the centrifugal and disruptive forces bequeathed by the Middle Ages: the fragmentation caused by the territorial nobility and the disintegration that resulted from the independence of the towns. It might be true, as Schmoller said, that the necessities of real life were driving society relentlessly towards the territorial form of organisation.[1] But the success attained in the political field was far more impressive than that achieved in the economic sphere.

The centralising forces went furthest in the France of Louis XIV. Here the countervailing forces to autocracy were temporarily neutralised. With the assistance of the Church and the bourgeoisie, the powers of the nobility were reduced to the retention of social and fiscal privileges. The Church was then virtually reduced to the level of a state department. The high court—the Parliament of Paris—did indeed

[1] Schmoller, *The Mercantile System and its Historical Significance*, p. 15.

advance the claim to control the absolute legislative power of the crown by making the registration of royal edicts and ordinances subject to its approval; but this claim had no foundation in law or in fact, and was disposed of in practice by the formal command of the king ordering it to proceed. The States-General, the parliament of France, was never convened during the long reign of the monarch.[1] The responsibility for local government was transferred, in typically autocratic manner, from the nobles to royal officials, the *intendants*, who were given greatly increased power to assess and collect taxes. The king's authority was even adequately boosted by the appropriate ideology. This was effected by the revival of the concept of Roman law that God directed the affairs of states through his chosen agents. A large measure of cultural and religious uniformity was also enforced. To such a degree was centralisation pushed that the king could, with a measure of truth, identify the state with himself.

But even in the France of Louis XIV the centralisation that was achieved was different from that of the East. This was due to different conceptions of human values and property relationships and to fundamental religious, legal, and national ideals. As regards the last, the states that arose in western Europe were national states, and one of the main factors that contributed to their rise was the spirit of nationalism that gradually emerged from the end of the fifteenth century. Not even in France or Spain, therefore, did the centralisation of power imply the complete subjection of the individual to the state, but was, on the contrary, compatible with the maintenance of a large measure of individual freedom.

In the countries that eventually came to be the most intimately associated with the exploitation of the opportunities offered by the opening up of a world market, England and the Netherlands, the various contestants for sovereignty were too evenly balanced for the assumption of autocratic power by the king.

In the Netherlands there was no central government. Sovereignty resided in the provinces, and the States-General was a congress of delegates of autonomous states. The postal system and many taxes were farmed out and a central system of finances was completely lacking.

In England, parliament during the course of the Middle Ages, gradually acquired a national representative character. First it gained a measure of control over taxation, then the right to initiate legislation, and finally it claimed immunity from royal interference in its deliberation of public affairs. The judiciary also affirmed its independence of the central authority and asserted the supremacy of the common law against the royal power.

The weakening of the royal power in these countries was associated with the growth of the middle class in wealth and power. As this class, a highly differentiated group, was easily accessible, it was continually invigorated by the infiltration of the more enterprising elements from below. Intermarriage and the purchase of land and titles by successful businessmen, on the other hand, affiliated it to an increasing extent with the stratum above. More than any other section, the bourgeoisie came to shape the destinies of the modern world, and the eighteenth century, especially, was dominated by the 'progressive' thinking of this class.

The eighteenth century has been described as the age of the enlightened despots. These rulers were often genuinely desirous of improving the living standards of their subjects and of improving the efficiency of their administrations. But though some of them might have been enlightened, according to the light of the times, none of them could be described as a 'despot' in the accepted sense of the term.

---

[1] After 1614 the States-General was not summoned for 175 years.

The French monarchy also became discernibly weaker in the eighteenth century. By the end of this period no state in western Europe could, indeed, be described as a political democracy. But neither did it have a political system in which there were no checks on what the established rulers could and wished to do.

Economic disintegration

Formidable obstacles to the effective centralisation of the state's power were presented by the centrifugal and disruptive forces bequeathed by feudalism in the economic sphere—that is, the fragmentation caused by the interests of the territorial nobility—and the disintegration that resulted from the independence of the towns. The internal barriers to economic unity in the form of urban regalian rights, urban economic control, and a disintegrating system of customs, coinage, and weights and measures, powerfully backed by poor means of communication and strongly rooted in vested local interests, were only very partially overcome, and as a rule they were too strongly entrenched for the early modern state to dislodge.

During the Middle Ages numerous functions of control had been usurped by towns and feudal rulers, who imposed restrictions for their own ends. The most obstructive of those that remained in the early modern period were undoubtedly the enormous number of tolls imposed on transit between provinces, on rivers, and on highways. On all the great rivers there were customs barriers at intervals from ten to fifteen kilometres, at each of which successively the merchant was fleeced. England, with its strong central power, attained its economic unity early and with comparative ease. Sweden was the only other European country to obtain a similar measure of customs unity. According to Adam Smith, the absence of internal tolls was 'perhaps one of the principal causes of the prosperity of Great Britain'.[1]

In the other countries of Europe the work of unification involved the creation of national customs systems. But here the state did not meet with much success. In Germany the territorial powers seldom succeeded in removing the internal tariff barriers or even in always bringing the tolls under government control. This was partly because of their inability to overrule vested local interests; but to an even greater extent it must be ascribed to their inability to dispense with this source of revenue.

France in this respect occupied an intermediate position between Germany and Great Britain. By the tariff of 1664 Colbert succeeded in combining the *cinq grosses fermes*—an area comprising three-eighths of the country—into a single customs territory. This was probably the greatest achievement of mercantilism in the creation of national unity. But this unity was achieved only in regard to the interprovincial customs. The river and highway tolls presented insuperable difficulties, and the customs between the other provinces were left entirely untouched. This impotence of the so-called absolute state is the more remarkable since the French Revolution in one night swept away these and a host of other medieval barriers.[2]

Even less success was attained in unifying weights and measures—a purely technical task. In this respect, too, Britain led the way towards unification, though even in the British Isles complete unity was by no means attained. The French monarchy initially dared go no further than to systematise weights and measures within individual provinces. At the end of the *ancien régime* the state openly acknowledged its

[1] *Wealth of Nations*, bk v, ch 2 pt 2, 4; 'Mercantilism', *Encyclopaedia of the Social Sciences*.
[2] Heckscher, i, 46 ff; Schmoller, pp. 18 ff.

inability to obtain national uniformity and resigned itself to the unassuming task of drawing up tables showing the relation between the weights and measures of different parts of the country. This was all that could be accomplished after 450 years of struggle. Germany, in this field as in every other, proved completely incapable of mastering the confusion.[1]

A fair measure of uniformity was attained in French coinage through the simple operation of Gresham's law whereby the bad money of the local powers was driven out by the still worse currency of the king. In Germany the territorial rulers were strong enough to resist this competition. When the small duchy of Oldenburg was annexed by Napoleon in 1810 it still possessed four independent currency systems. Nor was this the only source of confusion. The depreciation of the English coinage was stopped in the sixteenth century. On the Continent rulers exercised their talents to manipulate the currency for their own benefit and to the loss of everybody else. So bewildering was this currency confusion in central and northern Europe that commerce sought relief, as we have seen, in the creation of an ideal bank money, a unit of account based on a given weight of precious metal.[2]

Taxation was another field in which there was a complete absence of unity. Increased sources of royal revenue did indeed enable the kings to maintain standing armies and a paid bureaucracy, important factors in the creation of the modern state. This work of consolidation was however partly neutralised by extravagant military policies. These no doubt furthered capitalist enterprise by the introduction of standardised processes, though they hampered development by the waste of resources and the risks and hazards that they introduced into business life. No less than two-thirds or more of the revenues of western countries were absorbed by military expenditure, and it was the problem of military expenditure combined with inadequate sources of revenue that eventually brought about the eclipse of the highly centralised French administration.

The financial straits of mercantilist governments made them follow the principle of fetching their revenue when and where they could, or, in the words of Colbert, of so plucking the goose as to obtain the greatest quantity of feathers with the least amount of hissing. Feudal privileges in the form of exemption from taxation were maintained by the nobility and the Church. This inequality represented one of the most pernicious aspects of the *ancien régime* and was largely responsible for its undoing. The inability of the so-called 'absolute' state to levy adequate direct taxation induced it to heap indirect taxes on sales, imports and exports; persons, land, cattle and harvests were burdened; titles and monopolies were sold, and the currency depreciated. The policy of farming out the taxes withdrew an important sphere of finance from the central administration, with injurious effects on both the taxpayers and the treasury.

Another serious source of disintegration was the municipal regulation of industry. Mercantilism has been described as the extension of the exclusive gild policy to the whole state.[3] If that were so, the first duty of mercantilism would have been to concede to all citizens of the state the privileges that had hitherto been enjoyed exclusively by the burghers of the individual towns. The special advantages of burgesses as a whole as well as the privileges monopolised by individual towns would have had to disappear. All attempts by the communes to form mutually exclusive entities, to control economic activities for their own ends,

[1] Heckscher, i, 111 ff.

[2] *Ibid.*, i, 118 ff.

[3] Cf. Sombart, *Der Moderne Kapitalismus*, i, 363.

and to prevent the competition of rural areas would have had to be suppressed. All urban interests would have had to be rigidly subordinated to the larger advantages of the state. Such a policy would doubtlessly have contributed powerfully to liberating resources for economic development within the larger national units.

But mercantilism must be credited rather for what it attempted than for what it attained in this direction. Little was accomplished in Germany in surmounting municipal exclusiveness. Even where political and economic conditions were more favourable, as in France, little was done towards creating greater internal unity, and the measures adopted were a hindrance rather than a help to industrial development. Services rendered by the state to rural industry were probably due as much to enforced passivity, to the inability of applying the code of industrial regulation in the country districts, as to tolerance and active encouragement.

If, however, mercantilist policy did not succeed to any marked extent in overcoming the economic disintegration of the Middle Ages, it so firmly laid the foundations of that unity that the spiritual and material forces freed by the Industrial and French Revolutions could effect without any conscious effort the changes for which mercantilist statesmen had striven deliberately but ineffectually for several hundred years.

The creation of productive powers and the policy of restriction

The name 'mercantilism' was given by the physiocrats and popularised by Adam Smith to designate the economic policy applied by the early modern state to stabilise and to extend its power.

According to Adam Smith and his followers, the essence of mercantilism consisted in the identification of wealth and treasure, in the belief 'that wealth consists in money, or in gold and silver'.[1] It would be easy to find in mercantilist literature sufficient statements to support this view. Money was considered to be more or less identical with capital, and because it was believed to yield a return in much the same way as land does, nothing was more natural than that it should be coveted to an unlimited extent.[2] It would however be a travesty of the truth to foist on all mercantilists this confusion of wealth with money. The more enlightened of them appreciated the fact that the value of money consisted in its use as a circulating medium, 'to keep the wheels of the machine in motion'.[3] Hoarded treasure is useless. To serve a useful purpose it must remain in continual circulation, fertilising commerce and industry by combining the means of production.[4]

The accumulation of treasure was therefore merely a means to an end. The primary concern of mercantilists was to strengthen the state. In the first place, treasure was needed because it constituted the sinews of war. In the second place, mercantilists seem to have appreciated the influence of an abundance of currency and a low rate of interest as a spur to investment. Finally, and above all, money was needed in the seventeenth century to prevent a fall in prices and to stimulate production; hence the mercantilists' concern to keep the currency in circulation.

---

[1] *Wealth of Nations*, bk iv, ch 1.
[2] Heckscher, *Economic History Review*, vii, no. 1.
[3] Davenant, *Works*, i, 448.
[4] Mercantilists also pointed out again and again that a country with relatively less money than others is induced to 'sell cheap and buy dear', that excessive competition might turn the terms of trade against a country. Heckscher, ii, 235. Hence the attempts to secure favourable terms of trade by the manipulation of the market.

The monetary circulation of European countries could be maintained and increased either by prohibiting the export of bullion or by securing a favourable balance of trade. The bullionists tried to increase the treasure of their countries by prohibiting the outflow of bullion, whereas the mercantilists believed that the only way to attain the desired end was to secure an excess of exports over imports. Bullionist policy had prevailed in the Middle Ages and was maintained everywhere, with greater or less tenacity, up to the second half of the seventeenth century. Then the mercantilist theory generally gained the upper hand in all the leading countries of Europe. It became the accepted doctrine of policy that the government should regulate, not the flow of precious metals, but the stream of commerce, leading it into channels which would ensure a favourable balance of trade. 'The conception of "a well-ordered trade" dominated the thought of the seventeenth century.' The balance of trade became the barometer of a country's prosperity, the assumption being that it would be possible, with the defective trade statistics of the time and the still more defective theoretical notions, to ascertain what the balance of payments was in fact, and to shape public policy accordingly.

It soon became apparent however that trade was seldom bilateral, and that the balance between any two countries was therefore a very 'fallible and erroneous' criterion of commercial advantage. All that was required was that a country's balance of trade should be favourable with the world as a whole. Mercantilist policy seemed to Adam Smith to have turned 'from one fruitless care . . . to another care much more intricate, much more embarrassing, and just equally fruitless'.[1] According to him the mercantilist concern with the export of gold was futile because the import of commodities would be paid for by the export of goods and services. But what he failed to appreciate was the fact that the problem of the mercantilist state and its preoccupation with the balance of trade arose precisely because western Europe wanted more goods from outside its own area than could be paid for in goods acceptable to foreigners, and that the deficit had to be paid by the continuous export of precious metals, with all the effects attendant on such a drain.

Naturally, the efforts to create a favourable balance of trade led to protection. Economic self-sufficiency became the kernel of mercantilist policy. This was in direct contrast with the medieval policy of provision, which encouraged imports and discouraged exports. Mercantilism, on the contrary, aimed at the creation of productive powers. Mercantilist conceptions in this respect showed an advance on medieval ideas by dispelling the belief that consumers necessarily benefited by conditions that created momentary plenty. People began to recognise that the extension of the market might be a better guarantee for securing adequate provisions because it maintained production on a higher plane. Mercantilists, however, and especially the more typical representatives of the *Beamtenstaat*, were not interested primarily in maximising consumers' satisfaction. What they demanded of international trade was that it should increase the wealth, that is, the productive powers, of the state.[2]

Protection, in so far as the facts are known, began in the towns of north Italy in the thirteenth century. It passed to the Netherlands in the middle of the following century, and to France and England a century later. But it was not before the effects of the price revolution had worked themselves out by about the middle of the seventeenth century, and till contraction had succeeded the expansion, that

[1] *The Wealth of Nations*, bk iv, ch 1.
[2] 'Mercantilism', 'Protection', in *Encyclopaedia of Social Sciences*; Heckscher, *Mercantilism*, ii, 104 ff; Sombart, ii, 934 ff.

mercantilism really entered on its protectionist phase, and that tariffs mounted and commercial wars began.

More direct measures than mere protection were also adopted to encourage enterprise. This encouragement took the form of the granting of loans, subsidies, and even titles of nobility to entrepreneurs, the establishment of state undertakings, the issuing of orders that certain commodities should be consumed, and the reservation of the home market for certain services. The best known of these last measures were the famous Acts of Navigation of 1651 and 1660 respectively, which provided the framework of English naval policy for nearly two centuries. These acts aimed at building up the British mercantile marine by securing the colonial, coastal, and fishing trades for English ships, and by ousting the Dutch as intermediaries in the commerce of the country. They were never stringently enforced. Naturally it is extremely difficult to disentangle the effect of these laws from the general conditions affecting the trade of the time. Adam Smith regarded the Acts as prejudicial to commerce but justified them on political grounds. 'As defence, however, is of much more importance than opulence the Act of Navigation is, perhaps, the wisest of all the commercial regulations of England.'[1]

A typical method of encouraging new industries or the application of new processes was the grant of patents of monopoly,[2] though the primary object of granting monopolies was often fiscal rather than economic. According to mercantilist ideas all economic activity was 'privileged'. The state claimed the right to allow or to prohibit enterprise at its pleasure. The practice made its appearance in the 'first modern state', the Sicily of Frederick II, which claimed for itself the monopoly of all commerce in grain, salt, iron and raw silk. In the fifteenth century the states of Italy claimed a monopoly of foreign trade. Portugal and Spain monopolised the colonial trade in the sixteenth century.

More frequently these privileges were delegated to individuals, corporations or towns. The ordinary Englishman, in about 1600, could trade with only three countries: France, Spain and Portugal. Commerce with the rest of the world could be carried on only by the members of specific companies, to whom exclusive spheres of influence had been assigned. The colonial trade was monopolised by chartered companies, which were accorded important state functions as well. Industrial monopolies were equally common. Old industries often became the monopolies of existing gilds. New industries became the privileged possessions of courtiers or inventors.

In general the system of monopolies was restrictive rather than promotive, both by reason of the exclusiveness of the rights granted and by reason of the narrow and often ill-judged circle on whom the rights were conferred. Public disapproval of the abusive price practices of monopolists in England led to their partial correction by the Statute of Monopolies of 1624, then to their final removal when parliament assumed the right to cancel obnoxious grants in 1642, and finally to the abolition of the royal prerogative of granting monopolies in 1689. In France these practices reached their highest development in the eighteenth century, and in Germany they continued till late in the nineteenth century.

---

[1] *Wealth of Nations*, bk iv, ch 2.
[2] Monopoly may further the performance of this function in two ways: first, by affording an assured and profitable market it provides an incentive to the bearing of uncertainties that may not otherwise have been undertaken; secondly by facilitating the accumulation of entrepreneurial capital, it may provide the means with which the desired innovation can be gradually effected.

The regulation of industry

Finally the state tried by a system of minute regulation to direct industry into the desired course. The tradition of authoritarian control in industry was inherited from the medieval gilds. Such regulation required an efficient administration, and mercantilists believed in the necessity of a sound civil service as a necessary condition of prosperity. Colbert realised this condition in France by the organisation of a centralised bureaucratic system for the purposes of administration in general and of industrial regulation in particular. England, on the other hand, lacked such a service, and the very multitude of laws intended to standardise industry defeated their own purpose.

The system of industrial legislation introduced by Colbert represents the most imposing attempt at regulating industry during this period. But it simply consisted in the application of medieval principles to a larger area, without due consideration of the requirements of the new capitalist industry. It was inspired by the same fear of innovation, by the same craft bias, and by the same insistence on the meticulous copying of traditional processes. However well-intentioned initially, it became with the lapse of time more and more 'a meddling tyranny'. The objectives and methods of administration became obsolete, irrelevant and corrupt. Bureaucratic tyranny and corruption paralysed enterprise, and innovation was smothered by official obstruction and victimisation. The energies of the bourgeoisie were deflected from trade and industry to tax-collection and the legal profession, services which always flourish in a bureaucratised society. Colbert himself seems to have been aware of the dangers associated with his policy. He referred to some of his measures as 'crutches' to be cast aside when industry had attained maturity, and he formulated the argument for economic freedom in the significant words: *Il faut laisser faire les hommes.*[1]

The principles of economic regulation in Britain did not differ materially from those on the Continent, though the administration required for their efficient application was lacking. Many important districts also fell outside the scope of this control. Since most of these regulations were of a kind that interfered with the development of capitalist enterprise, they were actively resisted not only by merchants and landed gentlemen in parliament, but also by many of the magistrates interested in the progress of large-scale industry, magistrates placed in the position of having to enforce legislation that as private persons they found it desirable to evade. The difference between France and England was not so much in the nature of their industrial legislation as in its enforcement. 'In France the officials were so vigorous about enforcing the laws that craftsmen sometimes tried to massacre them for their zeal. In England the officials were so lax that workmen sometimes struck in an effort to remind them of their duty.'[2]

Whereas English mercantilism was initiated primarily by private interests from below, French mercantilism was imposed by the bureaucracy from above. The concern of the bureaucracy with industrial development can be appreciated from the fact that the idea of international conflict and power was inherent in mercantilist dogma, that this was a period of falling prices with its depressive effect on

[1] Wilson, in *The Cambridge Economic History of Europe*, iv, 522 ff; Birnie in *European Civilization*, ed. Eyre, v, 285. The dyeing ordinance of 1671, for example, contained no fewer than 317 articles and was 'less a code than a dyer's manual'. Chaptal, Napoleon's minister, who was himself a chemist, described it as the best contemporary treatise on the dyeing art (Birnie, p. 280).
[2] Nef, *Industry and Government in France and England, 1540-1640.*

enterprise, and that it was a period during which the expansion that was achieved was brought about, not by the introduction of innovations but by the spread of existing methods, which took the form of imitation, repetition and the expansion of the range of commodities produced. Expansion could therefore best be achieved by the combined drive of private interest and public policy. Where Colbertism failed was in its stifling effect on enterprise. And when, with the advent of the Industrial Revolution, the accent moved to the introduction of new methods in one sphere of industry after the other, the system facilitated the transfer of industrial leadership to Great Britain, whose entrepreneurs had succeeded in surmounting the obstacles to innovation and in which the whole system of regulation was already in complete decay.[1]

Colonial policy

In the attempts to increase the economic power of the state the colonies played an integral part. According to mercantilist conceptions the colonies had to complement the mother country and not, on any account, to compete with her. They had to direct their development along lines that were most advantageous to the parent country and had to supplement its efforts to attain economic self-sufficiency. The English Staple Act of 1663 referred explicitly to the need for developing 'a greater correspondence and kindness' between the colonies and the motherland, but at the same time required the colonies to remain 'in firmer dependence upon it'.

The execution of such a policy required 'a nice alternation of encouragement and restraint'. The trade of the colony was in principle monopolised by the government, by a chartered company, or by the citizens of the mother country. In practice the monopoly was circumvented and supplemented by smuggling, the normal lubricant of the old colonial system. The development of colonial industries that might compete with those of the mother country was deliberately impeded. On the other hand, colonial products enjoyed partial or complete immunity from customs duties and were thus guaranteed a virtually monopolistic priority in the markets of the home country. Occasionally native enterprise was even checked in favour of the colonies. Examples of this were the prohibition of tobacco culture in England and the exclusion of English fishermen from the waters of New England. The iron industry affords a good example of the mercantilist conception of the function of the colonies. In order to break the English dependence on supplies from northern Europe, colonial smelters were given a free market for their products in Britain (in 1750). Colonial ironmongers however, were forbidden to manufacture iron goods, because that would reduce the demand for English hardware.[2]

The exploitation of the colonies assumed slightly different forms according to national temperament and methods of administration. The Portuguese and the Spanish possessions were administered as state monopolies, and the interests of the colonies were subordinated to the object of transferring the maximum quantity of precious metals to the mother country. The system suffered from a lack of flexibility and from the still more serious difficulty that, owing to the lack of industrial development in the home countries, the needs of the colonists could not be adequately supplied. To plant active and self-dependent societies in the countries

[1] Heckscher, i, chs 5, 6; Nef, p. 136 ff; Wilson, iv, 522 ff.
[2] Lipson, iii, 154 ff.

that they had conquered was an ambition alien to the genius and the history of the Iberian governments of the time.

French colonial policy was almost as restrictive as that of Spain and Portugal and tended equally to repress rather than to promote the development of the colonies. The administration was centralised in Paris, and the government exercised a rigid political and economic control over the overseas settlements.

The Dutch colonies were founded by chartered companies, with the result that the emphasis was laid almost exclusively on immediate commercial advantage. The government of the Dutch East India Company substantiates the verdict of Adam Smith that 'of all the expedients that can well be contrived to stunt the natural growth of a new colony, that of an exclusive company is undoubtedly the most effectual'.[1]

Although England allowed her American colonies considerable freedom in developing their political institutions, she also adopted the typical mercantilist system of regulation. But there was this important difference between Britain and other countries that until 1763 this control was only very imperfectly enforced. England was also the natural market for most of the wares of her colonies, and this territorial specialisation, supplemented by open evasion, no doubt on the whole proved beneficial to both parties. But the lax administration of the system brought the authority and prestige of the mother country into disrepute, and stimulated the spirit of independence that made the subsequent attempt to enforce the law look like a gross act of tyranny.[2]

Mercantilist interest was centred largely in tropical islands and coastal belts. These were what were known as the 'supply colonies', which provided the staple articles of commerce: precious metals, sugar, spices, and slaves. The great continental areas within the temperate zone were valueless for the commerce of those days. As ends in themselves these 'colonies of settlement' finally succeeded. But the early modern states valued them merely as outposts for defence and attack in the European conflict. Sully maintained in 1600 that no kind of wealth could be expected from any country in the new world beyond latitude 40. Voltaire dismissed the loss of Canada with a contemptuous reference to 'a few frozen acres of land'. The West Indies were considered to be far more valuable than the North American colonies. According to Sir Josiah Child, emigration to the West Indies should be encouraged, for they provided employment to the workers of the mother country by purchasing her wares and freighting her ships. The North American colonies, he suggested, should be neglected and restrained in every possible way. Between none of these colonies and the mother countries did any strong bonds of sympathy exist, and most of them ultimately seceded when the opportunity arrived.

---

[1] *Wealth of Nations*, bk iv, ch 7, pt ii; Geyer, *Das Wirtschaftliche System der Niederländisch-Ostindischen Kompagnie am Kap der Guten Hoffnung.*

[2] The position was quite different in India and in Ireland. The former was exploited by the East India Company. The natural resources of the latter were similar to those of England, and she was largely dependent on that country for a market for her textiles and dairy produce. The import of Irish manufactured woollens, cattle and dairy produce into England was, however, prohibited in the seventeenth century, and Irish wool could be exported to England only. At the same time the Irish parliament was compelled to discourage local woollen manufacturers. The object of these regulations was obviously to suppress any vestige of Irish competition—a policy that was only too successful in its application.

The gradual development of economic freedom

In the commercial democracies of the West the entrepreneurial classes were making more and more insistent demands in the eighteenth century that they be left a free hand to conduct their own business, that it was vain to think that trade could be 'ruled and circumscribed by art', and that it would be better to let it 'take its own natural course'.[1] Naturally, however, the kingdoms with central administrations tried to conserve their systems of bureaucratic control against the corroding influences of commercialism, and as long as they retained their power the development of economic freedom was a very gradual process.

In Holland the entrepreneurial and ruling classes were virtually identical, and the country consistently followed a liberal economic policy. Import and export duties were kept low so that the carrying trade could be encouraged. The merchants vehemently resisted the granting of protection to any industry, and only the cloth industry was able to secure a certain measure of protection.[2] This liberalism was confined to the European trade, and Dutch policy differed from that of the other countries in temper, form and method rather than in basic principle.

In Britain in the seventeenth century the monarchs proved to be increasingly powerless to prevent the encroachment of the entrepreneurial class that was intent on sweeping away the traditional framework of the corporative society. The absence of a civil service and of an adequate system of inspection made it impossible for the state to enforce measures of industrial control. After the Revolution of 1688 the employers were allowed a much freer hand in industry, and with the growing economic individualism of the eighteenth century attempts to fetter the unrestricted freedom of contract between employer and employee were increasingly resisted and ignored. Parliament, in 1702, pronounced the maxim, which was to mould its policy during the rest of this period, that 'trade ought to be free and not restrained'; and by the end of this period Britain was well on the way towards the adoption of a policy of *laissez-faire*.

From an ideological point of view, mercantilism also had within itself the germs of its own undoing. Its object was to encourage commerce and industry as a means of obtaining a favourable balance of trade and, consequently, an abundant circulation of money. A circulation sufficient to prevent a fall in prices and to maintain a low rate of interest would indeed serve as an inducement to invest. The maintenance of a continually favourable balance in any specific country would, however, encourage price inflation, which would have an unfavourable effect on its competitive position. If, therefore, money is not an asset in itself, but merely a medium necessary to maintain the prices of essential commodities intact, then as Petty, North, and Stewart pointed out, the quantity of money circulating in the national economy should be neither too small nor too great. This raises questions of the relation of the quantity of money to goods and services, of the optimum supply of money required, and the problem of inflation. These issues undermined the spontaneous acceptance of the central thesis of mercantilism the necessity of the constant activity of the balance of trade and, consequently, the necessity for the state to promote national strength by the application of an appropriate economic and power policy. As the optimum supply of currency in circulation would appear, with the technical and analytical equipment available at the time, to be indeterminate, the only sensible thing to do would be to leave the supply of money to find its own level.

---

[1] Lipson, iii, 84 ff.
[2] Cf. Poelman, in *Het Huiselyk en Maatschappelyk Leven Onser Voorouders*, p. 243.

The physiocratic reaction to mercantilism went even further. Colbert had tried to encourage industry and the export of industrial products as a means of ensuring a favourable balance of trade. But a sound agricultural basis is a necessary condition for sustained industrial growth. Any balanced development of the economy must obviously begin with the largest sector, which must be able to produce surpluses for the market and thus become firmly integrated in the market economy before it can serve as a basis for general expansion. This was the basic thesis of the French physiocrats, who insisted on the necessity of organising agriculture on an efficient and capitalist basis. 'The advantages of agriculture', said Quesnay, 'depend on the amassing of land in great farms, brought to their highest value by rich farmers. . . . We do not envisage the farmer as a labourer who works the soil himself; he is an entrepreneur who commands'. Quesnay was therefore the logical successor of Colbert. But whereas Colbert had prohibited the export of corn as a means of keeping down the cost of living of the urban workers, Quesnay based his programme of agrarian reform on the assertion that economic prosperity required a large and remunerative market for the staple agricultural products, and that this could be obtained only under free trade. Freedom of production and freedom of the market constituted the natural order. State intervention in economic affairs was unnecessary, for, in the words of the older Mirabeau, laws that conform to nature are unnecessary and laws that contradict it impracticable. The concept of an economy that functions in accordance with its own inherent laws was well on its way to becoming an ideological reality.[1]

---

[1] Stark, *The History of Economics*, p. 18 ff. The physiocratic domination of French thought, as reflected in the Eden Treaty of 1786, was a temporary phenomenon, as contrasted with the much more permanent influence exercised by the liberal economic philosophy in Great Britain.

Part 7
The Free Enterprise Economies Come to Fruition

Last quarter of the eighteenth century to third quarter of the nineteenth century

20

The generation of self-sustained growth

The Industrial Revolution

The slow growth during the early modern period was due primarily, as we have seen, to the slow development of technology and the weakness of both the inducement and the ability to invest. With the dawn of the Industrial Revolution, the development of technology, the emergence of new industries, the building of railways and of cities, the opening up of new continents, and the rapid growth of population, provided such scope for new investment that the full employment of productive resources was assured, and therefore too the maximum income possible under the prevailing standards of technical development. This growth was both rapid and self-sustained. The period of the Industrial Revolution has, in fact, been described as a 'vast secular boom'.[1]

It has been maintained that this transformation should be regarded as the quickening of an agelong evolutionary process rather than a violent break with existing practice. The Industrial Revolution was neither sudden nor violent. It was spread over a whole century, and its origin can be traced far back into the previous period. The series of inventions that heralded the movement merely marked a stage in the long development of a new mechanical technology. They were the result, not of accident, but of the systematic thought directed to industrial problems in consequence of the accumulated knowledge, increased specialisation and growing technical ability of the previous centuries.

The changes effected in the cotton industry were the most revolutionary because it was relatively easy to solve the problems of this trade by mechanical and chemical means. Yet thirty years elapsed between the invention of the spinning machines and the final triumph of the spinning factory over the domestic worker, while the powerloom did not completely oust the handloom in Great Britain before the middle of the nineteenth century. The older and more rigid branches of the textile trade—wool, linen and silk—were even slower to adopt mechanical equipment and to assume the factory form of organisation. The same applied to the metal industries. It was not until Cort's puddling process was patented an 1783 that the problem of substituting coke for charcoal in the final processes of iron manufacture was solved, though the production of iron remained a crude and cumber-

[1] Hicks, *Value and Capital*, p. 302.

175

some process till well into the nineteenth century. The other industries were even slower to adopt improved processes of manufacture.[1]

The concept of the generation of self-sustained growth, though of value in explaining the difference in the means and rate of economic advance before and after the Industrial Revolution, should obviously not be dramatised to give the impression of a complete break in the continuity of historical processes. But, while there is evidence that the process of economic development had gathered considerable momentum in Britain before the Industrial Revolution, the index of industrial output of British industry prepared by Walther Hoffmann nevertheless shows that whereas the annual rate of increase had fluctuated between zero and 2 per cent from the beginning of the eighteenth century until 1780, it subsequently rose to a level of 3-4 per cent and, except for a slight setback during the Napoleonic Wars,

---

[1] Usher, *An Introduction to the Industrial History of England*, ch 10; Clapham, 'Economic change', in *Cambridge Modern History*, x. The year 1760 is usually accepted as marking the commencement of the new period because in that year the Carron works were founded and Roebuck's blast furnaces were built with a view to the use of coke. This advertisement for the new process led to its rapid adoption by works in other centres. This date may therefore be taken as marking the beginning of the transfer of the centre of gravity from the organic textile trades to the inorganic mining industries. Cf. Toynbee, *The Industrial Revolution of the Eighteenth Century in England*; Cunningham, *Growth of English Industry and Commerce*, p. 524; Sombart, *Der Moderne Kapitalismus*, ii, 1137 ff. From the point of view of the production of iron, however, it seems that the year 1775 'marks more clearly than most dates selected as boundary-stones the end of one economic period and the beginning of another'. Up to that time the output of iron had increased by an average of not more than 1 per cent per annum. Within the next few years the rate of increase was multiplied manyfold through the inventions associated with the names of James Watt and Henry Cort. Ashton, *Iron and Steel in the Industrial Revolution*. This year also saw the revolt of the American colonies against British mercantile policy, and was followed by the publication of Adam Smith's *Wealth of Nations* in the following year. The date 1760 is also significant because of the rapid increase in the decade beginning in this year of the mechanical inventions that heralded the Industrial Revolution, as well as of many important changes in agriculture, industry and transport. The number of patents of invention issued an Great Britain in the eighteenth century was as follows:

1700-1709 ... 22   1730-1739 ... 56   1760-1769 ... 205
1710-1719 ... 38   1740-1749 ... 82   1770-1779 ... 294
1720-1729 ... 89   1750-1759 ... 92   1780-1789 ... 477

The records of the British Patent Office also provide evidence of the new mechanical interest not only in respect of the increase in the number, but also in the greater variety of the new inventions. Moreover, whereas the 'early patents were issued in many cases not for definite, finished inventions but for mere ideas and suggestions, for vaguely defined processes or devices, in some instances not far removed from the occult arts of the middle ages', those after 1760 show the tendency to become more definite and concrete. 'The contrast may be explained in part, no doubt, by the increase in scientific and technical knowledge.' (Bowden, *Industrial Society in England Towards the End of the Eighteenth Century*, pp. 9 ff). The invention of Hargreaves's spinning-jenny in 1764 is usually said to mark the beginning of the industrial age in the textile trades, and the textile industry was the most characteristic industry of the Industrial Revolution. The output of cotton textiles, however, did not begin to expand very rapidly before the 'eighties of the century. During the first half of the century the imports of raw cotton grew at a little more than 1 per cent per annum; between 1750 and 1780 the rate increased to about 3 per cent. Then, in the 'eighties, the rate jumped to some 20 per cent per annum, after which, for half a century or so, the rate settled at around 8 per cent. It is for this reason that Rostow, 'with a sense of the considerable violence done to economic history', adopts the years 1783-1802 as best indicating for Great Britain the period of the so-called 'take-off into self-sustained growth' (*The Stages of Economic Growth*, ch 4). Finally, Hoffmann has shown that only in the 1780s did the annual percentage rate of industrial output increase to such an extent as to leave little doubt that there had been a significant change in the fundamental conditions of production. 'The change in the rate of production which occurred about 1780 was so definite that it clearly marks an epoch in the evolution of Britain's economy' (Hoffmann, *British Industry*, 1700-1950, pp. 31 ff).

remained at this level until the middle of the nineteenth century.[1] This does indeed represent a very significant increase in the rate of growth, and although this first achievement of self-sustained growth must be conceived as having occurred over a period of years, there can be no doubt of its telling influence in bringing about the structural transformation first of the British economy and society and then of the rest of the world. So farreaching and pervasive were these changes in their economic effects, so dramatic in the outlets for human energy they provided, and so profound in the possibilities for economic progress they supplied, that the process can only be described as revolutionary.

Britain assumes industrial leadership

The beginnings of the Industrial Revolution must be sought in the expansion of commerce, the gradual improvement of technology, and the increasing capitalistic organisation of the preceding period. The extension of the market and the growing accumulation and investment of capital favoured industrial specialisation and the introduction of improvements in technique. The colonial markets demanded simple standardised wares, like cotton cloth, which lent themselves easily to machine production. The needs of the market stimulated inventive research on these lines and facilitated the adoption of mechanical improvements. The English cotton industry was a comparatively new branch of production and was therefore free from the restrictions of craft custom and government regulation. It could adopt the technique and organisation best suited to its needs. Similarly the scarcity of wood stimulated experiments in the use of coal. Coal was available in abundance and in close proximity to the iron ore. Sometimes the coal and the iron were embedded together, the coal being mined as a necessary byproduct, and there was therefore a strong incentive to using it. Britain's markets for manufactured goods, both at home and overseas, were growing and these opportunities were seized by a business community that was becoming increasingly sophisticated commercially, increasingly cost conscious, and increasingly responsive to the opportunities offered by economic development. Above all the British market was becoming more cohesive and competitive pressures were becoming more effective in inducing the adoption of technical innovations. In every sphere the Industrial Revolution manifested itself as a response to the challenge offered by the economic conditions of the time. The inventions must not be regarded as isolated events but as a continuous and inter-related process, because new methods in one industry effected changes in other industries, and were in turn affected by these developments.

England was especially well placed to take advantage of this combination of favourable circumstances. She had assumed the lead in science and technology. Her political and commercial supremacy gave her the virtual monopoly of the new colonial markets. Her social system had been freed from the worst abuses of feudalism and now gave free scope to the energies of the bourgeoisie. Good means of communication by water and the absence of internal customs barriers stimulated domestic trade. What nature bestowed, man had improved, and from the middle of the seventeenth century there had been a continuous and growing investment in improving the means of transport. The country was fortunate in the abundance of its natural resources. Large coal and iron-ore deposits laid the foundation of her

---

[1] Hoffmann, *British Industry, 1700-1950*, pp. 31 ff.

industrial supremacy in the nineteenth century. The increased production of wool after the enclosure movement provided the raw material for the expansion of the woollen industry. Cotton was indeed not grown on the island, but the uniform humidity of Lancashire's climate became a decisive factor in the development of the textile industry. Above all, there was present in England a class of businessmen with the initiative and knowledge necessary for the introduction of novelties. The comparative shortage of labour and the relatively high wages of the country encouraged the use of mechanical means of production, and the nature of her manufactures facilitated the use of those means. England also possessed abundant capital, and low rates of interest and rising price levels in the second half of the eighteenth century undoubtedly stimulated investment in improved methods of production. Finally, in Britain the whole system of industrial regulation had broken down, and the new doctrines of economic individualism taught that only by the production of goods that were better and cheaper than those of other countries could new markets be opened up and the old ones be retained. Seldom has such a unique combination of circumstances assured a country the leadership and hegemony of the business world.

Structural changes brought about by the Industrial Revolution

The Industrial Revolution brought with it not merely a change in the scale of economic activity but also fundamental and permanent changes in the industrial structure, first of Great Britain, then of western Europe and, finally, of the whole world.

The first of these was a change in the content of the national product. In the process of development, primary production came to have a gradually but steadily declining share of the national product while the share of industrial output and of transport consistently increased. This pattern of growth has been followed, since the Industrial Revolution, in virtually all countries. It involves a shifting of productive resources from low yielding industries, operating under conditions of diminishing returns, to high yielding sectors of the economy enjoying rapidly increasing returns.

Secondly, there was a change in the organisation of production, which was reflected in the changing roles of capital and labour. The transition from an agricultural to an industrial economy involved the mechanisation of manufacturing processes, the construction of new means of transport, the building of cities on a hitherto unprecedented scale, and the provision of the necessary social overhead expenditure. All these activities entailed capital formation on an extensive scale—an increase in the ratio of capital formation to national income from say 3 per cent during the first half of the eighteenth century to 5 per cent in 1780, 7 per cent at the beginning of the nineteenth century, and 10 per cent by the middle of that century.[1] This ratio of investment to national income was not high when judged by present-day standards, but the efficiency of investment—that is, the increment in output per unit of investment—was high because of the new technological advances, the increased knowledge of the practical problems involved in production, the better methods of organisation, the generation of internal and external economies, and the creation of large new markets through the process of industrialisation.

Thirdly, economies became more closely integrated internally and in the inter-

[1] Deane and Cole, *British Economic Growth*, ch 8.

national economy. The nineteenth century saw an increased specialisation in the industrial countries, on the one hand, and in primary producing countries, on the other hand. The rapid growth that took place first in Britain and then on the continent of Europe was then again transmitted to the rest of the world through a vigorous increase in the demand for primary products, and was associated with the export of capital to most of the primary producing countries.[1]

Above all, the expansion brought about by the Industrial Revolution differed structurally from that of all previous periods in being of an irreversible and cumulative nature. Before this era economic progress had been extremely slow and undependable, and had been dependent primarily on the discovery of new resources. The new industrial countries now succeeded in building a compound rate of growth into their economic systems, and even though the rate of increase was moderate, its impact over a period of time resulted in massive and assured economic expansion.

New industries and new sources of power and raw material

The textile industry was the first to be affected by the new methods of production, and, because of the high income and price elasticity that existed for cotton textiles in the European and colonial markets, growth in this industry was transferred to other industries, and especially to the chemical and the iron and producers' goods industries. Nor was industry the only sphere to be affected. Significant also was the use of new sources of power and new raw materials: the substitution of inanimate for animate sources of power and the use of new and more abundant raw materials, and especially the substitution of mineral for vegetable and animal substances.

Before the Industrial Revolution the use of machines had been impeded by the absence of a good motive power. Wind was intermittent and unreliable, and the use of water power placed severe limitations on the location of industry. These limitations were removed by the invention of the steam engine. The increased depth of mining had led to the improvement of pumping machines and finally to the adoption of steam power. But the first steam engines were limited to pumping in mines until Watt made them capable of producing the rotary motion necessary for driving machines. During the course of this period the steam engine displaced the other sources of power as a prime mover, and made possible the general adoption of machine methods of production. 'The new form of power and, no less, the new transmitting mechanisms by which this was made to do work previously done by hand and muscle, were the pivot on which industry swung into the modern age.' The steam engine became the central feature of the Industrial Revolution, supplying the indispensable basis for mass production by machinery, for which the expansion of overseas trade had previously provided the economic inducement. Above all, it also created the necessary market for the products of the producers' goods industries through the role which steam power came to play first in the textile industry and then in the producers' goods industries themselves, and the important external economies which were generated for the whole economy in the process.[2]

Coal and steam liberated industry from the limitations of organic nature. The world was no longer confined to the annual income of the sun's energy embodied in

[1] Cole, *The Cambridge Economic History of Europe,* vi, The Industrial Revolutions and After, pt i, pp. 44 ff.
[2] Ashton, *The Industrial Revolution*, p. 70; Ohlin, *American Economic Review*, May 1959, pp. 338 ff.

animal and vegetable life, and could exploit the resources of energy that had been stored up in mineral matter over millions of years. The world could live on its capital.[1] The application of steam power to the manufacture of textiles had the important effect of reducing costs in this industry and of generating important external economies in the producers' goods industries. Everywhere it served as a growth point in economic development by making possible and accelerating the adoption of innovations that could not otherwise have been applied.

Coal and iron became the source and the symbol of nineteenth century civilisation as wood had been of all previous centuries. Coal dust polluted the atmosphere of the new industrial centres. Valuable combustible materials escaped as soot, and the byproducts of the coke ovens and the gases of the blast furnaces spoiled the surroundings of manufacturing towns. But such things were of small account to a world fascinated by the new sources of power. Artists discovered a peculiar beauty in this world of twilight, fog, and smoke. The effusion of filth became the symbol of prosperity, a clear sky in an industrial district the sign of a strike or a depression.

Iron became the characteristic material of the new age. It combines great strength with malleability and is strong not only under compression but also in tension. If it oxidises fairly easily it has the compensating advantage of being, next to aluminium, the commonest metal on the earth's crust. But the importance of the iron industry during this period must not be exaggerated. In regard to the number of men employed, the capital invested, the value of the output, and the rate of growth it could not compare with the cotton industry. But the growing supply of cheap metal did greatly facilitate the mechanisation of other industries, the movement from water to steam power and, eventually, the metamorphosis of the means of transport.

The centralisation of industry

Until the eighteenth century there had been no very marked territorial differentiation in industry, nationally or internationally. The various industries were spread evenly over the country, either because they were domestic or because they had to have easy access to power and to raw material.

With the advent of the Industrial Revolution the gap in development between Britain and the Continent widened. The first half of the nineteenth century saw the gradual diffusion of the new methods across the channel, first to Belgium, then to France, and finally to Germany. During the second half of the century industry on the Continent came of age, and by the end of this period, as the result of a generation of drastic institutional changes and selective investment, a number of industries in western Europe could already compete with those of Great Britain on the export markets of the world.[2]

A second aspect of the centralisation of industry was its movement from the country to the towns and its location in certain specific areas. With the introduction of power driven machines, mechanical power could be transferred to the towns. The people of London, Manchester, and Liverpool, Boulton said, went 'steam-mill mad'. Industries concentrated in regions offering special inducements in the form of a convenient labour supply, cheap raw materials, motive-power, transport facilities and easy access to markets. The coal and iron fields especially became the new

[1] Sombart, *Der Moderne Kapitalismus,* i, 122.
[2] Landes, in *The Cambridge Economic History of Europe,* vi, pt i, p. 458.

centres of industry. This territorial specialisation often produced a lopsided development, in which regional opportunities and the advantages of a well diversified economic and social structure were neglected. The rapid aggregation of human beings produced problems of housing, town planning, and welfare that were beyond the powers and vision of the contemporary administration. The centres of the creation of wealth everywhere became the saddest spectacles of squalor and environmental destruction.

Rise of the factory system

Mechanical power and machinery produced the factory system. Machines need a substantial capital outlay, and as the productive process is divided into a number of mutually dependent processes, it can be effectively organised only in a central establishment. Machines, moreover, can be installed only in a place where power is available, and when the power is kinetic the location must be near the source at which the power is generated. The factory also offers good facilities for the supervision and the division of labour, and these become essential if automatic processes are to be efficiently used. The hours of labour, the assignment of individual tasks, the speed and regularity of performance all have to be precisely regulated. As Ure pointed out, the main task of the new factory managers consisted in the 'distribution of the different members of the apparatus into one co-operative body, in impelling each organ with its appropriate delicacy and speed, and above all, in training human beings to renounce their desultory habits of work and to identify themselves with the unvarying regularity of the complex automaton'.[1] The factory, in fact, encourages the rational organisation of work—the use of resources in such a way as to minimise costs and to maximise returns—as the outstanding purpose of the undertaking. The factory system, finally, facilitates the adoption of innovation by its inducement to efficiency, the experimentation with new methods, and the application of scientific procedures.

The displacement of the domestic by the factory system proceeded slowly. It was not until the first quarter of the nineteenth century that the factory had finally established itself in the British textile trade; by the middle of the century it dominated the metal trades. But by the end of this period the factory had made little progress in the British clothing and leather industries, while boot and shoe-makers, saddlers, goldsmiths, watchmakers and cutlers still stood aloof from the system. On the Continent Belgium was the only country to follow close on the heels of Great Britain in adopting the new forms of industrial organisation; France and Germany did not make rapid headway until the second half of the century.

The factory system effected the final divorce of the worker from the means of production and established a simple and direct relationship between employer and employee. A means of organisation had been evolved which was especially suited to the needs of the capitalist system.

Most of the more unfortunate consequences of the factory system were immediate in effect and transitional in character. Such a rapid and fundamental transition could not, at the time, have been effected smoothly, especially as it coincided with a period of almost continuous warfare. Early factory conditions were bad. There were few sanitary facilities and little ventilation; safety devices were unknown. The hours of labour were long and the wages low. There is today,

---

[1] Ure, *The Philosophy of Manufactures*, p. 15.

however, general agreement that, as far as material standards were concerned, the condition of the majority of workers did improve. But if the influence of the new forces was on the whole beneficial, their impact on important sections of workers was decidedly detrimental. Those, for example, who sought to compete rather than to cooperate with the new technique fought a losing battle, and brought much suffering on themselves and their families.

The introduction of machines facilitated the employment of women and children. Men were at first loath to enter the factories, and these were only gradually introduced in branches of industry that were the chief spheres of male employment. It has been estimated that at least three-quarters of the employees in the early cotton factories were women and children. But the use of child labour was by no means initiated by the introduction of machines, for the employment of children was an integral part of the older industrial society. Similarly the long hours of labour were a legacy of the domestic system, under which a working day consisted of twelve hours' toil.

Fortunately the worst aspects of the factory system were remedied during the course of the nineteenth century. And once the period of transition was over, it was better for the worker to work regular and shorter hours in a well ventilated factory than to work in a crowded tenement littered with the refuse of his labour. The Industrial Revolution had two important effects on material welfare. In the first place, investment in the new inventions stimulated the demand for labour and created a high level of employment. Secondly, the substitution of mechanical for human power greatly increased man's dominance over nature and helped considerably to relieve want. Machines not only perfected the work of human beings but performed tasks they could not do. The result was a great improvement in the standard of living, reflected in the increase, betterment, and cheapening of the commodities and services available to the masses. The decline in mortality is everywhere the most decisive indication of the improvement in living conditions that accompanied the Industrial Revolution.

The new means of transport

The revolution in industry was associated with a no less important metamorphosis of the means of transport. In no respect, perhaps, did this period more clearly surpass its predecessors than in the conquest of space. The new means of conveyance took the form of improved roads and canals, of railways and of steamships. In Great Britain and America these were provided for the most part by private enterprise. On the continent of Europe, where there was an ingrained tradition of state enterprise, pressing military needs, and lack of capital, they were supplied mainly by the state.

The second half of the eighteenth century introduced the classical phase of road construction in Europe. Hard-surfaced highways, capable of bearing traffic all the year round, were constructed. A considerable increase in speed and a corresponding reduction in cost were the result.

The building of railways caused a comparative decline in the importance of roads. They were reduced to purely local significance, their main function being to act as feeders to the new form of transport. The existing methods of construction were adequate for the demands made on them, and not until the appearance of the automobile in the twentieth century did standards of grading and surfacing on the best roads advance much beyond the work of the engineers at the beginning of the nineteenth century.

Until the introduction of the railway, transport by water was the only cheap means of moving commodities in bulk. Countries like England and Holland, with extended coastlines and excellent systems of internal waterways, were therefore in an exceptionally favourable position to develop their trade.

The great age of canal construction, however, did not begin before the middle of the eighteenth century. Then a veritable fever of canal building swept Great Britain and covered the country with a network of waterways. The direct stimulus for their construction was supplied by the needs of Britain's expanding industries, which required facilities for the transport of heavy and bulky commodities such as coal, iron and clay. Factories were built along the canals just as they were later to be erected along the railroads. The canals thus relieved the roads of a large part of the growing traffic and even enjoyed a considerable share of the passenger service.

On the Continent the canals, like the highways, were constructed mainly by the state, in contrast to England where they were built almost exclusively by private enterprise. They were therefore more highly standardised, and as they were mostly toll-free they continued to play an important part in transport even after the building of the railways.

The railways supplied what neither the road nor the canal could provide: a rapid and cheap means of transit for men and material. They became the new arteries for the economic and political life of countries, reducing the time and cost of movement, opening up continental regions, revolutionising commerce, differentiating countries economically while uniting them socially. By lowering transport costs they expanded markets everywhere. Above all they played a central part in the expansion of the iron and coal industries, first in Great Britain, then on the continent of Europe, and finally in America. By the middle of the nineteenth century, indeed, railroad construction provided the most important single stimulus to industrial growth in the western world. The railways also enlarged the market for agricultural products and made the introduction of innovations in this industry possible. This in turn released labour for the development of other sectors of the economy. In view of the rapid economic development brought about by the railways, the traffic they came to carry was mainly new freight not previously moved by any other agency. At the same time they tended largely to displace the other means of transport not effectively protected against their competition. Thus the railways secured a position of dominance which they maintained unchallenged till well into the twentieth century.

This period also saw the application of steam power to navigation, though the displacement of the old means of propulsion took place much more gradually at sea than on land. The middle of the century, in fact, saw the rise of the American clippers, marvels of grace and speed, whose crowded sails and great lengths in proportion to their beams enabled them to attain remarkable speeds. As late as 1870 the merchant fleets of the world still consisted mainly of sailing vessels, but thereafter the steamship began to make rapid headway. The opening of the Suez route in 1869 seriously affected the clippers because they could not navigate the canal. Economies were gradually effected in the amounts of coal and water the steamers were required to carry. Coaling stations where steamships could replenish their supplies were established on the main ocean routes, and the consumption of coal was reduced by the invention of new types of marine engines. Because steam navigation offered signal advantages in certainty, safety, speed and cost, the sailing vessel was forced out of the most profitable carrying business, and, during the period that followed, was forced off the seas.

Innovations in agriculture

The changes in the secondary and tertiary sectors of the economy were effectively complemented by important innovations that were introduced in the primary sector. Without the innovations in agriculture, the revolutionary transformation of the rest of the economy could not have been implemented. Hitherto the most persistent problem of the farmer had been that of maintaining the fertility of his soil. This was achieved by the use of animal manure, fallowing, and the rotation of crops. Owing to the lack of winter-roots only a limited number of animals could be kept alive on hay during the winter months. The use of animal manure was therefore restricted. The universal means of restoring the fertility of the soil was to let it lie fallow every second or third year. This was supplemented by the alternation of crops.

The introduction of green crops and winter roots in Britain, a practice adopted from the Low Countries in the late seventeenth and early eighteenth centuries, enabled the farmer to dispense with the wasteful process of fallowing. The rapid increase in population acted as a strong stimulus to the general adoption of these measures, and the effects were farreaching. Nitrogenous plants such as clover, lucerne and alfalfa derive their nourishment from the air rather than from the soil. Planting the land with such legumes has the same effect as leaving it fallow, while the decay of the roots after the crop has been reaped, roots into which nitrogen has been absorbed from the air, enriches the soil with an essential element of plant growth. Farmers, therefore, could now sow their lands alternately with cereals, artificial grasses, and winter roots. Areas which had been permanent pasture could also be brought under the plough. A great increase in fodder, and consequently in the number of animals, with an abundant supply of manure, was the result. The maxim that 'a full bullock yard and a full fold make a full granary' was verified.

No less striking was the effect on the breeding of sheep and cattle. Both cattle and sheep had hitherto been valued mainly for their milk, draught potential or wool, but had not been bred specifically for meat production. As long as a large proportion of the cattle had to be slaughtered every autumn on account of the scarcity of fodder, and while those that remained were kept barely alive during the winter, scientific breeding was impossible. Roots and artificial grasses not only increased the yield of cereals but also supplied the winter keep, which facilitated improvements in livestock. Sheep, formerly rivals to tillage, became a valuable adjunct to arable farming. Cattle, instead of seeking a precarious existence on the fallow, were stall fed. The effect on the weight and quality of the animals was remarkable.

During the course of the nineteenth century the technique of agriculture was further improved by the introduction of agricultural machinery, artificial fertilisers, and efficient methods of storing and preserving food. Liebig's discoveries made the farmer more independent of animal manure and facilitated specialisation in those branches of agriculture for which the land was best fitted by nature and by economic circumstances. The introduction of agricultural machinery was the response to the challenge of conditions in America. The westward and urban drift of population made agricultural labour scarce and expensive at a time when the price of agricultural produce was falling. The farmer had to raise his labour productivity or else go out of business. The mechanisation of agriculture began in the West, but by the middle of the century it had become a national movement. It was the rural counterpart of the Industrial Revolution, which fended off the spectre of diminishing returns. Without it, improvements in the standard of living would have been inconceivable.

Throughout the first three-quarters of the nineteenth century agriculture in both the Old and the New Worlds was stimulated by the increased demand for agricultural products, a demand that came with the growing industrialisation and urbanisation of western peoples. There was a gradual transition from subsistence farming to production for the market. Except in a few areas, however, the farming population never became completely absorbed into the capitalist system. A large proportion of agriculturists continued to farm 'for a living' rather than 'for profit'.

Agrarian changes

The changes in agricultural technique were accompanied by changes in land tenure no less farreaching in their effects. The new methods of cultivation required a considerable investment of capital. They were incompatible with the open-field farming still practised over about half of England and most of the Continent. 'Village farmers could not introduce roots and grasses on open fields which after harvest were grazed in common, rest their exhausted arable, vary its cropping or grow fodder for their half starved stock whose scanty manure was wastefully distributed.' Changes were therefore effected in land tenure that brought about the final dissolution of the medieval village community and the displacement of collective husbandry by individualist farming.

The enclosure movement of the eighteenth century destroyed what remained of communal husbandry in Great Britain. Its place was taken predominantly by large single farms cultivated by capitalist tenant farmers, though the number of very small freeholds, awarded out of the collective farms, naturally also increased. Whereas the first enclosure movement in Tudor times had been made with the object of turning arable land into pasture, this second movement transformed the collectively cultivated open fields into compact farms on which the new scientific farming could be profitably conducted. In addition, much common and waste land was enclosed. The absorption of the commons, coinciding with the loss of supplementary earnings from domestic industry, induced many smallholders to sell their awarded freeholds. The state also favoured the process of concentration. Tudor governments had opposed enclosures for pasturage because these threatened the country with depopulation and famine. Hanoverian legislators encouraged enclosures for grain growing and stock raising because they increased employment and averted famine. English rural society, as a result, became typically differentiated into landlord, tenant and labourer. Nowhere else in the world was the agriculturist so completely dissociated from the land he cultivated.

The rural organisation of eastern Germany bore a close resemblance to that of Britain. The Prussian Junkers were efficient landowners and by purchase or forcible appropriation they had succeeded in building up large seignorial domains, which they exploited by means of servile labour. The emancipation of these serfs was not brought about suddenly and violently from below, as in France, but proceeded slowly and methodically from above. Legal servitude was replaced by economic subjection, so that the landowners were assured of both their regular and their seasonal labour forces. Whereas the French peasants freed themselves and paid no price for the privilege, the German landlords, according to Sombart, made the peasants pay heavily for restoring to them the freedom of which their ancestors had been robbed without the payment of any compensation.

Over the rest of the continent the agrarian movement tended to follow exactly the opposite course. The peasant was liberated from feudal restrictions and promoted to an independent proprietorship. Instead of the lord dispossessing the peasant, it was the peasant who dispossessed the lord. With the emancipation of the Russian serfs in 1861 the process of freeing the European peasantry can be said to have been completed. Thus by the end of this period European agriculture was carried on by vast numbers of small peasant proprietors, with, here and there, islands of large estates cultivated by landless labourers. The change in the status of the peasant, however, as a rule brought about little change in his methods of cultivation, which for the most part preserved their traditional character. And it did not prevent the continued presence on the land of a class of smallholders, a semi-proletariat who could not make a living from their holdings but were forced to seek employment with richer peasants or in local industries. Nevertheless this medieval residue of peasant proprietorships provided the capitalist system with a powerful conservative support, and provided a large part of the world with its surest guarantee of social stability.

Rapid growth of population

The changes in agriculture, industry and transport offered renewed scope for an increase in population. The mass of the European people had lived for centuries on the margin of subsistence and the means of existence had determined the size of the population. The table of nature, as Malthus said, was laid for only a limited number of guests, and those that came uninvited had to starve.

With the new developments in transport and in food production the basis of existence was enlarged, while progress in the technique of hygiene improved sanitary conditions,[1] and advances in medical knowledge reduced the incidence of disease. The coincidence of high fertility and of a reduced rate of mortality was phenomenal. During the century that preceded this period (1650-1750) the population of Africa and America had remained stationary or had actually dwindled, while that of Europe had increased by only 40 per cent. During the next century-and-a-half the population of Europe nearly trebled itself. The inhabitants of the United States increased from about 4 million in 1790 to approximately 76 million in 1900. The population of the world between 1650 and 1900 is estimated to have increased as follows (in millions):[2]

Continent	1650	1750	1800	1850	1900
Europe	100	140	187	266	401
Asia	250	406	522	671	859
Africa	100	100	100	100	141
North America	7	6.3	15.4	39	106
South America	6	6.1	9.2	20	38
Oceania	2	2	2	2	6
Total	465	660	836	1098	1551

People of European descent enjoyed a disproportionate share of the world increase. The nineteenth century was a period essentially of European and largely of Germanic expansion.

[1] By the use of iron pipes sewage could be kept separate from drinking water; this innovation did much to make the populous centres of the nineteenth century possible.
[2] Willcox, *International Migrations*, ii, p. 78.

Growth of the working class

For capitalism to reach its mature condition, says Karl Marx,

> Two very different kinds of commodity-possessors must come face to face and
> into contact: on the one hand, the owners of money, means of production,
> means of subsistence, who are eager to increase the sum of values they possess
> by buying other people's labour-power; on the other hand, free labourers, the
> sellers of their own labour-power. . . . The capitalist system presupposes the
> complete separation of the labourers from all property in the means by which
> they can realise their labour.[1]

Marx was generalising from English conditions, though the process was more
complex than he realised. The second enclosure movement did indeed tend to
separate the agricultural worker still further from the soil. At the same time the
decline of domestic industry cut the peasantry off from a traditional source of
supplementary employment. But the technical developments in agriculture were, at
least initially, not of a labour-saving kind. Until the middle of the nineteenth
century the number of workers engaged in agriculture in England increased rather
than decreased. Rural migrants to urban centres must on the whole, therefore, have
been drawn from the natural increase of the agricultural population, and it is as true
to say that they were attracted to manufacture as that they were repelled from
agriculture.[2]

The most important source of industrial labour was provided by the rapid
increase in population. This increase was due to the improved conditions brought
about by the application of the new technical methods and the enhanced opportunities of employment offered by investment in these methods. In a significant
sense, therefore, industrial capitalism can be said to have provided its own labour
force, just as it largely provided its own capital through the reinvestment of
reserves.

The slow growth of the factory system, the survival of the individualist traditions of the artisan and the craftsman, the ambition of many workers to rise to the
position of small employers, were all factors that retarded the development of
labour organisation and the growth of class consciousness. There was a corresponding lack of combination among employers. The absence of organisation and the
desuetude of labour legislation imparted mobility and elasticity to the labour force
and allowed unfettered free trade in the labour market, which were optimum
conditions for a rapidly expanding industrial capitalism.[3]

There still remained the problem of training the requisite labour force in the skill
and discipline required by machine production. This was no easy task. The worker
had to give up his 'desultory habits of work' and discipline himself to the order and
the regularity implicit in the new methods of production: he had to become a
useful factory hand. Because women and children were more easily available and
proved to be more amenable to factory routine the labour force was initially largely
recruited from this source.

The more basic requirements of training, which, at successively higher levels, are
represented by the provision of elementary education, the acquisition of the
working skills of the mechanic, the engineer's combination of scientific knowledge
and applied training, and finally, the provision of university training in the pure and

[1] Marx, *Capital*, pp. 737 ff.
[2] Ashton, *The Industrial Revolution*, pp. 60 ff.
[3] Cf. Dobb, *Studies in the Development of Capitalism*, pp. 265 ff.

applied sciences, were in Britain, with the peculiar English partiality for decentralised empiricism, initially left very largely to private enterprise. It was only gradually during the course of the nineteenth century that the state began to provide the necessary facilities. Germany in this respect was more progressive, and her policy yielded its rewards during the succeeding period when, with the growing complexity of industrial technology, a formal education became increasingly essential.[1]

The entrepreneurs

The Industrial Revolution gave great scope to the energies of the bourgeoisie, and this class played a dominant role in determining the economic and political destinies of the period. It triumphed in the struggle for power against the old feudal-agrarian interests; and the proletariat had not yet appeared on the horizon as a threatening rival. The new methods of industrial organisation provided unique opportunities to individuals of 'motor' temperament, capable of winning through in the competitive struggle for existence. 'The social foundations of progress', says a Liberal report, 'were the liberation of the energies of the middle classes, the scope offered to their enterprise, their talents, and their thrift, and the honour paid to success in business life.'[2]

During this period economic activities were still conducted on a relatively small scale, both technically and financially. The source of enterprise was easy to locate; it was associated with the entrepreneur. The entrepreneur was a capitalist who risked his own wealth in an undertaking which he himself directed. The small beginnings from which he started assured him a thorough mastery of details. The qualities demanded of the business undertaker were powers of organisation, a keen wit, inventive power, a knowledge of the technical processes of his industry, and acquaintance with the general conditions of the market. The entrepreneur in economic literature was the independent self-employed manager, the one who carried the risks and claimed the gains of the enterprise.[3]

Most of these men started from very modest beginnings. This was made possible by the simplicity of the equipment required. Sometimes they were merchants who had become manufacturers, sometimes they were drawn from agriculture or the service trades, but as a rule they were recruited from industry itself. This was to be expected, since the centre of gravity was shifting from marketing to the technical and managerial problems of production. Industry was assuming the lead, procuring the capital, bearing the risks, overcoming difficulties of technique and organisation, and producing commodities in a quantity and of a quality hitherto unknown. This was the era of industrial capitalism.[4]

The new entrepreneurial class was alive to the possibilities offered by technical innovation, eager to find new markets and receptive to new ideas. Newcomers into an industry could easily oust their already established competitors if their methods of rendering the services were superior. The ownership of the business gave the entrepreneur unfettered control in the management of his own affairs and facility

---

[1] Landes, in *The Cambridge Economic History of Europe*, vi, pt 1, 566 ff.
[2] *Britain's Industrial Future*, Report of the Liberal Industrial Inquiry (1928), p. 6.
[3] Marshall, *Industry and Trade*, p. 355.
[4] 'Thus the manufacturer, being at the same time a capitalist, a works manager and a merchant, set a new pattern of the complete business man. Often enough he was nothing else' (Mantoux, *The Industrial Revolution in the Eighteenth Century*, p. 386).

in taking decisions; the personal ownership of the business supplied the stimulus to succeed. The new man of business was interested, not in the enjoyment of income, but in the accumulation of wealth. 'He worked day in and day out with the consciousness of the hell of penury on one side, and the paradise of huge possessions on the other.'[1] This developed a fighting spirit, the sense of playing for a stake, an individualism that tolerated no outside interference. But it also stimulated the qualities of thrift, resourcefulness, and perseverance that are usually associated with the bourgeoisie.

Commerce

The Industrial Revolution had farreaching effects on commerce, and the expansion of commerce in its turn had a profound effect on the development of this period. The large and elastic markets provided by exports imparted the dynamic character to the changes that inaugurated the period, first in the textile industry and then, more gradually, in the producers' goods industries and in other sectors of the economy. The rapid growth of the European economy in its turn was transmitted to the underdeveloped countries of the world through the vigorous increase in the demand for primary products and the concomitant investment of capital in these countries.

The most general feature of the trade of this period was one of expansion. Official values of the imports and exports of Great Britain during the period 1613 to 1760 reflect an average annual rate of increase of 1.1 per cent, and Britain's foreign trade during these years expanded more rapidly than that of any other major economic power. The twenty-three years between 1760 and 1783 were years of protracted warfare, during which the country's imports showed only a moderate increase and the exports actually tended to decline. But during the next sixty-seven years (1783-1850), the average annual rate of increase of Britain's foreign trade advanced to 3.7 per cent. World trade during the following thirty years (1850-80) increased by 270 per cent, which represents an average yearly increase of 3.4 per cent.

The French Revolution removed the internal barriers to trade, the railways further facilitated the creation of larger economic entities, and the reduction of tariff barriers stimulated international trade. The collapse of the old colonial system opened the markets of Asia, Africa and America to world trade. The number of commodities exchanged between countries increased and their general character changed. The place of the luxuries that had featured so prominently in the commerce of all previous centuries was taken by articles of mass consumption. International trade was no longer concerned primarily with the condiments but with the aliments, no longer with spices and seasonings but with the staple foods. The staple articles of production no longer had a purely local significance but obtained a world market. Commerce became increasingly regular and certain. Capital locked up in goods in transit and in warehouses decreased in relation to the amount of business transacted. Markets became increasingly sensitive, the currents of commerce changing with the slightest variations in price.

Economic resources thus became effectively integrated through a system of price-making markets, which spread the effect of prices to markets other than those directly affected. The large number of small undertakings in each major industry,

[1] Webb and Webb, *The Decay of Capitalist Civilisation*, p. 73.

the absence of tariff restrictions on the exchange of goods, and the prevalent belief in the efficacy of competition, assured a very large measure of effective competition. Economists generally assumed that such conditions prevailed and were unanimous in their praise of the advantages to be derived from them. These consist in the advantageous distribution of resources among different uses, the elimination of the least efficient firms, the necessity of adopting the best available means of production, and the provision of goods and services to the consumer at prices just sufficient to allow normal profits to efficiently organised undertakings.

Money and banking

These developments would have been impossible without important improvements in the sphere of money and banking. Initially, Britain was the only country on the gold standard; throughout the rest of the world silver currencies or bimetallic standards prevailed. Various attempts were made to introduce a certain measure of uniformity in the currencies of the Continent. Germany succeeded in reducing her monetary confusion by the establishment of a monetary convention in 1857, although a uniform German currency was not secured until the establishment of the Empire. The convenience of the French monetary system based on the decimal principle led to its adoption by eleven other European states. With the formation of the Latin Currency Union in 1865 a number of these countries agreed to regulate their currencies in common. During the second half of the nineteenth century bimetallic countries suffered severe inconvenience from fluctuations in the output of the precious metals, and opinion veered strongly toward the establishment of a gold standard. Such a standard was well on its way to being established by all the leading powers of the world at the end of this period.

The old-fashioned deposit banks of the leading commercial centres, which gave no credit and issued no notes, were declining rapidly in the eighteenth century. Note-issuing banks of a semi-public character, modelled on the Bank of England, had been established during the eighteenth century in almost every state of Europe. These lost much prestige during the Revolutionary and Napoleonic wars through the issue of inconvertible paper money, and their subsequent reorganisation was both slow and difficult. Gradually, however, modern banking systems evolved, resting ultimately on state banks that were largely responsible for the control of credit and solely responsible for the manipulation of the currency. In Britain there developed around the Bank of England an efficient system of banking, with modern facilities such as the regular use of banking accounts, cheques and clearing-houses, which enabled it to mobilise funds and to extend commercial credit. But these facilities only very gradually spread to the leading commercial centres of the Continent.

The provision of capital

The fixed capital required in most branches of enterprise was small, and the initial outlay as a rule came from the savings of the entrepreneur, supplemented perhaps by funds provided by a partner. But, as the Bubble Act of 1720 restricted the ordinary partnership to six members, each of whom was fully liable for all the debts of the concern, it was not easy to induce men of substance to assume such risks. Hence it was more usual to raise the necessary funds by mortgaging the factory buildings, and mortgages remained one of the most important instruments of industrial finance throughout this period. Supplementary loans could sometimes be secured on personal security from friends, and merchants were often willing to risk their resources in the undertakings of industrialists whose products they handled. But, on the whole, long-term capital for industrial ventures tended to remain local and confined.

Capital for expansion was provided by the ploughing back of profit, which was virtually the only means of ensuring success in a period of keen competition and rapid expansion, and the first generations of factory-owners were mostly men of thrifty habits, who had few interests outside their own spheres of activity.

The British banks of the eighteenth century were small private concerns, and only in London did they have control over any appreciable funds. There is little evidence that they were initially in a position to finance the exploitation of inventions and still less evidence that they were prepared to do so. The shortage of liquid resources was at first a serious handicap to industrial expansion. But gradually during the course of the nineteenth century a specialised system of banking institutions arose, which mobilised capital and placed it at the disposal of manufacturers for financing their working expenses by way of overdrafts and the discounting of bills. Short-term capital thus became impersonal and highly mobile.

It was in comparatively few spheres of enterprise that undertakings were on a scale to necessitate associated capital and recourse to incorporation as a means of acquiring outside capital.[1] Because of the shortage of capital on the Continent, however, there developed a new form of banking, the joint stock investment banks, which were eventually to play an important role in economic development in general and in industrial development in particular. These banks combined deposit and investment functions, and were accordingly subject to great hazards, but they were also a source of great potential strength. Their main advantage lay in their ability to mobilise capital and to channel it into industry. Because of their close association with the enterprises which they financed, both as financial partners and as economic consultants, they enabled these to expand rapidly in times of prosperity and sustained them in times of adversity.

The slow growth of corporate enterprise

On the whole this was a period of small-scale industry and atomistic competition. Industrial and commercial enterprises were organised predominantly in the form of individual proprietorships and partnerships. Incorporation was still restricted to a comparatively small sphere of business enterprise.

In England the power of the partnership to raise capital was hampered by the fact that all the partners were subject to unlimited liability. In the continental *société en commandite*, on the other hand, the liability of the passive partners was limited to the loss of their investment. This facilitated the task of the entrepreneur in raising outside capital. The funds supplied by the sleeping partner were divided into equal shares in the eighteenth century, and early in the nineteenth century these were made transferable. Thus there arose the sleeping partnership with share capital—the *société en commandite par actions*—in which only the active partners shared unlimited liability. Such partnerships were easy to form and subject to little

[1] Ashton, *The Industrial Revolution*, p. 94 ff.

state control. The institution was liable to much fraud but served a useful purpose in mobilising capital for business enterprise.

The corporation, on the other hand, was subjected to such onerous restrictions that its development was severely handicapped. The British Bubble Act of 1720 forbade the formation of companies with transferable shares without the special grant of a charter from the Crown or from Parliament. Such a charter was difficult and expensive to obtain, and the formation of joint-stock companies was thus effectively restricted. This provision was removed in 1825, but the unlimited liability of all the shareholders for the company's debts was retained. As a company therefore had no advantage over a partnership, there was no inducement to adopt the corporate form of organisation. It was not till 1856 that Parliament legalised the principle of limited liability. Finally, in 1862 incorporation was made easy and the last impediment to the development of the joint-stock company was thus removed.

It was, however, not until the 1870s that public flotation for industrial purposes became frequent and that firms came generally to appeal to the security market for funds. It was only gradually that a market for non-specific savings developed during the course of the nineteenth century. Initially, industry and agriculture each still had a capital market of its own, and each undertaking was largely restricted to its own private sources of supply. Apart from the inner circle of merchants and financiers, the habit of investing developed only slowly during this period.[1]

The same conditions prevailed in other countries. In the United States, legislation was passed by New York in 1811 to substitute a general incorporation law for the process of negotiating with the state legislature for each charter. By 1850 such laws were common, and by 1875 they provided for the usual method of incorporation. The conception that incorporation was a special concession specifically granted by the government to specific enterprises was maintained in France until 1867 and in Germany until 1870. In spite, therefore, of the corporate organisation of undertakings such as railways, banks, insurance societies and gas companies, activities that have a public or quasipublic character, and large-scale undertakings such as mining and ironworks, it was not until the following period that the corporation became the typical form of business enterprise.[2]

The triumph of laissez-faire

Rapid and sustained growth came with the Industrial Revolution. But dramatic as was the progress of technology, it proceeded in an essentially orderly way in accordance with a pattern dictated by the prevailing needs and the existing condition of the country. It could therefore be implemented under an essentially *laissez-faire* regime.

In Britain the whole system of industrial regulation had, since the seventeenth century, been in gradual retreat before the insistent demands of the entrepreneurial

[1] Postan, *Economic History Review*, vi, no. 1; Hunt, *The Development of the Business Corporation in England 1800-1867.*
[2] *Annals of the American Academy of Political and Social Science*, Nov. 1939, p. 161 ff; 'Corporations', *Encyclopaedia of the Social Sciences.* 'The year 1875 is a fitting date at which to drop from consideration corporations created by special acts and to concentrate attention on charters issued under general laws', *Business Incorporation in the United States, 1800-1943*, National Bureau of Economic Research, p. 31. By that time constitutional provisions requiring incorporation under general laws had become widespread in the United States.

class for greater economic freedom, and after the revolution of 1688 employers had been allowed much greater liberty in the management of their own affairs. Owing to the absence of a civil service and of an adequate system of inspection, much of the industrial legislation that had been passed had, in fact, always remained a dead letter. At the beginning of the eighteenth century Parliament laid down the principle that trade ought to be free and not restrained, and this tenet formed the basis of British policy from that date onwards. The relaxation of industrial restraints was therefore already an accomplished fact when Parliament, in 1756, placed the formal seal of legislative approval on it by renouncing the policy of regulating the conditions of employment.

The whole system of industrial regulation bequeathed by mercantilism was gradually discarded, not only in Britain but also in the rest of the western world. The abuses in public administration, which had discouraged the accumulation of capital through extortionate taxation and the mismanagement of public funds, were remedied. The national unity that the *ancien régime* had striven in vain to secure was attained without any conscious effort by the French Revolution. All internal tolls, provincial, municipal and gild privileges, and the practice of selling offices were abolished, taxes were equalised, and weights and measures were standardised throughout the country. Other countries followed the French precedent. Thus in 1818 the customs barriers between the different Prussian provinces were removed, and in 1834 all the tariffs between the eighteen states constituting the *Zollverein* were swept away and a single uniform tariff established for the whole area. During the next thirty years the area of the *Zollverein* was gradually extended until it included almost every state in Germany. Everywhere the new means of communication also established a measure of national unity hitherto unknown.

The new economics

The developing capitalist system had therefore marked out its own appropriate course, and the principle of economic freedom was firmly entrenched in state policy. But it had yet to be buttressed by the requisite economic ideology. This was supplied by the physiocrats in France and by the classical economists in Great Britain.

The doctrine of *laissez-faire* followed naturally from the belief of the physiocrats that human societies were governed by natural laws that serve the needs of society better than any system of controls. The work of the legislator should therefore be to aid in the discovery of and to conform to these laws, not to interfere with their operation by the imposition of artificial restraints.

In opposition to the political and economic paternalism of the autocratic state, Adam Smith advanced the novel idea that socio-economic coordination could best be achieved by means of spontaneous competitive controls. 'This represents an intellectual accomplishment of such magnitude that not even the now outmoded social philosophy and psychology which Smith and his school confused with it can detract from its significance for the whole of social science.'[1] Smith and his successors clearly formulated the tenets and implications of this policy, and laid the foundations of a social code that was to serve as the basis of liberal policy during the nineteenth century.

The new economics conceived the industrial system as an automatic self-

[1] Dahl and Lindblom, *Politics, Economics and Welfare*, p. 195.

regulating mechanism, which was kept in equilibrium by its own appropriate system of checks and balances operating through a system of price-fixing markets. Economic activity was conceived as the exchange of goods and services at prices determined in the market. Price—or value—became the focus of attention, and buying and selling the essential phenomena to be studied. Economics became a science of price relations.

The forces of the market determine the present material welfare of society, conceived as the value of the annual flow of goods and services, and the future progress of the economy, conceived as the flow of capital funds into investment channels. All goods and services, both consumer goods and the means of production, are made available through the market mechanism and therefore have objectively determined prices. All forms of income are derived from the sale of goods and services. The acquisition of purchasing power converts the process of meeting requirements into an allocation of the scarce productive resources between alternative uses. Classical economics thus gave a clear formulation of the laws that determine the division of the national product among the factors that participate in its creation.

Economic order is preserved by the opposing forces of demand and supply. The competition of buyers forces prices up; the competition of sellers forces them down. The 'normal' price—the point of equilibrium—is the point where these forces balance. Thus 'normalcy' is dependent on the existence of competition. Competition became the key principle of economic theory; the maintenance of competition its chief tenet.[1]

What is more, since supply creates its own demand, so that the whole of the cost of production is spent in the aggregate, directly or indirectly, on purchasing the output of the economy, equilibrium, with the full employment of resources, is assured.

Since all economic decisions are based on prices and all movements of economic significance become effective through prices, the concept of a self-equilibrating system of markets provides a single but comprehensive means of explaining the economic process. The choice of the goods to be produced and the means of producing them, and thus the allocation of resources between uses, the remuneration of the factors of production, the choice between consumption and investment, and even the effects of social and political decisions on the economy, can all be explained within the comprehensive framework of the market economy.

The prices the classical economists were interested in were primarily relative prices and not absolute ones. The function of money was conceived as purely neutral and monetary policy consequently of very limited application. In accordance with Say's law that supply creates its own demand in the sense that the whole of the costs of production must necessarily be spent in the aggregate on the purchase of the product, the only functions of money that were recognised were those of the medium of exchange and the unit of account. The function of the store of value, and consequently the means of hoarding, was ignored. John Stuart Mill in his *Principles of Political Economy* could therefore express the view that 'There cannot be intrinsically a more insignificant thing, in the economy of society, than money. . . . It is a machine for doing quickly and commodiously, what would be done, though less quickly and commodiously, without it.[2]

---

[1] By the middle of the nineteenth century experience in Britain had, however, shown that attempts to maintain competition in the field of public utilities were futile.
[2] Mill, *Principles of Political Economy* (1929 edn), p. 488.

Thus it may be said that whereas mercantilist theory had been concerned primarily with questions of power and progress, the new economics was interested mainly in the allocation of resources according to scarcity and consumer choice. The equilibrium concept obtained a teleological content as the state towards which forces tended naturally to move under conditions of free competition, a movement that measures of policy could temporarily obstruct, but which they could not permanently overcome. This created a basic harmony of interests in the economic sphere, a state best served by the *laissez-faire* policy of leaving things alone.

Free trade

The advantages of the free employment of resources do not stop at national frontiers. Under a system of free trade each country exports commodities that are relatively abundant and therefore cheap, and imports goods that are relatively scarce and therefore dear. From the point of view of the goods already produced, the effect of free intercourse is consequently to maximise the satisfaction derived from their consumption. From the point of view of production, international trade will lead to an increase in the flow of goods available to society because it encourages specialisation. Each country will tend to specialise in the production of those things in which it has the biggest relative advantage and exchange them for those in the production of which it suffers the greatest relative disadvantage. Free trade will therefore lead to the best selection of opportunities by each country. Competition will lead to a more or less equal distribution of the advantages of specialisation among the different participants.

The Industrial Revolution gave Great Britain a dominant position in the world market. The country was becoming thoroughly industrialised in a world that was still primarily agricultural. The interests of her manufacturers no longer lay in protecting the home market, where they had no competition to fear, but in securing easier access to foreign markets. Such access could be obtained only by accepting agricultural produce in return. Industry therefore combined with commerce to agitate for the removal of obstacles to the expansion of foreign trade. This ideal was ultimately realised by Gladstone's tariff laws of 1853 and 1860. Import duties were henceforth retained on a few commodities solely for the raising of revenue. The repeal of the Corn Laws (1846-49) marked the final recognition of England's transition from an agricultural to an industrial and commercial state. The immediate advantages of extreme specialisation were preferred to the ultimate advantage of a more diversified and better integrated economic system with the easy fatalism which characterised the policy of the period. 'If you had to constitute new societies, you might on moral and social grounds prefer cornfields to cotton factories, an agricultural to a manufacturing population', said Peel, 'but our lot is cast and we cannot recede.'

The advantage of freer trade with Britain to countries with industrial possibilities of their own was much more dubious, and the victory of free trade was never as complete elsewhere as it was in England. The movement for reform was at first local. In Germany industry was very little developed before the 1870s, and the landowners and the merchants of the north were much more powerful than the manufacturers of the south. The Prussian landowners were opposed to any increase in tariffs that might have an unfavourable effect on the export of grain. The *Zollverein*, from its inception in 1834, therefore followed the lead of Prussia in adopting a liberal commercial policy.

French public opinion was still strongly protectionist, but the establishment of the Second Empire in 1852 put an end to constitutional government, and Napoleon III, who had lived in England and was first and foremost a theorist, was favourably disposed to a liberal commercial policy. A series of commercial treaties, by which French tariffs were considerably reduced, was negotiated with the chief European powers.

In other countries there was also a movement towards freer trade. Holland, between 1845 and 1872, gradually eliminated all her duties except 5 per cent on manufactured goods retained for revenue purposes. Belgium repealed her corn laws in 1850, and by 1857 was practically a free trade country. The Scandinavian countries followed the same course. Russia moved towards lower duties between 1825 and 1875, and Italy under Cavour went far on the road to commercial freedom.

During the third quarter of the century a comparatively mild fiscal regime was thus established throughout most of Europe. Export duties disappeared, prohibitions were dropped, and import duties reduced. Measures designed to favour merchant shipping were reformed. Europe was covered with a network of liberal commercial treaties. These usually embodied the most favoured nation clause by which a participant in a treaty shared any reduction that might be made to other states. The slightest concession to any party therefore effected a general reduction in duties over a large part of the Continent. The prosperity of Britain lent prestige to free trade doctrines. Improvements in transport were facilitating international trade, and a country that secluded itself commercially seemed to be renouncing the opportunity of sharing in the march of progress.

Social policy

With regard to social legislation, on the other hand, industrialisation and the rapid growth of cities created problems of employment and housing, health, and the provision of services, which the existing institutions were ill-adapted to solve and which necessitated state intervention in many spheres. Policy-making was hesitant at first, and inspired largely by political rivalry. The Industrial Revolution, indeed, added greatly to the number of the industrial proletariat, concentrated them in cities, and made them more specifically a class and more dependent on the employing class. But their political power remained limited, for the franchise was only very gradually extended to the lower classes, and it was only towards the end of this period that labour associations became fully legalised in the various European countries. The poor were still a problem rather than a power in politics.

Great Britain was the first country to introduce legislation to protect the worker against the evils of the new industrial system because it was here that the problem was most acute. Gradually, from the 1830s onward, a series of Factory Acts secured the ten-hour day as well as factory inspection, safety appliances, better sanitary conditions, and the removal of the worst evils attached to child and female labour, while housing conditions were improved and compulsory slum repairs instituted. These efforts to deal with the more serious abuses of the new industrial system aroused strenuous opposition from the supporters of free enterprise, who saw in it the revival of paternalism. The reforms consequently took years to accomplish, were always at best only partial in their application, and were often frustrated in practice by the failure to provide adequate machinery for their enforcement. The advocates of economic freedom did not deny that the state had a duty to protect the weak, but insisted that the onus of proof lay 'not on those who resist, but on those who recommend, government interference. *Laissez-faire*, in short, should be the general practice: every departure from it, unless required by some great good, is a certain evil.'[1]

This policy was perhaps more conspicuous for what it left undone than for what it accomplished. But it should not be forgotten that the civil service of the time was in its infancy, that until 1835 many British manufacturing centres had no adequate municipal government, and that local services were virtually non-existent.

Achievement of the period

The achievement of this period was unique. It has been estimated that real wages in Britain doubled during the first half of the nineteenth century, and that they doubled again during the second half. During the same time the working population was more or less quadrupled. There was, therefore, something like a 1,600 per cent increase in the production and consumption of wage goods during the period. If we are to judge by the condition of the working population at the end of the century, its lot a hundred years previously could not have been an enviable one. According to Sombart, there were, with the exception of the landed nobility, hardly 1,000 persons in the whole of Germany in 1800 with incomes of £500 and more. The great mass of the working people lived in a state of chronic destitution. They lacked even absolute necessities.[2]

The process of innovation, the growth of population, and the opening up of new resources introduced a period of rapid expansion. The process of innovation created a continually changing complex of end products and gave rise to complementary investment, which generated income and supported more innovation. These factors combined to raise the marginal efficiency schedule of capital and, with the relatively cheap capital available in Britain at the beginning of the Industrial Revolution, induced a rate of investment sufficiently high to ensure self-sustained growth. The growth of real investment took the form of a deepening and widening of capital. The former process meant that more capital was used per unit of output; the latter that capital formation grew correspondingly with the output of finished goods. Such scope was supplied for new investment that the process of capital formation was conducive to the securing of a high and stable level of employment, and therefore the maximum income possible under the prevailing standards of industrial technique.

Under such conditions the dynamic impetus of a compounded rate of growth, the cumulative impact of building compound interest into an economic structure, could attain its full effect. In such an environment the idea of progress, vaguely conceived as a rapid improvement in general prosperity, became a living reality. In the new inventions progress became something tangible, visual, and concrete.

> The common man, before whose eyes the marvels of science and invention were constantly displayed, noted the unprecedented increase in wealth, the growth of cities, the new and improved methods of transportation and communication, the greater security from disease and death and all the conveniences of domestic life unknown to previous generations, and accepted the doctrine of progress without question. [3]

[1] Mill, *The Principles of Political Economy,* (edn 1929), p. 950.
[2] Sombart, *Die deutsche Volkswirtschaft im neunzehnten Jahrhundert,* p. 428 ff.
[3] 'Progress', in *Encyclopaedia of Social Sciences.*

Part 8
Structural Changes in Free Enterprise Economies

*From the last quarter of the nineteenth century to the
Great Depression of the early 1930s*

21
The growth of corporate and public enterprise

Introduction

From the last quarter of the nineteenth century onward important changes began to take place in the free enterprise economies of the world, changes that affected basic aspects of their structure and function. Often they took place below the surface of publicity, but they were no less potent for their lack of prominence.

During the previous period industry had been conducted on a relatively small scale. The source of enterprise was easy to locate; it was associated with the entrepreneur. He was a capitalist who ventured his own wealth in an undertaking which he himself directed. Business was financed almost exclusively by the individual proprietor and the partnership, supplemented by loans from banks and private individuals. Unincorporated enterprise was the characteristic form of organisation, not only in commerce and industry but also in mining and shipping, as well as in banking and insurance. The entrepreneur in economic literature was the independent, self-employed proprietor, the man who bore the risks and claimed the gains of business enterprise.

The position has changed fundamentally since the last quarter of the nineteenth century. The individual proprietor has been largely displaced by the corporation. To this day there are, of course, numerous businesses owned by individuals, but they are relatively insignificant from the point of view of both the number of men employed and the value of services rendered. Corporate organisation has become the characteristic form of modern business enterprise.

The advantages of the corporation are obvious. It facilitates the acquisition of large amounts of capital and by dividing and limiting their liability gives relative security to shareholders. Capital has become impersonal, divisible, and easily transferable between different places and occupations—the ideal factor of production visualised by economists. The corporation also gives endurance and stability to the individual business and facilitates the drawing of new blood into management. Usually it is privileged in regard to taxation as well.

The differentiation of functions in the corporation

The differentiation and delegation of functions are features of the corporation. In the individual proprietorship there is a very clear allocation of responsibility. In the modern corporation, on the other hand, the making of decisions has been diffused and delegated to a whole hierarchy of directors and executive officials.

The executive officials are primarily responsible for business leadership in the modern corporation. They, as a group, initiate the decisions which determine the volume and direction of investment, formulate price policies, and make all the other important decisions on which the destinies of the undertaking depend. With the increasing size and complexity of business organisation, and the consequent necessity for delegating authority and responsibility, there has also been a tendency for decision-making to be diffused throughout the whole group of executive personnel. The board of directors, on the whole, play a rather passive role, exercising their authority primarily in such matters as large capital expenditures, new security issues and the declaration of dividends.[1]

Control of the corporation

The directorate is legally responsible to the shareholders. The effectiveness of this responsibility depends primarily on the dissemination of the shares. The number of small stockholders in large corporations has greatly increased. The function of risk-bearing, formerly undertaken equally by all shareholders, has been broken up and distributed among different types of shareholders. Stockholders themselves distribute their investments among a large number of companies on the principle of not having all their eggs in one basket. All these developments have tended to decrease the interest of shareholders in the affairs of the concerns they own.

Most large companies have passed out of the effective control of their shareholders. As is reflected, for example, in the number of votes cast at elections, the majority of the holders of shares are both indifferent to the affairs of the concerns that they own and incapable of influencing the choice of directors. The directorate, elected in theory by the stockholders, is in practice elected by 'proxies' or agents delegated by the shareholders to act for them at the annual elections. These proxies are suggested to shareholders by the management, and stockholders rarely attend meetings or name proxies other than those proposed by the management. 'The election of directors is nominal, their re-election automatic, their vacancies filled by co-option.'[2]

Where the ownership of shares is widely diffused, control can thus be maintained by those who own only a small proportion of the capital. And this is not all. Through the device of the holding company, control can be exercised over a large number of corporations through the possession of only a small proportion of their combined capital. This is effected through the control of one corporation by a second smaller corporation, the second by a third still smaller company, and so on. Thus by a process of pyramiding, a tremendous aggregate of corporate capital can be effectively governed by a comparatively modest investment. By such means the control of companies remains in the hands of the promoters, who constitute a self-perpetuating oligarchy.

This divorce of ownership from control represents a significant change in the capitalist system. Private enterprise assumes ownership of the means of production by a person who has complete property rights and control over these instruments;

---

[1] Gordon, *Business Leadership in the Large Corporation*, chs 4–6.
[2] Plant, *Economica*, Feb. 1932.

the enlightened self-interest of the owner being regarded as the best guarantee of economic efficiency. With the separation of ownership from control, however, the dependability of the individualistic profit incentive as an automatic propellent towards economy and efficiency in the conduct of business enterprise is weakened. The property holder, in whom control is theoretically vested, has, on the other hand, been degraded from a controlling proprietor to a mere dividend receiver. Instead of holding tangible assets which he can use at his discretion, the owner now holds pieces of paper representing right to and expectations of future income. This evaporation of the material substance of ownership, it is maintained, has taken the life out of the idea of property. In the place of the physical entity—the office, the factory, or the ship—for the ownership and control of which the owner would be prepared to make the greatest sacrifice, there now appear parcels of shares, which involve no functional relationship and arouse no sentimental attachment. Gradually therefore, it is maintained, the bourgeois mind is being prepared for the social control of resources.[1]

The taking of decisions

The technique of arriving at decisions is also substantially different in the new form of organisation. The success or failure, the life or death of the small establishment depended on the correct insight, the clear grasping of things in the near future, and on the promptness with which the entrepreneur acted on his intuition. The taking of decisions remains the primary function of the modern executive. But more and more this has become a collective affair, the chief executives merely approving and coordinating decisions that flow up to them from their subordinates. The insight, the power of divination, or the vision of the entrepreneur has been tempered by the calculations of the expert. The specialisation and the coordination of management functions into a smoothly operating entity have become the major problem of administration. The result is greater caution and more red tape, but also the more rational handling of management problems. This is reflected in the increased emphasis on planning and research, in the development of accounting techniques, and in the attention paid to problems of internal organisation. This routinising and mechanisation of the taking of decisions means an important modification of capitalist enterprise. Capitalism had hitherto been an essentially free and individualistic system. The growth of impersonal control within the establishment and the great extension of the size of corporate entities during this period gradually introduced the more hierarchical control of economic activities.

The motive force of expansion in corporate enterprise has come largely from the accumulation of reserves. Profits that were reinvested in business, together with the funds saved by the rich, no doubt always formed the chief source of new capital. In the corporate organisation they have obtained a new and significant character. Probably between one-half and two-thirds of the total capital accumulations in modern industrial societies represents the sums held back and reinvested by business corporations and by public authorities.

With the increased dissociation of management from the ownership of the enterprise, corporate savings have been forced by the executive on the helpless shareholders. Whether to meet heavy taxation or to obtain funds for expansion, dividends have been sacrificed and reserves maintained. This source of capital

[1] Schumpeter, *Capitalism, Socialism and Democracy.*

supply has become inelastic and bears little relevant connection with the returns yielded by new investments. Reserves often provide both the means and the incentive for experimental investment, since the failure to yield returns does not threaten the business with cuts in dividends or with bankruptcy.

The dissociation of management from ownership

The building up of reserves at the expense of dividends is the outcome of the dissociation of management from ownership. The business has become an objective personality with its own proper interests. From the point of view of the executive, the paying-out of funds as dividends may be considered as a dissipation of the resources of the enterprise; the expansion of the undertaking, on the other hand, as a means of self-expression.

There has thus arisen a class of business executives whose position has not been achieved through ownership. The responsibilities of business leadership have devolved upon men who are professional managers. Both by training and tradition these men are different from the nineteenth-century entrepreneurs. They are salaried personnel trained in the field of business management. Though they are only trustees of funds and exercise delegated authority, they are responsible to a certain extent for making the decisions that affect not only the dividends that are paid to shareholders, but also the prices paid by consumers, the wages paid to workers, and the level of output and employment in their firms and in the economy as a whole.

The system of incentives to which the salaried executives are subject is also a far cry from the entrepreneurial remuneration of the previous period. The corporation offers a wide range of incentives to the executive personnel, from salaries and bonus payments to a variety of non-financial attractions. But the traditional reward of entrepreneurial achievement, the profits arising from business ownership, is not a primary incentive to the executive official, though the making of profit and the growth of the enterprise are still the leading incentives and the criterion of success of the business undertaking. The role assumed by executive officials has therefore required new and appropriate methods of training and indoctrination to ensure the identification of their own interests with those of the corporate entities that they control, as a means of ensuring that market cues will elicit the appropriate responses, for without these appropriate responses the system of free corporate enterprise cannot function.[1]

The gradual growth of public enterprise

An outstanding feature of this period was the spread of the Industrial Revolution and of sustained growth, first throughout the western world, and then also to some of the countries of the East. A significant fact was also that whereas the conditions for rapid growth developed spontaneously in Great Britain, the industrialisation of the late-comers to the industrial stage, and especially of countries such as Germany, Russia and Japan, was largely the result of conscious acts of policy. Questions of

[1] Gordon, pt iii.

national prestige and political power ranked equally with purely economic considerations in the formulation and implementation of this policy.[1]

But even in those countries in which economic development continued to be
promoted primarily by private enterprise there was a renewed, if modest, growth of
public enterprise during this period. This comprised the services rendered by central,
state and local authorities.

By the end of this period public authorities in almost all countries were operating the postal services and seeing to the upkeep of roads, harbours, and waterways.
Over one-third of the railroad mileage of the world at the end of this period was
publicly owned and the rest rigidly regulated and controlled. Municipalities were
responsible for water supply and sewage disposal, and generally operated local
transport, light, and power supply services. Numerous mixed works had been established by states, provinces, and consumers. Most states were vitally interested in
land reclamation, irrigation, and afforestation, while the public works schemes of
governments had assumed very large proportions. Education, research and the
protection of life and property were mainly in the hands of collective enterprise. To
a much smaller extent public authorities furnished competitive services such as
banking, mining and manufacturing.

Ideological considerations, the inadequacy or the unsatisfactory nature of
private business, and the difficulty of obtaining the necessary funds for capital-
intensive undertakings through private channels, all combined to cause the expansion of collective enterprise. It was rarely fiscal. The services supplied by public
bodies are generally of an intangible character and often cannot be divided into
separate units to which a definite price can be attached. They are services that
maintain the organised life of society, providing as they do for defence, public
safety, the administration of justice, the control of business, or the facilities for
carrying it on, such as the means of transport. They are often of general cultural
and human value, so that private enterprise cannot be expected to invest as much in
these services as is socially desirable. This is true of educational and health services,
recreation, housing, and so forth. The public ownership of forests, minerals and
oilfields has been motivated largely by the desire for conservation. Irrigation and
land reclamation schemes have been developed extensively because agriculture has
been regarded as an industry which is outstandingly desirable socially. The more
commercialised public undertakings are predominantly monopolistic in character.
In granting monopolies to private companies such stringent regulations have
to be devised to prevent the exploitation of the public, and such elaborate
negotiations entered into in regard to tariffs, services, and wages that, rather than
assume a complicated control, public bodies have often preferred to render the
services themselves. In many cases private initiative has not been forthcoming at all.

Finally, a significant and, to the West, ominous development emerged towards
the end of the First World War. In Russia, after the Communist Revolution, all
private property was expropriated and the first centrally administered economy
made its appearance on the modern world scene.

---

[1] Especially significant from the point of view of economic growth was the fact that whereas
Great Britain had left technical training, like primary education, to private enterprise, the new
countries, and especially Germany and Japan, initiated and maintained a whole range of educational institutions deliberately to promote technical and general education.

22

The concentration of economic activity

Large-scale production

The process of concentration can take the form either of an increase in the size of the individual establishment, that is of the single plant or factory, or of an increase in the scale of management.

The term 'large-scale production' was first used to characterise the transformation brought about by the abandonment of handicraft methods and the introduction of mechanical processes and factory organisation in industry. The movement began in Great Britain and then spread to the continent of Europe, to the United States, and eventually to the rest of the world.

It was in the United States that large-scale production developed most spectacularly. Here, as everywhere else, the movement first manifested itself in the textile trades. But, from the beginning of this period, the textile industries were displaced in significance and as the representatives of large-scale operations by the heavy industries, while this type of organisation also spread to many other branches of industry. Census statistics show that as far as American manufacturing is concerned, and as judged by the criteria of the number of employees, capital investment, and volume of output, the process of mechanisation made most rapid headway during the two decades from 1870 to 1890, and by the end of that time had substantially run its course. Large-scale operations had become characteristic of American industries, and since then there has been a distinct slowing down in the rate of growth and a tendency towards stabilisation of the size of the average establishment.[1]

William Thorp, in a census monograph published in 1924, came to the conclusion that the tendency in American industry at the time was to operate on all scales of production. Certain industries apparently were tending to operate on a larger scale, but others seemed to be following exactly the opposite tendency; and these were by no means the industries that were losing in importance so far as the total number of wage-earners was concerned.[2]

Though the census statistics are very difficult to interpret, it seems that much the same movement has taken place in other countries. Thus in Sweden the size of the average establishment increased over the period 1896-1912, and thereafter

[1] 'Large-scale production', in *Encyclopaedia of the Social Sciences.*
[2] *Industrial Society*, ed. Marshall, pp. 862 ff.

showed a fairly rapid decrease. In Great Britain, as in the United States, there was a decline in the smallest and the highest groups. In Germany the lowest group, comprising quite small establishments, showed a strong relative rise between 1925 and 1933, whereas the highest group, containing the largest number of workers per establishment, showed a corresponding fall. There also appeared to be a tendency for the prevailing size of factory to be the same in the United States, Great Britain, and Germany.[1]

The combination movement

Not only the tendency towards large-scale production but also the tendency towards economic concentration seems, in the twentieth century, to have substantially run its course.[2] Combinations vary considerably in regard to the measure of control exerted over the individual units, but broadly they can be divided into three groups: mergers, concerns or combines, and cartels.

The merger represents the most thorough form of combination. The manufacturing plants, financial structures, and commercial organisations of the combining firms are merged into a single new enterprise, while the productive processes of the individual plants are unified by a plan worked out for the enterprise as a whole.

Unlike the merger, the concern does not place primary emphasis on the technical integration of the individual establishments. The unity merely extends to the financial and commercial activities of the combining units, while their other functions remain free from direct control. The formation of concerns is greatly facilitated by the creation of holding companies. These do not legally own establishments but merely hold the shares of the nominally independent undertakings, which continue to do business under their own names. Often the concern has no separate legal existence at all, the units being combined financially through the mutual exchange of stock. By means of the holding company device, one institution can obtain control over a large network of companies through the establishment of a pyramidal series of holding companies in each of which the possession of a proportion of the stock is sufficient to assure control over the subordinate units. The law of the land, as well as the psychology of its business men, has contributed to making the concern the typical form of American combination.

The cartel, finally, is an association of independent enterprises in the same branch of trade, formed with the object of increasing the profits of its members by subjecting their competitive activities to some form of common control. The sales policies of member firms are controlled, but the units retain complete independence in regard to their internal financial and manufacturing operations. Cartels are based on contractual agreements between independent firms to adopt certain procedures that are definitely limited in purpose and scope. Their object is to exercise monopolistic control through price-fixing, the limitation of supply, and the allocation of markets. The detailed specification of procedure is determined by periodical negotiations in which all the members participate on an equal footing. Successful agreements are therefore reached by unanimity rather than by majority vote. In the case of the more firmly organised cartels the members often have to transfer part of their functions, especially in regard to sales, to a syndicate. But, as all members

---

[1] Ohlin, in *The World's Economic Future*, pp. 97 ff; Jewkes, *Economic Journal*, June 1952. On the other hand, the average scale of Soviet industrial establishments increased significantly in all industries between 1928 and 1960.

[2] Cf. Penrose, *The Theory of the Growth of the Firm*, p. 250 ff.

participate as equals, they are, even in the most rigidly organised cartels, liable only to financial penalties and are free to violate agreements if they find it to their advantage to do so. The cartel has therefore generally not been a very permanent form of combination.

Agreements among producers with the object of checking competition have tended to occur at all times and in all countries whenever conditions appeared favourable. But the Germans with their genius for organisation have gone beyond everyone else in making these agreements far more general, more ingeniously elaborate, and more frankly accepted as a necessary means for the coordination of economic activities.

In English-speaking countries a restriction of competition has been attempted by trade associations. These associations differ greatly in internal organisation, the extent to which they are representative of different industries, and in the scope of their activities. But besides functions such as the promotion of efficiency in production and distribution, they also attempt to eliminate price competition, to control the channels of distribution, and even to regulate output. They may therefore be described as very loose cartels. Trade associations have even tried to formulate their own appropriate ideology, and edifying codes of business ethics have been enunciated, which have tried to justify the elimination of price competition and to elevate the new 'cooperative competition' to an acceptable principle for the shaping of business policy.

Generally it can be said that the combination movement, which began in the field of raw materials and manufactures, spread to every sphere of economic activity during this period. How far the movement has proceeded in the United States, the country which must still be regarded as most characteristic of capitalist organisation in the western world, is shown by the investigations of Berle and Means. According to them the 200 largest non-banking corporations, at the end of this period, controlled about one-half of the corporate assets, over one-third of the business wealth, and about one-fifth of the national wealth of the United States.[1]

Nor does this reflect the full measure of concentration. Centralised control has been made more effective by means of financial measures such as stock ownership, interlocking directorates, and common affiliations with financial institutions. The National Resources Committee found that in 1935 eight interest groups controlled at least 106 of the 250 largest corporations in the country and that these interest groups were related in various ways to one another.[2]

A relatively small number of large corporations therefore controlled a very considerable proportion of the total assets and accounted for a relatively large share of the economic activity within the sphere of corporate enterprise in the United States at the end of this period. Concentration was particularly marked in manufacture, communication, public utilities, and contract construction. Wholesale and retail distribution, the service activities, agriculture and the professions, on the other hand, were much less concentrated. Nor was the United States unique in this respect. From studies made in Canada and the United Kingdom, it would seem that the share of economic activity accounted for by large firms was at least as big in these countries as in the United States.[3]

---

[1] Berle and Means, *The Modern Corporation and Private Property*
[2] National Resources Planning Board, *The Structure of the American Economy*, i.
[3] Mason, *Economic Concentration and the Monopoly Problem*, p. 36 ff.

Is the process of concentration progressive?

Nutter has attempted to measure the degree of concentration in the American economy, as indicated by the share of the product output in different spheres of the economy accounted for by the largest firms, over a period of time. His estimates would seem to show that concentration ratios, as far as the non-government sector of the American economy is concerned, have not increased in the twentieth century.

Nutter took as his starting point a list of highly concentrated industries in the year 1899. As concentration ratio he took the proportion of the industry's output produced by the four largest firms, and his criterion of 'monopoly' was a concentration ratio of 50 per cent or more. Monopolies then accounted for about 19 per cent of non-governmental production while workably competitive industries accounted for about 81 per cent.

The share of the total national income acruing to monopolistic industries in 1937, on the other hand, was 13 per cent. But by using a somewhat wider concept of monopoly and a somewhat different set of data available only for recent years, this percentage was increased to 21. If an average of the two sets of estimates for 1937 is taken, the fraction of the national income that originated in privately organised monopolistic industries fell from 17 per cent in 1899 to 15 per cent in 1937, while the share that originated in privately organised competitive industries fell from 76 to 60 per cent. The balance was accounted for by non-profit organisations.[1]

Economists have generally maintained with little or no evidence that an economy in which 'competitive' elements were formerly preponderant in most markets has gradually been supplanted by one in which 'monopolistic' elements prevail.[2] If the view that the previous period was characterised by small-scale 'atomistic' competition is correct, then the process of concentration, which presumably started during the last quarter of the nineteenth century, must by the end of the century have substantially run its course.

Concentration and monopoly power

It is generally assumed that the large measure of concentration that exists in certain sectors of the economy, and especially in the sphere of manufacture,[3] confers on big business a large measure of monopoly power.

Thus it is maintained that a characteristic feature of the free-enterprise economy of the previous period had been the existence of numerous small firms, which independently decided what to produce and in what amounts, in response to consumer demand. Prices were determined by the forces of supply and demand on the open market, each seller being responsible for such a small part of the total output that he accepted these prices, since no action of his could influence the prevailing condition.

[1] Nutter, *The Extent of Enterprise Monopoly in the United States 1899-1939*, pp. 19 ff.
[2] Cf. the view of the Temporary National Economic Committee: 'Industrial consolidation is a fact. . . . Sixty years ago it was only a prospect. A century ago, aside possibly from a few patent monopolies, there was no single enterprise controlling the output, much less the distribution, and still less the price, of as much as ten per cent of any product manufactured in this country' (*Mon. no. 13*, 1940, p. 134).
[3] According to Nutter's estimate, the ratio of concentration in American manufacturing in 1937 was 39 per cent.

The characteristic feature of the industrial organisation of the present period, it is asserted, has been the growth of firms that market such a large proportion of the total output that each cannot fail, in determining the scale of his production or his price policy, to take account of the effect of his actions on the market as a whole. Price and production policies have therefore, in a significant sense, come to be administered by business executives themselves, though in doing so they are influenced by the policies of their rivals as well as by the responses of the consuming public. Their decisions are, however, no longer dictated to them exclusively by the automatic forces of the market; their price and production policies, on the contrary, have an important effect on the market. Even in industries with a low degree of concentration, price-fixing arrangements have, it is said, often tended to bring about a substantial administrative element in price and production policies.

But in the sphere of manufacture, as contrasted with agriculture, prices must always have been 'administered', whatever specific connotation might be given to this word. In the large concern, which is burdened with large overhead costs and produces a multiplicity of products, this is admittedly a more complicated procedure and demands that more consideration be given to factors relevant to the internal organisation and administration of the firm than in the small undertaking. This does not necessarily imply, however, that big businesses are able to maintain prices that are out of alignment with current market prices and that they will not be induced to adapt their price and production policies to given market situations. Nor does it necessarily imply that the effectiveness of competition, from a long-period point of view, has declined. For executives would naturally realise that, should they desire to maintain prices, they would have to effect cost reductions or an improvement of their products as a necessary means of ensuring the continuance of their competitive position.

Admittedly the size of the firm in relation to the market is an important element in determining the degree of monopoly power that can be exercised in a market. But it is not the only factor. It is conceivable, therefore, that the large measure of concentration attained in manufacturing industry, the tendency to 'administer' prices, and the increased protection extended to local industries during this period may have been partially neutralised by factors that tended to make competition more effective. Thus markets as well as firms tended to grow in size during this period, improved facilities of transport and communication tended to convert local and regional into national and international markets, and the great proliferation of products tended to reduce the 'gap in the chain of substitutes'. Price competition was also supplemented to an ever increasing extent by non-price competition. The high rate of innovation moreover tended continually to destroy monopolistic elements in any given market situation for, as Schumpeter pointed out, a temporary privileged position in a progressive economy is, as a rule, no bed of roses. Such a position, in fact, invites and is always threatened by competition, whether 'actual or potential, direct or collateral, domestic or foreign'.[1]

The issue that is important from our point of view is whether the large measure of concentration that has been attained in certain sectors of free enterprise economies has impaired the effectiveness of the market mechanism as a means of fixing prices, allocating resources, and remunerating the factors of production. Are these substantially different under the present system from what they would have been if the process of concentration had proceeded less far than it has done in fact? This is a question to which it is unfortunately impossible to give an explicit answer.

---

[1] Schumpeter, *Capitalism, Socialism, and Democracy*, p. 102.

'Admitting' [says Mason] 'that the existence of one or a few large firms in a market produces a situation in which some or all of them attempt to take account of the effect of their own policies on the market situation or on the policies of their rivals, does this lead to a serious departure from competitive standards in the determination of price, output, and investment policies? If we are to rely on facts rather than a highly abstract theory for the answer to this question, it is astonishing how inadequate that answer must be.'[1]

There still remains the effect of collective combinations on prices. The primary purpose of cartels has been the control of prices, and it is through price regulation that they have exerted their most important influence on the economic system.

Cartels have generally aimed at maintaining prices above the competitive level, though few well-organised cartels have followed the aggressive policy of charging what the market will bear. The fear of potential competition, domestic or foreign, has always loomed in the background. Nor has any elaborate national price policy been developed anywhere by collective combinations. Executives in their attempt to control prices are, in fact, likely to act like ordinary human beings, with all the shortsightedness, cleverness, and vision that characterise the species, to an extent which makes generalisation about the effect of combination on prices extremely hazardous.[2]

The control of prices has necessarily involved the control of output in order to prevent the individual producer from encroaching on the preserves of his associates, and in order to adjust supply to demand. The only criteria of output that cartels have been able to devise, however, have been the fixing of members' quotas in accordance with past production. The inevitable results have been the suspension of the process of selection and the maintaining of the high cost units at the expense of the low cost ones. Cartel policy has been primarily concerned not with increasing the efficiency of their members, but with mitigating the effects of over-capacity. It has, however, not been conspicuously successful in regulating the expansion of productive capacity in accordance with the trend of market needs. Member firms have been encouraged to make speculative investments in plant when the time approaches for a renewal of the quota assignments, with the result that the flow of investment funds has been diverted into channels other than those dictated by competitive efficiency.

During the depression of the early 1930s the governments of most of the leading countries organised control schemes for the regulation of the export of commodities such as wheat, sugar, tea, coffee, tin and rubber. For some of these commodities international agreements were concluded, in terms of which price and export quotas were fixed and certain countries agreed to limit domestic production. These pools, controls and valorisation schemes were not conspicuously successful in furthering the cause of economic stability. They were comparatively successful as means of temporarily readjusting supply to demand but not as permanent means of control. The experience of the 'Great Depression' made it clear that attempts to secure price stability through the use of collective monopolies can be relatively successful only if the underlying market situation is favourable. This situation can be brought about only by favourable economic conditions in general and by policies that succeed in bringing about full employment.

---

[1] Mason, p. 50.
[2] Nourse, *Proceedings of the Academy of Political Science*, xviii, no. 2, 134 ff.

International trade and investment before the First World War

The preceding period had been an era of quantitative expansion in international trade as in every other sphere of economic activity. Whereas the period had been characterised by free competition between individuals within the same countries, the commerce between different countries had been complementary rather than competitive in character. International trade had consisted mainly in the exchange of raw materials for manufactured products, and had been dominated by British manufacturing, shipping, commercial, and financial enterprise. No country had as yet built up an economic structure that necessitated recourse to general measures of protection. Britain was able to extend her markets as rapidly as she could increase her productive capacity, and when other countries began to enter the industrial field there was still sufficient scope for all of them.

These conditions now began to change. The total volume of world commerce expanded considerably less rapidly from the beginning of this period, a change that is reflected in the following percentage figures:[1]

	1850-1880	1880-1913	1928-1958
Increase in the volume of world trade	270	170	57

Not only did the rate of expansion of world trade tend to slow down, but Britain also steadily lost her monopolist position as the universal provider of manufactured goods. Industrialism spread from England to Belgium, France, Germany, and the United States. Before the end of the nineteenth century there were a great many industrial centres in the world, all of which had developed powerful interests in commerce, shipping, and finance, as well as in industry.

The expansion of these countries at rates conforming to their growing ability to produce and to save became increasingly difficult. Their governments therefore attempted, by means of protection and more assertively by the acquisition of

[1] Nurkse, *Patterns of Trade and Development*, p. 19. 'The end of high prosperity after 1873 and the persistent malaise of the following decades signed in effect the evening of the Industrial Revolution; whereas the hinge of the 1890s marks the beginning of a new career' (Landes, in *The Cambridge Economic History of Europe*, vi, 463).

spheres of influence, to secure full employment for their labour and capital. Owing to the increased importance of the heavy industries, promising openings for commercial and political penetration were found in young and weak countries that needed investment in railways as well as in mining and other equipment. The rivalries fomented by the search for these concessions constituted an important source of friction during the era that preceded the First World War.[1]

Before the war there was still a very pronounced territorial specialisation. The highly industrialised regions of western Europe supplied the rest of the world with manufactured commodities, with banking and other facilities, and with transport services. The less advanced regions provided cheap foodstuffs and industrial raw materials. These imports saved Europe from the threat of diminishing returns in agriculture, and removed one of Malthus's positive checks to the growth of population. The exchange of tropical products for those of the temperate zone, which constituted one of the earliest forms of international trade, also retained some of its significance. The densely populated regions of the East, on the other hand, contributed spices, silks and other luxuries in exchange for the products of western manufacture.

The interchange of goods among the industrial countries of Europe, however, was of considerably more importance than their trade with the producers of agricultural commodities. This reflected the greatly increased importance of industrial goods in the modern economic system and was based on differences in natural resources, technical equipment, and industrial tradition in the main producing centres.

Until the First World War, however, the world's commerce still expanded fairly regularly by 3 per cent annually.[2] Population was still increasing rapidly, while migration afforded relief to the relatively overpopulated countries of Europe and a welcome addition to the productive powers of the new countries overseas. The gradual penetration of capitalist enterprise into every corner of the globe created a demand for goods that could not be produced at home, as well as the corresponding stream of exports to pay for them. Owing to the economies of large-scale production, competitive pressure to reduce costs led to the expansion of one industry after another beyond the capacity of the home market. By the beginning of the First World War there was hardly a major industry which was not dependent on the world market for an outlet.

The movement of commodities was closely connected with the export of capital in the form of short-term loans and long-term investment funds. The capital exported represented the surplus of developed European communities loaned to open up the large undeveloped resources of new countries. These resources consisted of transport facilities to link the regions with foreign markets, of agricultural and of mining facilities, as well as of processing and fabrication plants such as meat-packing and milling, all of which furnished desirable supplements to the production of the creditor countries. The development of these assets in the new countries supplied the means of liquidating the debts. Capital movements and the movement of goods were therefore complementary.

European foreign investment reflected the formidable capitalist penetration of the newer or more backward countries and contributed a powerful support to the

---

[1] Cf. Salter, *World Trade*, p. 19 ff.
[2] From the late 1870s up to 1913 indices of manufacturing production of the principal industrial countries appear on a diagram as an almost straight line rising at the rate of approximately 3½ per cent per annum. World trade increased only slightly less rapidly (League of Nations, *Industrialization and Foreign Trade*, ch 2).

international commercial structure of the period prior to the First World War. The almost universal adoption of gold-standard currencies at the beginning of this period facilitated both international investment and world trade. The functioning of this standard before the war was to a certain extent automatic, especially in Great Britain, and owing to the dominant position of London in international finance, the world was, in a sense, on the sterling standard. Banking systems were loaned up to the practical limits set by their reserves. Gold movements were therefore accompanied by changes in the bank rate, which were followed by the transfer of funds and more slowly by changes in price and in income levels. International debts had been incurred over a long period, and trade channels and capital movements had been organised to adapt themselves to existing conditions. These long-term loans represented the surplus funds of industrial societies made available for the exploitation of the undeveloped potential of the newer countries, and the development of this potential provided the means of liquidating the debts. The movement of capital and the movement of goods therefore mutually supplemented each other. The relative flexibility of wage rates and the comparative absence of restrictions on trade facilitated the transfer of commodities. Gold movements, as a result, remained small and were followed by their own correctives.

The comparative smoothness with which the prewar monetary mechanism functioned was the more remarkable because it was so largely self-regulating. Not the least influential of the conditions that made this possible was the gradual opening up of new markets which, together with the expansion of the home populations, prevented the demand for the output of Europe's factories from reaching saturation point, or the rate of interest from falling to a level that would encourage hoarding. In this expanding market the adjustment of supply to demand could be effected by the movement of prices under the pressure of competitive forces. Overinvestment in any particular industry corrected itself, without the drastic penalties of prolonged unemployment or the scrapping of plant, merely through the temporary discouragement of new investment brought about by falling prices, until the expanding market had re-established an effective demand for the product.

With the growing competition of Germany on the world market and the increased participation of the United States in international trade, the formerly almost unlimited market became more cramped in relation to industrial capacity. It became increasingly difficult to maintain the conditions necessary for the full employment of productive resources. The struggle for foreign markets became intense—a struggle in which the leading states played an increasing part, either in the form of tariff policy or more assertively through the partition or division into spheres of influence of the still unappropriated parts of the world's surface.[1]

The interwar period

The First World War greatly accentuated these difficulties by accelerating the rate of growth of the forces involved. It afforded the most effective protection to home industries in every country, stimulating especially the industrial development of former European markets—the New World, the Far East, and the British Dominions—while the European productive system was thoroughly disorganised by the demands of the war economy. Europe's share of the world's commerce diminished. The magnitude of foreign investment, its distribution between creditor and

[1] Salter, *World Trade*.

debtor countries, and the direction of capital movements, all changed radically as a result of the conflict. The old international indebtedness was greatly reduced by repayment and the depreciation of foreign balances. English capital abroad was reduced by about a quarter, mainly through the repatriation of American securities, while the French lost about a third of their foreign investments as a result of state bankruptcies. Most of Germany's foreign investments were lost. At the same time enormous new obligations were incurred by the former creditor countries in the form of reparations and inter-allied debts.

Increased territorial differentiation and policies to attain industrial self-sufficiency became characteristic features of the postwar period. The newer industrial countries progressed from the stage of development in which they manufactured only the simpler goods destined for immediate consumption to one in which industries producing intermediate and capital-equipment goods became of prime importance.

Especially remarkable was the rise to power of the United States which, by the end of the nineteenth century, had taken the lead as the greatest producer of manufactured goods in the world. The First World War supplied a tremendous fillip to her industrial development, and the postwar period up to 1929 was one of almost sustained prosperity for most sections of the community. By that year the power of the United States to produce economic goods and services was nearly as great as that of the next four most important world powers, and exceeded that of the whole of continental Europe. Inhabited by 7 per cent of the world's population, the United States produced a third of the world's coal, a third of its iron and steel, and 60 per cent of its oil, and generated a third of its electric power. Productivity in American industry was the highest in the world. It was more than twice as high as in the United Kingdom, and its level of productivity was approached only in some of the British dominions.[1]

This expansion, however, was not transmitted to the still undeveloped countries of the world by a corresponding increase in the demand for primary products. The tendency during the interwar period, on the contrary, was for the proportion of raw materials in world trade to decrease and for the share of finished manufactures to increase. Thus whereas the rapid growth in the demand for primary products had given a tremendous stimulus to the development of new countries in the nineteenth century, the tendency for industrial expansion in the West to be transmitted to the still undeveloped countries of the world was now retarded by the inelastic demand for most of the primary export staples. This represented a significant structural change in the world's economy.

Commercial and monetary policies

The postwar reconstruction effort was directed primarily towards the re-establishment of prewar conditions. State control was curtailed and conditions favourable to private enterprise were restored. Everywhere there was a return to the gold standard, and budgets were so regulated that currencies could be kept on it. Everywhere attempts were made to reduce or to stabilise tariffs, to restore foreign investment by the settlement of war debts, to reconstruct the weaker countries by cooperative effort, and to relieve distress at home by the extension of social services. Finally an attempt was made to improve and stabilise international rela-

[1] Hitch, *America's Economic Strength*, chs 1–3.

tions by the creation of a supernational organisation that would supplement national sovereignty and the traditional social and economic system without fundamentally modifying them. The prosperity of the postwar period seemed to justify these measures. A decade after the conflict, the prewar system had been formally re-established everywhere in the western world, and prewar standards of prosperity had been surpassèd.

The temporary success of these measures masked the influence of structural changes that were to make a permanent return to the pre-World War I economic system virtually impossible. The maintenance of an international monetary standard demands that the price and income structures of the different countries should be kept in a certain relation to one another. This necessitates a very high degree of flexibility in the system. It functioned effectively as long as the appropriate government policies, labour organisation, and expansive conditions continued to exist. But gradually a large part of the price structure became inflexible because organised economic forces presented obstacles to a decline in their rates of remuneration. At the same time the falling away of the expansive forces of new markets and of a rapidly increasing population made the problem of the coordination and full employment of resources more difficult.

After the First World War the gold standard to a much larger extent became a managed currency. Central banking policy and the desire to maintain stability contributed to the creation of a greater rigidity in the economic system. The development of central banking created a surplus of reserves above ordinary requirements that broke down the necessary connection between gold movements, bank credit, and prices. In most countries there was a tendency not to associate the credit structure too closely with the state of the reserve funds. The new capital indebtedness created during the war, however, required great flexibility in the movement of both goods and money. But the difficulty of effecting such transfers was greatly increased because these transfers represented the export of capital from countries in which it was urgently required to countries in which it was relatively abundant. Many countries also reacted to the desire for economic self-sufficiency, so powerfully stimulated by the war, by raising their tariffs far above the prewar levels. In the creditor countries the inflow of gold exerted no inflationary effect on the credit structure. In the debtor countries, on the other hand, adjustment to the outflow of gold was hindered by the desire to maintain price and income levels. Such conditions were not conducive to bringing about a distribution of gold reserves that would enable debtor countries to maintain their currencies on the gold standard. This highly artificial situation could not be maintained. With the onset of the depression in 1929 the debtor countries were gradually drained of their gold reserves, a process which increased in momentum until, by 1931, a large part of the world had been forced off the gold standard. One of the main strongholds of the old international economic order had broken down.[1]

---

[1] 'I regard gold as a bulwark of human freedom. If the liquidity problem is looked after exclusively by other methods, gold will come to play a progressively smaller part in the totality of world reserves. This means that countries will depend to a progressively greater extent on "by your leave" accommodation for dealing with their troubles. Foreign-exchange reserves are owned and earned reserves; but there is no reason to suppose that the quantum of these will increase much, and in that case this component of total reserves will also diminish proportionately. Eventually almost all reserves will be of the "by your leave" variety. We shall all be subject, in fine, to a gaggle of governesses' (Harrod, *Reforming the World's Money*, pp. 172–3).

24
Policy

Structural changes in mature economies

The previous period saw the rapid transition in western economies from predominantly agricultural and commercial to predominantly industrial societies. The process
of technological innovation, the growth of population, and the opening up of new
resources created such scope for new investment that a high level of employment
was assured and a rate of development attained that had hitherto not been equalled
anywhere in the world. The period in fact represented a continuous investment
boom. The market mechanism under such conditions achieved the satisfactory
coordination of resources. Governments representing the dominant middle classes
were imbued with a basic optimism—they knew what they wanted and where they
were going, and their leadership was justified by the obvious concrete results that
were obtained.

In the mature economies of the present period there emerged important new
issues that called for solution. These were represented by the unsatisfactory coordination of resources effected by the market mechanism in certain spheres of the
economy and during times of recession, and the unsatisfactory rates of growth
obtained by some of the more mature economies towards the end of this period.
The growing political power of the working classes and the spread of socialist
doctrines were reflected in increasing criticism of the way capitalist economies
functioned. In the western world middle-class governments were, however, still in
almost complete control throughout this period.

Labour legislation and the provision of social services

A characteristic development during this period was the attempts of governments to
prescribe minimum conditions of employment for the working masses. The rise of
organised labour, as well as the fact that gradually virtually all the gainfully
employed in western countries have become employees, has favoured the passing of
labour legislation to protect working conditions—a state of affairs which the
employer-dominated societies of the previous period would never have tolerated.
By the end of this period the conditions of employment of nearly all employees in
the secondary and of large sections of employees in the primary and tertiary sectors

of the economy were determined by collective bargaining, statutory regulations and arbitration awards. The tendency was to remove the settlement of employment issues from the market and to impart to it a social and ethical quality which required public control. This was reflected in the view expressed by the Commission on International Labour Legislation of the Peace Conference at Versailles that 'the labour of a human being should not be treated as merchandise or an article of commerce'.

Attempts to control employment conditions were not equally successful in all countries and in all trades. The demand for the products, and therefore for the labour, of any one country is naturally more elastic than the demand for the similar products of all countries combined. As all trades are not equally effectively protected against the competition of foreign goods, a discrepancy arose in western countries, during this period, between the level of wages of employees working in sheltered home industries and of employees producing for the international market.

Because an attempt by any one country to raise the distributive share of labour creates a competitive advantage for its rivals, unless it is accompanied by an immediate corresponding improvement in the efficiency of its workers, it was argued that effective legislation could be attempted only on an international basis. The establishment of the International Labour Organisation by the Treaty of Versailles would, it was hoped, provide such a basis.

The work achieved by the International Labour Organisation during this period, however, was disappointing. Only a small number of countries ratified the most important convention, that of establishing an eight-hour day in industry, and their ratification of this convention was conditional on similar acceptance by other specified nations. This was the more remarkable as the existing legislation of a number of member countries partially conformed to the provision of the conventions. The value of legislation on an international scale is also open to question. Each country has its own peculiar problems to which it must largely adapt its labour policy. It is obviously impracticable to transfer the social legislation of the leading industrial countries of the West to countries at a different stage of economic development and with different standards of living. Attempts to make the conventions so pliable or so generalised as to suit the specific conditions of all countries would make them lose much of their moral force. To have stressed the moral obligation of ameliorating the conditions of labour has indeed been the main achievement of the Organisation. By disseminating information about the effects of the legislation already in force, it has helped individual countries to provide the means of solving their own specific problems.[1]

Labour legislation has been effectively buttressed by the provision of social services. The process began with the creation of national schemes of elementary education and has been gradually extended to cover other services: insurance against unemployment, accident, sickness and old age, housing facilities, maternity allowances, nutrition services and family allowances. Not only have services been increased in number but the generosity of their provisions has been extended as well, and an increasing proportion of the burden has been borne by the state. These services represent a collective reaction against the insecurities of the capitalist system. The risks of unemployment, sickness or invalidity are no longer regarded as purely individual affairs but have been socialised.

Social insurance schemes serve a useful function in the free enterprise economy, for they offer a means of satisfying the desire for security as a right, while setting a

[1] *The Work of the International Labour Organisation*, National Industrial Conference Board; Thomas, *Handw. der Staatsw., Ergänzungsband.*

limit to the economic and financial risks involved in this guarantee. Such schemes are complementary to the other main objective of economic policy—the maintenance of a satisfactory level of employment—because they can function effectively only when a reasonably high and stable level of employment is assured and the total income is sufficient to provide civilised standards of living to the masses of the people. Prolonged mass unemployment at the end of this period wrecked the actuarial basis of most contributory insurance schemes and reduced them merely to agencies for the government transfer of incomes.

The gradual expansion of state control

A significant feature of this period was the gradual and reluctant assumption by western governments of major responsibilities for the control, guidance and promotion of their economies. From playing a comparatively passive part devoted primarily to the maintenance of law and order, governments came by degrees to exercise an active influence on almost every sphere of the economy.

The reversion to protection

The beginning of this period witnessed a general reversion to protection. The immediate cause was the appearance of cheap American wheat on the European market. Agriculturists, who had consistently supported free trade as long as protection had been confined to industry and they themselves had little to fear from foreign competition, now became enthusiastic supporters of the new cause. This conversion of one of the largest and most powerful groups was of decisive importance for the success of the new policy. Organised consumers' opinion was conspicuously absent. Labour, though nominally in favour of free trade, was actuated primarily by its interest as producer. The merchant class, the natural upholders of free trade policy, steadily lost importance during the second half of the nineteenth century. Continental and American industrialists looked on the British sponsorship of free trade as a clever means of maintaining their superiority by denying other countries the opportunity of rising to industrial greatness.[1]

Technical improvements during the last decades of the nineteenth century led to large-scale production, to broadened markets, and to intense international competition. The differential advantages enjoyed by industrial countries in the production of particular products were reduced. International trade became less complementary and more competitive.

[1] Classical trade theory, indeed, is difficult to reconcile with growth theory, for the simple reason that comparative advantage is a static concept, whereas growth theory is based on the interaction of a number of dynamic factors in the interrelated sectors of the economy. Economic growth in developing countries is, in fact, largely dependent initially on import replacement, and this requires the application of the requisite protective policy on the part of the government. The view has also been expressed that international trade, as far as Britain was concerned, was not based to any appreciable extent on a system of comparative advantages during this period. The gain that it secured by specialisation derived from the terms of trade that subsisted everywhere between manufactures and primary products. Over the greater part of this period there was an advantage to almost every economy that moved resources out of agriculture into industry and exported manufactures and imported primary products (Robinson, 'The changing structure of the British economy', *Economic Journal*, September, 1954, p. 451).

Protection, like free trade, is to a certain extent self-propagating. At home the granting of protection to one industry necessarily entails a demand from others. In the international field the adoption of protection by one country produces a natural reaction in other countries, partly by force of example, partly through the commercial burden it thus imposes, partly as a means of retaliation. Dumping (the sale abroad of goods at lower prices than those demanded on the home market) became important with the development of capital intensive industries, the combination movement and industrial protectionism, and necessitated the imposition of protective measures in the form of anti-dumping duties. Nationalist feeling intensified economic antagonism. This manifested itself in increased protection, which in its turn aggravated political belligerency. Militant nationalism was transformed into a new economic imperialism that manifested itself in the scramble for Africa in the 1880s and in the division of all the unappropriated parts of the earth among the great powers.

Against such a combined front of sentiments and interests *laissez-faire* theories proved to be increasingly powerless. The layman, at heart always protectionist, supported the new cause. Economists began to formulate principles of national solidarity, stressing the advantages of a well-balanced economic system and the dangers of overspecialisation.

Protection, before the First World War, was on the whole comparatively mild. Advocates of protection accepted the main free trade assumptions, namely that the balance of payments would regulate itself and that a reasonably full level of employment would be assured. A series of commercial treaties was made under the leadership of Germany. The most-favoured-nation clause, which during the previous period had been an important means of extending free trade, now became an instrument of protection. In the case of most-favoured-nation treatment, reductions in duties accrued not only to the contracting parties but to all the countries that had bargained for the most-favoured-nation treatment. But though this provision no longer promoted free trade, it helped to prevent discrimination against particular countries, so that, despite protective tariffs, commerce followed much the same course as it would have done under free trade.

After the First World War, protection passed far beyond its prewar level. The war left many legacies of restriction on commercial intercourse, while political antagonism between the former belligerents retarded the restoration of normal commercial relations. Depreciating currencies forced countries to raise their tariffs as a means of equilibrating their balance of payments. New political entities or countries where new industries had developed during the war erected tariff barriers to protect and foster industrial development, while in the old industrial countries the desire for self-sufficiency was greatly strengthened. Russia broke away from the international capitalist commercial organisation and instituted a state monopoly of foreign trade.

There was, nevertheless, also a tendency towards greater freedom through concerted action. On the basis of the new tariff systems innumerable bilateral conventions, which incorporated the most-favoured-nation principle more uniformly than before the First World War, were entered into. But the most-favoured-nation clause now laboured under serious disadvantages. Under a system of low tariffs this clause secures equality of treatment and helps to avert causes of friction. When countries with high tariff systems claim most-favoured-nation treatment, however, the result is that reciprocal negotiations rapidly become impossible, because two moderate tariff countries are not likely to negotiate for mutual tariff reductions when these reductions have also to be accorded to countries whose tariff systems are much higher than their own and offer no advantages in return. The result was a growing disinclination after 1927 to negotiate bilateral agreements for the reduction of tariffs and an increasing antipathy to the most-favoured-nation clause. The only alternative method of obtaining an all-round reduction in tariffs was through multi-lateral action by collective conventions. All these attempts foundered not merely because of the inherently different angles of approach adopted by developing and developed countries, but also because of the inherent difficulty of bringing a number of different tariff systems, each complicated in itself, into a unified scheme, and of finding a principle on which tariff reductions could be based.

Attempts to establish greater commercial freedom were completely wrecked by the financial difficulties that came with the depression. There followed a period of intense restriction, during which not only tariffs but prohibitions, quotas, and exchange prohibitions were mobilised with the primary object of protecting national currencies and the secondary motive of protecting the home market. The cumulative effect of this restriction was to change the basis of international trade in many countries from one of individual freedom tempered by tariff restrictions to one in which trade was tolerated only under special permission. Particularly important was the imposition of substantial protective tariffs and the subsequent adoption of a comprehensive system of protection with Empire preference by Great Britain in 1931. This complete reversal of her commercial policy was the more significant because, ever since the introduction of Sir Robert Peel's budget in 1842, she had so consistently maintained and propagated a free trade policy.[1]

Monetary policy

Before the First World War the monetary mechanism possessed the pliability required of an international standard. The functioning of the gold standard was to a certain extent automatic, especially in Great Britain and, through the dominant position of London in international finance, the world was, in a sense, on the sterling standard. Banking systems made loans up to the practical limits set by their reserves. Gold movements were therefore accompanied by changes in the bank rate, and these were followed by the transfer of funds and more slowly by changes in price and income levels. International debts had been incurred over a long period, and trade channels and capital movements were organised to adapt themselves to existing conditions. The capital exported represented the surplus of developed European communities that was lent to open up the large undeveloped resources of new countries. The development of these resources supplied the means of liquidating the debts. Capital movements and the movement of goods were therefore complementary. The relative flexibility of wage rates and comparatively low tariff structures facilitated the transfer of goods. As a result gold movements remained small and were followed by their own correctives.

Circumstances changed after the First World War. The gold standard became to a much greater extent a managed currency. Central banking policy and the desire to maintain stability made the economic system much more rigid, because the development of central banking created a surplus of reserves above ordinary requirements that broke down the necessary connection between gold movements, bank credit and prices. On the other hand there was the desire to dissociate internal

[1] Salter, *World Trade*, chs 1, 2, 3; League of Nations, *World Economic Surveys*, 1931–2, ch 10; 1932–3, ch 7.

credit policy from the preoccupation with reserves. The creation of new capital indebtedness on a vast scale as a result of war debts, however, required an extreme flexibility in the transfer of funds. The difficulty of making these transfers was greatly increased, for they represented the export of capital from countries in which it was urgently needed to countries in which it was relatively abundant. But the movement of goods was restricted. Creditor countries refused to accept media other than gold for the payment of their debts, and the effect of the import of this gold on their price structures was neutralised by central banking policy. The inflow of gold therefore lost its largely automatic power of restricting further imports of the metal. In the debtor countries, on the other hand, adjustment to the outflow of gold was hindered by the desire to maintain price and income levels. Such conditions were not conducive to bringing about a distribution of gold reserves that would enable debtor countries to maintain their currencies on the gold standard.

The maintenance of stability

The capitalist system functions best during periods of rapid expansion with numerous and tempting investment outlets. Such an era was inaugurated by the Industrial Revolution. The process of technical innovation, the growth of population, and the opening up and exploitation of new resources created exceptional opportunities for profitable investment which, with the prevailing feeling of optimism, were fully utilised in the West.

These factors supplied such scope for new investment that the process of capital formation was conducive to securing the fairly full employment of productive resources and, therefore, the maximum income possible under the prevailing standards of technical development. The effect of such conditions was to minimise the risks of business enterprise. Industry provided mainly for the primary, non-deferable, calculable needs of a rapidly expanding population. If undue optimism had caused a temporary overinvestment in any particular sphere, the expansive factors would soon restore the equilibrium. Overoptimistic businessmen could anticipate the future and make capital outlays for plant, railways, or building construction that were not justified by the existing demand but would soon be raised to a profitable level by the process of expansion. Depressions were shortlived; recovery was easy and spontaneous. During the depression, opportunities for new investment outlets would accumulate and the supply of resources would become more elastic. As a result the contraction would soon lose momentum and become more responsive to expansive stimuli. The ordinary risks inherent in a period of rapid change could, therefore, be easily assumed in a rapidly expanding economy.

These conditions gradually changed during this period. Technological change indeed was still proceeding at a rapid rate, but it tended to be of a type that required a relatively less substantial investment of new capital. It is doubtful whether there was much 'deepening' of capital in the western world during the first third of the twentieth century in the sense of an increase of capital-intensity per unit of output. At the same time the field for territorial expansion was narrowing and the rate of population growth slowing down. New sources of capital accumulation seeking investment, on the other hand, became apparent as more countries reached the stage of industrial maturity. Not only did increased wealth bring about an increased accumulation of private savings as conditions of full employment were reached, but increasing sections of the economy were financed from internal sources owing to the enhanced importance of corporate savings. The result was a growing pressure on the available investment outlets, which became noticeable from the beginning of this period, and which became especially acute at the end of the period.

These factors reduced the ability of western economies to recover spontaneously from the effects of the business cycle and increased the necessity for government regulation. At the same time the instability of the economic system was increased by the fact that a growing instability of demand was accompanied by a growing rigidity in the mechanism of supply. The demand became more transient and undependable because, with rising standards of living, a smaller proportion of national incomes was spent on goods and services that satisfied imperative human needs, and a growing proportion on passing wants, the demand for which was more eclectic and fickle. A growing proportion was also spent on durable consumer goods with a slow rate of obsolescence, the replacement of which could always be postponed. During periods of depression everyone is inclined to economise on such goods with the result that the depression is intensified. The demand for these goods is also more difficult to estimate so that errors in business forecasts are increased, and such errors have even more unfortunate effects in that these goods can be provided only by an elaborate mechanism made up of minutely specialised and rigidly fixed cost elements.

Any economic system would, under such conditions, experience great difficulty in securing the necessary correspondence between the various flows of incomes and services that bring about the effective equilibrium of economic forces. These flows are the spontaneous savings of the community and the investment decisions of entrepreneurs, the demand for consumption goods and the production of these goods, and, finally, the stream of money incomes and the stream of goods and services. The ineptitude of the monetary policy applied by the Federal Reserve Board over the years 1929 to 1933 allowed the discrepancies between these flows to become greatly accentuated. The Board allowed a banking and liquidity crisis to develop by permitting the stock of money to fall by over a third. More than one-fifth of the commercial banks in the United States holding nearly one-tenth of the volume of deposits at the beginning of the contraction suspended operations because of financial difficulties. The lack of leadership within the Board was as remarkable as the absence of vigorous and informed criticism from outside.

> Hence, as events proceeded, it (the Board) was increasingly inclined to look elsewhere for the solution, at first to hope that matters would right themselves, then increasingly to accept the view that crisis and boom were the inescapable product of forces in the private business community that were developing beyond the system's control.[1]

Because of the weak, passive and vacillating policy pursued by the monetary authorities the cumulative effect of the recession was allowed to develop into the major tragedy of the Great Depression, with farreaching economic, social and political consequences for the whole world.

[1] Friedman and Schwartz, *The Great Contraction*, p. 123.

Part 9
The Present — A Period of Co-existence

25
Conflicting ideologies

Marxian dialectics

The term *socialism* was first used in its modern connotation in 1827 to denote tendencies opposed to liberalism.[1] As a proletarian ideology, the appeal of socialism developed spontaneously out of the conditions brought about by capitalist organisation. The agrarian and industrial revolutions recast the framework of society. The corporative relationships of the handicrafts and the collective self-sufficiency of the village community were destroyed. Peasants and craftsmen were torn away from communal relations which had given their lives a content and a meaning and congregated in amorphous masses in the large industrial centres.[2] Two sharply differentiated classes appeared in society, the proletariat and the bourgeoisie. Machine production tended initially to reduce the workman to a more standardised collective type. The emotional aspects of his life—his religion, traditions, and national consciousness—were weakened; his intellectual faculties and especially his critical faculties, on the other hand, were greatly developed. The proletariat acquired a moral and mental outlook that offered an extremely propitious setting for socialist doctrines.

Socialist theory, which till the time of Marx and Engels had been confined to the speculation of isolated individuals, received a synthesis and a dynamic impetus from these two writers that made it a world proletarian movement. Their precursors had

---

[1] The word 'socialism' is no less misleading than the word 'capitalism'. As a socialist economy is diametrically opposed to a capitalist economy, it implies the collective ownership and central administration of the means of production, distribution and exchange, and therefore denotes a state operated economy. Many so-called western socialists however want to retain the private enterprise economy but subject it to controls in regard to its operation and the distribution of incomes.

According to Marxian mythology, socialism is an intermediate stage between capitalism and communism. Communism represents the ultimate goal of historical evolution. In the communist collectivity the state would have withered away and a classless society emerged, to the support of which everyone would contribute according to his ability and be compensated in accordance with his needs.

[2] It was undoubtedly this dehumanising effect of the technological and organisational changes of the nineteenth century—the estrangement of the worker from his social and economic environment so eloquently sermonised by Karl Marx—that provided the most deep-seated basis for the proletarian reaction to the capitalist system.

enveloped their work in a highly religious and metaphysical atmosphere. Marx and Engels regarded the appeal to transcendental values in order to find a solution to the social problem as the subtle insinuation of an opiate into the minds of the working masses. The new ideology abandoned the principle of social solidarity and glorified the class struggle as the means of liberating the proletariat. This emancipation and the attainment of equality had to be brought about by the workers themselves. The working class was acclaimed as the class entrusted with the historic mission of bringing about a better order.

Such doctrines had an immediate and dynamic appeal. The proletariat, which had always been neglected, now attained a new self-consciousness and spiritual pride. The checks and restraints of traditional religion and morality were removed, and the new proletarian movement was given the character of an inevitable, predetermined, 'religious' process by the materialistic interpretation of history. Communism in its turn became an opiate as intolerant and as impervious to reason as any theological creed.

According to Hegelian dialectics the inner contradictions inherent in every social system are the driving forces that cause the supplanting of one historical phase by another. Through the conflict and opposition of elements inherent in each situation, institutions are gradually transformed by negation into their opposites. Out of theses and antitheses there emerge new syntheses. According to Hegel's idealistic world view, 'ideas' are the activating or creative forces of the real world, thought being conceived as an autonomous, independent process.[1]

Marx, though he rejected the substance of Hegel's philosophy, retained the method. He also conceived of conflict as the dynamic of social change. Ideas, however, are not the formative forces of history; these are derived, dependent, secondary. The history of mankind, according to Marx and Engels, is determined not by human ideas but by a gradual economic evolution that moves on irresistibly according to its own inherent laws.[2] 'The mode of production in material life', says Engels, 'determines social, political, and spiritual evolution in general. It is not the conscious thought of mankind that determines its modes of existence, but on the contrary, its modes of social existence that determine its conscious thought.' The spiritual embellishments of society—law, religion, art, and philosophy—merely form an ornamental superstructure based on the material, productive forces of mankind. [3]

---

[1] A similar view was also expressed by John Maynard Keynes: 'The ideas of economists and political philosophers, both when they are right and when they are wrong, are more powerful than is commonly understood. Indeed the world is ruled by little else' (*The General Theory of Employment* . . ., p. 383).

[2] It has been pointed out that Marx had no justification for using the Hegelian method while rejecting the substance, since it makes sense only in terms of thought. 'In Hegel's system it has a place. But there are no grounds for supposing that material phenomena exhibit in their change and development the same process of logical interrelation as that which governs the idea. What Marxist-Leninists do, however, is arbitrarily to select any two dissimilar phenomena, and then represent them as logical contradictions to which the laws of the dialectic apply, thus contravening the principle of formal logic that while propositions and statements may be contradictory, things and events cannot be' (Hunt, *Marxism: past and present*, p. 13).

[3] Hence the attempts of communists to found a new order not only in the economic field but also in the sphere of philosophy, morality, science and art. But as these are products of the human mind and of human culture in the widest sense and not merely of a particular economic system, they can be transformed and superseded only in their own appropriate spheres and by their own inherent causes, and not by changes brought about in the economic field alone. These proletarian endeavours have therefore been characterised by their aberrations rather than by any genuine contributions to their respective fields. Cf. Croce, *Politics and Morals*, ch 7.

Historical materialism professes to offer a unique interpretation of the forces responsible for social change. These forces must be sought in the ever present tension between the development of the powers of production on the one hand, and the prevailing relations of production on the other. The former comprehends the existing stage of technique and organisation and the prevailing degree of human rationality. The latter refers to the social conditions under which production takes place, the methods of distribution and control, the social stratification and the prevailing ideologies. The forces of production tend to be highly dynamic. Driven by the quest for profit or the desire to improve the standard of living, by the expansion of human knowledge, or by the mere growth of numbers, the forces of production tend continually to gain in strength, depth and scope. The relations of production, on the other hand, tend to be conservative. The prevailing systems of appropriation and social organisation favour certain classes at the expense of others, and they tend to crystallise into political institutions with their appropriate codes and ideologies. Initially, the productive relations tend to be in harmony with the productive forces, thus enabling these to produce effectively. But in the course of time the productive relations tend progressively to lag behind the development of the productive resources and eventually become a drag on their full utilisation, which gives rise to increasing friction and tension.

The basic thesis of Marxian doctrine is centred in the labour theory of value. The *value* of a commodity is defined by Marx as the labour-time required to produce it.

A use-value of a good (a useful article) has value solely because abstract human labour has been embodied or materialised in it. How are we to measure this value? In terms of this quantity of 'value-creating' substance it contains—the quantity of labour.[1]

This is not a scientific proposition in the sense that commodities actually tend to be exchanged at prices proportional to their *values* as defined in this way, which Marx knew to be incorrect. It is, on the contrary, a dogmatic statement, which serves as the cornerstone of the argument that explains the functioning and the inevitable collapse of the capitalist system.

As labour alone creates *value*, the aggregate value of economic output, the 'quantity of value', that can be produced is determined by the quantity of wage labour, the 'socially necessary labour-time' that is employed. By the use of additional capital equipment the *physical* product can indeed be increased, but this would not add to the *value* of the output. If therefore the amount of equipment grows faster than the labour force, the rate of profit must fall, unless wages fall. With the accumulation of capital that accompanies the development of capitalism profits can be increased or maintained only by the continually intensified exploitation of labour.

It follows that, because of this exploitation and the consequent decline of purchasing power, there is a constant overproduction of 'values' that cannot be realised, and thus the failure to use the creative powers unleashed by modern techniques. Thus the injustice of capitalism is also its weakness, since it prevents profits from being realised. Capitalism creates powers of production which it cannot employ.[2] This constitutes the inner contradiction of the capitalist system,

---

[1] *Capital*, i, ch 1, p. 7 (Everyman ed.). The value of a commodity is defined by Marx as the quantity of labour-time or labour-power embodied in its production.
[2] Hence the importance of credit creation, a typical capitalist invention to push sales, but which merely has the effect of accentuating the severance in the chain of turnover by the generation of recurring crises of ever-increasing severity.

which prohibits its continuation and which it is powerless to reform. Hence the class struggle must intensify, the rate of profit must fall, and capitalist economies must eventually collapse.

The carrier *par excellence* of the transformative principle, the channel for its transmission and the most dramatic form of its expression, is the class struggle, the stratifying factor consisting in the ownership, or the exclusion from ownership, of the means of production. Ultimately all fundamental social struggles are derived from conflicting class interests and clashes. Other conflicts and groupings—national, religious, ideological—play a secondary role. In the constant and pervasive pressure exercised by economic conditions, all other differences are effectually effaced.

As the process of historical development moves forward by its own inexorable force, capitalist evolution must, because of its inner contradictions, inevitably encompass its own destruction. According to the immanent and immutable laws of political economy, the growing accumulation of capital and the increasing relative misery of the masses must inevitably lead to the expansion of industrial capacity in excess of the requirements of the market, and consequently generate more and more devastating crises. Growing competition for the market leads to the continual concentration of capital in fewer and fewer hands. This progressive diminution in the number of capitalists will be accompanied by a corresponding increase in the mass of oppressed and enslaved workmen, a process that will facilitate the expropriation of the remaining capitalists and the transfer of their property to the state. Goaded by recurring crises of unemployment, the proletariat will finally be driven to seizing the means of production.

> Along with the constantly diminishing number of the magnates of capital, who usurp and monopolise all advantages of this process of transformation, grows the mass of misery, oppression, slavery, degradation, exploitation; but with this too grows the revolt of the working class, a class always increasing in numbers, and disciplined, united, organised by the very mechanism of the process of capitalist production itself. The monopoly of capital becomes a fetter upon the mode of production, which has sprung up and flourished along with it, and under it. The centralisation of the means of production and the socialisation of labour at last reach a point where they become incompatible with their capitalist integument. This integument is burst asunder. The knell of capitalist private property sounds. The expropriators are expropriated.[1]

The primary objective of the proletariat must therefore be the revolutionary overthrow of the capitalist system and its transformation into a socialist economy, in which the productive resources of humanity, hitherto suppressed, will be released, because capital equipment will be employed for the production of 'use value' and not of 'exchange value'. Every conceivable means must be used by the proletariat to achieve this end. Measures of reform must be regarded only as auxiliary means of overthrowing the bourgeois state. Class interests are inherently irreconcilable. No compromise must therefore be regarded seriously, no agreement permanently honoured. In the revolutionary struggle the working class must not be hindered by considerations of conventional justice and morality. Marx, indeed, in the words of Croce, has shown himself as a 'most remarkable continuator of Machiavelli', though both men would most strongly have repudiated the affinity.[2]

---

[1] Marx, *Capital*, ch 24 (7).
[2] Croce, *Matérialisme historique et economie Marxiste*, p. 179; Sombart, *Der proletarische Sozialismus*, i, 333 ff; 'Socialism', in *Encyclopaedia of Social Sciences*.

Marx, as Henry Smith has pointed out, became the prisoner of his own scheme of thought, though in later life he became increasingly sceptical of the internal consistency of his system.

The dialectical process necessitated that the conflict of forces set up by the emergence of capitalism (itself the synthesis of an earlier conflict) could not be resolved within the system which created them, only by the creation of a new system, a new synthesis. Science was, for Marx, the capacity to understand the determinate process of history according to his own rules. Therefore it was impossible for him to admit that conflict could do anything but become intensified within the economic system which created it. He *had* to find proof that things could not improve.[1]

Herein lies the tragedy of this in many ways brilliant man. As a decrier of the capitalist system he was unique, even though his basic tenets were fallacious. His positive contribution to the new socialist state, whether in the political or the economic sphere, on the other hand, was elementary and the dogmatic nature of his thinking often a hindrance rather than a help.[2] The verdict of Croce is therefore not without foundation; that the originality of Marx was that neither of the philosopher nor of the economist, but of the creator of political ideologies or myths. But then Marx wanted to play the role of the prophet rather than of the philosopher, and in the realisation of this ideal he was phenomenally successful.

The Fascist reaction

Futurism and archaism, as Toynbee has pointed out, are typical reactions of a society which faces the danger of social disintegration.[3] The former seeks relief from the present by the creation of an ideal futurist state; the latter tries to achieve the same object by going back to the happier state of a no less illusory past. Both, therefore, seek goals that are intrinsically unattainable. Marxism represents the futurist response, and Fascism the archaistic reaction to the problems and pressures presented by the capitalist economy, polity and society.

The Fascist and Nazi regimes can be explained historically as a reaction against the socialist movement and its immediate antecedent, the liberal democratic state. As such the national socialist movement has its roots deep in the 'reactionary' tendencies of the eighteenth and nineteenth centuries.

The essence of democracy is government by discussion and compromise; the departing point is the possibility of a rational solution that will be acceptable to the majority. In the democratic scheme of values, human personality occupies a central position. The individual has a natural 'imprescriptible' right to freedom. Society is conceived as an association of individuals, and a clear distinction is drawn between society and its organised expression, the state. The development of a harmonious and full social life requires that each individual should have the right to make decisions and to bear responsibilities. The powers of collective organs over their members must therefore be circumscribed within narrow bounds. The tradition of toleration, freedom of speech and discussion, and freedom to organise for a wide

---

[1] Miller and others, in *Communist Economy under Change*, p. 214.

[2] 'So for Marx capitalism was chaos and to abolish this chaos there had to be central planning. He did not, of course, say how to plan, since he did not in the least understand the subject. On this single omission seems to rest the whole myth that he said nothing about the socialist future. (Wiles, *The Political Economy of Communism*, p. 59).

[3] Toynbee, *A Study of History*, abridgement by D. C. Somervell, pp. 505 ff.

variety of purposes without being subjected to state supervision constitutes the basic elements of liberal patterns of thought and of 'western' civilisation. Its most extreme expression in the economic sphere was found in *laissez-faire* policy. The interventionist tendencies of the late nineteenth and early twentieth century, however, considerably weakened its appeal as a means of propaganda and its force as a directive of social policy.

Socialism, in theory, inherited this liberal tradition. It developed an entirely lay conception of the state, its ultimate object being the creation of a society of free individuals living in peaceful cooperation. The state, according to Marxian doctrine, is merely an instrument of class oppression, and when classes disappear the state will also wither away.[1] Socialism is frankly supranational and cosmopolitan. It believes in the equality of all members of mankind, and does not look at the differences that have divided them in the past but towards a future in which a worldwide community of free men will emerge.

In contrast to the libertarian world view, German philosophy has always tended to place the community rather than the individual in the centre of the scale of values. Under the strain and stress of a nationalism quickened by Napoleon's defeat of Prussia, the German Romantic Movement developed into a reaction against liberal ideas and democratic institutions—in fact, against all the influences that had shaped the western world since the fifteenth century and had finally been embodied in the Age of Reason. For its inspiration the movement turned to the Feudal System, 'that enchanted unity derived from collective authority'.[2] According to the Prussian view the individual cannot be conceived as something apart from the community of which he is a member. The community is not merely an association of individuals but an organism of which the members form an integral and functional part. The state, according to Hegel, the 'harvester of the romantic crop', represents the principle of absolute reason and spiritual power that bestows on man whatever value he has. The social whole is both logically and historically antecedent to the individual. Far from losing his liberty in the collective whole, the individual is integrated into a higher sphere in which his real will is realised. As the state is the embodiment of absolute power, political policy must not be judged in terms of 'subjective morality'. Power is the basic fact of political life, and the political order must be judged, and justified, within its own terms.[3]

Fascist and Nazi ideologies represent the historical culmination of these doctrines, only vulgarised and adulterated, as is inevitable with popular movements.[4] Of the two, Fascism was the older, but Nazism the more 'dynamic' and

---

[1] Both Marx and Engels had a deep distrust of the state. According to Engels 'the modern state, whatever its form, is essentially a capitalist machine'. But a planned socialist economy is inconceivable without the state. Lenin escaped from the dilemma by maintaining that once the state became proletarian, the Marxist objection would no longer be valid. 'The state is an organ or apparatus of force to be used by one class against another. So long as it remains an apparatus for the bourgeoisie to use force against the proletariat, so long can the slogan of the proletariat be only—the destruction of the state. But when the state has become an apparatus of force to be used by the proletariat against the bougeoisie, then we shall be fully and unreservedly for a strong state power and centralism' (*Will the Bolsheviks Retain State Power?*, 1917).
[2] Sombart, *Der proletarische Sozialismus*, i, 31.
[3] Hegel, *Philosophy of Right*, sec. 257 ff.
[4] Fascist theories have been greatly influenced by the German Romantic Movement. According to McGovern 'when we read the writings of Alfredo Rocco, perhaps the most important of the "official" Fascist philosophers, we almost feel that we are reading Hegel's *Philosophy of Right* denuded of its metaphysical background', McGovern, W. M., *From Luther to Hitler; the History of Fascist-Nazi Political Philosophy*, Houghton Mifflin, Boston, 1941.

ruthless. It was only after 1933 that the Italian movement took over the more extreme tenets of its German neighbour.

Both liberalism and socialism conceive the ultimate object of society as consisting in securing the welfare and happiness of the individual, and both regard the state as merely a means to the attainment of that end. Where they differ is in regard to the means that should be adopted to attain this objective. According to totalitarian ideology, on the other hand, the community is infinitely more than the mere aggregate of individuals who constitute the social group at any given time. Individuals are merely the temporary expression of the life of the nation that goes on for ever. The interests of the nation transcend and may be directly opposed to those of the individuals that compose it at any given time. Organised society does not exist primarily and solely for the individual; it is the individual who exists for the organised collectivity that is the state. The totalitarian state is all-inclusive and omnipotent. There is in principle no single aspect of public or private life that does not concern it. Nor can it tolerate within itself any force that is indifferent to it. The state completely controls all the ideas, values, and activities of its subjects; all economic activity, all political, social and cultural life is in theory coordinated, canalised, and directed.

Apart however, from an all-pervading control, the economic theory of totalitarianism does not differ from that of other non-socialist regimes. Private initiative and private ownership of the means of production are valued and maintained. National socialism was never a socialist movement in the sense that it strove to socialise the means of production. Thus the original Nazi programme embodied socialist principles such as the abolition of unearned incomes, the socialisation of trusts, the sharing of labour in the profits of companies, the break-up of large estates, the abolition of ground rents, and the prohibition of speculation in land. But when the party came to power the radical elements were liquidated, and the socialist principles were watered down to the general principle that the common good transcends private interest.

The totalitarian state, however, greatly accentuated the tendency towards control. The state, according to Fascist ideology, has a direct and authoritative interest in every phase of a people's economic existence. Any economic liberty granted to the individual is not an absolute right but merely a concession granted in the interest of society, a concession that may be revoked whenever necessary and is always conditional on its not interfering with the aims of national policy. Fascism, in the words of Alfredo Rocco, 'does not refer economic problems to individual needs, to individual interest, to individual solutions. On the contrary it considers economic development and especially the production of wealth, as an eminently social concern, wealth being for society an essential element of power and prosperity'. Ultimately all spheres of activity, the economic sphere included, would be coordinated into a new 'total' order, a planned entity that would radiate over the whole life of the nation. Meanwhile neither Fascism nor Nazism had a clearly conceived plan, far less a concerted and long-range programme of action. Everything was subordinated to the all-important military needs, which had the immediate justification of making the depression-paralysed economic system function at full blast once more. The period of extreme totalitarian domination was moreover too short to judge the effect of the multiplicity of controls on the system of priceforming markets and the creation of basic disequilibria within the pricing system.

The tendency of totalitarian ideology was to give the concept of socialism a purely idealistic content. It came to mean social solidarity: society conceived as an organism of which individuals and classes were functional members. The organic theory of society is very old. Throughout history it has served as a conservative weapon. From the conception of society as an organism of which individuals and groups are functional members there naturally follows a static conception of social life. Class differences are necessary and must remain. Social change can come about only very gradually as a process of organic evolution; for any internal conflict may endanger the existence of the whole organism.

The most original contribution of totalitarian thought to the social problem is the tendency to idealise economic relations. An attempt is made to sever the connection between social and economic status and to found a social hierarchy outside the realm of economics. Each function is equally indispensable and there-fore of equal importance in the life of a people. The peasant represents the biological backbone of the people; the worker symbolises the qualities of sacrifice, self-discipline, and self-abnegation; and the middle class are the 'standard-bearers of national culture', symbolising the heroic principle of personal leadership. Compulsory labour service symbolises the dignity of work. Labour is no longer a mere factor of production bought and sold in the open market: it is a social duty, a contribution that the individual must make to the economic life of the nation. But if labour has this obligation towards the state, the state has the corresponding duty to ensure its just reward, the security of employment, and the amenities of a civilised existence. The interests of labour and capital are identical. Both are employed by the nation and must cooperate for the common good. Through the integration of all groups as functional members in an organic entity, the division of society into classes with conflicting interests is eliminated.[1]

The spiritual bonds of the corporative state function exclusively within the individual nation. As historical growth represents the highest level of organic growth, so the nation represents the highest realisation of organic unity. Class conflicts are transferred to the international sphere. The real struggle is not between proletariat and bourgeoisie but between different national entities. The totalitarian state, like the mercantilist state, redirected policy from considerations of welfare to considerations of power, only infinitely more systematically and effectively. In the totalitarian state the primacy of politics is complete.

Western revisionism

The decline of liberal economic philosophy. The mood of the western world at present is reflected by the fact that there have been numerous attacks on liberal *laissez-faire* policy as a means of effecting the coordination of economic resources, and imputations against the weakness of the liberal appeal as an expression of the needs, aspirations and interests of the masses.

The classical economists discovered the coordinating effect of spontaneous competitive forces operating through the market mechanism and laid the founda-tion of the social code that formed the basis of liberal policy in the nineteenth century. Adam Smith had taken the detailed working of the price mechanism for granted, and his advocacy of *laissez-faire* policy was consequently not hedged in with the numerous qualifications that could have been expected in a more compre-hensive exposition.

The neo-classicists came to see the economy as an interrelated and integrated

[1] Cf. Trivanovitch, *Economic Development of Germany under National Socialism*, ch 1.

system of price-forming markets and developed the concept of a general equilibrium. In an optimum equilibrium position the marginal returns on resources in all the different fields of application would be equal. A position is consequently reached in which it would not be possible, with the available inputs, to increase the output of any commodity without sacrificing the output of another.

As this was a proposition of formal economic logic, independent of any specific organisation of the economy, a Marxist like Lange had no difficulty in showing that such a result would also be characteristic of the optimum allocation of resources in the ideal socialist economy. In fact, as the socialist economy would not be distorted by the existence of monopolies and the unequal distribution of incomes, this optimum position was more likely to be attained, on a trial and error basis, in a perfect socialist market economy than in a capitalist economy. The fact that ideally competitive conditions exist neither in a capitalist nor in a socialist economy, but only in the imagination of economists, did not detract from the ideological significance of his conclusions.

Marshall was the first of the neo-classicists to indicate the serious limitation of the price-market mechanism, as a means of the efficient allocation of resources, when faced with the problem of industries subject to decreasing costs. Under such conditions it might indeed be beneficial for the state to subsidise these industries at the expense of those subject to increasing cost.

His successor, Pigou, could therefore argue that, even though equality in the values of marginal social net products of resources in all different uses was an *essential condition* for the optimum allocation of resources, state action might be needed to jerk the industrial system from one relative maximum to another higher absolute level. Characteristically, he considered state action in the form of a *temporary* bounty or temporary protection.

Pigou also laid the ideological basis for another strong argument for state intervention by drawing a distinction between *private* and *social* net product, but the revolutionary implications of this distinction were not pursued. The cases where intervention was justified were put forward as exceptions to the rule that *laissez-faire* would ensure maximum welfare. All that was required was that readjustments be made here and there to ensure the most efficient possible distribution of resources between uses.

It was becoming increasingly clear, however, that ominous cracks were appearing in the impressive structure of neo-classical static economic theory, and especially in one of its basic theorems—the intimate logical connection between a system of perfect competitive markets and the efficient allocation of resources.[1]

The Keynesian revolution. The liberal philosophy had been built up primarily to explain and justify England's hegemony in the economic world of the nineteenth century. The difficulties that she experienced after the First World War raised serious doubts as to the efficacy and the general validity of the doctrine. Thus as early as 1926 Keynes, in his *Essays in Persuasion*, cast doubts on the very foundation of *laissez-faire* ideology:

> Let us clear from the ground the metaphysical or general principles upon which, from time to time, *laissez-faire* has been founded. It is *not* true that individuals possess a prescriptive 'natural liberty' in their economic activities. There is *no* 'compact' conferring perpetual rights on those who Have or those who Acquire. The world is *not* so governed from above that private and social interest always coincide. It is *not* so managed here below that in practice they coincide. It is *not*

---

[1] Bliss, 'Prices, markets and planning', *Economic Journal*, March 1972.

a correct deduction from the Principles of Economics that enlightened self-interest always operates in the public interest. Nor is it true that self-interest generally is enlightened; more often individuals acting separately to promote their own ends are too ignorant or too weak to attain even these. Experience does *not* show that individuals, when they make up a social unit, are always less clear-sighted than when they act separately.

We cannot, therefore, settle on abstract grounds, but must handle on its merits in detail, what Burke termed 'one of the finest problems in legislation, namely, to determine what the State ought to take upon itself to direct by the public wisdom, and what it ought to leave, with as little interference as possible, to individual exertion'. We have to discriminate between what Bentham, in his forgotten but useful nomenclature used to term Agenda and Non-Agenda, and to do this without Bentham's prior presumption that interference is, at the same time, 'generally needless' and 'generally pernicious'.[1]

Keynes, however, was still basically in agreement with the neo-classicists that the cases that justified state interference were exceptional. The great change not only in emphasis but in basic thinking came with the virtual collapse of the market as a means of coordination during the Great Depression of the early 1930s. A large part of the resources of capitalist economies was unemployed. Keynes, in his General Theory, diagnosed the cause as a deep-seated defect in the coordinative mechanism of the capitalist system, and enunciated the view that saving, instead of being invariably both a private virtue and a public benefit, could actually be a social vice if investment failed to use savings effectively. Thrift, in fact, is an aid to economic growth only if the propensity to invest is strong; if it is weak, thrift will tend to make it all the weaker.

Keynes thus exploded the doctrine of the harmony between private and public interests that formed the corner stone of nineteenth-century liberalism. These different and often conflicting interests could no longer be relied on automatically to produce full employment. On the contrary, a deliberate act of policy is required if this effect is to be ensured. The maintenance of a satisfactory level of employment becomes an object of public policy.

Keynes was indeed optimistic about the possibility of harmonising the adjustments that had to be made with the fundamental assumptions of the capitalist system. Apart from the necessity for central controls to bring about an adjustment between the propensity to consume and the inducement to invest, matters could best be left to 'the free play of economic forces'. There was no need for the farreaching socialisation of economic life. The existing system with its advantages of efficiency and freedom could, in the main, be retained.[2]

Not since the days of Adam Smith have the ideas of an economist exerted such farreaching effects on economic policy. Both Smith and Keynes lived at decisive turning points in the evolution of the capitalist system, both were the products of their times, yet both were also powerful influences in shaping the forces of institutional change. The implementation of Keynesian theories has led to a very large degree of government involvement in the national economy and has exerted a profound effect in ensuring its stability. It is now generally accepted in the western world that it is the government's function to maintain a high level of aggregate demand, and that if private demand should flag and falter, it has to be revived and stimulated by government spending.

During the postwar years, however, there came the realisation that high levels of

[1] Keynes, *Essays in Persuasion*, pp. 312 ff.
[2] Keynes, *The general Theory of Employment, Interest, and Money*, pp. 378 ff.

employment would be associated not merely with *high* but with continually *rising* levels of wages and prices.[1] How then can an economy simultaneously enjoy full employment, price stability, and free markets? The western world today faces the problem of cost-push as well as of demand-pull inflation, and it is groping for an answer to this problem. Where the cost-push elements are strong, exclusive reliance on the use of monetary and fiscal measures to depress the demand would ensure a greater measure of price stability only at the expense of creating unemployment and excess capacity. A more radical solution could be sought in the use of direct price and wage controls. If this policy could be successfully applied, it would ensure a greater measure of stability, but only at the cost of major interference with the market mechanism, with all its attendant problems.

Susceptibility of the free enterprise economy to criticism. Whereas certain societies, such as collective communities, tend to integrate people and to include and embrace them in the social collectivity, western societies tend to be selective and exclusive in their groupings, and the free enterprise economy, by the intellectual liberty which it ensures and the misfits which it engenders, facilitates the rise of a certain class of individuals who are exceptionally prone to organise resentment and to heap abuse upon the system. A liberal education inevitably contributes to making certain sections of society unfit for employment and the earning of incomes that conform with their 'legitimate' hopes and aspirations, and is therefore a fertile field for the breeding of resentment. The class stratification, lack of 'organic' unity, and want of security in capitalist societies, and the presence of penalised groups in the western world have all contributed to the generation of friction and animosity. Jews, especially, have played a conspicuous part as decriers of the capitalist system, to the development of which they, as a people, have contributed so much. This attitude can no doubt be explained largely by the resentment of a penalised people, who try to assert themselves against the existing institutional framework of a society of which they do not feel themselves to be an organic part.[2] It has, however, also been maintained that communist teaching is Judaistic in a deeper, spiritual sense. [3]

Moral relativism. One of the most significant intellectual developments in the western world during the twentieth century has been the tendency to move away from 'dogma' and towards the assessment of the relativism of all values. There are no means by which the scientist can determine the superiority of some ends to others in 'absolute' terms; all that he can examine is their 'relative' superiority as means for the attainment of other, ulterior or ultimate, ends. But to determine which of several competitive ends is superior to the others is beyond the scope of science. The result has been a tendency in scientific literature to eschew all statements that express evaluations and preferences in absolute terms.

This withdrawal of science from moral judgments came at a time when all the important political values that had been implicitly accepted in the West were about to be subjected to their severest challenge and to categorical denunciation. This involved the principles that government should be based on respect for the dignity

---

[1] Friedman (in 'The role of monetary policy', *American Economic Review*, March 1968, p. 2) has shown that for more than two decades after the appearance of the *General Theory* it was believed that monetary policy had served its purpose. This view gave rise to the cheap money policy that was generally pursued after the Second World War, but which had to be drastically changed in the fifties because inflationary pressures could no longer be ignored.

[2] Cf. Sombart, *Der Proletarische Sozialismus*, ii, ch 5; Schumpeter, *Capitalism, Socialism and Democracy*, pp. 143 ff.

[3] Russell, *A History of Western Philosophy*, pp. 363 ff.

of the individual, should promote the greatest happiness of the greatest number, and should uphold the right of the individual to realise himself to the best of his ability in the economic, social and political fields, to enjoy freedom of expression and of conscience, and to organise for a multiplicity of purposes without intervention by the state. Thus science was left impotent to defend western civilisation by referring to the validity of fundamental principles. For there was no scientific basis for stating in absolute terms—that is without reference to a specific value system—that the new competitive creeds should be condemned because they were 'immoral', 'unjust' and 'evil'. Belief in the democratic political system and the free enterprise economy, like the belief in any other system, according to the new view, is merely a 'dogma' and an 'ideology'. It is, in fact, nothing more than a 'myth'.

This is the philosophical justification of the permissive society. A characteristic feature of this society has been the reaction among certain sections against the traditionally accepted values of western civilisation. The new ideologies are the result of disillusionment with the achievement of a culture that is considered as concentrating too unilaterally on material values, of a society that has become oversystematised, overindustrialised and overurbanised, and of a creed that venerates rationality, with its strong appeal to self-discipline, self-reliance, and dedication to vocational achievement. The new ideology appeals, on the contrary, to spiritual and especially to emotional values, spontaneity, permissiveness and the removal of constraints on personal freedom, and propagates general spiritual, moral and social anarchy.

These views represent the negative response to the challenge of the increasingly hierarchical organisation of society. A more positive and more universal reaction is reflected in the demand for an increasing participation by individuals at all levels of association: the involvement of workers in the management of business enterprises, of students in the academic administration of universities, of citizens in the way political issues are handled and things are run by central and local authorities. It is a call for a wider distribution of power and a broadening of participation by individuals in controlling their own lives and work. The claim is for a more even distribution of responsibility and a greater use of persuasion by discussion in the conduct of human relations and a corresponding diminution of anonymous, formal and impersonal methods of government. It involves the greater decentralisation of the process of decision-making, the reassertion of the worth and dignity of the individual, and an insistence on the greater effectiveness of democratic institutions.[1]

The socialist movement and the free enterprise economy. Ideological differences in the West have created a deeply divided society. At the beginning of the twentieth century there was still a broad measure of agreement in regard to the policies to be pursued and the types of organisation to be encouraged, an accordance supported by the appropriate institutional framework and ideological perspective. The free enterprise economy dominated the world scene.

Today all this has changed. There is an almost infinite variety of economies and polities and allegiance to systems has become fluid. Socialist parties of different grades of persuasion dominate the political scene even in the West.

An especially serious challenge to the continued effective performance of the free economy and the free polity has been the growth of a militant leftist trade union movement. Economically, by the imposition of excessive demands and the organisation of strikes it could seriously impede the efficient functioning of the

[1] Ways, 'More power to everyone', *Fortune*, May 1970.

self-equilibrating market mechanism. Politically, by fostering emotional and irrational animosities and by undermining the respect for justice, the spirit of compromise, and the maintenance of law and order, it could even become a threat to the survival of parliamentary democracy. The only effectual countervailing policy that conservative governments have been able to muster against these tendencies has been the creation of conditions necessary to ensure economic growth, together with the maintenance of high and stable levels of employment, the implementation of policies designed to extend the advantages of the welfare state, and the formation of a framework within which western societies could become progressively deproletarised and socially mobile.

Basically the free and open society is non-doctrinal, pragmatic and results-orientated. This is the reason for its inherent flexibility and accounts for its powers of adaptation and capacity for survival in societies in which there is the appropriate motivation and consequently the resilience of mind and temperament to effect the necessary innovational and policy changes. Probably an even greater potential challenge to the continued effective performance of free economies and free polities than the leftist labour movement, therefore, would be the growth among the middle classes of economic lethargy and an indifference to the assumption of political responsibility. It would indeed seem as if influential and well-educated sections of the upper middle classes in western societies are becoming increasingly bored with the generation of wealth and the attainment of national objectives and that there is a corresponding dissatisfaction among both blue and white collar workers with unchallenging and routinised work, both of which would threaten gradually to sap the economic and social strength of western nations. Ideological support for this attitude ranges from the growing popularity of non-growth population and economic theories to the spontaneous generation of world-denying mythical movements that present a new vision of consolidation, of harmony and of correspondence rather than of expansion, and a new hierarchical and antidemocratic system. It is significant that the world's first free societies were overwhelmed, not by external pressures, but by the gradual deterioration of the quality of the people and the loss of their will to govern and to create, with a corresponding proliferation of eastern cults. Western societies no doubt have far greater sources of inherent strength than the free polities of antiquity, but they will also be presented with far more formidable challenges.

26

The centrally administered communist economies

Historical background

The Communist Revolution after the First World War imposed a highly centralised administrative system on the Russian polity. A similar system was also forced upon the satellite countries after the Second World War, and was adopted in China after the success of the Communist Revolution and in a number of other countries both in the Old and in the New World. In all these countries the market mechanism has been supplanted as a means of coordination by central planning.

Autocracy and orthodoxy had always been characteristic features of the Russian polity. A perennial and pervasive centralising influence was exerted by the Byzantine Church. From the time of the Christianisation of Russia to the Communist Revolution—a period of nearly a thousand years—the Orthodox Church played a great and creative part in the history of Russian culture and the formation of the Russian state. As the only educational agency, it controlled the spiritual life of the people, and it became the chief exponent of the idea of national unity. When, in the late Middle Ages, the princes of Moscow undertook the political unification of the country, it not only took a direct part in the work of national consolidation but provided them with the theory of a divinely ordained royal absolutism, obtained from its Byzantine precedents. An intimate and indissoluble alliance evolved between Church and State, though the Church in Russia was always prepared to serve as the subordinate member of the alliance.[1]

A secondary centralising force, which connected the Russian with the Chinese polity, was provided by the Tartar invaders, who during their conquest of China had become thoroughly acquainted with Chinese culture and especially with Chinese forms of government.

Important factors contributing to the rapid growth of autocracy were also the constant pressure exerted by foreign enemies and the absence of a fully developed feudal system and of strong and prosperous urban communes.

The Russian polity developed typical dirigiste tendencies, and especially the creation of a centralised and routinised bureaucracy, functioning not in the interest of the public but of the state, and whose primary function was conceived as the maintenance of order.

[1] Karpovich, 'Church and state in Russian history', *Russian Review*, iii, no. 3, 1029.

A politically submissive population—a mass of peasantry living near the level of subsistence—with a small but assertive group of intellectual activists to raise resentment, an unprogressive and often absentee class of large landowners, the absence of a large urban bourgeoisie, and a government composed largely of conservative and routinised bureaucrats, all these factors combined to provide the ingredients for a revolutionary solution of the social problem. After each major international setback the weakness of the system was vividly revealed, but it survived because of the absence of a sufficiently strong and well disciplined opposition, with an alternative policy and a militant ideology. With the collapse of the bureaucratic system towards the end of the First World War this vitalising factor was provided by the emergence of the Communist party.

The movement of events in China followed a parallel course. The existence of a mass of peasants living on and often below the level of subsistence, the unequal and excessive parcellation of the land, the absence of an urban middle class, and government by a routinised and unprogressive bureaucracy of the scholar-landlord class set the stage for social conflict.

The position of the peasantry apparently deteriorated rapidly in the eighteenth and nineteenth centuries. A rapid increase in population with little or no increase in the cultivated area led inevitably to the excessive subdivision of holdings, to interest and rent indebtedness, and to the build-up of mass underemployment. The ruling caste of scholar bureaucrats and landed gentry were unwilling to initiate and unable to implement the necessary reforms, while the impact of western imperialism merely helped to highlight the helplessness of the government.

This society in the process of disintegration obviously required a solution of the agrarian problem, the replacement of the existing bureaucracy by a more modern-orientated and dynamic administration, the evolvement of a militant ideology to propagate the necessary changes, and the imposition of a strong centralised government to implement these changes.

The Empire was dissolved at the beginning of this century, but the new government continued to rely on the old bureaucracy, which effectively precluded the introduction of the necessary reforms. The Japanese invasion presented the conditions necessary for a revolutionary solution. It dissolved the sedate society, broke down time-honoured conventions, dislocated the existing economic structure, and created an atmosphere propitious for the generation of new values and new perspectives, which called for the implementation of new policies.

Mao Tse-tung's clear-sightedness lay in his perception of his country's main problem and the pertinence of his conclusions to the realities that confronted Chinese society. Inspired by Marxian and Leninist teachings, he had the ability to weave these into an integral but workable unity, to activate the peasant masses, and to plan the strategy for spearheading the revolution and creating a new order.

The Communist Revolution created an authoritarian socialist state with a strong central government patterned on the experience of Soviet Russia, with power centred in the party machine. Because of the existence of minute and hopelessly sub-economic holdings among the majority of the peasant proprietors, the government was able gradually to overcome the ingrained resistance of the peasants to the communalisation of their holdings. This facilitated the rationalisation of production and the transfer of massive funds from agriculture to finance the industrialisation of the country. The socialisation of commerce and industry presented no problem. Here there had always been a considerable state sector, which was expanded by the subtle process of 'using, restricting, and transferring' private enterprises to the public sector. A coordinated policy was initiated with the inauguration of a series of five-year plans based on Russian experience in 1953. As in Russia, there has been a unilateral concentration on manufacturing industry in general and on the heavy industries in particular.

In the rest of this chapter the analysis will concentrate primarily on the Russian economy as the oldest and most advanced of the modern centrally administered systems.

The centralisation of power

According to Marxian mythology each society, in the course of its evolution, must pass through certain clearly prescribed stages of development. In each stage political power is exercised on behalf of the dominant class. This process would, however, terminate with a socialist revolution, because eventually no suppressed class would remain to be exploited. With the emergence of the classless society, the state would therefore tend to wither away.

Although the withering away of the state has remained an integral part of communist mythology, all communist states, and especially Soviet Russia, have moved systematically towards a policy in which the maintenance and enlargement of the state's power and its centralisation in the hands of a dictator or a small oligarchy representing the party leadership has become the primary objective of government policy. This centralisation of political power was indeed the inevitable counterpart of the imposition of the centrally administered economy.[1]

The first step in the process was the centralisation of the state's authority. The fully collectivised economy had to be effectively organised on an authoritarian hierarchical basis.

After preliminary experiments, the Soviet economy took definite shape with the introduction of planning in 1928. Its dominant features have been the centralisation of economic leadership, the nationalisation of the non-labour factors of production, and the planning, coordination, and control of economic activities on the basis of plans worked out for the economy as a whole.

The administration of such a state requires a centralised bureaucracy. The whole Soviet economy can, in fact, be conceived as an enormous authoritarian pyramid. Within this pyramid there is relatively little communication horizontally, even between firms, but there is a large flow of information and orders in a vertical direction. Everywhere in the Soviet hierarchy, lower bodies have been subordinated to higher-information flows upward and decrees downward, and all decision-making powers have been transferred to the Council of Ministers. Lines of communication therefore tend to be long, with consequent delays in the adjustment to changing conditions.

Communist ideology did indeed originally contain certain important elements of a general democratic nature: the right to free assembly, free and secret elections, the inviolability of the person and of the home, freedom of conscience, of speech, and of the press, and the right to strike. But this 'humanistic baggage', completely

---

[1] The stateless society has therefore been conveniently relegated to the next world by the subtle distinction between 'socialism' and 'communism' (see first footnote ch 25). Lenin supplied the justification for the centralisation of power. The assumption of political power by a single dominant figure is vindicated by his knowledge of Marxist theory and the correctness of the decisions that he would take in terms of the prescribed course of history. Hence the infinite squabbles among the true believers over questions of interpretation of Marxist theology.

foreign to the requirements of a centrally administered economy, was dispensed with soon after the Revolution.

The process of consolidating the power of the central government in fact has had an important effect on all communist institutions, all of which have gradually been divested of executive policy-making powers and converted into mere bureaucratic agencies for the implementation of state policy. The first organisation to be stripped of authority was the Communist Party. This was achieved by transforming the party from an elective into a co-optive body, which ensured its effective domination. Gradually the Party as such, as distinguished from the party leadership,[1] ceased to be an organ for the formulation of policy and was reduced to a propaganda organ for the implementation of policy. At this level party members play the important role of mobilising the employees for the purpose of fulfilling the plan and of checking on directors to ensure that they act 'correctly'.

The assimilation of the other organs into the state bureaucracy was much easier: the army, the secret police, and the trade unions.[2] Finally, all professional, scientific and literary personnel were strictly controlled and mobilised to reinforce state policy. The expression of an idea that is in conflict with the current official, and therefore orthodox, line would indeed subject the rash concipient to the dangers of immediate denunciation by his colleagues and to liquidation by the state.

Objectives of policy

The objective of policy has been the maximisation of economic growth in general and of industrial growth and military strength in particular. Since the inception of the planning era in 1928, Soviet economic policy has systematically aimed at the fastest possible growth of industry and especially of the heavy industries, the mobilisation of a high proportion of national income for capital investment, and a corresponding depression of the levels of consumption, at large-scale training in technical, scientific and vocational skills, and at the attainment of economic self-sufficiency.

There is a unilateral concentration on the allocation of as large as possible a proportion of the gross national product to investment; a singleminded emphasis on growth-inducing and technologically well-equipped industries, and a corresponding neglect of the consumer industries and the retention of consumer standards on a minimum compatible with the maintenance of the efficiency of the labour force. The main emphasis has therefore fallen on industry as against agriculture, on heavy industry as against light industry, and, within the sphere of heavy industry, on machine construction, which is regarded as the ultimate determinant of the pace of economic development.

Administrative planning

After the Revolution, the Soviet regime had to decide on the future organisation of the new economy. Not only were all the non-labour factors of production national-

---

[1] The party leaders are, of course, also the highest government officials.
[2] The function of the trade unions is to press for maximum labour productivity in the interest of the economy. As the communist regime combines public ownership with executive power and the management of the economy, any serious conflict is conceived as treason against the state.

ised,[1] but it was also decided deliberately to reject the market mechanism as a means of coordinating resources and to resort to central planning. Planning, according to communist dogma, would provide the magic formula that would introduce order and stability and promote the rapid development of the economy.

Administrative planning was adopted, partly for ideological reasons, partly from necessity. Thus in the Russian economy today, all economic activities are, at least in theory, controlled by a unique system of instructions, which consists of the plan figures supplemented by prescripts, rules and limiting provisions. The system operates through a number of constituent, directing and controlling institutions. The whole economy is, in principle, coordinated by the central plan.

The most important economic and political instrument is the development plan drawn up by the various planning organisations in collaboration with numerous bodies concerned with the planning process. The development plan consists of a number of targets drawn up for the duration of the planned period. However, whereas the long-term plan is concerned primarily with problems of development and investment and represents the targets to be achieved, the short-term plans have to do mainly with the attainment of equilibrium between the supply of and demand for goods and factors of production, and transform the development policy embodied in the long-term plan into directives that have to be fulfilled. Since all these plans have to be closely coordinated and since the assumptions on which the development plans are based have to be modified in the light of changing conditions, planning is a continuous process.

The dominance of central controls under the Soviet system is reflected in the predilection for plans drawn up in physical terms. In its conceptual framework, the plan is simply 'a sum of administrative orders'. The tendency has been to conceive planning in purely technological and engineering terms by estimating production requirements on the basis of technological coefficients and by using physical balances to equate sources and uses of intermediate and final products. Thus the main instrument of Soviet planning is a very detailed system of material balances in quantitative terms—tons of steel, thousands of tractors, and so forth by means of which the supply of and demand for each product are equated and internal consistency in the short-term plans is maintained. It ensures that all the requirements for individual factors or commodities are matched by the available goods—a function that in the free enterprise economy is performed by the market mechanism. This represents the most bureaucratic of all methods of planning in the sense that all the constituent elements—output orders, inventory changes, or the allotment of materials to the various production units—depend on administrative decisions.

After the Revolution all effort was concentrated on the primary objective of mobilising the country's resources for the attainment of targets set by the government, which visualised the rapid transformation of the Soviet economy. Where a fundamental re-allocation of resources has to be effected, prices, costs and profits may, in fact, not afford adequate criteria on which to adjudicate the most efficient long-term distribution. In such circumstances the whole scheme may, indeed, have to be conceived largely in physical terms.

---

[1] Private property was limited to income and savings, some dwelling houses, household articles, and goods for personal use. Each household on a collective farm is also allotted a small plot of land and is allowed to own some livestock, poultry, and minor agricultural implements. Artisans are permitted a precarious existence. But it is illegal for a private citizen to employ anyone to produce a commodity for sale or for an individual to sell anything that he has not produced himself. Though these prescriptions are evaded on an extensive scale by semi-legal and illegal activities, they nevertheless profoundly affect the organisation of the Soviet economy.

The financial side of the plan is handled by a single monolithic State Bank, whose functions are mainly of an auditing and controlling nature. The money stock consists of a flow of credit in the production sector and a flow of currency in the wage and consumer sector. The objective of policy is to ensure that money plays a purely passive and neutral role in the economy and that the flow of money is, as far as possible, merely the reverse of the flow of goods and services. The point of contact between the flow of credit and the flow of currency is under strict control. The use of money, in accordance with Marxian ideology, is in fact restricted to a bare minimum and every effort is made to accelerate its return to the banking system.[1]

In spite of the compulsion and waste involved, administrative planning has succeeded in effecting the high rate of development of the Russian economy. It has had its greatest success in the basic industries: in steel, coal, oil and electricity—with outputs that are relatively homogeneous and inputs that are few in number and relatively easy to determine both in quantity and in quality. The misdirection of resources inherent in the system has tended to be absorbed by the general growth of the economy. Errors in planning have, in practice, been cushioned by the maintenance of centrally held stocks, by imports, and by the existence of non-priority sectors, such as consumption and agriculture, which take the brunt of shortages and have to make do with what remains after the important sectors have taken their shares.

A central problem of administrative planning is that a system of instructions lacks an all-embracing criterion of effective performance, such as is provided theoretically by profits in a capitalist economy. The criteria of the extent to which the objectives are attained in the Soviet economy—the so-called 'success indicators'—tend to be comparatively simple while the economy is still in a relatively developmental stage, but naturally become more complex as the economy becomes more sophisticated and mature. Thus, in a differentiated economy, a quota which represents the purely quantitative fulfilment of the target may be qualitatively unacceptable to the consumers, whether these be ultimate or intermediate. The cost at which the target is achieved would be another very relevant criterion of the success attained. As the results registered by these indicators are likely to conflict, it would become increasingly difficult in a complex society to formulate the system of instructions in unequivocal terms.

As the Soviet economy has become more mature, more sophisticated, and more highly diversified, the planners have become increasingly perplexed by the task of planning the interconnections between the enormous number of individual production units and products and of ensuring the internal consistency of the different portions of the plan.

> The sheer volume of work requires it to be divided between different institutions, or different offices within the same institutions. The supply plans often fail, at micro level, to match with one another or with the production plan, creating headaches and holdups at enterprise level for which the planners are responsible. Plans for costs, labour productivity, profits, calculated in yet other offices, may not match output or supply plans, or one another. Investment plans, a vital aspect of the longterm growth plan, are not properly geared into the current production and material allocation plans, so that machinery is not ready for installation, building materials fail to arrive, and there is an alarming rise in unfinished construction. All this is complicated by the fact that the

---

[1] Nieuwenhuizen, 'n Vergelykende Studie van Geldverskynsels in die Sowjet-Unie en die Westerse Kapitalistiese Volkshuishoudings (D. Com. thesis), pp. 360 ff.

leadership is pursuing several objectives at once; so that the priorities have become blurred or at least difficult to enforce. Thus planners find it remarkably difficult to give priority treatment to the list of 'especially important investment projects' which they themselves have drawn up.[1]

The centralisation of economic decisions indeed has certain definite advantages. But one must not be misled by the success achieved by the Soviet economy in the coordination of 'naturally centralised' production processes, such as the manufacture of space vehicles and war equipment, and fail to realise also its serious defects. The frequent changes to which the planning organisation has been subjected, the incessant demands of Russian economists for reform, and the reforms actually effected in the satellite countries and in Yugoslavia, are adequate proof that these defects are in-built in the system of the command economy.

The tendency in the Soviet economy has hitherto been to meet the problems of coordination inherent in the system of administrative planning by expanding the bureaucratic apparatus, rather than by attempting to improve the planning procedure or to effect genuine decentralisation through the market mechanism.

Considerable improvements in planning procedure could be effected through the application of modern scientific techniques developed in the West in the fields of activity analysis and operations research and in the sphere of programming techniques. But the effective application of these techniques requires as an essential prerequisite the formulation and imposition of a realistic, coherent and logical theory of value, which is basic to the problem of rational resource allocation and the coordination of economic activity. This can only be done if the planners are prepared to free themselves of the limitations imposed by Marxian theory.

Until comparatively recently the use of mathematical techniques was frowned on by the political hierarchy. Much work is, however, at present in progress in Russia on the development of information systems to collect and process data for planning, on the development of mathematical programming methods, and on the use of computing techniques and machines.[2]

Because of the size of the economy attempts have also been made to effect administrative decentralisation on a regional basis. The advantages that would accrue from such a process would be greater speed and fidelity in the transmission of information and the lower cost of its processing, better and quicker adaptation to changing conditions, the resolution of conflicts at a lower level, and greater opportunity for the dispersal of initiative.[3]

Attempts at administrative decentralisation have also been a characteristic feature of planning in the other large communist economy. Central planning in China, in fact, generated problems even more serious than those with which the Soviets had to cope. Administrative decentralisation here aimed not only at improving economic coordination by reducing central controls, but also at the more basic

---

[1] Nove, 'The prospects for economic growth in the U.S.S.R.', *American Economic Review*, May 1963, pp. 544—5.

[2] Thus there has been an elaborate expansion of nodal stations in which a very extensive computer capacity has been developed. The problem, however, is the assembling of information indicative of the relative scarcity of resources. For whereas the objective of the macromanager is to reveal, that of the micromanager is to conceal. This concealment has provided a measure of elasticity, without which the system would at times have threatened to come to a standstill. But the result is also that the information supplied and the instructions issued often contradict one another, and this problem may become accentuated with the growing complexity of the Soviet economy.

[3] Grossman, in *Comparative Economic Systems*, p. 146.

problem of creating conditions that would activate and speed up economic development at the most basic and inert levels of the economy, namely in agriculture and in small-scale industry. One of the major problems of controlling Chinese industry has been that of bringing an enormous number of small-scale production units, using widely divergent techniques, into a unified plan without entangling them completely in bureaucratic controls and thus stifling their initiative. The favoured method of attaining this end has been the granting of greater authority to local and regional authorities.

The difficulty with administrative decentralisation, however, is that the greater the latitude left to the individual plants or to the local and regional authorities, the more difficult it becomes to ensure effective coordination on a national basis. The partial decentralisation of planning and management may, in fact, do more harm than good by injuring the balance of the economy. Virtually complete decentralisation on a purely administrative basis would make the maintenance of mutual consistency in the various production targets impossible in a command economy. It is nevertheless essential that a proper balance should be maintained between centrifugal and centripetal forces. The problem of centralisation versus decentralisation is a real one even in the large private corporation. In the administratively organised economy it is a perennial, pressing and vital issue.

A more effective method of overcoming the rigidities of the centrally administered economy would be to substitute economic for administrative procedures and consequently to allow greater initiative to the individual production units. Thus, if freely negotiated inter-unit contracts and supply arrangements were permitted, the central planners would be freed from much of the detailed operational work that at present threatens to overwhelm them. Professor Liberman has devised a set of criteria for judging the success of an industrial unit by the profit it makes rather than by the traditional test of meeting assigned production quotas. By basing incentives on profits, following a drastic change in the price system, central planning, he maintains, would be freed from the necessity for supervising enterprises in detail and from wasteful attempts to control production not by economic but by administrative methods.

Such means would be effective only if a meaningful price system, which adequately reflects underlying scarcities, were introduced. In the Soviet economy the price and market mechanism, as a coordinating device, has hitherto been relegated to a purely subsidiary role, though it has tended to insinuate itself spontaneously along various devious and non-official channels. The prices of producers' goods are conceived as a means of securing compliance by the managers of production units with the plans drawn up by the planners, and of evaluating the performance of firms in the execution of their tasks. The prices of consumer goods are conceived primarily as distributive devices that will equate the volume of goods produced with the income distributed. The extension of costing to all the factors of production has also been seriously impeded by Marxian doctrines of value.[1]

In order to perform allocative functions, however, scarcity prices, and not merely accounting prices, are required. Only such prices would make it possible to eliminate, at least partially, detailed physical planning in regard to production units and the rationing of producer goods by administrative allocation, and make possible the decentralised operation of production units in accordance with the profit maximisation criterion advocated by Liberman and his supporters. At the same

---

[1] Spulber, *The Soviet Economy*, p. 36; Bornstein, 'The Soviet price system', in *Comparative Economic Systems*, p. 278 ff.

time scarcity prices would enable the authorities to allocate resources effectively in accordance with the planners' preferences. Since the function of scarcity prices is to equate supply and demand and to determine opportunity costs, the imposition of such prices would also be required on all the factors of production—on capital and land as well as on labour.

The institution of such a price system would, moreover, be of great help in the conduct of international trade, both between communist and capitalist countries and between the communist countries themselves, because it would enable the policy makers to decide which goods could be economically imported and exported. The double handicap of irrational internal price structures and arbitrary foreign exchange rates has hitherto prevented the planners in communist countries from making precise calculations of comparative advantage in their foreign trade relations. Decisions to import and export are therefore made largely in physical terms, as part of the physical planning process. Interstate commercial treaties within the communist bloc are indeed based on agreements of 'friendship and mutual aid', and have a political as well as a commercial objective. But trade even between communist countries takes place at world market prices, or at negotiated prices based on those prevailing in the free market, and therefore require the retention of such a market.[1]

Tentative attempts have been made, first in Yugoslavia and more recently in Czechoslovakia and other satellite countries, to improve the effectiveness of their economies by the institution of market controls. Since 1950 a movement has taken place towards the institution of a much freer type of 'market socialist economy' in Yugoslavia. While public ownership of all but the smallest production units in industry and trade and peasant plots in agriculture has been retained, greatly increased scope has been allowed for the free exercise of their initiative by consumers, farmers, and business firms, whose activities are increasingly coordinated through the market mechanism, instead of by detailed planning and administrative orders in physical terms issued by the central authorities. Prices, with some exceptions, are determined by market prices, and business enterprises try to maximise their profits.

Central economic planning in Yugoslavia operates increasingly through measures of fiscal and investment policy and decreasingly through direct intervention. It is concentrated largely on determining, or at least influencing, the allocation of resources between saving and consumption, the geographical and sectoral distribution of new investment, the degree of participation in foreign trade, and the distribution of national income between different groups of the population and different public authorities. This has however necessitated the retention of certain strong central controls. An important feature of the system is the high level of taxation which, supplemented by the savings of enterprises, provides the funds to finance a high level of investment.[2]

These developments reflect a significant tendency for communist economies of the advanced type to become more closely affiliated with the free enterprise economies of the West. The very strong ideological and vested interests in the Russian command economy that would militate against such a tendency should, however, not be overlooked. Many of the difficulties now being faced in centrally

[1] Nove, *The Soviet Economy*, p. 192; Spulber, 'The Soviet-bloc foreign trade system', in *Comparative Economic Systems*, p. 344 ff.
[2] Fleming and Sertic, 'The Yugoslav economic system', in *Comparative Economic Systems*, p. 230 ff.

administered economies are inherent in a system that is completely irresponsive to consumer preferences. A more rational approach to planning would require a clear break with the existing administrative measures, would involve the effective separation of the functions of government from those of economic management, the introduction of meaningful price systems for both producer and consumer goods, and the distribution of the goods through the market and not by means of physical allocation. It would also necessitate the elimination of arbitrary central commands and of interference with plant managers, and a much greater reliance on economic incentives.

Not only would the political leaders and the bureaucracy fear that a shift from detailed physical planning to more aggregative value planning would mean a loss of control by the central authorities to the managers of production units, who would tend to develop independent sources of power, but it would involve an important ideological deviation from the traditional Marxian conception of the 'anarchic' operation of the decentralised capitalist economy.

It seems more likely that the greater recognition of demand, scarcity, and marginal calculations in planning and pricing will come about through the development of mathematical models to implement planners' preferences than through a movement toward competitive market socialism. New concepts and methods will have to be justified in Marxian terminology—as examples of 'creative Marxism'—and their 'fundamental' differences from both bourgeois economic theory and capitalist practice will be stressed. For Soviet economics cannot, for political as well as ideological reasons, simply adopt Western theories of value, prices, and allocation. It must either adopt them, carefully reframing them in Marxian terms, or indeed discover them.[1]

Vested interests as well as the many basic ideological differences between free and controlled economies will ensure that any convergence that may take place between the two systems will be very gradual and vacillating. It certainly will be neither rapid nor dramatic.

[1] Bornstein, 'The Soviet price reform discussion', *Quarterly Journal of Economics*, February 1964.

27
The newly developing economies

Differences in income between developed and underdeveloped economies

One of the outstanding features of the economic history of the world in recent times has been the deliberate attempts of underdeveloped and traditionally organised countries to expedite their rate of economic development.

Economists during the postwar years became acutely aware of the wide gap in per capita incomes that exists between the highly industrialised peoples of the West and the poor and predominantly agricultural societies of Asia, Africa and Latin America. This awareness was accentuated by the fact that incomes expressed in money tend to overstate differences in real income and economic welfare. The grouping together of all underdeveloped societies into a residual and still more into a more or less homogeneous entity could moreover be considered as analytically suspect, because in many ways these societies represent highly diversified units as far as their aptitudes and attitudes and the nature of their social and political institutions and policies, and therefore their capacities for economic development, are concerned.[1]

Vicious circles of poverty as the cause of the problem and balanced growth as its solution

Characteristic of the immediate postwar years was not only the fact that the world became conscious of the wide difference existing between the developed and underdeveloped parts of the world, but also the dramatic causes advanced for the phenomenon of underdevelopment and the heroic measures proposed for its solution.

The central problem of the existing poverty and the potential progress of underdeveloped societies, it was maintained, must be sought in a series of interlocking vicious circles of poverty. The most important circular relationship is that which

---

[1] The fact must also be stressed that the emphasis placed on the requisite abilities and attitudes to ensure economic progress does not represent an ethical valuation. The qualities required to promote material success may indeed not necessarily be those that have always been most highly esteemed by moralists.

affects the accumulation of capital. This circle runs from the low income level of the community to the small capacity to save; this leads to a lack of capital, which in its turn engenders low productivity and, therefore, a low real income per head: and so the circle is complete.

As the conditions favouring spontaneous economic development are present only to a small degree in most underdeveloped countries, governments should, it is held, enter the promotional field in order to overcome the limitations imposed by the market and thus ensure more rapid growth. The allocation of resources can, as has been repeatedly pointed out, take place in two fundamentally different ways: by spontaneous application through the market mechanism and by the planned allocation.

Entrepreneurs under the price system distribute their resources on the basis of the marginal principle—that is, they invest new resources in such a way that marginal, or additional, increments cannot obtain a higher net return from any one application than another. In this way progress is obtained on all fronts simultaneously and equally, in accordance with consumer demand and the profit motive. This is the capitalist method of allocating resources. However, it is held that this method cannot, by itself, effect a rapid transition from an economy that specialises predominantly in the production of primary products to a more differentiated structure, unless the prevailing combination of circumstances is extremely favourable. It does not operate effectively where the economic system has to be coerced or jerked from a given distribution of resources to an alternative and fundamentally different arrangement, even though the new allocation may ultimately be of much greater advantage to that system. This is reflected, it is maintained, in the fact that the great development of international trade in the nineteenth century stimulated a broad growth of productivity together with a widening of markets in only a limited number of countries, whereas it left the greater part of the world in an almost unchanged backward state, with only a few isolated sectors of high productivity that were complementary to those of the developed capitalist economies.

As the newly developing countries cannot rely on an expansion of world demand for their exports of primary products to stimulate adequate economic growth from the outside, they must seek a solution to the growth problem in an expansion of the domestic market. Domestic markets, however, are limited because of mass poverty owing to low productivity. This discourages private investment in any one industry. The solution therefore must be sought in a balanced pattern of investment in a large number of different industries.

If all industries and, in fact, all sectors of the economy are developed simultaneously, each expanded sector, operating more productively with more capital and improved techniques, will provide the others with the necessary markets and complementary facilities. Through the diversified growth effected by the 'big push', a pattern of mutually supporting investments in different lines of production can enlarge the size of the market and help to fill the vacuum in the domestic economy of low income areas. This, in brief, is the notion of balanced growth.[1]

Furthermore, external economies are likely to be effected by industries and sectors through cost reductions or demand increases in other industries or sectors of

[1] Nurkse, *Lectures on Economic Development*, pp. 170 ff. The initial emphasis on the investment of physical capital as a means of rapid development must undoubtedly be ascribed to the fact that, in accordance with the static classical tradition, the state of knowledge and of the arts was assumed as constant.

the economy. Such cost reductions may result from the entry of economies of scale, from increases in productivity, or from the introduction of new technologies. These would raise the efficiency of the whole economy and thus lower the cost of differentiation. Similarly, investment in the necessary infrastructure of services would be socially profitable even though the rate of return might be modest, because it would make possible and profitable industries and sectors that utilise these services and that could not otherwise have been developed. Such investment therefore helps to induce economic development that is self-sustained and cumulative in its impact.

Limitations of balanced development

It is pointed out in the Appendix that planning on the communist pattern could probably make its most significant contribution in bringing about the forced industrialisation of a developing country. The 'big push' version of balanced growth is, however, likely to operate effectively only in countries that have large internal markets, possess large and diversified material resources and a favourable ratio of resources to population, dispose over the necessary political, social and institutional apparatus, and, above all, have the human resources necessary successfully to initiate and at each stage to complete the pattern of balanced investment.[1]

The less developed countries of the world today show marked differences among themselves. Some economies are small and have a very limited potential, while others are large and have diversified human and material resources. The economies of Africa and Latin America have, on the whole, a low ratio of population to material resources, while the Asian economies generally suffer from the pressure of population on the means of existence. Some have a high ratio of exports to national income and can therefore enjoy the advantages of international specialisation, while others have a low ratio. Above all, the underdeveloped countries are at very different stages of general economic development.

But economists like Hirschman and Myint have pointed out that the administrative machinery of most underdeveloped countries is notoriously weak. Balanced development of the 'big push' variety would therefore hopelessly overstrain the existing apparatus by imposing on it the burden of new entrepreneurial and managerial functions before it can effectively execute its basic administrative functions of maintaining law and order, providing essential public services and collecting the necessary revenue. As Hirschman has pointed out, the balanced growth approach makes an impossible demand on the underdeveloped countries by expecting them to provide, all at once, the necessary entrepreneurial and managerial ability to operate a whole host of new industries. But if these abilities were available, the countries would not be underdeveloped in the first instance. While a newly developing country should indeed aim at balance as an investment criterion, this alternate objective could, according to these economists, be best obtained by initially promoting certain strategic investments, which could indeed by themselves cause further imbalance, but which would generate the stimuli and pressures needed to induce further growth. The important issue is to determine the proper sequence

[1] The problem is that where private enterprise is scarce, the same would almost certainly also be the case in regard to public enterprise. Enterprise is a question not merely of the sufficiency of the supply of capital for investment or the availability of bright ideas, but of experience, organisational ability and creativity.

of investment decisions that would most effectively promote growth in the correct direction.[1]

Problems of development—balanced or unbalanced

Economic development, as has already been pointed out in chapter 19, consists to an important extent in the generation of sufficient savings and their conversion into productive investment projects. This requires, in the first place, the provision of sufficient voluntary or forced savings. It needs, in the second place, the availability of profitable investment opportunities into which the savings can be channelled. Finally, and above all, it calls for the ability to transmute the available savings into specific investment projects. Measures to stimulate economic growth can therefore be directed towards speeding up the ratio of savings to national income; to obtaining greater clarity or to programming the data in regard to the facilities that can be developed; and, finally, to facilitating the process of converting savings into concrete production facilities.

The provision of capital

It is usually maintained that, depending on the incremental capital output ratio and the rate of population growth, a rate of invested savings approximating probably to at least 10 per cent of a nation's income is needed to keep production ahead of growing population, so as to permit of a steady increase in consumption and to ensure the growth of the capital base of the economy. Even though this percentage may be exaggerated,[2] it would, except in exceptionally favourable circumstances, be very difficult for an underdeveloped country to attain a high rate of capital formation spontaneously and without outside loans, and thus to set out on the road towards self-sustained growth. Most of these countries are poor agricultural communities with low incomes and low standards of consumption. There is indeed often a surplus of agricultural labour that could be mobilised for industry without harm to the economy. But the effective mobilisation of domestic-saving potentials and their utilisation for purposes of economic development would require strong and effective measures, on the one hand to keep down consumption leakages and to improve agricultural methods, and on the other hand to channel the available funds into the desired investment projects.

Industrial development must be preceded by, or at least be closely associated with, the development of agriculture, for, in a very significant sense, the people who really have to finance initial industrial development in newly developing countries are the farmers. The individuals engaged in producing industrial commodities and services have to be fed. Unless agricultural productivity is rising, the feeding of increasing numbers of such people may not be possible without putting tremendous strain on the economy. The first requirement is therefore to increase agricul-

---

[1] Hirschman, *The Strategy of Economic Development*, chs 3-6; Myint, *The Economics of the Developing Countries*, ch 7.

[2] Incremental capital output ratios of the order of 3:1 would seem to be representative of both developed and underdeveloped countries today. With an annual population increase of 2 per cent, an annual saving of 6 per cent of national income would be required to keep per capita income stable. A saving of 10 per cent would provide a per capita increase in income of 1.33 per cent, which must be considered as moderate.

tural production. The second is to mobilise the agricultural surplus for investment in the other sectors of the economy. The third is to effect the export of part of the output in order to obtain the necessary industrial, transport, and service equipment from abroad. Each of these essential prerequisites is associated with a series of very serious problems.

The pattern of economic growth

Countries in the course of development from per capita incomes of under $100, a category which at present includes most of Asia and Africa, to per capita incomes of approximately $1000, tend to follow the same broad pattern of growth. The share of the national product that accrues to primary production tends to decline from almost 50 per cent to about 10 per cent. The share that goes to industrial output, which includes construction and the provision of power, on the other hand, tends to rise from about 15 per cent to nearly 40 per cent, while the share received by transport tends to double over the same range of incomes.

Economic development therefore requires the transfer of resources from·the primary to the secondary and tertiary sectors of the economy, which in a newly developing country as a rule also implies the transfer of resources from the predominantly self-sufficing to the predominantly capitalist sectors of the economy. This may be no easy task and the position will differ in different countries according to the ratio of population to resources, the international demand for primary products produced, or the means of persuasion or coercion at the disposal of the central government.

So far as the secondary and tertiary sectors of the economy are concerned, industrialisation and investment in the necessary social overhead expenditure have usually been relied on to act as the prime movers to bring about the required economic differentiation. But whereas the balanced growth approach on the communist model favours a crash programme and a big push forward simultaneously on all fronts, the unbalanced growth approach, which has been typical of capitalist development, represents the application of a smaller but steadier push or pull to certain selected sectors of the economy, which are likely to respond to a concentrated force sustained over a period of time.

The most obvious and historically the oldest method of selecting the activities to be promoted is to choose those industries that fit into an import replacement scheme and that can therefore be more or less effectively insulated, at least during the initial stage, from outside competition. Such industries must obviously be carefully selected with a view to market requirements and possibilities and the dictates of comparative advantage. They in their turn lead to further investment through the development of complementarities and external economies, and the income thus produced in turn spills over into derived-growth sectors, according to the requirements of income-elasticity. In this way, through backward and forward linkage and side effects, they act as growth points in the country's general economic development.

Small countries with limited resources and great dependence on foreign trade have usually been induced to pay attention to comparative advantage in the selection of industries to be developed. The larger the economies, on the other hand, the more the stress that has usually been placed on the requirements of balanced growth rather than on the dictates of comparative advantage. In large stagnant economies, without ready access to foreign outlets for excess production and the corresponding foreign sources of supply of income-elastic consumer goods and equipment, balanced growth would seem to offer a more seductive appeal for the rapid differentiation of economic activity.

Investment efficiency

The relation of a population to the efficiency of investment has both a quantitative and a qualitative aspect.

So far as the quantitative aspect is concerned, it has been maintained that the problem with most underdeveloped countries is that the too-rapid increase in population does not give enough time for capital accumulation or technical innovations to catch up and help them on the road to self-sustained growth. For rapid population growth both slows down the rate of capital formation and reduces the efficiency of its application. The crux of the matter, says a recent review of the relation of population growth to economic development, is not so much whether the world can adjust to the present high rates of population growth, but rather how much better the prospects for development would be if these rates could be reduced.

A representative sample of less developed countries shows that over 65 per cent of total investments are devoted to maintaining the level of per capita income at a constant level, whereas the corresponding figure for a sample of developed countries was less than 25 per cent. To reduce this gap, a developing country can either increase its national income and/or reduce its population. In terms of the resources required to achieve a given increase in living standards, these will be many times lower if they are used to reduce fertility than in any alternative investment. This is ultimately the basis of the need for population control.[1]

So far as the qualitative aspect is concerned, it is now generally recognised that the most serious limiting factor holding back the development of the less advanced countries is the deficiency of their human rather than of their physical capital. In order to be able to participate in modern economic development, a people must be possessed of an appropriate cultural and intellectual background. This involves, as a primary requisite, the breakthrough from a preservation-motivated to a profit-motivated society, and the development of cultural attributes such as the will to achieve and to create, and the affiliated characteristics dependent on personality and character. But technological development is above all dependent also on the practical knowledge how to run and service a highly sophisticated and differentiated economy, and the non-availability of these qualities results in a limited capacity to absorb capital in productive equipment. In the words of Professor Kuznets, 'the major capital stock of an industrially advanced country is not its physical equipment; it is the body of knowledge amassed from tested findings and the capacity and training of the population to use this knowledge effectively'.[2]

As essential as the intellectual and cultural attributes are the requisite political and administrative abilities, attitudes, perspective and vision. Economic development therefore requires, as a necessary condition or concomitant, the major social and political transformation of society as a means of ensuring the effective utilisation of its capital resources.

---

[1] Zaidan, 'Population growth and economic development', *Finance and Development Quarterly* no. 1, 1969. The threat presented by exponential growth to the world's resources is of course an even more serious long-term issue.

[2] *Processes and Problems of Industrialization in Underdeveloped Countries*, United Nations, p. 5.

The higher the level of enterprise and managerial ability required, the more difficult it is to overcome the deficiency within a reasonably short time. The position is the same with the complementary ability required in the fields of public administration and government. But modern technological development is also making continually more exacting demands for technically trained personnel. Advanced western technology, with the demand that it makes on the scarce resources of capital and skilled labour, is indeed by no means ideally suited to the requirements of underdeveloped economies. Nothing in fact is more symptomatic of the modern economy than the highly diversified and differentiated abilities that are required for its effective performance.

The size of the market

The scope for industrial specialisation and differentiation is determined by the size of the market. The small-scale consumer goods industries, processing plants and 'last-stage' assembly plants, which alone can find an adequate market for their output in most newly developing countries, do not by themselves provide the growth nuclei essential for modern industrial development. Such nuclei are constituted by economic complexes which, through their linkages with many sectors of the economy, stimulate the overall growth of the economy. These complexes must therefore be large enough, and the rate of growth in demand for their products rapid enough, to have a substantial impact on the entire economy.

Individually and separately, the markets of most newly developing countries would be too small to obtain the full advantages of development into the more sophisticated spheres of industrial development, which would provide the best opportunities for rapid and sustained growth of incomes and standards of living. Separately, with divided resources and limited markets, each might plan an autarchic national development based on import substitution, usually of articles in which there is intense international competition. Or they might concentrate on the increased export of primary agricultural commodities, or of a few mineral products. This would entail continued dependence on a limited array of slowly growing export sectors, on a few relatively high-cost consumer and construction goods industries with a low growth potential, on foreign economic assistance, and on uncoordinated foreign investment.

A solution to this serious problem could, of course, be sought in greater market unification, which would enable the planned development of a number of countries on a coordinated and integrated basis. But the organisation of such economic blocs always faces serious difficulties. Thus the existing infrastructure of services in each area would invariably have been conceived and constructed to meet the needs of a specific country or, at best, of a limited number of countries, and with a view to the promotion of overseas imports and exports. The existing infrastructure would consequently have to be basically modified and structured to promote the opening up of the bloc as a whole. Its formation would also involve the problem of the equitable distribution of the gains of unification among all the partners. Any durable scheme of cooperation would, in fact, seem to be doomed to eventual failure unless it involved some form of political union.

The role of the government

'The intensive study of the problem of economic development', says Hirschman, 'has had one discouraging result: it has produced an ever lengthening list of factors and conditions, of obstacles and prerequisites. The direction of the inquiry has proceeded from thoroughly objective, tangible, and quantitative phenomena to more and more subjective, intangible, and unmeasurable ones.'[1] One of these intangible but essential prerequisites of economic development is a stable and enlightened government.

The Second World War saw the disappearance of much of the old colonial system and the growth of political freedom over an ever-increasing part of the world. The rise of political freedom went hand in hand with a nationalist zeal for greater economic opportunity in countries hitherto organised on a traditional basis.

The colonial governments had concerned themselves largely with the maintenance of law and order and the provision of basic welfare services. In the economic field the activities of the state had been concentrated primarily on the provision of essential means of transport, irrigation, and other essential utilities. Direct participation in agricultural, industrial or commercial pursuits was rare, and the development of the import and export sector was left almost entirely to private enterprise. For the rest, governments restricted themselves to the provision of basic facilities, including information, education and research. But they did perform the useful function of incorporating the colonial countries in the world economy; as a result these countries were in many ways better prepared to meet the requirements of economic growth than some of the countries that had never lost their independence or had acquired it at a much earlier period.[2]

The newly developing polities tend to conform to authoritarian types governed through an administrative apparatus, with occasional caesarist links with the relatively amorphous and politically passive mass of citizens. The government thus tends to become personalised, that is, incorporated in the person of the ruler, who tends to lose contact with the masses and therefore to become very susceptible to the influences exerted on him by the various faction leaders within his party. But because of their lack of contact with the masses, and because of the weak institutionalisation of the government apparatus, the leaders are liable to be ousted by opposing factions. Hence the strength and the frequent interference of the army in the political life of these countries. As the only highly institutionalised and organised body, the army is indeed often tempted, and in fact compelled, to act as a stabilising force and to assume the function of a caretaker or alternative government.

Imbued with the objective of economic and social development, the new governments have all stressed the need to make the most efficient use of their national resources. Because of the appeal of socialist doctrines to the masses, who have neither the taste nor the capacity for an individualistic system with its personal dedication to the achievement of economic aims, most governments have indeed declared that their economic objectives are directed towards the attainment of a socialist society. But in none of the newly developing countries, outside the communist bloc, has indigenous private enterprise been deliberately eliminated. Foreign owned mining, industrial, commercial and banking concerns have however been forced in a number of countries to cede control to the native authorities,

[1] Hirschman, *The Strategy of Economic Development*, ch 1.

[2] Thus, as far as the tropical colonies were concerned, Arthur Lewis (in *Tropical Development 1880-1913*) has shown that, in spite of certain inhibiting factors, colonial governments laid the foundations of a social and economic infrastructure, sprouted a professional and middle class, improved their economic, legal and political institutions, and enhanced their overall productive capacity.

invariably without the payment of compensation. In all newly developing countries the role of the state, in its attempt to promote economic growth, has increased. But the sectors in which public investments has been primarily extended have been transport and communication, the provision of power, and in the expansion of agricultural facilities. Planning in these countries has dealt mainly with the major programmes that have to be implemented in the public sector; in only a few have production and investment targets also been set for the private sector.[1]

The important issue is naturally whether the newly developing countries will attempt to accelerate their future rate of economic development by adopting, on the whole, measures compatible with the maintenance of a free economy, whether they will opt for centrally directed policies, or whether they will espouse communist methods and ideologies to attain this end. The question is whether governments will be satisfied merely to create the necessary social overhead capital and the necessary conditions and climate for economic progress, and whether they will encourage private enterprise, whether foreign or domestic or a collaboration between these, as well as collaboration between private and public enterprise, or whether they will rely predominantly on massive government planning and investment to expedite the rate of development of their countries. This is an issue the effects of which will transcend the consequences of the economic activities directly concerned.

---

[1] Meier, *Leading Issues in Development Economics*, p. 440 ff. 'The pressure that international aid agencies have exerted on governments to prepare national plans and the priority that the governments have given these plans are misapplied. The priority belongs to building up a proper economic policy-making machinery and using it effectively. What is important is not to set a target in a document called a plan, but establishing the right economic policies and targets and then deciding on the action to carry them out. Once these are secured, an effective and realistic plan can be easily produced' (Kamarck, *The Economics of African Development*, p. 212).

28
The free enterprise economies of the West

The role of the state

Probably the most significant of the changes that have taken place in the western world during this period has been the increased scope of public action in the economic field. Whereas during the previous period the state had assumed limited responsibilities, which had only a peripheral effect on the economy, its functions have now become inextricably intertwined with the economic life of the people.

This has been effected, in the first place, by greatly expanding the controlling and regulating functions of the government. Not only have many new regulatory controls appeared on the scene, but the range of regulatory authority has been expanded into many new fields. The development of an elaborate administration has been both the essential means and the incentive for the expansion of these controls.

Governments have, in the second place, tried to stimulate economic activity by the extension of tariff protection, the stimulation of exports, the organisation of industrial relations, the provision of technical training, and the promotion of research. They have also become increasingly concerned with the more equal distribution of economic activity throughout their countries and with the conservation of their natural resources.

More directly the state has played an important part in the stimulation of economic activity by the direct operation of business enterprises in the fields of industry, finance, housing, and the provision of an infrastructure of services. Because of the many defects of departmental organisation, there has been a world-wide trend towards the establishment of public corporations to perform these tasks.

Significant, too, has been the development of a large range of 'mixed' agencies which, while individually constituting a slightly different combination of public and private controls in order to adapt themselves to the requirements of specific exigencies, blur the formerly clear distinction between private and public enterprise.

The important fact, from the point of view of the maintenance of a free enterprise economy, is that, although government participation in economic activity has increased, public enterprises are in most cases run in the same way as private concerns, and that their output and pricing policies are on the whole market orientated. Thus, while private businesses have tended to become more 'professionalised', government concerns have been granted a measure of independence approaching that of private corporations, and their approach has become more clearly affiliated to that of private business practices. The managerial practices and attitudes in the private and public sectors have thus become closely related.[1]

A third major factor in the economic development of the West has been explicit assumption of government responsibility to achieve objectives such as the maintenance of high and stable levels of employment and the highest rates of economic growth consistent with the preservation of equilibrium in the balance of payments and the containment of inflation. There has thus developed in western economies a 'web of mutual dependence which knits together the public and the private sectors of industry'.[2] Government activity has in fact assumed so important a role in western economies that its operations can be said largely to determine the general economic momentum. Thus, despite the primary role of private enterprise, government fiscal and financial policies and their timing now constitute one of the major influences that determine the state of employment, the level of production, and the rate of investment.

A fourth significant development in the expanding role of government action has been the rise of the modern welfare state. The provision of social services had its origin during the previous period. What is distinctive of the present period is the expansion in the number of these services, their rapid diffusion throughout the western world, and the transmission, through welfare services and pension schemes, of increases in the national dividend to those less fortunate sections of society that are not able to appropriate a direct share of the increased prosperity by means of their own earnings. By these means, and by the maintenance of high and stable levels of employment, the prosperity achieved in the postwar world has been diffused among wide sections of the population.

The scope of the public sector in western economies has thus assumed such proportions that it exerts a crucial influence on the way these economies function. The public sector spends between 30 and 40 per cent of the gross national product and accounts for about the same percentage of capital expenditure, and employs up to a quarter of the total labour force.

The appropriation by the state of such enormous tax revenues and their transfer to the public sector raise vitally important issues in regard to the effect on private enterprise.

In a predominantly free economy, marginal rates of taxation of more than 50 per cent can have a detrimental effect on individual enterprise and effort because the government becomes the major 'shareholder' in income attracting taxation above this level. So far as corporations are concerned, the major source of company financing has always come from retained profits. With high rates of company taxation the question therefore arises whether, especially during periods of inflation, the net profits after taxation will be sufficient to provide for the payment of dividends that will continue to attract new equity capital and leave adequate funds for expansion. The deleterious effects could, of course, be offset by generous investment allowances. The final effect would naturally depend on the socio-

---

[1] Nationalisation of the major industries, once a cornerstone of socialist programmes, would seem to have been largely abandoned by democratic socialist parties as a general objective because it can, by itself, contribute little towards removing the shortcomings of capitalist economies and towards the attainment of stability, labour peace, and the more equal distribution of incomes. It may, on the other hand, reduce democratic liberties by concentrating more power in the hands of the state.

[2] Grove, *Government and Industry in Britain*, p. 78.

economic yields provided by public expenditure and on the ability of governments to stem the pressures making for increased consumption and their success, in spite of the high taxation, in maintaining high rates of economic growth.

Private enterprise

In the field of private enterprise a significant feature has been the development of hierarchical agencies. It has, in fact, been said that 'one of the most striking features of western society today is the vital and ubiquitous role of hierarchical organisations'.[1] More and more areas of life are thus being subjected to the norms of rationality, limited and specified responsibility, and defined areas of competence.

In the large corporation, whether private, public, or mixed, the management tends to become professionalised. This has important social and economic effects. The objective of optimising profit—the leading characteristic of business enterprise in the era of the owner-entrepreneur—is still of prime importance to the management as a means of winning professional and social prestige and of ensuring the success and growth of the undertakings which they administer, but it is being increasingly supplemented by other considerations. Employer-employee relationships are receiving growing attention. Time horizons have lengthened and corporate policies are being directed towards ensuring future performance and management continuity. Long-term planning has developed as an integral part of the techniques of scientific management. Finally, the salaried management and the corporation it controls have come to identify their interests to a degree that is quite remarkable.

The large business enterprise has come to be regarded to an increasing extent as 'affected with a public interest', rather than as merely the private concern of the management or the stockholder. As such it is expected to conform to certain standards of public performance in respect of the quality of its management, its leadership in business innovation, the maintenance of adequate standards of remuneration, advanced methods of organisation, satisfactory rules of business conduct, and, indeed, the achievement of the economy as a whole. It is therefore no coincidence that one of the characteristic developments of this period has been the growth of organisations devoted to promoting understanding of the art of management and the growth of research into the art of management.

Another significant feature of the 'organisational revolution' is the increasingly institutional character of the savings-investment process. In addition to retained company profits and depreciation funds, an increasing supply of investment funds is being derived from institutional channels, such as life insurance companies, pension funds, state funds, building societies, and similar sources. This reflects the growth of the capacity for saving to be found among the lower and middle income groups, which are accustomed to invest their savings through institutions rather than directly through the market. It implies that investment decisions are today very largely made, not by individual investors, but by the managements of institutions, and this must have important effects on the direction of investment, the continuity of the investment process, and the stability and progress of the economic system. Above all it means that the market itself, so far as capital funds are concerned, is being largely institutionalised.

But here again the free enterprise economy has shown its remarkable powers of resilience and adaptation to changing circumstances. The creation of more func-

[1] Dahl and Lindblom, *Politics, Economics, and Welfare*, p 230.

tions of money and the more complete utilisation of each function have made banking institutions far more dynamic in their approach and operation. Commercial banking has become organised in a few large hierarchical organisations, but this has facilitated the rise of numerous specialised institutions, whose activities cannot easily be incorporated in the institutionalised processes of commercial banking. A very elastic credit creating mechanism has accordingly arisen, which can bring about a disparity between the monetary sector and the less elastic 'real' sector of the economy. The result has been the growing attempts of central banks, institutions exogenous to the private banking sector, to control their activities by controlling their liquidity. These attempts have not been conspicuously successful, with the result that these controls have had to be gradually increased in order to induce the financial sector to conform to policies designed to curb inflationary pressures. But, because of the highly diversified and dynamic nature of the financial sector, on the one hand, and the continuation of inflationary pressures and the pursuit of independent economic policies by governments, on the other hand, the problem is going to be a perennial and increasingly difficult one.

Technology

In the field of technology the most significant development has been the growth of coordinated and systematic research. During the previous period, organised industrial research had been the exception rather than the rule. Invention and the development of innovations had been the work of individuals. During the present period, these functions have become systematised and routinised. This involves the close collaboration of scientists and engineers working in well-equipped laboratories, the coordination of work performed in different centres, whether private, mixed, or public, and the institution of central public research organisations.

The most outstanding achievement of the new methods of research and development has been the harnessing of nuclear power. The cost and risk of innovation in this field have been so great that the incentives of the price system have been inadequate to induce the necessary response. It is significant that the great investment in capacity and equipment and the organisation of the necessary intellectual and physical resources required for harnessing this revolutionary form of power have been made possible and have been contributed almost entirely by government agencies. But even apart from expenditure on nuclear research, governments have today become the major source of technical research and development expenditure, and they have come to play a leading role in innovation in such diverse sectors of the national economy as agriculture, secondary industry, transport, and the generation of power. For only governments can afford to support the study of problems on a very large scale, and especially studies that offer no promise of specific or immediate commercial results, but which are nevertheless needed for the advancement of science and technology.[1]

A profound change has also taken place in the attitude of private corporations towards research, development and innovation. The discovery that specialised technological research pays is a recent one. But today it may be said that research has become a necessity and development a business imperative. Research has indeed

---

[1] 'The British Government supplies nearly two-thirds of all the money spent on industrial research and development—about the same proportion as in the United States. In France the proportion is even higher' (Shonfield, *Modern Capitalism*, p. 373).

become a major instrument of competition, research strategy having both 'defensive' and 'offensive' objectives in view. This helps to ensure that technological development will be self-sustaining and that the rates of innovation and obsolescence will proceed at a high level. Research and development programmes, especially those involving basic research, also introduce a strong inducement to subject all phases of an organisation to a careful long-range plan.

Private corporations and governments have moreover become far better organised for converting new discoveries into commercial propositions. The result has been that the average period intervening between the discovery of a new process and its application in industry and placement on the market has been greatly reduced. This is reflected also in the reduced calculated working life of newly installed plant and equipment, because experience has shown that plant becomes technically obsolescent much faster than was formerly the case. Research and innovation therefore create a built-in drive towards development that has greatly revitalised mature economies. The business community, and indeed western society as a whole, have accepted the idea of technological development as one of its major goals, and communist competition will impel the West to invest ever increasing resources in the attainment of this objective.

Research has also been directed to an increasing extent towards enhancing the efficiency of management. Originally aimed mainly at increasing the productivity of labour, scientific management has been extended to include all the basic problems of management. These comprise, first, the technical function: the division and coordination of labour, the determination of optimum working conditions, the scientific layout of the plant, attempts to make the productive process continuous, and so forth; secondly, administrative functions such as control, costing and budgeting; thirdly, the commercial functions involved in purchasing, selling and advertising; fourthly, methods of financing; and finally, the human factor in industry. In all these spheres the former empirical methods have been replaced by a scientific approach that first observes and records the data of the phenomena concerned, then analyses them and deduces conclusions, and finally applies these conclusions to the prediction of results.

These developments have had a significant effect on productivity. According to Professor Kendrick, at least three-quarters of the increase in output per man-hour in the United States during the twentieth century can be attributed to technical progress rather than to the formation of capital. European studies corroborate these views. These studies point to the conclusion that the rise in total productivity has been caused largely by intangible investments in research and development and in education, investments that have had the effect of advancing and diffusing technical knowledge, as well as by improved methods of organisation, such as the increased specialisation of workers, equipment and plant.[1]

A development that is likely to be of great and increasing concern to the western world in future will be the effect of exponential growth on the availability of raw materials and especially of energy resources. This will require directed and coordinated planning and research for the conservation and use of scarce materials as well as the development of alternative sources. Policies aimed at achieving these results are likely not only to involve economic decisions but also to have serious social and political repercussions.

---

[1] Kendrick, *Productivity Trends in the United States*; Williams, 'Technical invention—the key to faster growth?', *The Times Review of Industry*, December 1962.

Organisation

In a book published in 1932 Berle and Means found that between 1909 and 1928 the 200 largest nonfinancial corporations in the United States had increased their gross assets about 40 per cent more rapidly than all nonfinancial companies, and came to the following significant conclusion:

> Just what does this rapid growth of the big companies promise for the future? Let us project the trend of the growth of recent years. If the wealth of the large corporations and that of all corporations should each continue to increase for the next twenty years at its average annual rate for the twenty years from 1909 to 1929, 70 per cent of all corporate activity would be carried on by two hundred corporations in 1950. If the more rapid rates of growth from 1924 to 1929 were maintained for the next twenty years 85 per cent of corporate wealth would be held by two hundred huge units. . . . If the indicated growth of the large corporations and of the national wealth were to be effective from now until 1950, half of the national wealth would be under the control of big companies at the end of that period.[1]

This rather sombre prediction has not materialised. In chapter 23 it was shown that, although there was a very high measure of concentration in some of the sectors and sections of western economies, there was no evidence of a compelling historical force at work that led inevitably to an increase in the proportion of economic activity accounted for by the largest firms.

This conclusion has been substantiated by postwar studies. Thus Nutter found that immediately before the outbreak of the Second World War monopolistic industries accounted for only one-fifth of the national income in the United States, government and governmentally supervised industries for another fifth, and competitive industries for three-fifths. Monopolist conditions were most common in contract construction, communication, and public utilities, and were least common in transport, services and trade.

There was no evidence that the degree of monopoly had increased between 1899 and 1939. These conclusions were supported by the findings of Stigler and were substantiated by Adelman for the period up to 1947. The conclusions reached in subsequent investigations, though conflicting, seem to indicate that there is no conclusive evidence that the trend of concentration in the United States during the postwar period has been upward, and that there has been a diminution either in the vigour or the extent of competition.[2]

The stabilisation of the process of concentration can no doubt be ascribed partially to the restraining effect of anti-trust legislation in the United States. Major influences that have restricted the growth of monopoly, however, have been economic and technological forces such as the expansion of market areas, continual innovation, and the growth of the service sector. 'Compared to fifty years ago, the

---

[1] Berle and Means, *The Modern Corporation and Private Property*, p. 36.
[2] Nutter, *The Extent of Enterprise Monopoly in the United States, 1899-1939*, pp. 19 ff; Stigler, *Five Lectures on Economic Problems*, Lecture 5; Adelman, 'The measurement of industrial concentration', *Review of Economics and Statistics*, Nov. 1951; Kamerschen, 'Changes in concentration in American manufacturing industries', *Zeitschrift für die Gesamte Staatswissenschaft*, Oct. 1971. In a recent work, (*Enterprise Monopoly in the United States 1899-1958*, p. 90) Nutter and Einhorn came to the conclusion that, considering enterprise only and not the labour monopoly, and excluding the role of 'pure' cartels, there was no evidence of a significant increase in the extent of monopoly relative to either the economy as a whole or the competitive sector of the economy between 1899 and 1958.

economic scene has become far more open and fluid in such fundamental matters as market entry, access to capital, and consumer receptivity to new names, new methods, new ideas, and new products.'[1]

The problem with all the investigations hitherto undertaken in regard to the measure of concentration, however, is that static criteria cannot by themselves indicate the degree of monopoly power that actually exists in a market. The important fact is that a large measure of concentration does exist in the modern economy. Studies in regard to western Europe, Canada and Japan would seem to indicate that the process has proceeded at least as far in these countries as in the United States. At the same time trade unions have developed into a powerful and highly organised movement, with the ability to exercise a pervasive influence on the process of wage and price determination.

An important development from the point of view of the effective functioning of the free enterprise economy, has consequently been the growth of bargaining as an alternative or adjunct to controls exercised through the price system and mandatory price controls imposed by governments. This has significantly and to an increasing extent become a matter of negotiation among relatively few hierarchical organisations, and it means that policies tend to be shaped by the demands of those that are highly organised. Negotiations between management and labour are today no longer the purely private concern of the parties directly involved, but affect the economy as a whole: its price structure, its competitive ability, its balance of payments position, as well as the consuming public.

Competition between large concerns as a rule does not focus on price but on product quality, terms of sale, delivery conditions and other non-price dimensions. Oligopolists try to wean customers from one another not with reductions in price but with advertising, customer service and product design. Rivalry has in many spheres been intensified by rapid technological progress, which has increased the range of mutually substitutable products, by the increased scope of international trade, which has tended to intensify competition across national frontiers, and by improvements in the means of transport and communication, which have widened markets enormously in terms both of area and of population. The growth of oligopolistic competition in many sectors of the economy raises important issues in regard to the continued effective performance of the market economy in these sectors.

In the free market society it is the consumer who ultimately determines the allocation of resources. The first question that has been raised is therefore whether, under the conditions created by competition between the few, corporations still provide for the wants of the consumers, or whether they themselves create these demands by massive marketing methods and induce the public to buy the products they themselves decide to produce. The second question is whether the new form of competition ensures that the consumer will be able to buy the goods and services generated by the economy at the lowest price compatible with the continued flow of production.

In reply to the first issue it could be maintained that since the emergence of the Palaeolithic caveman economic development has involved the creation of new means of satisfying human needs. In defence of advertising it could be replied that, although a considerable proportion of the enormous outlays for this purpose does indeed consist of what Alfred Marshall referred to and condemned as 'combative' advertising, a very large percentage consists of what he called 'constructive' advertis-

[1] Max Ways, *Fortune*, May 1970, p. 290.

ing for new products, of which he approved.[1] The experience of advertising people also seems to indicate that factual, informative advertising is more effective than persuasive advertising in terms of sales results. That information about new products is essential is admitted even in Soviet Russia. Thus according to Mikoyan:

> The task of our Soviet advertising is to give people exact information about the goods that are on sale, to help to create new demands, to cultivate new tastes and requirements, to promote the sale of new kinds of goods and to explain their uses to the consumer. The primary task of Soviet advertising is to give a truthful, exact, apt and striking description of the nature, quality and properties of the goods advertised.[2]

In reply to the second issue it would no doubt be conceded that price administration does indeed try to maintain prices and profits higher than those that exist under conditions of free competition. But it could be contended that, if price competition tends to be largely absent from oligopolistic competition, there are nevertheless pressures that enforce a large measure of price discipline. These forces are the countervailing power exerted by large buyers, the massive chain of inter-product competition, and the greatly enhanced effect of international competition.[3]

It could also be maintained in defence of large corporations that they have usually been in the forefront of research and the adoption of improvements in management, production and marketing techniques. Thus many Japanese economists see the intense competition between large firms as one of the causes of the rapid growth of the Japanese economy during the postwar period.[4]

Finally, it could be contended that the concentration of industry should be seen not merely as a departure from the 'ideal type' of the market economy, but also as an attempt to adapt that system to the needs of the new technology, which impels important sectors of business towards large-scale operation.

The large corporation has therefore become an integral part of the free enterprise economy, bringing about basic modifications in its structure and posing a number of serious social and economic problems.[5]

Policy

Perhaps the most significant of the changes in recent years, from the point of view of the evolution of the economic system, has been the transformation of the function and role of government, and especially the development of new techniques of control, which has been described as probably 'the greatest political revolution of our time'.[6]

---

[1] Alfred Marshall, *Industry and Trade*, pp. 304 ff.

[2] Quoted, Ogilvy, *Confessions of an Advertising Man*, p. 147.

[3] Concerning Japan, Bieda says that 'The competition between the single-firm oligopolies and the multiple-firm oligopolies (as the *keiretsu* perhaps could be called) has reduced the costs, mark-ups and prices, but maintained profitability by increasing efficiency and the scale of operation. Indeed, the large firms and the *keiretsu* members do not try to maximise profits but fight to increase their share of the market. This business behaviour is called "excessive competition" (*The Structure and Operation of the Japanese Economy*, pp. 185 ff).

[4] *Ibid.*, p. 186.

[5] Cf. Heilbroner, *The Making of Economic Society*, pp. 112 ff.

[6] Dahl and Lindblom, pp. 16, 233 ff.

No doubt the most important single factor that has led to the greatly increased participation of public authorities in the direction of the economic system has been the failure of mature capitalist economies to ensure satisfactory levels of employment. The achievement of a high and stable level of employment was therefore initially the central theme of economic policy, along with the problems of inflation and the maintenance of international equilibrium attendant on the achievement of this objective.

Instability in free economies is caused by substantial changes in total expenditure: spending by consumers, investment by businesses, foreign investment and government expenditure. Changes in total spending effect changes in employment and the price level. As the result of Keynesian theories, it is generally agreed today that it is the responsibility of the government to ensure high and stable levels of employment by an active fiscal and monetary policy. Most western economies have been remarkably successful in carrying out this policy. 'There is every reason to believe', says Maddison, 'that the successful experience of Europe in managing demand represents a permanent sophistication in the technique of managing a capitalist economy with fairly general policy instruments.'[1]

The maintenance of high and stable levels of employment has however resulted in creeping inflation in all western countries. Inflation has been both of the cost-push and the demand-pull variety. Cost-push inflation has resulted mainly from the action of pressure groups seeking to further their own economic interests, with the consequent over-compensation of labour. Demand-pull inflation has been partly an expenditure reflection of cost-push inflation, partly the effect of overinvestment by the private sector on capital equipment and by the public sector on defence and social services, which has resulted in inflationary methods of finance, with multiple effects on consumer outlays. Policy measures have therefore ceased to be concerned exclusively with the management of demand and have come to influence the process of income determination as well.

The process of demand inflation can be checked by depressing demand by the use mainly of fiscal and monetary measures, though invariably at the cost of economic growth. Because of the importance of the cost-push factor, it has appeared to most governments that the problem of price increases must also be tackled by direct interference with the process of price and wage fixation. It is, however, much more difficult for governments to carry out an incomes policy than it is to control demand, because this touches on the freedom of participants in the production process to bargain freely and on fundamental problems of social equity. It is indeed true that the task of maintaining stable prosperity would be greatly facilitated if a way could be found to combine a steady and gradual upward trend in money wage rates that corresponded to the average overall growth in productivity. The process of price fixation through the market nevertheless requires a degree of flexibility, even under conditions of general expansion, to allow for changes in the conditions of supply and demand. The Dutch Economic and Social Council, after the failure of the Dutch incomes policy, consequently came to the rather pessimistic conclusion that

there is increasing unanimity in thinking that wage trends really depend on a large number of factors, which are so diverse that they cannot be reduced to a

[1] Maddison, *Economic Growth in the West*, p. 18.

single formula. . . . In determining wages, these factors can best be appreciated in the first instance by private enterprise. But this means that private enterprise must have adequate freedom of action in this field.[1]

This is no doubt true. The fact nevertheless remains that trade unions today represent by far the most powerful and best organised pressure group in western societies, and have the power by the exercise of undue pressure in the bargaining process to prevent the effective functioning of the self-equilibrating market mechanism. The strike weapon especially, which in a highly integrated economy represents a complete anomaly, can be used by militant and irresponsible labour leaders to disrupt the economy. Unless organised labour is therefore prepared to align wage demands to increases in productivity, the governments of free societies will be obliged to resort to the imposition of some form of incomes policy.

A prices and incomes policy on a wide front can obtain the requisite support from all sections of the population only if it is associated with an overall growth policy. Whereas in the 1950s policy was directed primarily at dealing with the short-term anticyclical problems of full employment and stability, policy in the 1960s was directed more deliberately towards the attainment of an explicit growth objective. Policy has been directed at the deliberate fostering of savings and investment, the improvement of education and research, the maintenance of effective competition, the stimulation of international trade, and the maintenance of equilibrium in the balance of payments. The result has been that the rate of growth attained in Soviet Russia only by the imposition of drastic control measures has been achieved by the use of much more general policy measures and with far less sacrifice by some of the more dynamic countries of the West.

The benefits of the prosperity achieved have also been widely diffused among all sections of the population. Under conditions of full employment and a rising demand for labour, average wage earnings have risen at least as fast as the national product. Deliberate efforts have also been made, by means of welfare services and pension schemes, to extend the benefits of the higher standards of living to those members of society that do not participate automatically in increases in productivity.

To be logically consistent, a growth policy must aim at the attainment of certain long-term objectives. This is greatly facilitated by the drawing up of long-range forecasts of targets for the economy as a whole. The policy of 'planning' or 'programming', which started in France in the 1940s, represents the most elaborate and detailed planning in the western world.

The plans that have been drawn up have been indicative, and not mandatory, projections of the optimum possible course of development rather than policy blueprints. They consist of two processes: forecasting the activities of the private sector and translating national policy goals into concrete patterns of government action. Such planning has two main advantages. On the one hand it establishes a target rate of growth for the economy as a whole and a projection of future output figures for the different sectors of the economy. This gives a lead to individual sectors as well as to units within each sector in regard to the assumptions on which they have to base their own expansion programmes. For the public sector, again, it indicates broad policy goals, especially in respect of their investment plans. Planning shows the interdependence of all the branches of the national economy and thus helps to prevent uncoordinated and ill-conceived action. It facilitates the application of investment to those parts of the system that will produce high rates

[1] Quoted by Shonfield, *Modern Capitalism*, p. 216.

of return by the careful timing of the interconnected capital requirements of the economy and the prevention of bottlenecks that may threaten to hold up development over a much wider front. Above all, it tends to promote economic growth to the rank of a major aim of economic policy.[1]

Economic programming is consistent with the maintenance of a free enterprise economy in so far as it provides information about the economy on a national basis and thus facilitates the effective coordination of resources through the market. The danger inherent in the system is, of course, that failure to achieve the visualised objectives might induce governments gradually to modify its scope by placing it on an imperative rather than a purely indicative basis.

Policies of full employment and growth have, as we have seen, been associated in most western countries with the problem of rising prices. The threat of this inflation to growth and stability has been not only internal but also external. In countries as dependent on foreign trade as are the western nations, and with export products that have such close substitutes, export markets are easily lost if costs and prices in any one country rise more rapidly than in others. Loss of export markets, again, leads to balance of payments difficulties, which may impede economic growth. These difficulties have been persistent in certain countries during the postwar period.

The western countries are closely associated with one another by commercial ties. One of the outstanding features of the international economy since the Second World War has been the institution of a system of relatively free trade between the major industrial powers. The result has been that world trade since the 1950s has tended to grow faster than world income, and the liberalisation of trade has, in its turn, given a powerful impetus to rapid growth in the West.

The liberalisation and expansion of international commerce has raised the problem of ensuring an efficient international currency system, which will allow world monetary liquidity to expand smoothly and automatically, as required by the expanding volume of trade. What the western world needs is an effective and reliable reserve currency in which to trade, invest, intervene in exchange markets, and hold part of its reserves, and relatively fixed parities between the currencies of the leading trading countries. Before the First World War this function was performed by sterling, adequately buttressed by adherence to the gold standard by the leading economic powers. Since then this function has been taken over increasingly by the dollar. But the role of the dollar as an international currency has been undermined by the refusal of the United States to subordinate its economic, fiscal and monetary policies to the obligations of being a reserve currency country, and the enormous balance of payments deficits accumulated by it over the years.

The problem of maintaining international liquidity and an effective international standard of value could be met by a system of mutual accommodation between central banks, by an increase in the price of gold, by the rehabilitation of the dollar, by the creation of a new reserve unit, and by the basic transformation of the International Monetary Fund from a credit-transferring to a credit-creating institution. Any workable solution would in practice require a combination of these methods.

---

[1] In Japan, as in the West, there are only moral or psychological sanctions to conform to the indicative plan. But because of the patriotism and discipline of the Japanese, the moral sanctions to conform are stronger. The 'announcement effect' of the national plan is therefore very substantial and private planners tend to use it as a basis for their own plans. Bieda, pp. 59 ff.

The urgency of the problem is reflected in the fact that a shortage of reserves may, on the one hand, lead to an increasing reluctance to extend intergovernmental credit, and in an increasing tendency to seek credit in preference to parting with reserve assets. A general scarcity of reserves may also encourage a tendency to make the maintenance, the increasing or the restoration of reserves the overriding objective of economic policy, measures that may take priority over other fundamental objectives such as the maintenance of a high level of employment, economic growth, and freedom of international trade. If, on the other hand, reserves are made too readily available this may discourage the imposition of the necessary discipline on deficit countries to bring their balance of payments into equilibrium and on all countries to curb inflation. As postwar policy objectives and international codes of behaviour require a high degree of liquidity but also promote continuous inflation, measures of currency reform present the free enterprise economies of the western world with what is perhaps their greatest challenge in the economic sphere.

New developments in political economy

Both classical and neo-classical economics were basically static, with their emphasis on the maintenance of timeless equilibrium and their predilection for *laissez-faire* policy at home and free trade policy abroad. Neither the neo-classical analysis of the allocation of given resources between various uses nor the Keynesian short-period analysis of the employment of given resources could form the basis of development economics. For this a dynamic long-run analysis of how resources could be increased was obviously required.[1]

On the basis of Keynesian economics, however, theories of growth have been developed showing the interactions over time and the relationships among macro-economic groups such as producers, consumers, and investors that have to be complied with if capacity is to be fully utilised and if desirable rates of growth are to be attained. Growth theories for underdeveloped countries have concentrated on the sequence of expansion of production and factor use in interrelated sectors of the economy as a whole and in its various sectors, rather than on conditions of general equilibrium in which the classical economists have been traditionally interested. Both in respect of mature and of underdeveloped economies, therefore, the earlier economic theory, with its exclusive reliance on the self-regulating price mechanism, its reliance on the stable-equilibrium approach, and its predilection for *laissez-faire* policy, has been fundamentally modified.

An outstanding feature of the development of economic policy in recent years has been the trend towards a more global orientation. In considering macro-economic measures, however, it is necessary for governments to possess quantitative data in regard to the most important relations of the economic process. Emphasis has accordingly been placed on the diagnosis and prognosis of economic conditions, particularly with a view to identifying the factors that may be influenced by the application of an economic policy directed towards a high and stable utilisation of

[1] The successors of Adam Smith and especially the neo-classicists eschewed issues of technological change by the simple expedient of assuming 'a constant state of the arts'—i.e. the absence of any advance in technological knowledge. This simplified the analysis. But since technological change is one of the most important determinants of economic growth, their conclusions when applied to practical issues were often unrealistic and sometimes ill-conceived, because the limitations of the assumptions on which their conclusions had been based were not appreciated.

the human and material resources of a country. Economists have aided the policy makers by providing them with the necessary analytical tools. Through the identification and projection of economic trends on the basis of economic accounting data, they have helped them to deal more effectively with problems of economic stability and growth. The development of fields such as operations research, and especially of programming techniques, has provided extremely valuable aids to integrating the macro-economic approach with the underlying micro-economic factors and relationships that necessarily have to be observed in the execution of comprehensive and effective economic policies.

The greatly increased share of the national product appropriated and expended by public authorities has given rise to the issue of the efficient allocation of scarce resources between alternative social ends and the effective provision of collective goods and services. This raises questions in regard to the comparative rates of return on intangible and tangible investments, both in the public and the private sectors of the economy, which necessitate the analytical projection of the economy into future time periods. Cost-benefit analysis represents a practical way of assessing the desirability of projects in cases in which it is important to take a longer point of view and to include the social as well as the purely economic factors involved. It attempts, in other words, to make an evaluation of all the relevant costs and benefits over a period of time and reflects the increasing importance of the attainment of social and long-term objectives in economic analysis and in government policy and planning.

APPENDIX

Models of free enterprise and of centrally administered economies

The use of models

The socio-economic systems that have emerged on the world scene have ranged from centrally administered economies on the one hand to free enterprise economies on the other, and from monolithic societies and polities to pluralistic ones. But never in the history of the world has the coexistence of these two polar systems been thrown into such strong relief, their differences so openly proclaimed, and their advantages and disadvantages as alternative methods of political, social and economic organisation so loudly, uncompromisingly and militantly propagated as in the world today.

The evaluation of socio-economic systems presents formidable difficulties because of the proneness of the proselyte to compare the functioning of his system under theoretically ideal conditions with the imperfect performance of any other system in practice. Unfortunately, also, the use of normative concepts in the writing of history is unavoidable, for language invariably introduces words that reflect behavioural predispositions and thus carry normative implications derived from cultural associations.

These difficulties can, to some extent, be overcome by the use of models. Models are simplified abstractions from the complex reality of actual historical economies. They show how a certain type of economy would function under certain prescribed conditions. Thus the model of a free enterprise economy shows how such an economy would perform if the basic conditions necessary for the free operation of the system—the existence of a self-equilibrating system of price-forming markets—in fact pertained, and the activating forces of economy could consequently function effectively and without obstruction. Models accordingly enable us to distinguish and compare the basic features, performance and problems of different economic systems, and they place in sharp perspective the alternative solutions of the fundamental problem of the coordination of resources in the economy. They also reflect the deviations that could occur in the different systems from their ideal performance because of inherent weaknesses in their methods of operation, and which in turn would induce governments to provide the necessary means of support or rectification. They also show the degree of success that could be expected from the application of these measures and the effect that this would have in transforming the character of these systems.

Model of the modern free enterprise economy

How the modern free enterprise economy functions. The free enterprise economy, in its pure form, is essentially a market-orientated and self-equilibrating system. It is an economy in which all economic decisions are based on prices and all movements of economic significance become effective through prices.

The free enterprise economy is essentially a 'demand' economy in contrast to the centrally administered 'command' economy. The decisions of consumers in choosing between goods and services, saving and spending, work and leisure, ultimately determine the allocation of resources between the various productive uses. The investment decisions involved in applying the factors of production to the satisfaction of consumers' choice—the determination of the types of goods and services to be produced and the methods of production, distribution and finance—as well as decisions in regard to imports and exports and the adoption of innovational changes are made by business firms. The coordination of all these individual decisions is effected in a largely spontaneous and automatic way by the mechanism of the market.

To describe the process as automatic does not therefore imply the absence of human volition, but the limitation of planning primarily to the sphere of the individual enterprise. There is no centralised, unified, and compulsory control of economic life. In the completely free economy, as contrasted with a completely controlled regime, there is above all no unison of the whole productive process by means of a deliberate, unified and mandatory plan.

Price relationships regulate all the major economic decisions in the free economy. Changes in price reflect changes in the relative scarcity of commodities, changes in costs show changes in the relative scarcity of the factors of production, and their reaction provides a sensitive index for the distribution of productive resources. Naturally, the mechanism does not function equally effectively in all spheres.[1] But in a broad way price relationship and price movements determine which goods shall, and which shall not, be produced, and regulate the distribution of the goods already produced. They draw or repel the workers necessary to implement these decisions. They also control the measure in which present consumption shall be restricted in the interest of greater future abundance, and regulate the distribution of investment funds between the various uses. A very effective system of coordinated and interdependent markets is thus provided for determining the allocation of resources, their conversion into goods and services, and the remuneration of the factors of production.

All these decisions are based on rational cost-profit calculations, a procedure that culminated historically in the invention of double-entry bookkeeping. All activities are basically focused on their efficacy in attaining the best results with the smallest outlay. This method of comparing means and results numerically in turn exerted an important influence in rationalising every aspect of life, from modern experimental science (the rise of which corresponded significantly with that of modern capitalism) to religious ideas, aesthetic appreciation, and the outlook on life.

Economic rationality in the free enterprise economy is directed basically towards the efficient organisation of the individual undertaking, the criterion of success being the profit of the enterprise. In this sense it can be said that profit is

---

[1] The limitation of the price-market mechanism as a means for the efficient allocation of resources in the case of industries subject to decreasing cost was referred to in chapter 25.

both the motive power and the mechanism by which the direction of production is determined in the capitalist system.

Advantages of the free enterprise economy. Production for profit explains the peculiar nature of capitalist enterprise because it is the factor that lends to the system both its democratic and its dynamic character.

The charge is usually levelled against the capitalist system that it organises production for profit instead of the provision of services to the community. In fact, however, the profit incentive serves as an important means of ensuring that the objectives of the individual firm conform with those of society as a whole. Since profit is the difference between value produced and value used up, it is an important criterion of net value created. Increasing net value means enhancing the national product. This is a socially legitimate objective; it is, in fact, one of the main objectives of all societies. Naturally, whether what is good for the firm is also good for society would depend not only on the objectives pursued but also on the services provided and the prices charged. Even in a centrally administered economy, therefore, the provision of profit must be an important micro-economic aim.[1]

The profit motive also has the macro-economic advantage that it forces production to conform very largely to consumers' choice.[2] Thus, whereas in a centrally administered economy the allocation of resources can be made to comply very largely with the wishes of the government, in a free economy it has to conform to the scale of values ruling in the market, as determined by the desires of all the members of the public that have the necessary purchasing power.[3]

The driving forces of free competition and business enterprise ensure that the capitalist economy is a highly dynamic one. In a stationary economy and under conditions of free and effective competition, profit—both total and marginal, and as distinguished from rent and compensation for managerial services—would tend to disappear. It is only by change and innovation, and by the expansion of the economy that profit can be retained. Continuous expansion may therefore be said to be a historically essential condition for the effective functioning of a free

[1] Cf. Grossman, *Economic Systems*, pp. 109 ff.

[2] It has been maintained by Galbraith in *The Affluent Society* that this choice is very largely manipulated and perverted by advertising. Since most people do not know what they want, manufacturers can produce what consumers do not really need. It is then left to the advertiser to 'synthesise' new desires—to bring into being wants that previously did not exist. Thus 'the production of goods creates the wants the goods are presumed to satisfy', and, 'since the demand would not exist if it were not contrived, its utility or urgency is zero'. It may indeed be true that people cannot want specific goods if they do not know of their existence. But economic development since the emergence of the Palaeolithic caveman has meant precisely the provision of continually better means of satisfying men's basic needs. And even in our so-called affluent society, if a product does not meet some existing need, no advertising in the world will create a demand for that product; the advertiser will, on the contrary, merely have wasted his money. Galbraith may therefore, in his turn, be accused of having inverted the truth, and that it is not so much advertising that 'synthesises desires', as desires that synthesise advertising.

[3] The general arguments formulated against consumers' sovereignty are that consumers do not know what is best for them, that they are unduly swayed by waves of mass suggestion and by advertising, that they unduly discount the future, and that effective demand is weighted in favour of the rich by the unequal distribution of income. As against these views, the supporters of consumers' sovereignty point out that the object of production is to provide for the needs of the people and that their preferences should therefore ultimately determine what is to be produced, and that they are in the best position to decide what is good for them—and certainly better than any dictator. They admit that consumers' tastes could obviously be improved by education, and that consumers should be protected against deliberate adulteration and deceit. Cf. Grossman, *Economic Systems*, p. 10.

economy. This was appreciated by Karl Marx. 'The bourgeoisie', he says in the Communist Manifesto, 'have played an extremely revolutionary role upon the stage of history . . . they cannot exist without incessantly revolutionising the instruments of production, and consequently, the relations of production.'

The competitive economy indeed has the advantage of offering unequalled opportunities for the exercise of individual choice, judgment, and responsibility. The consumer is free to spend his income as he thinks best, the entrepreneur to invest his resources in the fields that offer the best returns, and the labourer to work where he can get the most satisfactory return for his services. By a simple but effective system of rewards and penalties, the promises of wealth and the threats of penury, each individual is tied to his task. Errors of judgment bring their immediate penalty and their own incentive to correction. The adoption of improvements is induced by the competitive struggle for existence, which offers a very effective method of eliminating the inefficient and of stimulating enterprise, individuality, and self-reliance. The careful consideration of cost-return valuations is imposed as a continuous necessity. Finally, a semi-automatic and objectively determined standard is established for rewarding each productive agent more or less in accordance with the value of his services in the productive system.

An autonomous system of coordinated and interdependent markets thus has the advantage of spontaneous adjustment to the constantly changing data of economic life. This rapid and continuous adaptation of output to changes of demand, to methods of production, and to the relative availability of resources assures the maintenance of equilibrium in a highly differentiated economy. Through the decentralisation of initiative and responsibility, enterprise acquires an elasticity and vigour that would be hard to instil and still harder to maintain in a centralised bureaucracy.

The free economy has the advantage of a wide diffusion of initiative. Every individual, to a certain extent, is an entrepreneur, a planner and an organiser. There can be no doubt that, in a highly differentiated economy, a competitive system with a multiplicity of independent sources of initiative would be more conducive to the generation of new ideas than a centrally administered economy. Professor Hayek has advanced cogent arguments why, in a highly complex and differentiated economic structure, arrangements arising from the spontaneous adjustment of individuals reacting to one another through market processes tend toward harmonies too complicated for any individual to grasp, and are better than any that can be planned, because planners, however wise, must be ignorant of many relevant facts and, indeed, cannot foresee the consequences of their decisions. An economy based on individual freedom and the rule of law, he says, is dynamic. It allows both the proliferation and the testing of many varying and conflicting ideals. Progress is not towards a goal preconceived by leaders, whether well-meaning or power-drunk, whose vision is necessarily conditioned by their education, the state of existing knowledge, and the conventional wisdom of the day. A free society is complex, morally variegated and unpredictably progressive. Those who seek to bring it under central control, on the other hand, are necessarily reactionary: they extend the area of coercion, impose a single moral scheme in line with their views of right and wrong, and diminish the possibilities of progress.[1]

The free enterprise economy, in its pure form, also presents favourable conditions for the attainment of a large measure of political and personal freedom, though this freedom has throughout history tended to be very unequally distri-

---

[1] Hayek, *Constitution of Liberty*, pts i and ii.

buted between the different sections of the population. This is the result, in the first place, of the large measure of control exercised by the public over those who direct affairs in a system that relies on competitive price controls rather than on government prescription. Liberty is, in fact, best maintained in societies in which power is least concentrated, and private property and the market are very effective institutions for ensuring the dispersal of power in society and the maintenance of independent sources of power. It is the result, in the second place, of the opportunities provided for alternative sources of employment in the private sectors of the economy and of the alternative sources of information and leadership available in an individualist system. It follows naturally, in the third place, from the policy of the capitalist state of leaving things alone and of allowing people to live their own lives, provided that these do not follow an antisocial course. Hence the freedom of religion, of education, of speech, of the press, and of association for a large number of ends that the system affords, and the development of individuality, responsibility and self-reliance that the system on the whole impels. Where the scope of state action is thus restricted, little pressure can be exerted by governments to induce human beings to conform to preconceived patterns.

The free enterprise economy, in its pure form, finally, allows a very large measure of freedom in the international field. It allows each economy to specialise in the production of those articles and services in respect of which it has the greatest relative advantage. It allows each country free access to the raw materials of the world on an equal footing with other countries, irrespective of the political allegiance of each country to the area producing the raw materials, which under a pure free enterprise regime is largely irrelevant, the flow of commodities being determined primarily by questions of commercial calculation.

Limitations of the system. Spontaneous coordination through the market mechanism has failed to offer a generally acceptable solution to certain very important economic issues, such as the distributional problem, the provision of certain services, the maintenance of economic stability and the assurance in certain circumstances of a satisfactory rate of growth, and the attainment of certain long-term social objectives.

The unequal distribution of incomes is a reflection not only of merit, but also of opportunity, chance and inheritance. This distribution has remained remarkably stable in all modern free societies. It seems, for example, to have been much the same in the large commercial centres of the late Middle Ages as it is in the western world today. Economic inequality no doubt provides a powerful stimulus to the capitalist economy, both by the capital accumulation that it facilitates and by the spectacular prizes that it holds out to everyone, but that are, in fact, attained only by the favoured few. The unequal distribution of incomes, however, implies that choice may not always provide a fair means for the satisfaction of wants in the order of their importance because, as Robertson puts it rather histrionically, 'wants which cannot clothe themselves in money are left undetected and unsatisfied and the luxurious fancies of the rich exert a stronger pull on the productive resources of the community than the stark needs of the poor'.[1]

The free enterprise economy also may not push the provision of certain types of services as far as is considered socially desirable; or may tend to over-accentuate the provision of other types of services. This is due to the fact that some of the benefits which the firm performs for society do not accrue to it and that, conversely, some

[1] Robertson, *The Control of Industry*, p. 87.

of the detrimental effects are not charged to it. A legitimate field is therefore open to public control, both to promote certain types and to discourage other types of entrepreneurial activity, or to provide certain services on a collective basis.

Moreover the success of a system depends not only on its ability to ensure individual freedom, opportunity, and economic progress, but also on its ability to provide a large measure of stability and security. Here, however, we are confronted with another weak aspect of the spontaneous coordination of resources through the market mechanism. Because of the freedom of decisions by economic subjects in the capitalist system there is no assurance that the necessary correspondence between the various flows of money incomes and goods and services that bring about the effective equilibrium of economic forces will be maintained. These flows are the spontaneous savings of the community and the investment decisions of entrepreneurs, the demand for consumer goods and the production of these goods, and, finally, the stream of money incomes and the stream of goods and services. So far as the last of these is concerned, the asset function of money has indeed become of steadily increasing importance in free economies. From this function there has evolved a whole series of assets, with varying degrees of liquidity, in which purchasing power is temporarily stored. Changes in the liquidity preferences of individuals in the financial sector—their decisions to enter or to withdraw from the market—can therefore exert a marked influence on the 'real' sector of the economy.

Freedom of choice in regard to consumption, saving and investment may not only fail to secure the equilibrium of the economy at a level that ensures the reasonably full employment of resources, but may also fail to procure a satisfactory rate of growth for the economy as a whole. In a free enterprise economy saving is determined by the preferences of individuals, as contrasted with a centrally administered economy, in which the central authorities decide on what part of the national income should be used for investment purposes. But since it is consumer satisfaction rather than consumer sovereignty that is the essence of economic welfare, it may be necessary in the interests of the consumers themselves to secure larger future resources by a measure of forced saving, rather than greater immediate satisfaction by the exercising of free consumer choice. Growth may therefore conflict at certain points with consumer sovereignty.[1]

Finally, it is not merely in regard to the maximisation of the national product over a period of time and the problems associated with the attainment of this objective that a system of private preferences may be found wanting, but also in the achievement of certain long-term social objectives. Because of the limited time horizons of individuals, the market, which is a reflection of the way in which people spontaneously value their individual wants and services, may in fact not be an adequate means of evaluating their real long-term requirements over an extended field of social experience. It may therefore be necessary to supplement the spontaneous decisions of individuals by those made by organised society on the basis of long-term planning.

Necessity for the provision of certain controls in the free enterprise economy. In the model of the pure free enterprise economy government intervention would be absent or negligible. Because of the factors mentioned above, however, certain services in all free enterprise economies have had to be provided by group decisions that operate through the political process, rather than by individual decisions determined by the market mechanism. These services fall into two main categories: on

[1] Wiles, 'Growth versus choice', *Comparative Economic Systems*, pp. 19 ff.

the one hand there is the provision of communal wants for which prices either cannot or ought not to be charged, or services that are needed for the attainment of certain social objectives; on the other hand there are measures designed to ensure that the functions of private economies are properly regulated. Among the former is the provision of defence, police protection, educational facilities, or other types of social overheads, and the achievement of long-term social goals; among the latter, measures designed to ensure the effective functioning of the system of private enterprise, such as the maintenance of healthy credit conditions, of aggregate demand at a suitable level, or of a suitable degree of competitiveness in the economy. The nature and scope of these activities would vary in different societies and in the same societies at different times, and it would obviously be impossible to determine *a priori* how far they could proceed without undermining the basic conditions for the survival of the free enterprise economy. In general it can be said that the regulation of private economic activity should concentrate on procedures rather than on substantive issues, should be indirect rather than direct, and should support the forces of the market rather than interfere with their effective operation.[1]

The tendency in the western world in recent times for more and more market functions to be taken over by administrative processes, which impede the elasticity of response of the market mechanism and penalise its functioning procedures, therefore poses serious problems in regard to the continued effective performance of free enterprise economies.[2] The increasing involvement and participation by governments in economic affairs at the same time raise issues in regard to the ability of political institutions that evolved under conditions of *laissez-faire* to subject the growing government bureaucracies to effective democratic control, and the ways in which individuals can be adequately protected against the growing range and penetrating power of public authority and given a more effective participation in controlling this authority and their own destinies. But, finally, it also raises the problem of eliciting the vision and planning required to effect the coordination between the public and private sectors to ensure the attainment of long-range social objectives.

---

[1] Direct controls are those that order, permit or forbid certain specific economic measures or activities, whereas *indirect controls* are those that create situations, by means of fiscal or monetary measures, which encourage or induce businessmen to pursue certain courses of action and dissuade them from engaging in others, because market conditions render the former profitable and the latter unprofitable.

[2] For, besides the factors mentioned in the previous paragraph, 'there seems to be in human societies a set of social and psychological factors favouring intervention in the market. . . . One of them is the impatience of idealists and would-be reformers with the working of the market, and their desire to take direct action to improve things, according to their criteria of improvement: this attitude reflects the intellectual arrogance typical of reformers. The attitude is reinforced by the fact that the defects of market organisation seem obvious to anyone, or can be made to seem so, whereas the socio-economic functions of the market are obscure and difficult to appreciate' (Harry G. Johnson, 'Planning and the market in economic development', in *Comparative Economic Systems*, pp. 427 ff).

Supporters of the free enterprise economy have indeed expressed the fear that, because of the tendency to extend administrative controls to meet specific exigencies, the capitalist system could gradually be converted into a socialist regime by the subtle process of *inadvertent transformation*.

Model of the modern centrally administered economy

How the modern centrally administered economy functions. The centrally administered economy is a command economy. The material means of production are owned by the state and are used by the government for whatever purpose it may be deemed advisable or expedient to use the resources at its disposal. The preference functions of the leaders and not the preference functions of consumers determine the allocation of resources. Since the productive resources are owned and operated by the state, all the decisions made in the free enterprise economy by entrepreneurs on the basis of the market mechanism are made by the government on the basis of an all-embracing plan, and are issued as administrative commands.

The completely controlled, like the completely free, economy of course represents a limiting case. Between these two extreme types of economic organisation many intermediate forms are conceivable. One such form would be a socialist market economy, which would attempt to combine conscious social planning with consumers' sovereignty. A model of a perfectly competitive socialist economy has been conceived by economists in which static efficiency would be achieved by means of the market mechanism. The individual socialist firms would compete with one another and the allocation of resources would ultimately be determined by free consumer choice. But consumers' sovereignty would naturally be effective in directing the allocation of resources in a 'socialist market' only if price systems were established which were determined primarily by the forces of supply and demand, and if adequate incentives were introduced to induce the productive and distributive units of the economy to respond to market requirements. If this could be achieved, an ideal socialist market economy would function very similarly to a free enterprise economy under conditions of perfect competition. Unfortunately, both of these exist only as the figments of the imagination of economists.

In the centrally administered economy reliance is not placed on market forces to ensure that what is needed is available 'at the right time, at the right place, and in the right quantities'. The allocative function, on the contrary, is fulfilled primarily on the basis of a unified and all-inclusive plan, which coordinates all the activities of the economy.

The first problem of planning is to ensure the correct balance in the use of the existing means of production. It has to ensure that the available productive resources are effectively employed and that they are distributed between the different sectors of the economy and within each sector in such a way that the correct proportions are observed in the output of the different branches of the economy. Thus each sector and each unit within each sector has to be given the means to fulfil its share of the planned production, and the quota allocated to each unit has to be aligned with those of all the other units. All these activities have to be coordinated by the plan in such a way that the creation of bottlenecks, on the one hand, and of unemployment, on the other hand, is eliminated.

The second task of the planned economy is to determine the appropriate rate of consumption and of capital formation, that is, to determine the rate at which the economy is to expand. Economic expansion can, in fact, be conceived as the result of a number of development decisions. These comprise decisions in regard to investment, research, technical education, organisation, the siting of services, policy, and so forth. In the free enterprise economy these decisions are made by numerous independent units, each of which has to make its investment decisions more or less in isolation from one another. A given market situation is the effect of all the previous independent decisions and in turn influences all future decisions. But investment decisions are based on future expectations and because no unit is able to predict the activities of all the other units with sufficient accuracy over any future period of time, even the most carefully planned decisions of entrepreneurs, when eventually tested in the market, may have resulted in the misallocation of resources. In the centrally administered system, on the other hand, all the means of production belong to the state, and the development must therefore be directed by deliberate state policy on the basis of centrally established priorities. Consequently it is theoretically possible to substitute for the *ex post* coordination brought about, often tardily and wastefully, by the fluctuations of the market, the *ex ante* coordination of the constituent elements in the development scheme.[1] Hence the ability and, in fact, the necessity for such an economy to plan for a considerable period in advance in order to achieve its long-term objectives.

Problems of central planning. But because the coordination of resources in the capitalist economy is obtained through the market mechanism, the individual enterprise is faced with a limited range of problems: to determine the nature and scope of its activity within a given price and cost structure.

One of the most difficult problems of capitalist enterprise and one that absorbs a not inconsiderable proportion of the energies of businessmen, as has been pointed out, is associated with the uncertainties that surround every decision. For the factors are unknown not only on the demand but also on the supply side. Every businessman usually has to act more or less in ignorance of the reactions, actual or potential, of his competitors. In a socialist economy, on the other hand, it is maintained, every central administrative decision is taken with the full knowledge of all other relevant decisions, because these all emanate from or are woven into the pattern of the planned economy. In fact, however, the centrally administered economy is faced with a far more formidable task—that of ensuring the effective coordination of all the country's resources.

In a comparatively simple economy, such as that of Ancient Egypt, this task should not have been an unduly onerous one. The inputs were comparatively few in number and relatively easy to determine both in quantity and in quality, the outputs were comparatively homogeneous in nature, and the flow of information to the central authority gave it reasonably trustworthy data on which to base its decisions. In the modern world, planning on the communist model has made its most significant contribution as an instrument for effecting the rapid industrialisation of the Soviet economy. In such an economy the objectives could be clearly determined, the necessary techniques could be adopted from the developed countries, the inputs and outputs were relatively uniform and easy to determine, and the demand was amenable to prediction, since it was dependent largely on the planner's own decisions.

But in the measure that an economy becomes more differentiated, the problems of central planning are accentuated because of the rapid increase in the number of planned interconnections. In the modern mature economy the inputs and outputs of thousands of individual enterprises have to be coordinated. To ensure the internal consistency of the plan under such circumstances becomes a formidable task indeed. Plans of costs, profits and productivity have to fit in with output allocations; investment plans have to be geared to the current production and material allocation plans; priorities for all spheres have to be carefully determined by the central authority. Planning, in fact, has to succeed in

[1] Dobb, *Soviet Economic Development*, p. 9.

fitting together in an immensely complex pattern the intricate economic inter-relationships between all the undertakings and organisations engaged in trans-lating paper directives into the realities of steel, paper, bricks, and the thousands of other commodities needed in a modern and increasingly sophisticated society.[1]

The sheer mass of the planning effort in a mature command economy may indeed necessitate all the effort of the planners being devoted to striving for the mere physical balance between the various resources, leaving little or no oppor-tunity for attending to their efficient allocation. It has been maintained that

> Coordinative planning as it is conducted in the Soviet Union does little by way of consciously steering the economy's development or finding efficient patterns of resource allocation. Its overwhelming concern is simply to equate both sides of each 'material balance' by whatever procedure seems to be most expeditious. It is apparently conducted with little reference to systematic, rational rules of choice or definite notions of efficiency. The concepts of economic calculation, efficiency, and optimality have been virtually absent from Soviet economics until recently. In any case, rational rules of choice would have been difficult to incorporate into the primitive, 'manual' procedure of adjusting the thousands of material balances simultaneously.[2]

Limited possibilities of administrative decentralisation. The difficulties involved in the central coordination of economic activity could be overcome by a greater measure of administrative decentralisation. The advantages of such a solution, as listed by Grossman, would be greater speed and fidelity in the transmission of information, a lesser volume and lower cost involved in the processing of informa-tion, a faster and better adaptation to changing circumstances, the resolution of conflicts at lower levels, and greater opportunities for the exercise of initiative in bringing about improvements and innovation. [3]

The problem with the administrative coordination of resources, however, is that central planning inevitably leads to the centralisation of authority and the taking of decisions, and requires the adherence of all the productive and distributive units to a rigid plan, with little scope for independent localised action and initiative. Only the central authority is able to adjudicate on the requirements of the economy and of society as a whole. Decentralised authorities—territorial bodies, trusts, or individual enterprises, charged with carrying out the plans—would naturally be ignorant of the overall impact of their decisions and actions on the economy. Greater decentralisation of decisions and activity therefore offers no easy panacea for the problems of the centrally administered economy.

Partial use of the market mechanism. A more effective method of decentralising decisions and initiative would of course be to relax the rigidities of central planning by resorting, at least partly, to the coordinating functions of the market mech-anism. This would, however, involve a serious encroachment on purely administra-tive practices, the curtailment of government dictation to economic management, the introduction of price systems reflecting underlying scarcities, and more recourse to economic incentives. It would, in fact, involve the partial displacement of the centrally administered by the socialist market economy.

[1] Miller *et al., Communist Economy Under Change,* pp. 21 ff.
[2] Grossman, 'Notes for a theory of the command economy', in *Comparative Economic Systems,* p. 142.
[3] *Ibid.,* p. 146.

The only feasible method of reconciling improvements in the efficiency of planning with the retention of the command economy, therefore, would be to perfect the techniques of central planning. These techniques could be greatly assisted by advances made since the war in the fields of activity analysis and operations research and the development of programming techniques. The application of these techniques would require the formulation and imposition of a logical, coherent and realistic system of values.

Stages in the development of the command economy. Three stages of development could be visualised in the provision of consumer goods in a command economy. In the first stage the consumers would be allowed to exercise their choice only in regard to such goods and in such quantities as the planners decide to make available to them, on a 'take it or leave it' basis. This would involve the permanent retention of a sellers' market in which the planners could dictate the nature and quality of the goods provided. Thus in Soviet Russia, where consumer goods have been deliberately kept in short supply, the basic mechanism of adjustment to a disequilibrium in the market for a particular article has been to adjust the demand to the supply, as contrasted with the adjustment of supply to demand, which would be the characteristic procedure in a capitalist economy.[1]

But in the measure that the economy succeeds in supplying more and more differentiated goods to consumers, a buyers' market would start to develop. The distributive agencies would therefore obtain a stronger bargaining position, because inventories of unwanted goods would simply accumulate on the shelves of shops and factories. In such an economy, therefore, consumer preferences would also be allowed to influence the types and quality of the goods that are produced, with resources made available by the planners, in the existing plants that produce consumer goods. This is the stage now being attained in eastern European countries.

The final stage would be reached in a mature command economy. The characteristic feature of such an economy would be the great proliferation of goods, and especially durable consumer goods, made available to the public. This would find its counterpart in the pattern of new investments in the plants that produce consumer goods, which would have to respond to consumer demand. Such a development would of course expose the command economy to the influences of consumer preferences, though the planners' preferences would still determine the overall magnitude of consumption, that is, the share of the national product devoted to consumption and the amount of investment made available to consumer goods industries.[2]

The allocation of producer goods. As regards producer goods, administrative planners have shown a predilection for the physical allocation of resources, which dispenses with the price mechanism in the allocation of resources. Prices do not express relative scarcities in such a system, but serve only accounting purposes. But in a highly differentiated economy the efficient allocation of the existing resources

---

[1] 'The quality of consumer goods has been consistently poor. For all its productive power, for all its feats in space, the Soviet economy seems unable to produce a doorknob that always turns, a door that closes properly, a light fixture that works on the first try, a toilet that flushes consistently. The average Russian's clothes are shabby, ill-fitting and expensive; it takes half a month's wages to buy a pair of shoes. His diet is dependent on the seasons and painfully monotonous' (*Time*, 10 November 1967).

[2] Drewnowski, in *Comparative Economic Systems*, pp. 117 ff; Bornstein, 'The Soviet price system', *American Economic Review*, March 1962, p. 90.

cannot be carried out on the basis of physical allocations alone. A meaningful price system, which reflects the underlying scarcities of the factors of production, is necessary to evaluate the competing requirements of different sectors of the economy as well as to measure the efficiency of individual firms and to ensure consistency and rationality in internal accounting. Without accurate pricing no comprehensive planning programme can be consistently and efficiently carried out in a complex economy.

Russian mathematical economists are becoming increasingly aware of the fact that the most pressing economic problem in the Soviet Union is to find a means of determining the optimum allocation of resources and of signalling relative scarcities to the planning authorities. They are reaching the conclusion that this can be attained only by means of some form of market simulation. This will, of course, entail the collection, collation and analysis of an enormous mass of economic data. But above all it will require the formulation of a realistic, logical and consistent theory of value.[1]

The rate of investment. An issue that is no doubt of even greater significance than the rational allocation of the existing resources is the question of the rate of progress to be attained by the controlled economy. Rapid growth, it has been maintained, can provide consumer satisfaction without consumer sovereignty, and can diminish the harm done by the violation not only of customers' sovereignty but also of the misallocation of resources by providing in due course the means of material plenty.[2]

Economic growth is a question of the *dynamic*, as contrasted with the *static*, efficiency of a system. Assuming a given state of technical efficiency, static economic efficiency assures the effective allocation of the available resources of an economy at a given point of time. Dynamic efficiency, on the other hand, is concerned with the growth possibilities of an economy. Different economies vary greatly in the rate of growth of their national product obtained from the same percentage increase in their use of resources. These disparities may be ascribed to differences in the selection of investments, to variations in the speed with which they generate innovations and the ease with which they adopt their own or foreign innovations, or to the differences in their static efficiencies that are effected by growth. Centrally administered economies have the advantage that they could specifically favour those sectors of the economy in regard to investment that ensure rapid growth, prestige and power. It applies not only to investment in machines and equipment, but also, and above all, to investment in research and the training of men. This advantage may, however, be at least partially neutralised by the readier adaptability of private enterprise economies to change and the response of private entrepreneurs to the challenge presented by competition. There would therefore seem to be no *a priori* reasons why the two systems should differ markedly in respect of their dynamic efficiencies.

[1] The basic need is very clearly stated by R. W. Campbell in the following words: 'Despite central planning there is still a tremendous need in the Soviet system for decentralised calculation of benefits and gains among alternatives, and these calculations must always be cast in terms of some common denominator of value. Economic theory bears the same relation to planning that physics does to engineering. It provides a model of concepts and interrelations that makes it possible to comprehend the dependence of consequences on other variables' ('Marxian analysis, mathematical methods and scientific economic planning: Can Soviet economists combine them?', in *The Soviet Economy*, ed. Shaffer, p. 352).
[2] Wiles, 'Growth versus choice', in *Comparative Economic Systems*, pp. 19 ff.

Growth is also affected by the ability of a system to appropriate as large a share of the national product as is consistent with the maintenance of efficiency, and to use it for investment. Here the centrally administered economy would seem to have a definite advantage over the private enterprise economy.

In the typically capitalist economy the rates of saving, spending and investment are determined predominantly by private individuals and institutions, and only to a minor degree by public authorities. In the centrally administered economy, on the other hand, these rates would be determined by the government. It would seem that in normal peacetime the government would be able to maintain a stable or a gradually rising standard of living and use the surplus for industrial development or military preparedness, or for whatever other purpose the central authority might wish to use it.[1] It would also be able to a very large extent to determine the direction of investment in human beings, that is, the type of training which the youth would receive.

The systematic coordination of resources to ensure full employment and the orderly distribution of investments through time would eliminate spurts of activity, with their consequent depressive reactions, though planning may of course produce its own instability by discrepancies between prescribed quantities and operational results, leading to disproportions or bottlenecks and the consequent unpredictability of results.[2]

A very high rate of investment could therefore be consistently maintained in the centrally administered economy by the simple, if drastic, expedient of preventing the living standards of the population from increasing in relation to increases in the productivity of the economy. If investment includes outlays on research, increases in productivity per head of the population could be obtained not only by capital widening and deepening[3] but also by technological progress.

But, apart from the social cost involved in rapid industrialisation, communist economists have recently stressed the fact that an optimum rate of investment may diverge very considerably from the maximum rate in the centrally planned

---

[1] According to Fellner, 'A totalitarian government, if it could establish itself in a country such as the United States, might not find it difficult to operate the economy at a level of consumption 20 to 25 per cent lower than our present consumption level, and then let consumption rise slowly with the rise of aggregate output. By such a policy, the present American net capital formation could be *more than doubled*, and it is quite likely that the annual economic growth rate of the United States could be *almost* doubled' (Quoted in *Comparative Economic Systems*, p. 10). The 'dynamic efficiency' of the Soviet economy, though good, has by no means been spectacular, and has been facilitated by the country's relatively favourable ratio of population to resources and the enormous size of the domestic market. Initially it was also greatly helped by the considerable industrialisation achieved before the communist Revolution.

[2] 'The business cycle has made unmistakable headway in East Europe, becoming so pervasive that communist economists who at first seemed to pretend that it did not exist, now openly admit that it is another unsolved problem of industrial development' (Mieczkowski, 'The unstable Soviet bloc economies', *East Europe*, Oct. 1967, p. 2).

[3] Capital widening means equipping additional workers with the same amount of capital per head as the average for the existing labour force, and capital deepening refers to investment that raises the average capital outlay per head above the existing level. The achievement of the United States in this respect has indeed not been outstanding during the postwar period. But the Soviet standard, whereby one-quarter of the national product is supposed to be devoted to new investment, does not appear to have put the rate of capital accumulation in the USSR significantly ahead of the more dynamic western European countries such as Germany and the Netherlands during the two postwar decades. Most of the others in fact attained approximately 20 per cent of their GNP (Shonfield, *Modern Capitalism*, p. 6). In Japan capital formation now exceeds 30 per cent of the GNP (Bieda, p. 273). If the expenditure on the education of their children by parents were included, the Japanese achievement would be even more remarkable.

economy. Too high a rate of investment may, in fact, be achieved at the expense of the maintenance of the existing equipment. Communist experience has also shown that when the demand for equipment is very high, because of the construction of new and the extension of existing plants, it may be difficult to introduce the benefits of technological change. Too high a rate of investment may, indeed, result in diminishing productivity through the diminishing efficiency of the investment process, diminishing efficiency of the whole productive process, increasing scarcity of labour, balance of payments problems, and the appearance of bottlenecks in some sectors. Communist experience, supported by investigations in western Europe and the United States, shows that, important as investment may be as a cause of growth of output per head of the population, its significance as a growth factor is dependent on the economic use of resources—the specific uses to which they are applied, and the efficiency with which they are administered and maintained.[1]

The command economy is an authoritarian economy. Finally, it must be pointed out once more that a command economy is necessarily an authoritarian economy. It would be impossible to conceive of a whole national economy organised on the command principle in a politically democratic milieu. The high values set on the attainment of certain national objectives, which form the basis of its ideology, the destruction of the other autonomous economic powers that its creation entails, and the enforcement of subservience to directives that its operation postulates, all necessitate the imposition of authoritarian rule. The problem of the central direction of economic activity is therefore important, not only in respect of the question of how far planned production would meet the basic requirements of the community, but also in regard to the more fundamental question of the maintenance of personal and political freedom.

---

[1] Fallenbucht, 'Investment policy for economic development', *Canadian Journal of Economics and Political Science*, Feb. 1963; Kendrick, *Productivity trends in the United States*, ch 3; OECD, *International Report on Factors of Investment Behaviour.*

Bibliography

Adelman, M. A. 'The measurement of industrial concentration', *Review of Economics and Statistics*, Nov. 1951.

Anderson, Sven A. *Viking Enterprise*, New York, AMS Press, 1936.

Appadorai, A. *Economic Conditions in Southern India A.D. 1000-1500*, 2 vols, Madras, 1936.

Arnold, W. T. *The Roman System of Provincial Administration*, Oxford University Press, 1914.

Ashton, T. S. *An Economic History of England: The eighteenth century*, New York, 1954 Methuen, 1955.

Ashton, T. S. *The Industrial Revolution 1760-1830*, Oxford University Press, 1957.

Ashton, T. S. *Iron and Steel in the Industrial Revolution*, Manchester University Press, 1951 (3rd edn 1963).

Bacon, Francis. *Novum Organum*, 1620.

Barker, Ernest. *Social and Political Thought in Byzantium*, Oxford University Press, 1957.

Barrow, R. H. *Slavery in the Roman Empire*, Methuen, 1928.

Baynes, N. H. *The Byzantine Empire*, Thornton Butterworth, Howe University Library, 1939.

Bechtel, H. *Wirtschaftsstil des deutschen Spätmittelalters*, Munich, 1930.

Becker, C. H. *Zeitschrift der deutschen Morgenländischen Gesellschaft*, vol. i, 1901.

Berle, A. and Means, G. *The Modern Corporation and Private Property*, New York, 1932 (rev. edn, Harcourt Brace, 1968).

Bieda, K. *The Structure and Operation of the Japanese Economy*, Sydney, 1970.

Birnie, Arthur, in *European Civilization*, 7 vols, vol. v, ed. Edward Eyre, Oxford University Press, 1935-37.

Bishop, A. W. *Origin of the Far Eastern Civilisation*, Smithsonian Institute, Washington, 1942.

Bishop, A. W. 'The rise of civilisation in China with reference to its geographical aspects', *Geographical Review*, Oct. 1932.

Bliss, C. J. 'Prices, markets and planning', *Economic Journal*, March 1972.

Bolkenstein, H. *Het economische Leven in Griekenlands Bloeitijd*, Haarlem, 1923.

Bornstein, M. 'The Soviet price system', *American Economic Review*, March 1962.

Bornstein, M. 'The Soviet price reform discussion', *Quarterly Journal of Economics*, Feb. 1964.

Bornstein, M., ed. *Comparative Economic Systems*, Irwin 1965 (2nd edn 1969).

Bornstein, M. 'The Soviet price system', in *Comparative Economic Systems*, 1965.

Bowden, Witt. *Industrial Society in England Towards the End of the Eighteenth Century*, New York, 1925.

Burns, A. R. *Money and Monetary Policy in Early Times*, Kegan Paul, 1927.

Busolt, G. *Griechische Geschichte*, 3 vols, Gotha, 1893-1904.

Cambridge Economic History of Europe, ed. M. M. Postan *et al.*, Cambridge University Press, 1942-65.

Campbell, R. W. 'Marxian analysis, mathematical methods and scientific economic planning: Can Soviet economists combine them?', in *The Soviet Economy*, ed. H. G. Shaffer, New York, Appleton, 1963.

Carcopino, J. *Daily Life in Ancient Rome*, Yale University Press, 1941.

Chi, Chao-Ting. *Key Economic Areas in Chinese History*, Columbia University Press, 1936.

Childe, V. Gordon. *Progress and Archaeology*, London, Watts, 1944.

Clapham, J. H. 'Economic change', in *Cambridge Modern History*, vol. x.

Cole, W. A. 'The growth of national incomes', in *Cambridge Economic History of Europe*, vol. vi, part 2.

Comparative Economic Systems, see Bornstein, M., ed.

Coulton, G. G. 'The mind of medievalism', in *Universal History of the World*, ed. J. A. Hammerton, London, 1928-30, vol. v.

Croce, Benedetto. *Matérialisme historique et économie Marxiste—essais critiques*, Paris, 1901.

Croce, Benedetto. *Politics and Morals*, Philosophical Library New York, 1945.

Cunningham, W. *Growth of English Industry and Commerce*, 3 vols, Cambridge University Press, 1915-21.

Dahl, R. A. and Lindblom, C. E. *Politics, Economics and Welfare*, Harper & Row, 1953.

Davenant, C. *Works*, 1771 edn.

Dawson, C. H. *The Making of Europe*, Steed & Ward, 1939.
Day, Clive. *A History of Commerce*, Longmans, 1929.
Deane, P. and Cole, W. A. *British Economic Growth*, Cambridge University Press, 1962.
de Roover, R. in *Annales d'histoire économique et sociale*, nos 44 and 45, 19.
de Roover, R. 'The organisation of trade', in *Cambridge Economic History of Europe*, vol. iii.
Diehl, Charles. *Byzance, grandeur et décadence*, Paris, 1928.
Diehl, Charles. *Les Grands problèmes de l'histoire Byzantine*, Paris, 1930.
Diehl, Charles. *Venise, une république patricienne*, Paris, 1928.
Dill, Samuel. *Roman Society in the Last Century of the Western Empire*, Allen & Unwin, 1933.
Dobb, M. H. *Studies in the Development of Capitalism*, Routledge, 1947.
Dobb, M. H. *Soviet Economic Development*, New York, 1948 (6th edn, Routledge, 1966).
Dopsch, A. *Wirtschaftliche und Soziale Grundlagen der Europäischen Kulturentwicklung*, Vienna, 1923.
Drewnowski, J. 'The economic theory of socialism: a suggestion for reconsideration', in *Comparative Economic Systems*, 1965.
Eberhard, Wolfram. *Conquerors and Rulers: social forces in medieval China*, Leiden, 1965.
Eberhard, Wolfram. *Social Mobility in Traditional China*, Leiden, 1962.
Encyclopaedia of the Social Sciences, ed. E. R. A. Seligman, Collier-Macmillan, 15 vols, 1948.
Endenburg, P. J. T. *Koinoonia en Gemeenschap van Zaken by de Grieken in den Klassieken Tyd*, Amsterdam, 1937.
Erman, A. and Ranke, H. *Ägypten und ägyptisches Leben im Altertum*, Tübingen, 1924.
Eyre, Edward, ed. *European Civilization*, 5 vols. Oxford University Press, 1933-37.
Fallenbucht, 'Investment policy for economic development', *Canadian Journal of Economics and Political Science*, Feb. 1963.
Farrington, B. *Greek Science*, Penguin Books, 1963.
Findlay, George. *History of the Byzantine Empire*, Dent, Everyman's Library, 1908.
Firth, R. W. *Primitive Economics of the New Zealand Maori*, Routledge, 1929.
Firth, R. W. *Primitive Polynesian Economy*, Routledge, 1939.
Fleming, J. M. and Sertic, V. R. 'The Yugoslav economic system', in *Comparative Economic Systems*, 1965.
Fowler, W. W. *The City-State of the Greeks and Romans*, Macmillan, 1919.
Frank, Tenney. *An Economic History of Rome*, Baltimore, 1920.
Frank, Tenney. *Aspects of Social Behaviour in Ancient Rome*, Baltimore, 1933-37.
Freudenberger and Redlich. *Kyklos*, xvii, 1964, no. 3.
Friedman, M. and Schwartz, A. J. *The Great Contraction 1929-1933*, National Bureau of Economic Research, Princeton University Press, 1969.
Friedman, M. 'The role of monetary policy', *American Economic Review*, March 1968.
Gadgill, D. R. *Industrial Evolution of India in Recent Times*, Oxford University Press, 1924.
Galbraith, J. K. *The Affluent Society*, Hamish Hamilton, 1958.
Geyer, A. L. *Das Wirtschaftliche System der Niederländisch-Ostindischen Kompagnie am Kap der Guten Hoffnung*, Munich, 1923.
Glotz, G. *The Aegean Civilization*, Kegan Paul, 1925.
Glotz, G. *Ancient Greece at Work*, Kegan Paul, 1926.
Goldenweiser, A. *Anthropology*, Harrap, 1937.
Gomme, A. W. *The Population of Athens in the Fifth and Fourth Centuries B.C.*, Glasgow, 1933 (rev. edn, Argonant 1968).
Gonda, J. *Ancient Indian Kingship from the Religious Point of View*, Leiden, 1966.
Gordon, R. A. *Business Leadership in the Large Corporation*, University of California Press, 1961.
Grossman, G. 'Notes for a theory of the command economy', in *Comparative Economic Systems*, 1965.
Grove, J. W. *Government and Industry in Britain*, Longmans, 1962.
Hamilton, Earl J. *American Treasure and the Price Revolution in Spain*, Harvard University Press, 1934.
Hamilton, Earl J. *Economica*, vol. ix. 1929.
Hasebroek, J. *Griechische Wirtschafts—und Gesellschaftsgeschichte*, Tübingen, 1931.
Hasebroek, J. *Trade and Politics in Ancient Greece*, Bell, 1933.
Harrod, Roy. *Reforming the World's Money*, Macmillan, 1966.
Hauser, H. and Renaudet, A. *Peuples et civilisations: les debuts de l'age moderne*, 4 vols, Paris, 1929.
Hayek, F. *Constitution of Liberty*, Routledge, 1960.
Heckscher, E. F. *Mercantilism*, 2 vols, Allen & Unwin, 1931 (2nd edn 1956).

Heckscher, E. F. *Economic History Review*, iii, no. 1. 1931-32.

Hegel, G. W. F. *Philosophy of Right*, trans. T. M. Knox, Oxford University Press, 1942.

Heichelheim, F. M. *Wirtschaftsgeschichte des Altertums*, Leiden, 1938.

Heichelheim, F. M. 'Welthistorische Gesichtspunkte zu den Vormittelalterlichen Wirtschaft-sepochen', *Festgabe für Werner Sombart*, Munich, 1933.

Heichelheim, F. M. *Wirtschaftliche Schwankungen der Zeit von Alexander bis Augustus*, Jena, 1930.

Heichelheim, F. M. 'Monopole', in *Paulys Realencyclopädie*, Stuttgart, 1894-1899.

Heilbroner, R. L. *The Making of Economic Society*, Prentice-Hall, 1964.

Heitland, W. E. *Last Words on Roman Municipalities*, Cambridge University Press, 1930.

Helleiner, K. F. 'The population of Europe from the Black Death to the eve of the Vital Revolution', in *Cambridge Economic History of Europe*, vol. iv.

Herodotus. *History*, 2 vols, Dent, Everyman's Library, 1933.

Herskovits, M. J. *The Economic Life of Primitive Peoples*, New York, 1940. (Reprinted as *Economic Anthropology*, Norton, 1965.)

Hicks, John R. *Value and Capital*, Oxford University Press, 1939.

Hirschman, A. O. *The Strategy of Economic Development*, Yale University Press, 1958.

Hitch, C. J. *America's Economic Strength*, Oxford University Press, 1941.

Hobhouse, L. T., Wheeler, G. C. and Ginsberg, M. *The Material Culture and Social Institutions of the Simpler Peoples*, London, 1930.

Hoffmann, W. *British Industry 1700-1950*, trans W. H. Chaloner and W. O. Henderson, Oxford, Blackwell, 1953.

Hull, C. H. *Economic Writings of Sir William Petty*, 2 vols, Cambridge University Press, 1899.

Hunt, B. C. *The Development of the Business Corporation in England 1800-1867*, Harvard University Press, 1936.

Hunt, R. N. C. *Marxism: Past and Present*, Bles, 1955.

Huntington, Ellsworth. *Civilization and Climate*, Yale University Press, 1935.

Huntington, Ellsworth. *The Character of Races, as Influenced by Physical Environment, Material Selection and Historical Development*, Scribner, 1924.

Jathar, G. B. and Biri, S. G. *Indian Economics*, Oxford University Press, 1932.

Jewkes, John. *Economic Journal*, June, 1952.

Johsnon, G. 'Planning and the market in economic development', in *Comparative Economic Systems*, 1965.

Jones, A. H. M. *The Later Roman Empire*, 3 vols, Oxford, Blackwell, 1964.

Jonkers, E. J. *Economische en Sociale Toestanden in het Romeinsche Ryk*, Utrecht, 1933.

Judges, F. in *European Civilization*, ed. E. Eyre, 7 vols, Oxford University Press, 1935-1937.

Kahrstedt, U. *Neue Wege zur Antike*, Munich, 1949.

Kamarck, A. M. *The Economcs of African Development*, Praeger, 1967.

Kamerschen, David. 'Changes in concentration in American manufacturing industries', *Zeitschrift fur die Gesamte Staatswissenschaft*, Oct. 1971.

Karpovich, Mikhail M. 'Church and state in Russian history', *Russian Review*, iii, no. 3.

Kees, Hermann. *Ägypten*, Beck, 1933

Kendrick, J. W. *Productivity Trends in the United States*, New York, National Bureau of Economic Research, 1961.

Keynes, J. M. *A Treatise on Money*, 2 vols, Macmillan, 1930.

Keynes, J. M. *The General Theory of Employment, Interest, and Money*, Macmillan, 1936.

Keynes, J. M. *Essays in Persuasion*, Hart-Davis, 1951.

King, L. W. *History of Babylon*, London, 1919.

Kulischer, J. *Allgemeine Wirtschaftsgeshichte*, 2 vols, Munich, 1928-9.

Kuznets, S. S. *Capital in the American Economy: Its Formation and Financing*, Princeton University Press, 1961.

Kuznets, S. S. 'Notes on the take-off', in *The Economics of Take-off into Sustained Growth*, ed. Rostow (see below).

Landes, David. 'Tehnological change and industrial development in Western Europe, 1750-1914', in *The Cambridge Economic History of Europe*, vi, part 1.

Latouche, Robert. *The Birth of Western Economy; economic aspects of the Dark Ages*, Methuen, 1961.

League of Nations. *Industrialisation and Foreign Trade*, Geneva, 1945.

League of Nations. *World Economic Surveys*, 1931-2; 1932-3.

Leemans, W. F. *The Old-Babylonian Merchant, his business and social position*, Leiden, 1950.

Lehmann-Hartleben, Karl. *Die Antiken Hafenanlagen des Mittelmeeres: Beiträge zur Geschichte des Städtebaus im Allertum*, Scientia, 1963.

Lenin, V. I. *Will the Bolsheviks Retain State Power?* 1917.

Leong, Y. K. and Tao, L. K. *Village and Town Life in China,* London 1915.

Letourneau, C. *Property, Its Origins and Development,* London, 1892.

Lewis, Arthur. *Tropical Development 1880-1913,* Allen & Unwin, 1970.

Liberal Industrial Inquiry Report. *Britain's Industrial Future,* 1928.

Lipson, E. *The Economic History of England,* 3 vols, A & C Black, 1945 (vol. 1, 12th edn 1962; vols 2, 3, 6th edn 1961).

Loane, Helen. *Industry and Commerce in the City of Rome 50 B.C.-200 A.D.,* Baltimore, 1938.

Loewe, M. *Imperial China, The Historical Background to the Modern Age,* Allen & Unwin, 1966.

Lowie, R. H. *The Origin of the State,* New York, 1927.

Maddison, A. *Economic Growth in the West,* Allen & Unwin,1964.

Mair, L. P. *An African People in the Twentieth Century,* Routledge, 1934.

Malinowski, B. *Crime and Custom in Savage Society,* Routledge, 1926.

Mantoux, Paul. *The Industrial Revolution in the Eighteenth Century,* Methuen, 1961.

Marshall, Alfred. *Industry and Trade,* London, 1921.

Marshall, L. C., ed. *Industrial Society,* 3 vols, University of Chicago Press, 1930.

Marx, Karl. *Capital,* 2 vols, Dent, Everyman's Library.

Mason, E. S. *Economic Concentration and the Monopoly Problem,* Harvard University Press, 1957.

McGovern, W. M. *From Luther to Hitler; the History of Fascist-Nazi Political Philosophy,* Houghton Mifflin, Boston, 1941.

Meier, G. M. *Leading Issues in Development Economics,* New York, Oxford University Press, 1964.

Meissner, B. *Babylonien und Assyrien,* Heidelberg, 1920.

Meyer, E. *Kleine Schriften,* Halle, 1924.

Mez, Adam. *The Renaissance of Islam,* London, Luzac, 1937.

Mickwitz, G. in *Vierteljahrschrift für Sozial- und Wirtschaftsgeshichte,* 32, i. 1939.

Mieczkowski, B. 'The unstable Soviet bloc economies', *East Europe,* Oct. 1967.

Mill, J. S. *Principles of Political Economy,* (1848), Longmans, 1929.

Miller, M. 'Studies in the theory and practice of markets and competition in Russia, Poland and Yugoslavia', in *Communist Economy under Change,* Deutsch, 1963.

Moreland, W. H. *India at the Death of Akbar,* London, 1920.

Moss, H. *The Birth of the Middle Ages,* Oxford University Press, 1937.

Myint, H. *The Economics of the Developing Countries,* Hutchinson, 1965.

Nabholz, H. 'Medieval agrarian society in transition' in *Cambridge Economic History of Europe,* vol. i.

National Bureau of Economic Research. *Business Incorporation in the United States 1800-1943,* 1948.

National Industrial Conference Board. *The Work of the International Labour Organisation.*

National Resources Planning Board. *The Structure of the American Economy.*

Neale, W. C. 'Reciprocity and redistribution in the Indian village', in *Trade and Market in the Early Empires,* ed. Polanyi (see below).

Needham, Joseph. *Science and Society,* xxiii, no. 1.

Needham, Joseph. 'Science and China's influence on the world', in *The Legacy of China,* ed. R. Dawson, Oxford University Press, 1964.

Nef, J. U. *Economic History Review,* vii, no. 2, 1936-37.

Nef, J. U. *Industry and Government in France and England 1540-1640,* Philadelphia, 1940 (repr. New York, Russell, 1968).

Nieuwenhuizen, P. J. ''n Vergelykende Studie van Geldverskynsels in die Sowiet-Unie en die Westerse Kapitalistiese Volkshuishoudings,' D.Com. thesis, 1972.

Nordenskiöld, E. 'The American Indian as an Inventor', *Journal of the Royal Anthropological Institute,* lix, July-Dec. 1929.

Nourse, E. G. *Proceedings of the Academy of Political Science,* xviii, no. 2, 1938-40.

Nove, A. *The Soviet Economy,* New York, 1962 (Allen & Unwin 1969).

Nove, A. 'The prospects for economic growth in the U.S.S.R.', *American Economic Review,* May 1963.

Nurkse, R. *Lectures on Economic Development.* Istanbul University, 1958.

Nurkse, R. *Patterns of Trade and Development,* Oxford, Blackwell, 1961.

Nutter, G. W. *The Extent of Enterprise Monopoly in the United States 1899-1939,* University of Chicago Press, 1951.

Nutter, G. W. and Einhorn, H. A. *Enterprise Monopoly in the United States 1899-1958,* Columbia University Press, 1969.

OECD. *International Report on Factors of Investment Behaviour,* Paris, 1950.

Ogilvy, David. *Confessions of an Advertising Man*, Longmans, 1964.

Ohlin, Bertil. *American Economic Review*, May 1959.

O'Leary, De Lacy Evans. *Arabia Before Mohammed*, London, 1927.

Ormerod, H. A. *Piracy in the Ancient World*, University of Liverpool Press, 1924.

Ostrogorsky, Georg. 'Die wirschaftlichen und sozialen Entwicklungsgrundlagen des byzantinischen Reiches', *Vierteljahrschrift für Sozial- und Wirtschaftsgeschichte*, 1929.

Ostrogorsky, Georg. 'Agrarian conditions in the Byzantine Empire in the Middle Ages', *Cambridge Economic History of Europe*, vol. i.

Pareti, Luigi, ed. *History of Mankind: The Ancient World*, Allen & Unwin, 1965.

Pearson, Harry W. in *Trade and Market in the Early Empires*, New York, Free Press of Glencoe, 1957.

Penrose, E. T. *The Theory of the Growth of the Firm*, New York, 1959, Oxford, Blackwell, 1960.

Pigou, A. C. *The Economics of Welfare*, Macmillan, 1921.

Pirenne, Henri. *A History of Europe from the Invasions to the XVI Century*, trs B. Miall, Allen & Unwin, 1939.

Pirenne, Henri. *Economic and Social History of Medieval Europe*, trs I. E. Clegg, New York, Harcourt Brace (London Routledge), 1937.

Pirenne, Henri. *Les Anciennes démocraties des Pays-Bas*, Paris, 1922.

Pirenne, Henri. *Muhammad and Charlemagne*, trans B. Miall, Allen & Unwin (1939), 1954.

Plant, A. *Economica*, Feb. 1932.

Pleket, H. W. 'Technology and society in the Graeco-Roman world', *Acta Historiae Neerlandica*, i.

Poelman, H. A. in *Het Huiselyk en Maatschappelyk Leven onser Voorouders*.

Polanyi, Karl, ed. *Trade and Market in the Early Empires*, Collier-Macmillan, 1957.

Polo, Marco. *The Travels*, Penguin Classics, 1968.

Postan, M. M. *Economic History Review*, second series, ii, no. 3; vi, no. 1, 1950.

Power, E. E. and Postan, M. M., eds. *Studies in English Trade in the Fifteenth Century*, Routledge, 1933.

Radin, Paul. *The World of Primitive Man*, New York, 1953 (repr. Dutton, 1971).

Rao, Ramachandra. *Decay of Indian Industries*.

Ricardo, David. *On the Principles of Political Economy and Taxation*, London, 1817.

Riepl, W. *Das Nachrichtenwesen des Altertums*, Leipzig, 1913.

Rivers, W. H. R. *Social Organization*, Kegan Paul, 1932. (n.i. of 1924 edn, Dawsons of Pall Mall, 1968).

Robertson, D. H. *The Control of Industry*, London, Nisbet, 1928.

Robertson, H. M. *Aspects of the Rise of Economic Individualism: a criticism of Max Weber and his school*, Cambridge University Press, 1933.

Robinson, E. A. G. 'The changing structure of the British economy', *Economic Journal*, Sept. 1954.

Romein, Jan. *De Lage Landen Bij de Zee*, Utrecht, 1934.

Rörig, F. *Annales d'Histoire Economique et Sociale*, 1930.

Rörig, F. *Mittelalterliche Weltwirtschaft, Blüte und Ende einer Weltwirtschaftsperiode*, Jena, 1933.

Rostovtzeff, M. I. *Social and Economic History of the Hellenistic World*, 3 vols, Oxford University Press, 1941.

Rostovtzeff, M. I. *Social and Economic History of the Roman Empire*, 2 vols, Oxford University Press, 1957.

Rostow, W. W., ed. *The Economics of Take-off into Sustained Growth*, Macmillan, 1963.

Rostow, W. W. 'The take-off into self-sustained growth', *Economic Journal*, March 1956.

Rostow, W. W. *The Stages of Economic Growth*, Cambridge University Press, 1961.

Russell, Bertrand. *A History of Western Philosophy*, Allen & Unwin, 1946 (2nd edn, 1961).

Salter, Arthur. *World Trade and its Future*, Oxford University Press, 1936.

Schapera, I. *Government and Politics in Tribal Societies*, Watts, 1956.

Scharma, J. P. *Republics in Ancient India: c. 1500-500 B.C.*, Leiden, 1968.

Schmidt, A. *Drogen und Drogenhandel im Altertum*, Leipzig, 1927.

Schmoller, G. F. *The Mercantile System and its Historical Significance*, New York, 1910.

Schumpeter, J. A. *Business Cycles*, New York, Mcgraw-Hill, 1939.

Schumpeter, J. A. *Capitalism, Socialism and Democracy*, New York, 1942. (paper back, Allen & Unwin, 1965).

Shonfield, Andrew. *Modern Capitalism: the changing balance of public and private power*, Oxford University Press for Royal Institute of International Affairs, 1965.

See, H. E. *Französische Wirtschaftsgeschichte*, 2 vols, Jena, 1930.
Seeck, Otto. *Geschichte des Untergangs der Antiken Welt*, 6 vols, Berlin, 1910-1920.
Seligman, E. R. A., ed., see *Encyclopaedia of the Social Sciences* above.
Slicher, van Bath, B. *De Agrarische Geschiedenis van West-Europa 500-1850*, Utrecht-Antwerpen, 1967.
Smith, Adam. *The Wealth of Nations* (1776), Dent, Everyman's Library.
Smith, Henry, in *Communist Economy under Change*, ed. Miller (above).
Smith, Vincent A. *The Oxford History of India*, Oxford University Press, 1961 (3rd edn 1968).
Sombart, Werner. *Die Deutsche Volkswirtschaft im neunzehnten Jahrhundert*, Berlin, 1925.
Sombart, Werner. *Der Moderne Kapitalismus*, 3 vols, Munich, 1916-28
Sombart, Werner. *Der Proletarische Sozialismus*, 2 vols, Jena, 1925.
Southern, R. W. *Western Society and the Church in the Middle Ages*, Penguin Books, 1972.
Spear, Percival. *A History of India*, 2 vols, Penguin Books, 1965.
Speck, E. *Handelsgeschichte des Altertums*, 3 vols, Leipzig, 1900-06.
Spulber, N. *The Soviet Economy: structure, principles, problems*, New York, Norton, 1962 (rev. edn 1969).
Spulber, N. 'The Soviet-bloc foreign trade system' in *Comparative Economic Systems*, 1965.
Stark, W. *The History of Economics in Relation to Social Development*, Kegan Paul, 1944.
Stigler, G. J. *Five Lectures on Economic Problems*, Longmans, 1949.
Stöckle, Albert. *Spätrömische und Byzantinische Zünfte*, Leipzig, 1911.
Strieder, J. *Studien zur Geschichte Kapitalischer Organisationsformen*, Munich, 1925.
Sumner, W. G. and Keller, A. G. *The Science of Society*, 4 vols, Yale University Press, 1927-29.
Temporary National Economic Committee. *Monograph no. 13*, Government Printing Office, Washington, 1940.
Thomas, *Handwörterbuch der Staatswissenschaften*, Ergänzungsband. Gustav Fischer, 1929.
Toynbee, A. J. *A Study of History*, 12 vols, Oxford University Press, 1933-61.
Toynbee, Arnold. *The Industrial Revolution of the Eighteenth Century in England*, Longmans, 1928.
Tregear, T. R. *A Geography of China*, University of London Press, 1965.
Trivanovitch, V. *Economic Development of Germany under National Socialism*, New York, 1937.
United Nations. *Processes and Problems of Industrialization in Underdeveloped Countries*, New York, 1955.
'Universitas', in *Dictionnaire des Antiquités Greques et Romaines.*
Unwin, George. *Studies in Economic History*, London, 1927 (new edn ed. Tawney, Cass 1958).
Ure, Andrew. *The Philosophy of Manufactures*, London, 1861.
Usher, A. P. *An Introduction to the Industrial History of England*, London, 1921.
Usher, A. P. *The Early History of Deposit Banking in Mediterranean Europe*, Harvard University Press, 1943.
Von Kremer, Alfred. *Kulturgeschichte des Orients unter den Chalifen*, 2 vols, Wien, 1877.
Von Soden, I. 'Leistung und Grenze sumerischer und babylonischer Wissenschaft', *Die Welt als Geschichte*, 11/5, 11/6.
Ways, Max. 'More power to everyone', *Fortune*, May 1970.
Webb, Sidney and Webb, Beatrice. *The Decay of Capitalist Civilization*, Allen & Unwin, 1923.
Weber, Max. 'Die Socialen Gründe des Untergangs der Antiken Kultur', *Gesammelte Aufsätze*, Töbingen, 1927.
Wiles, P. J. D. *The Political Economy of Communism*, Oxford, Blackwell, 1962.
Wiles, P. J. D. 'Growth versus choice', in *Comparative Economic Systems*, 1965.
Willcox, W. F. *International Migrations*, 2 vols, New York (London, Gordon & Breach), 1969.
Williams, 'Technical invention—the key to faster growth', *The Times Review of Industry*, Dec. 1962.
Wilson, C. H. 'Trade, society and the state', in *Cambridge Economic History of Europe*, vol. iv.
Wittfogel, Karl. *Oriental Despotism: a comparative study of total power*, Yale University Press, 1963.
Woolley, C. L. *Ur of the Chaldees*, Benn, 1929.
Xenophon, *Cyropaedia*, London, The Loeb Classical Library, 1947.
Yu-Lan, Fung. 'Why China has no science', *International Journal of Ethics*, April 1922.
Zaidan, G. C. 'Population growth and economic development', *Finance and Development Quarterly* no. 1, 1969.
Ziebarth, Erich. *Beiträge Zur Geschichte des Seeraubs und Seehandels im Alten Griechenland*, Hamburg, 1929.

INDEX

Note: The following abbreviations are used in the index. Dates are approximate.